Law Relating to

iPads, Tablets Smartphones & Smart Devices

The daring publisher, Universal Law Publishing Company, among the foremost in the law publishing field and progressive in venturing to bring out rare legal literature of avant garde *character has rightly enriched the* corpus juris *of India*

Justice V R Krishna Iyer
Random Reflections, page 14

Law Relating to

iPads, Tablets Smartphones & Smart Devices

Pavan Duggal

Advocate, Supreme Court of India

Universal

Law Publishing Co. Pvt. Ltd.

NEW DELHI - INDIA

2013 Edition

ISBN: 978-93-5035-347-9

Published by

Universal
Law Publishing Co. Pvt. Ltd.
NEW DELHI - INDIA

A-58, G.T. Karnal Road Industrial Area,
(Near Azadpur Metro Station), Delhi-110033
Tel. : 011-47082254, 27458529, 27215334 Fax : 011-27458529
e-mail: unilaw@vsnl.com

- Showroom : C-27, Connaught Place, New Delhi-110001
  e-mail: sales@unilawbooks.com
- Editorial : edit@unilawbooks.com
- Website : **www.unilawbooks.com**

Join us on Facebook www.facebook.com/unilawbooks

Recommended citation: Pavan Duggal, *iPads, Tablets, Smartphones & Smart Devices* (New Delhi: Universal Law Publishing Co. Pvt. Ltd., 2013).

Computer Typeset at Aesthetic and *Printed* at Afcon Enterprises, Delhi.

FOREWORD

After having worked in the area of Cyberlaw and Mobile Law for more than a decade, when my son Pavan came up with the idea of writing a book on legal aspects concerning mobile Smart Devices, I found that the said idea was most relevant in the current times, given the huge mobile revolution that our country as well as the world are currently witnessing.

Given the preferred focus of our lives on mobility, mobiles, smart phones, IPads and other Smart Communication Devices are redefining the way we live today. However, most of the lay mobile device users have very little clue on the legalities surrounding the use of mobile Smart Devices.

This book is an authoritative treatise, which gives us a deep insight into the emerging legal issues concerning mobiles, smart phones, IPads, tablets and other Smart Communication Devices and explains the relevant provisions of law in this regard, from the Indian perspective.

To facilitate a clear understanding for the readers, the book is written in a simple flowing language and contains a subject index for easy reference. It should be an invaluable asset for all those who are eager to explore the virgin area of Mobile Law for Smart Devices.

P.K. Duggal
Advocate

ACKNOWLEDGEMENTS

My grateful thanks to God for showing me the light ahead, to my father Mr. P.K. Duggal for his legal insights and guidance, to my mother for her inspiration, to my associates, for their untiring support, to my wife Sheffali for her understanding and encouragement and to several well wishers, whose blessings have given me the strength and conviction to author this book.

PREFACE TO THE FIRST EDITION

When I began working in the field of Cyberlaw, mobiles had just come on the horizon. Over a period of time, mobiles and communication devices are becoming more and more central to our lives and businesses. With ever increasing mobile penetration and content on mobile networks, it was evident that mobiles, communication devices and their usage would be regulated by law. Hence, I started working in the new area of Mobile Law.

With the transformation of the mobile into a smart device, innumerable disciplines have emerged in this field, owing to their autonomous nature. These mobile smart devices include I-Pads, Smart phones and Tablets. Mobility of Smart Devices has advantageously been availed in corporates *via* the BYOD – Bring Your Own Device – policy and cloud computing at large. Smart Devices have incorporated in them many new and interactive applications popularly known as mobile apps, the immensely popular ones being social media apps. All these functions of Smart Devices raise legal and regulatory issues that need to be addressed with immediate effect.

What inspired me to write this book was the absence of a book in this emerging field of legal discipline. This book aims to meet the urgent needs of mobile, smartphone and Smart Device users and mobility driven businesses to understand the diverse legal issues, which govern their day-to-day activities in the mobile ecosystem.

The coming into effect of the Indian Information Technology (Amendment) Act, 2008 heralded a new era and milestone in the growth of mobile law jurisprudence in India.

It is my sincere hope that the readers will be helped to become aware of the legal issues concerning mobiles, communication devices, Smart Devices, smartphones and the mobile environment and thus be able to protect themselves from the potential risks that the mobile ecosystem poses for all of us.

Pavan Duggal
pavan@pavanduggal.net
pduggal@nde.vsnl.net.in
pavanduggal@yahoo.com

CONTENTS

TABLE OF CASES

CHAPTER 1
INTRODUCTION

Today's world is a smart world, with Smart Devices. The word "smart" has various connotations but primarily brings to one's mind a sense of intelligence and brilliance to go around the day to day challenges. Smart Devices today are increasingly gaining centre stage attention for their efficacy, efficiency and reliance. These Smart Devices enable us to be smart in our day to day lives.

The word "smart" is defined by Oxford Dictionary as "informal, having or showing a quick-witted intelligence."[1]

Wikipedia defines the term "Smart Device" as follows:

> "A Smart Device is an electronic device that is cordless (unless while being charged), mobile (easily transportable), always connected (*via* WiFi, 3G, 4G etc.) and is capable of voice and video communication, internet browsing, "geo-location" (for search purposes) and that can operate to some extent, autonomously. It is widely believed that these types of devices will outnumber any other forms of smart computing and communication in a very short time. The most famous devices at the time of writing are the Apple iPhone and iPad, followed by devices such as the Samsung Galaxy tablet. The term can also refer to a ubiquitous computing device: a device that exhibits some properties of ubiquitous computing including artificial intelligence."[2]

Clearly, today is the world where we are surrounded by Smart Devices, whether it be smart phones, mobiles, tablets and hybrids between phones and tablets and a variety of other devices. These are devices which are mobile in nature, which help us to increase our efficiency and be on with the work while on the go and more significantly, help us to become far more productive. However, we are increasingly relying upon these Smart Devices not only for the purposes of generating publishing and transmission of our own personal data including sensitive personal data and information but also corporate data and information including the trade secrets and other data in our day to day business, profession and other activities. Consequently, we are finding that increasingly, Smart Devices are becoming more and more important in our lives. Why not so? This is so because these devices are intelligent, help us to do things in a multi-tasking manner and more significantly, carry among themselves, far more computing power, memory and the ability to multi task in a variety of places.

Today, once a person adopts a Smart Device, it becomes increasingly more and more important for the said person to denounce or give up the said Smart Device.

1. http://oxforddictionaries.com/definition/english/smart
2. http://en.wikipedia.org/wiki/Smart_device

That is the reason why Smart Devices are becoming more and more adopted in various parts of the world as also in India as well.

Let's have a look at what is the existing position pertaining to adoption of Smart Devices, smart phones, tablets and hybrids across the world. Globally, Smartphone Market grew 61% in 2011 with total shipment volumes reaching 491.4 million units in 2011, a whopping increase of over 304.7 million units in 2010. Smartphones are replacing feature phones at a much faster rate than expected, thanks to consistently falling prices.[3]

As per the survey of Mobitto Blog[4], there are 1.08 billion smartphones in the world. Some usage of smart phones highlights are as follows:

i. Android highest market share 46.9% vs. 28.7% iPhone

ii. 91% use of mobile web is social related (facebook, twitter, linkedin, foursquare)

iii. By 2013, Mobile phones will overtake PCs as the most common access to internet

iv. 95% users looked up local information

v. Facebook counts for 10% of all mobile data on iPhones

vi. 256% teens increased mobile data consumption vs. previous 12 months

vii. Apps will grow from a $6 billion today to $55.7 billion industry by 2015

viii. iPhone users download 48 apps/month

ix. 60% admit using Mobile phone while going to the toilet.

Further Go-Gulf.com recently published an infographic containing worldwide smartphone usage statistics which are as follows[5]:

(1) There are 91.4 million smartphones in the United States alone.

(2) Out of the 5 billion mobile phones in the world, 1.08 billion are smartphones.

(3) Android has the highest **market share** with 46.9% – the iPhone has 28.7%.

(4) 9 out of 10 smartphone users use their phone on a daily basis.

(5) The most popular smartphone activity is texting, followed by internet browsing and playing games.

(6) A higher percentage of Android users are below the age of 34 in comparison to iPhone users.

(7) People between the ages of 25 and 34 are more likely to own a smartphone (62%) than any other age group.

---

3. http://trak.in/tags/business/2012/02/16/indian-smartphone-market-growth-overview
4. http://blog.mobitto.com/smartphone-statistics-2012
5. http://ansonalex.com/infographics/smartphone-usage-statistics-2012-infographic

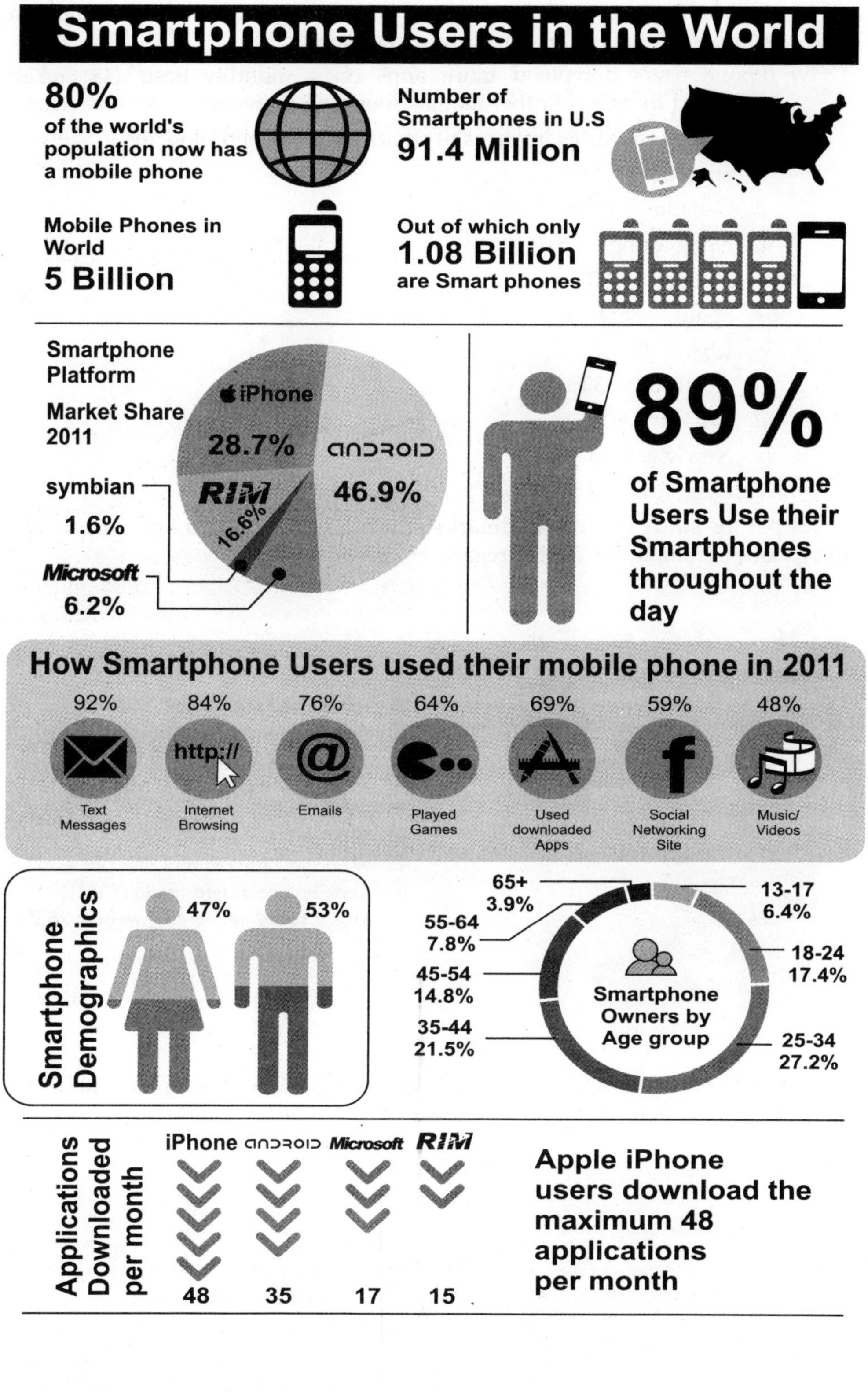
Smartphone Users in the World
80%
of the world's population now has a mobile phone
Number of Smartphones in U.S
91.4 Million
Mobile Phones in World
5 Billion
Out of which only
1.08 Billion
are Smart phones
Smartphone Platform
Market Share 2011
iPhone
28.7%
ANDROID
46.9%
RIM
16.6%
symbian
1.6%
Microsoft
6.2%
89%
of Smartphone Users Use their Smartphones throughout the day
How Smartphone Users used their mobile phone in 2011
92%
Text Messages
84%
http://
Internet Browsing
76%
@
Emails
64%
Played Games
69%
Used downloaded Apps
59%
f
Social Networking Site
48%
Music/ Videos
Smartphone Demographics
47%
53%
65+
3.9%
13-17
6.4%
55-64
7.8%
18-24
17.4%
45-54
14.8%
35-44
21.5%
25-34
27.2%
Smartphone Owners by Age group
Applications Downloaded per month
iPhone
ANDROID
Microsoft
RIM
48
35
17
15
Apple iPhone users download the maximum 48 applications per month

(8) Android users consume more data on a monthly basis (582MB) compared to users of other mobile operating systems.

(9) iPhone users download more apps on a monthly basis (48) when compared to users of other mobile operating systems.

(10) The top 10 countries in terms of smart phone penetration are:

i. Singapore – 54%
ii. Canada – 39%
iii. Hong Kong – 35%
iv. Sweden – 35%
v. Spain – 35%
vi. USA – 35%
vii. Australia – 33%
viii. Norwary – 33%
ix. New Zealand – 32%
x. Denmark – 31%

As per the study of 60 secondmarketer it has been revealed how people use smartphones, infographic in this regard are given as below[6]:

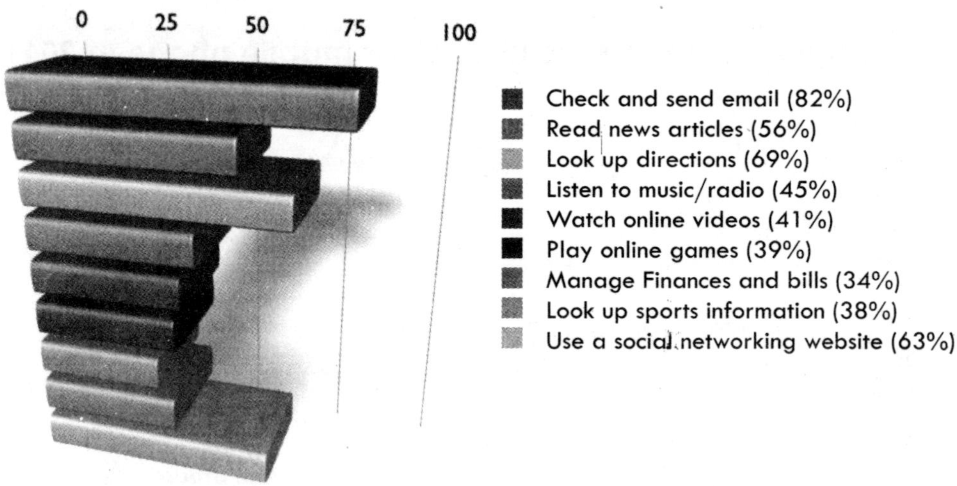

Snapshot of Digital India, 2012 by Ethinos Digital Marketing has published the statistics on usage of Tablet world wide, which are as below[7]:

6. http://60secondmarketer.com/blog/2011/08/16/how-people-use-smartphones-infographic

7. http://www.slideshare.net/Ethinos/a-snapshot-of-digital-india-May, 2012

Tablet Usage

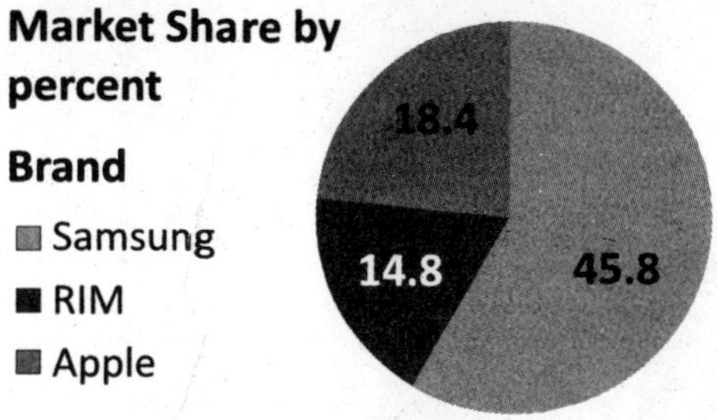

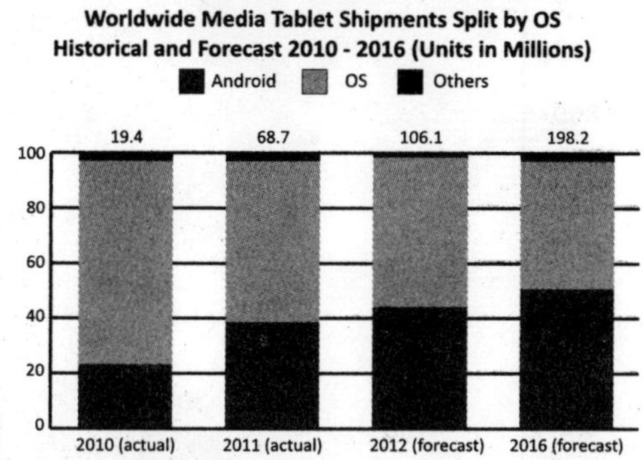

According to the eMarketer, half of the total US population will be using the internet *via* mobile by 2015. Further in USA, smartphones will reach 38% of mobile users and 28.8% of the overall population by the end of 2011. The number of smartphone users is expected to increase nearly 50% this year and smartphone user growth will continue at a steady double-digit pace through 2015. Just over 90 million US consumers will own a smartphone by the end of 2011; that number is expected to rise to nearly 150 million in 2015[8].

It is further pertinent to point out that rapidly penetrations of smartphones are causing to increase usage of smartphones application. The Research Guidance is predicting that global smartphone users will number 970 million by 2013. They also predict that this will cause app revenues to increase from US$ 1.94 billion (2009) to US$ 15.65 billion in only four years. The following figure gives a visual representation of installed base of smartphone application users[9].

8. http://therealtimereport.com/2011/08/26/us-mobile-internet-use-to-increase-25-smartphone-use-nearly-50-in-2011
9. http://www.mobilephonedevelopment.com/archives/996

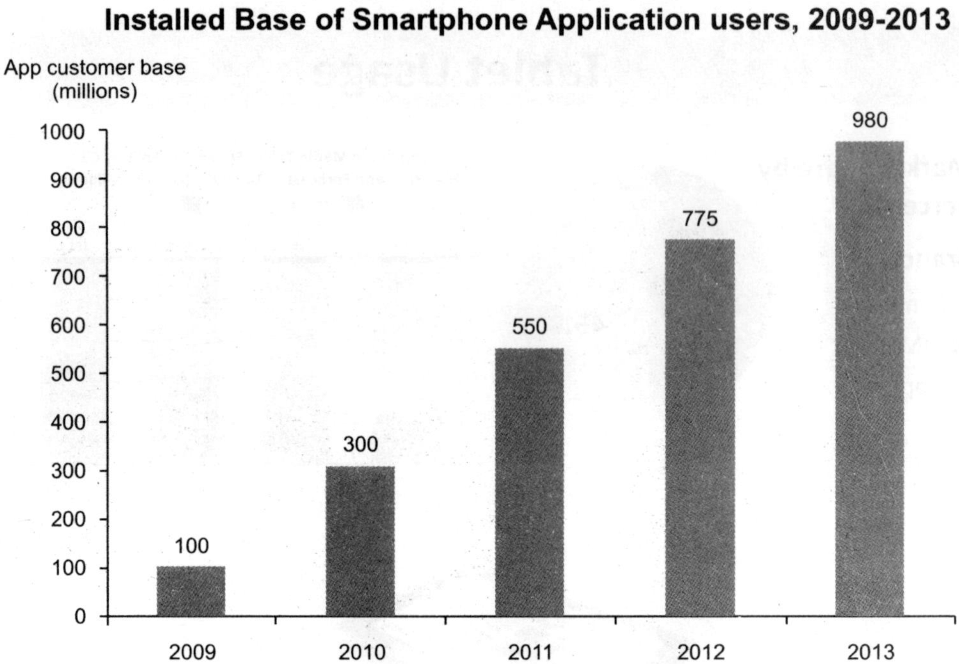

Online Publishers' Association has published the survey, 2012 pertaining to the adoption by operating system as below[10]:

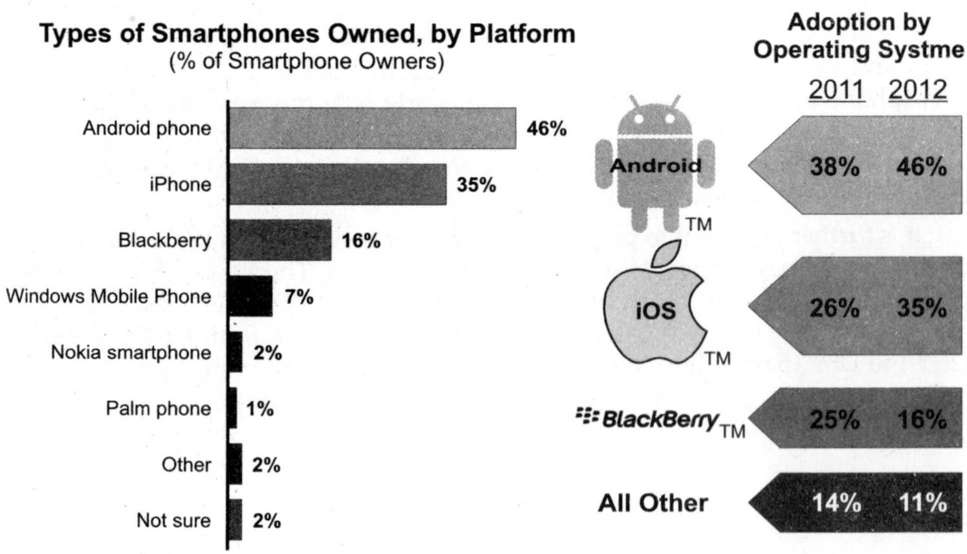

10. http://onlinepubs.ehclients.com/images/pdf/MMF-OPA_—_Portrait_of_Smartphone_User_August, 2012_(Public).pdf

Following figures show that the penetration of smart phones and feature phones among the various nations[11].

Italy has the highest smartphone penetration among 15-24

Smartphone v. Feature Phone, Age 15-24

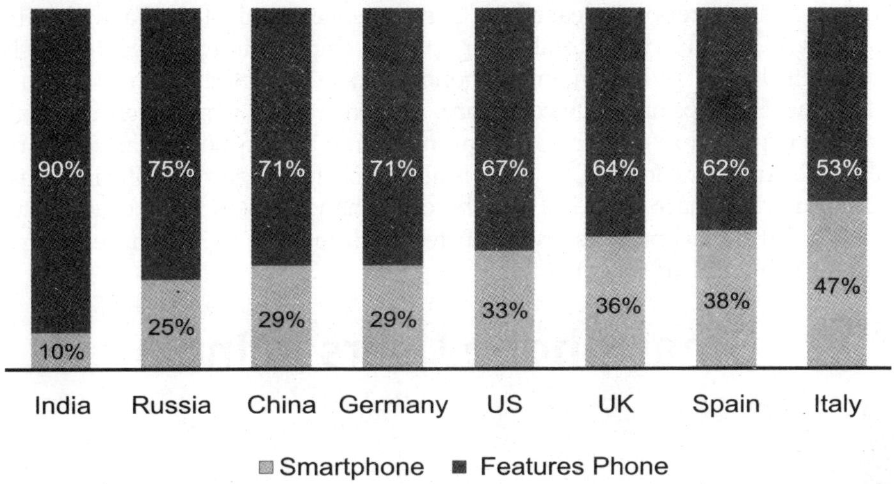

Smartphone users skew male everywhere but U.S.

Smartphone User, Age 15-24

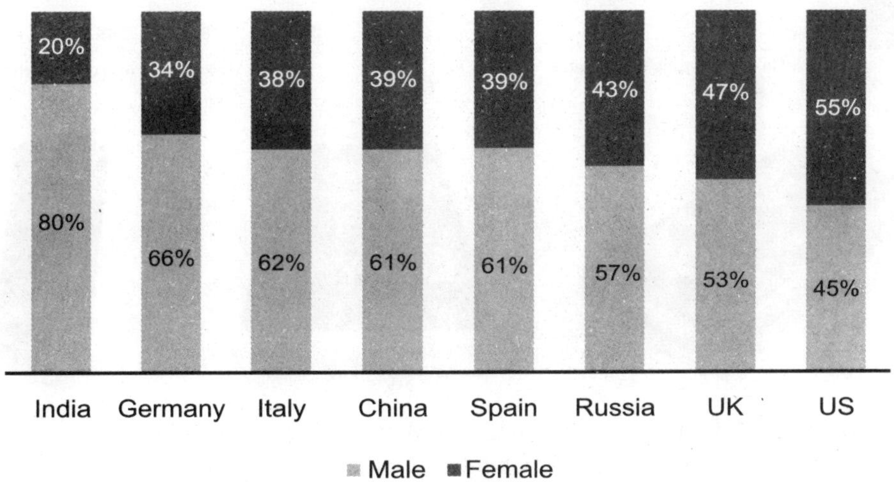

11. http://www.google.co.in/imgres?um=1&hl=en&biw=1024&bih=677&tbm=isch&tbnid=-RAkPN7DeGt6hM:&imgrefurl=http://blog.nielsen.com/nielsenwire/online_mobile/a-global-view-of-cellphones-and-youth/&docid=L2zk8TarjUxxeM&imgurl=http://blog.nielsen.com/nielsenwire/wp-content/uploads/2010/12/smartphone-male female.png&w=500&h=738&ei=fLWPUPGNG8L3rQf9mIDwCQ& zoom=1&iact= rc&dur= 0&sig= 100487755140654612808&page= 1&tbnh=207&tbnw=140&start=0&ndsp=12&ved= 1t:429,i:72&tx=45&ty=79

After having looked at the worldwide figures, we now examine as to what is the position pertaining to these smart devices in India in terms of their adoption.

As far as India is concerned, in comparison to Global Smartphone Market, growth in India is expected to be even higher. According to "India Smartphone Outlook for 2012" report released by Convergence Catalyst, India will witness 100% growth in 2012, with total smart phone shipments expected to reach 20 million units. In case of Indian Smartphone Vendor Market Share in 2011, Nokia's still led the Smartphone Market share. According to Convergence Catalyst, Android is expected to capture over half of Indian Smartphone Market Share by end of 2012. Another Mobile OS, Bada, is also expected to gain significantly taking its Indian market share to 10.2%. On the other hand, Nokia is expected to halve to 23.3% in 2012. Blackberry is also expected to slide from 13.3% market share last year to 9.9% by end of this year[12].

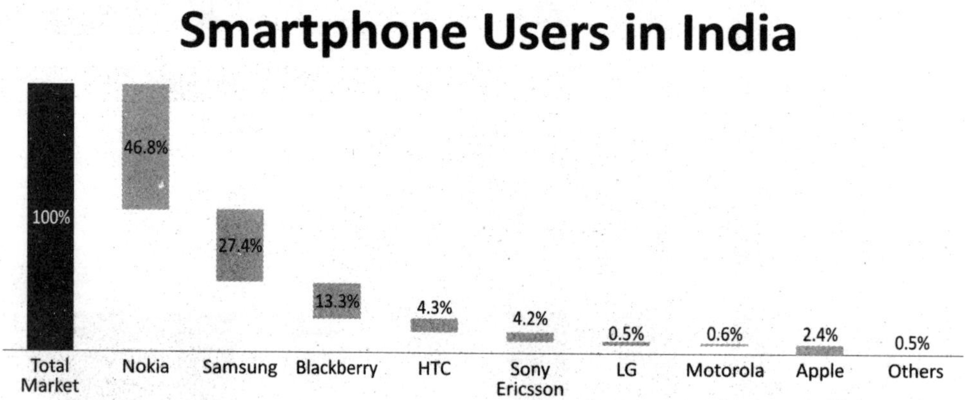

13

In case of tablets, as per the CyberMedia Research recent figures reveal that 158,000 tablets were sold between October, 2010 and June, 2011 (3 quarters). As per CMRI sales figures for India's tablets, 85000 tablets were sold between November, 2010 and March, 2011 and Samsung had 84.7% share, Apple 5.9% share and Olive has 8.2% share[14].

---

12. http://trak.in/tags/business/2012/02/16/indian-smartphone-market-growth-overview
13. http://www.slideshare.net/Ethinos/a-snapshot-of-digital-india-may-2012
14. http://trak.in/tags/business/2011/09/30/tablet-sales-india-overview-2

Further as per CyberMedia Research[15] Sales of Tablet computers in India touched 158,000 units in the 9-month period ending June, 2011 with some 10 vendors offering 27 brands between them. Samsung emerged as the best selling tablet brand in India. Olivepad launched the first media tablet in India in July, 2010. The first major international brand to launch followed in October, 2010 the Samsung Galaxy Tab. The Apple iPad, the most well recognized tablet, arrived in India only in January, 2011. Leading Vendors (in terms of unit shipments) are Samsung with a 45.8% market share; Apple with 18.4% and RIM with 14.8%. Top Ten Tablet vendors in India (alphabetical) are Acer, Apple, Binatone, HCL, HTC, Motorola, Notion Ink, Olive, RIM and Samsung.

A survey by Neilsen and Informate throws a few interesting perspectives as follows[16]:—

- There are 27 Million Smartphone users in Urban India 1 Lakh+ towns.
- 22 Million Social Networking and 16 Million Streaming Video users on the smartphone.
- Nearly 1 in 5 mobile phone users in Urban India has a smartphone (18%)
- The 18-24 age group has the highest incidence of smartphone ownership (13%).

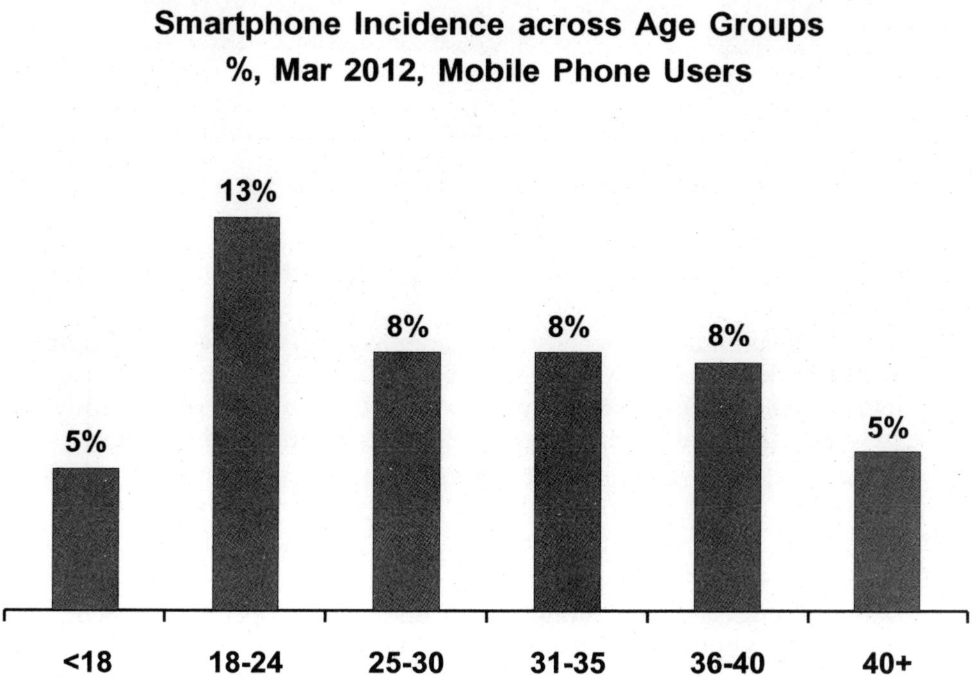

15. http://indiatechonline.com/cybermedia-research—tablet-market-in-india-579.php
16. http://www.pluggd.in/number-of-smartphone-users-in-india-297

Neilsen and Informate's survey further reveals the projected Smartphone Usage as below:

- 22 million use their smart phones for social networking;
- 24 million use it for running online searches.
- 19 million smartphone users are chatting and using webmail.
- 16 million users view streaming video, and use smartphones for maps and navigation.
- 8 million smart phone users use it for banking & finance, travel, shopping and accessing other web portals

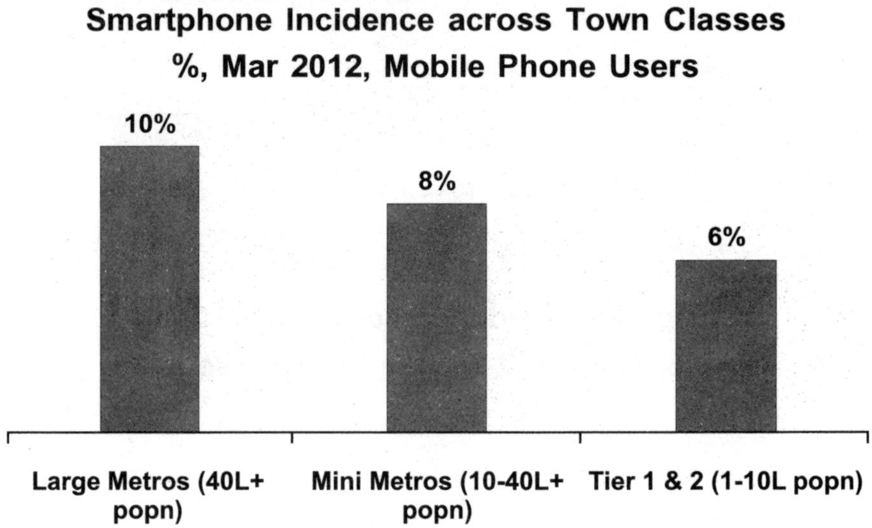

Further, more and more companies in India have started giving tablets to their employees.

The new culture that is currently being adopted across the world including in India is that of Bring Your Own Device (BYoD). This enables employees to bring their own specific devices to the work place for the purposes of efficiently and effectively carrying on the performance of their obligations and services.

The worldwide market and the Indian market have seen a booming of these smart devices. Let us look at some of the examples of these smart devices, as defined by Wikipedia, which are currently available in the worldwide and Indian markets, which are as follows:

A **smartphone**[17] is a mobile phone built on a mobile operating system, with more advanced computing capability and connectivity than a feature phone. The first smartphones combined the functions of a personal digital assistant (PDA) with a mobile phone. Later models added the functionality of portable media players, low-end compact digital cameras, pocket video cameras, and GPS navigation units to form one multi-use device. Many modern smartphones also

17. http://en.wikipedia.org/wiki/Smartphone

include high-resolution touchscreens and web browsers that display standard web pages as well as mobile-optimized sites.

The **iPhone**[18] is a line of smartphones designed and marketed by Apple Inc. The iPhone runs Apple's iOS mobile operating system, originally named "iPhone OS". The first iPhone was released on June 29, 2007; the most recent iPhone, the sixth-generation iPhone 5, was released on September 21, 2012. The user interface is built around the device's multi-touch screen, including a virtual keyboard rather than a physical one. The iPhone has Wi-Fi and cellular connectivity 2G, 3G and 4G (iPhone 5 only).

The **iPad**[19] is a line of tablet computers designed and marketed by Apple Inc. The iPad runs Apple's iOS operating system. The first iPad was released on April 3, 2010; the most recent iPads, the fourth-generation iPad and iPad Mini, are expected to ship on November 2, 2012. The user interface is built around the device's multi-touchscreen, including a virtual keyboard rather than a physical one. The iPad has Wi-Fi and cellular connectivity [2G, 3G and 4G (third and fourth generations and iPad Mini only)].

A **tablet computer**[20], or simply **tablet**, is a mobile computer, larger than a mobile phone or personal digital assistant, integrated into a flat touch screen and primarily operated by touching the screen and instead of using a physical keyboard it often uses an on screen virtual keyboard.

The iPads, Tablets, Smart Phones and Smart Devices are increasingly becoming the basis of our day to day existence and activities. Not only personal information is being stored on the Smart Devices but more significantly corporate information including confidential data and information is also being stored, published and transmitted using these iPads, Tablets, Smart Phones and Smart Devices.

In the Indian corporate sector, I find that almost all top management of all companies have some Smart Devices or the other with them. More and more people rely upon iPads, Tablets, Smart Phones and Smart Devices as tools, having very strong computing powers in their hands while they on the move. Carrying of laptop is now old fashion. It is the new Smart Device which defines the status of a person and also the increase of his estimation in the eyes of others.

There are variety of advantages of these iPads, Tablets, Smart Phones and Smart Devices:

Smartphones can do things much more quickly than their standard mobile phone and PDA precursors[21].

(1) **Keeping you organised** – smartphone handsets can function as personal organisers, with electronic diaries, contact lists, and automatic reminders.

18. http://en.wikipedia.org/wiki/Iphone
19. http://en.wikipedia.org/wiki/Ipad
20. http://en.wikipedia.org/wiki/Tablet_computer
21. http://www.is4profit.com/business-advice/it-telecoms/smartphones/the-benefits-of-smartphones.html

(2) **Flexible working** – as with a PDA, you can use your smartphone to take notes, review and edit your appointments, contacts and documents, all while you're on the move.

(3) **Information at your fingertips** – more and more services are being made available on smartphones, from access to maps, directions to television transmissions with news coverage or weather reports to traffic information and scheduling alerts which means your business can always stay one step ahead of what's going on.

(4) **Never out of touch** – you can connect to the internet for e-mail and web access 'on the move', or connect to your computer network to access relevant data, wherever you are, making it easier for remote workers, or a mobile workforce to stay in touch with the business.

(5) **Better information sharing** – considerably more data can be received and transmitted *via* a smartphone, such as large e-mail attachments or data files from websites. Previous mobiles could only manage small e-mails without attachments.

(6) **Greater functionality** – many models offer built-in digital cameras with immediate snap and send functionality, so remote workers or offsite staff can instantly photograph and send images or videos of anything from supplier's goods to site inspections or damaged warehouse machinery. Smartphones could offer you a new way of marketing to customers, Multimedia Messaging Services (MMS) lets you include animation, graphics and music in a message.

(7) **Faster communication** – web access is quicker than in previously available mobiles, making it easier to access e-mail and information from the Net. Some models and carriers offer an 'always-on' internet access service making connection easier

(8) **Multimedia Functions**[22]:— Smartphones not only allow you to store and play your entire collection of music, they allow you to download and watch movies and television shows. Favorite media is at your fingertips.

(9) **Applications**[23]: Perhaps the greatest advantage to owning a smartphone is the availability of thousands of small applications - called apps. A wide variety of apps can be downloaded from online stores, allowing you customize and personalize your phone. Games, photo utilities, online magazines and interactive reference apps can help enhance how you use your smartphone.

(10) **Remote Office**[24]: Many smartphones offer functions and apps so you can remain productive no matter where you go.

Further, there are also disadvantages that surround the use of these mobile devices.

---

22. http://techtips.salon.com/advantages-smartphones-3480.html
23. http://techtips.salon.com/advantages-smartphones-3480.html
24. http://techtips.salon.com/advantages-smartphones-3480.html

These are Smart Devices which are generally light, easy to carry and portable. But because of convenience of their sizes and portability, it is often possible that more people land up in losing their Smart Devices.

According to the Federal Communications Commission, the theft of cell phones makes up 30 to 40 per cent of all robberies nationwide. In New York City, thefts of iPhones and iPads rose 44 per cent through April of 2012, according to NYPD statistics, the New York Daily Newsreports. The city's website says mobile phones account for 81% of all electronic device thefts. The Chicago Tribune reports that police in the Windy City attribute an increase in robbery in 2011 to the theft of smartphones. In downtown Los Angeles, thefts of cellphones increased 32 per cent in the first quarter of 2012, reports the Los Angeles Times.[25]

According to a new survey, more than 8,000 devices are left at seven of the largest airports in the United States, including: Chicago, O'Hare, Denver International, San Francisco International, Charlotte Douglas, Miami International, Orlando International and Minneapolis/St. Paul.[26]

The survey by Credant Technologies reveals some of the downsides of mobile and the security issues raised when the devices get lost. Here's the breakdown of the devices getting lost:

- Smartphones and tablets: 3,444 (43.0%)
- Laptops: 3,576 (44.6%)
- USB drives: 996 (12.4%)

The biggest threat remains losing the device some 1,000 phones are lost in the UK every day. With an increasing number of smart devices used to access company servers, companies are risking contacts, emails and financial information falling into the wrong hands.[27]

The adoptions of iPads, Tablets, Smart Phones and Smart Devices have now brought in a new cultural revolution. Whether it is Doctors, Lawyers, Corporate Honchos, Academicians, Professionals, Government Employees or any other profession, these Smart Devices have re-defined the deliverance of the way, the people approach their day to day jobs providing professional services and more significantly trying to make themselves far more efficient as time passes by.

Further, these Smart Devices are now being exposed to various kinds of misuses. Increasing illegal and criminal use of these Smart Devices has provided far more different challenges pertaining to law enforcement agencies.

A confidential survey conducted by the International Air Transport Association, an airline trade group, and obtained by ABC News last year, found 75 incidents from 2003 to 2009, in which an electronic device was suspected to have interfered with a flight's controls, communications or other equipment. The

---

25. http://www.cbsnews.com/8301-504083_162-57511364-504083/iphone-related-crime-on-the-rise-as-smartphones-gain-popularity
26. http://techcrunch.com/2012/07/06/dont-put-down-that-ipad-8000-mobile-devices-left-at-top-u-s-airports.
27. http://www.nokiasiemensnetworks.com/news-events/insight-newsletter/articles/smart-devices-a-big-security-threat-for-consumers-and-enterprises.

report relied on anecdotal information from pilots and crews, however, and didn't confirm that any of the incidents was actually caused by a passenger's device. Given that 72,462,640 passenger flights departed from U.S. airports alone in that period, according to the Bureau of Transportation Statistics, this is hardly convincing evidence.[28]

It is in this context that the adoption of iPads, Tablets, Smart Phones and Smart Devices bring forward various complicated legal, policy and regulatory challenges.

This book aims to examine the legal nuances and aspects pertaining to use of iPads, Tablets, Smart Phones and Smart Devices in India and what are the legal ramifications concerning the same. This book further aims to provide to be a guide for all relevant stakeholders in the digital ecosystem who use these iPads, Tablets, Smart Phones and Smart Devices for the purposes of not just doing day to day communications but also the performance of their day to day activities.

Needless to say, these iPads, Tablets, Smart Phones and Smart Devices are becoming an integral part of our day to day existence.

This book seeks to address mysteries behind the legal aspects concerning the use of these iPads, Tablets, Smart Phones and Smart Devices.

---

28. http://www.bloomberg.com/news/2012-08-29/using-ipads-on-takeoff-landing-faa-should-consider-it.html

CHAPTER 2
MOBILE LAW IN INDIA

All iPads, Tablets, Smart Phones and Smart Devices are covered by the Indian law prevailing for the time being in force. This has come as a strange revelation to some people who believe that these iPads, Tablets, Smart Phones and Smart Devices are only couple of years old and yet it is hard to believe that the law is so well advanced to deal with all these kinds of iPads, Tablets, Smart Phones and Smart Devices. The fact still remains that there are various legal, policy and regulatory ramifications pertaining to use of Smart Devices in India.

The first fundamental clarity that we all need to have is that all these iPads, Tablets, Smart Phones and Smart Devices that we have talked about are communication devices, which are used to communicate audio, video, image or text and are nothing but a computer resource, since they all have computing capabilities with memory functions. Further all these iPads, Tablets, Smart Phones and Smart Devices deal with ultimately data and information in the electronic form and are essential to the digital ecosystem. Hence, all these iPads, Tablets, Smart Phones and Smart Devices are fully covered by the Indian Cyberlaw being the Information Technology Act, 2000.

Indian Cyberlaw, being the Information Technology Act, 2000, is India's mother legislation dealing with the entire issues pertaining to the use of computers, computer systems, computer networks, computer resources and communication devices as well as data and information in the electronic form. At this juncture, it becomes important to examine as to what the law says in the context of iPads, Tablets, Smart Phones and Smart Devices.

India's Mobile Law is the Information Technology Act, 2000 as amended by the Information Technology (Amendment) Act, 2008. The Indian Cyberlaw being the Information Technology Act, 2000 was originally meant to be a law aimed at providing the legal recognition for transactions carried out by means of electronic data interchange and other means of communication commonly referred to as e-commerce which involves the use of alternatives to paper-based methods of communication and storage of information. It further aimed to facilitate electronic filing of documents with the Governmental agencies and had sought to amend four different laws of India namely the Indian Penal Code, the Indian Evidence Act, 1872, the Banker's Books Evidence Act, 1891 and the Reserve Bank of India Act, 1934.

Indian Cyberlaw had given a very exhaustive definition of the term "computer' which had defined "computer" to mean any electronic, magnetic, optical or other high-speed data processing device or system which performs logical, arithmetic and memory functions by manipulations of electronic, magnetic or optical impulses and includes all input, output, processing, storage, computer software or communication facilities which are connected or related to the computer in a computer system or computer network. Clearly, the definition of the term "computer" was vast enough to include all kinds of mobile phones therein since all mobile phones are data processing devices or systems which perform logical, arithmetic and memory functions.

However with the widespread adoption of mobiles in India, the Government of India decided to amend the Information Technology Act, 2000. These new amendments will effect by means of the Information Technology (Amendment) Act, 2008. These amendments have had the effect of transforming India's Cyberlaw into India's Mobile Law.

By virtue of the new amendments very substantial provisions of law have been inserted as well as amended so as to incorporate therein all kinds of coverages pertaining to applicability of the said provisions to communication devices, mobiles, personal digital assistants, smart phones, etc.

I would now specifically deal with the relevant provisions under the Information Technology Act, 2000 which are applicable to mobiles, communication devices, cell phones, iPads, Tablets, Smart Phones and Smart Devices. Each of the said provisions are extremely relevant and pertinent from the perspective of their applicability to mobiles, communication devices, cell phones, iPads, Tablets, Smart Phones and Smart Devices

Definitions are most integral part of any book.

We now proceed to examine the various definitions to different terms relevant to iPads, Tablets, Smart Phones and Smart Devices, mobiles and communication devices that have been prescribed by section 2 of the amended Information Technology Act, 2000.

Section 2(1)(ha) of the Information Technology Act, 2000

> *Section 2(1)(ha)—"communication device" means cell phones, personal digital assistance or combination of both or any other device used to communicate, send or transmit any text, video, audio or image.*

The Information Technology Act, 2000 has been amended by the Information Technology (Amendment) Act, 2008. One of the most dramatic changes that the amended Information Technology Act, 2000 has brought forward is its specific explicit coverage of communication devices.

For the first time in the history of independent India, the phrase "communication device" has figured in a legislation which has also proceeded to give its detailed legal definition. The definition of the term "communication device" appears in section 2(1)(ha) of the amended Information Technology Act, 2000. The definition is both illustrative as well as generic. As per the said definition, communication device means the following:

(a) Cell phones.

(b) Personal digital assistants.

(c) Combination of cell phones and personal digital assistants, or

(d) Any other device which is used to communicate, send or transmit any text, video, audio or image.

A perusal of the said definition clearly shows that this is a very wide definition of the term "communication device". By specific reference to cell phones, all mobile phones, iPads, Tablets, Smart Phones, Smart Devices and aspects related thereto, have been brought within the ambit of the definition of the term "communication device". This would include also not just the basic cell phones but even smart phones and i-Phones of any make, description or manufacture of any kind whatsoever. In addition, lots of people today use personal digital assistants. These personal digital assistants help people not just to increase their productivity and efficiency but also assist them in leading their life in a far more orderly and disciplined manner. All these personal digital assistants including blackberries have been brought within the ambit of the definition of the term "communication device".

The real beauty of the definition given under section 2(1)(ha) of the amended Information Technology Act, 2000 clearly lies in its broad futuristic definition of the term "communication device". As per the said definition, any other device which is used to communicate, send or transmit any text, video, audio or image would also classify as a communication device.

According to Wikipedia:—

(i) "A text is a coherent set of symbols that transmits some kind of informative message.[29]

(ii) Video is the technology of electronically capturing, recording, processing, storing, transmitting, and reconstructing a sequence of still images representing scenes in motion.[30]

(iii) Audio is sound that is capable of being heard.[31]

(iv) An image (from Latin imago) is an artefact, for example a two-dimensional picture, that has a similar appearance to some subject—usually a physical object or a person[32]."

The term "information" has been defined under section 2(1)(v) of the Information Technology Act, 2000 in the following terms:

"Information" includes data, message, text, images, sound, voice, codes, computer programmes, software and databases or micro film or computer generated micro fiche.

"Data" is defined by section 2(1)(o) of the amended Information Technology Act, 2000 as a representation of information, knowledge, facts, concepts or instructions which are being prepared or have been prepared in a formalised manner, and is intended to be processed, is being processed or has been processed in a computer system or computer network, and may be in any form

29. http://en.wikipedia.org/wiki/Text.
30. http://en.wikipedia.org/wiki/Video.
31. http://en.wikipedia.org/wiki/Audio.
32. en.wikipedia.org/wiki/Image.

(including computer printouts magnetic or optical storage media, punched cards, punched tapes) or stored internally in the memory of the computer.

Since the term "information" includes data, message, text, images, sound and voice, any device which is used to communicate send or transmit data would qualify as a "communication device."

When one analyses the definition of the term "communication devices" in today's context, it becomes clear that the said definition of the term "communication device" is wider than the mere concept of iPads, Tablets, Smart Phones and Smart Devices. Further, since a computer is also used to communicate, send, transmit any text, audio, video or image, a computer would also qualify as a "communication device" within the meaning of the said definition. In that sense, the term "communication device" appears to be far broader than the definition of the term "computer" under section 2(1)(i) of the amended Information Technology Act, 2000.

The net result of this definition is that all kinds of communication devices of whatever make, nature, manufacture or character would qualify as communication devices defined under section 2(1)(ha) of the amended Information Technology Act, 2000. Thus, all mobile phones, cellular phones, smart phones, personal digital assistants, iPads, Tablets, Smart Devices and any electronic device of any description whatsoever, used to send, communicate or transmit data would qualify as a communication "device". This definition is in the widest possible amplitude and impacts all users of mobile phones, cellular phones, smart phones, iPads, Tablets, Smart Devices and other intelligent devices of any nature, which are used to send, communicate or transmit data.

The net effect of the introduction of the definition of the term "communication device" under section 2(1)(ha) of the amended Information Technology Act, 2000 clearly shows that the Indian Information Technology Act, 2000 is the relevant law that shall apply to all mobile, wireless, wire line and/or communication devices, iPads, Tablets, Smart Phones, Smart Devices and all activities concerning data and information resident therein, inclusive of all communications and transmissions of data and information inherent or resident therein, as well as data and information in the digital format on mobile networks. Considering that India has a huge penetration of iPads, Tablets, Smart Phones and Smart Devices which is constantly growing, iPads, Tablets, Smart Phones and Smart Devices users will now need to be more careful of their activities done using all kinds of iPads, Tablets, Smart Phones and Smart Devices, mobile phones, personal digital assistants as also other kinds of communication devices.

Section 2(1)(j) of the Information Technology Act, 2000

Another major path-breaking amendment to the Information Technology Act, 2000 has been in section 2(1)(j) of the Information Technology Act, 2000. The earlier language has been substituted by new language. Section 2(1)(j) reads as follows:

> *"computer network" means the inter-connection of one or more computers or computer systems or communication device through—*

(i) *the use of satellite, microwave, terrestrial line, wire, wireless or other communication media; and*

(ii) *terminals or a complex consisting of two or more inter-connected computers or communication device whether or not the inter-connection is continuously maintained.*

The net effect of this new amendment is that all inter-connection of one or more communication devices would come within the ambit of definition of the term "computer network". Earlier, the way the term "computer network" was defined under section 2(1)(j) was only with respect to inter-connection of one or more computers through various means. However, with the onset of huge adoption of iPads, Tablets, Smart Phones and Smart Devices and increasing usage of mobile networks, the term "computer network" has been defined to include the following:—

(i) Inter-connection of one or more computers and computer systems.

(ii) Inter-connection of one or more communication devices.

(iii) Inter-connection of one or more computers and communication devices.

(iv) Inter-connection of one or more computer systems and/or communication devices.

The aforesaid inter-connection can either be through the use of satellite, microwave, terrestrial line, wire, wireless or other communication media.

All kinds of inter-connection of communication devices through use of wire, wireless and other communication media have been brought within the ambit of the definition of the term "computer network". All mobile networks set up through wires as also connected through satellite, microwave, terrestrial line, wire, wireless or other communication media would also qualify as a computer network.

Further, the inter-connection of one or more communication devices through wireless would also qualify as a computer network.

The term "computer network" also includes the inter-connection done through terminals or a complex consisting of the following:

(a) Two or more inter-connected computers.

(b) Two or more inter-connected communication devices.

This is irrespective as to whether or not, the inter-connection is continuously maintained. Thus, even if there is a communication network consisting of two or more inter-connected computers or communication devices, it would still qualify as a computer network. Further, there is no need for the inter-connection to be continuously maintained in order for the said complex communication network to qualify as a computer network. The net effect of this definition is that all mobile networks, wire networks, wireless networks and wifi networks would qualify as a computer network as per the requirements of section 2(1)(j) of the amended Information Technology Act, 2000. This definition is of the greatest significance, since it has become extremely all comprehensive and incorporates within its ambit all kinds of computerized networks, including computer networks, wire networks, wireless networks, wifi networks as also networks that help, connect other communication media.

It is pertinent to note that section 2(1)(j) uses the phrase "other communication media". The phrase "other communication media" has not been defined under the amended Information Technology Act, 2000.

Wikipedia defines that "*In communication, media (singular medium) are the storage and transmission channels or tools used to store and deliver information or data. It is often referred to as synonymous with mass media or news media, but may refer to a single medium used to communicate any data for any purpose.*[33]

Thus, the aforesaid definition of the term "computer network" is huge and comprehensive in its ambit and incorporates all prevailing and perceived networks of digital/electronic format using computers, computer systems, computer networks, computer resources and communication devices.

Section 2(1)(nb) of the Information Technology Act, 2000

The amended Information Technology Act, 2000 has provided for new provisions for cyber security. For the first time in the history of legislative jurisprudence in India, the term "cyber security" has been given a legal definition. The said legal definition is enshrined in section 2(1)(nb) of the amended Information Technology Act, 2000.

Normally speaking, the term "cyber security" conjectures in one's mind, the image of security pertaining to computers in cyber space and security of procedures and/or transactions happening in cyber space and the Internet. However, section 2(1)(nb) has given far more wider definition of the term "cyber security" to also incorporate protecting information equipment, devices, computer, computer resource, communication device and information stored therein from unauthorised access, use, disclosure, disruption, modification or destruction.

Section 2(1)(nb) of the Information Technology Act, 2000 states as follows:

> *"cyber security" means protecting information, equipment, devices, computer, computer resource, communication device and information stored therein from unauthorised access, use disclosure, disruption, modification or destruction.*

Thus, cyber security is concerned with the protection and preservation of the following:—

(a) Information,

(b) Equipment,

(c) Devices,

(d) Computer,

(e) Computer resource,

(f) Communication device, and

(g) All information shared therein.

All the aforesaid need to be protected from the following activities:

(a) Unauthorised access,

(b) Unauthorised use,

(c) Unauthorised disclosure,

33. http://en.wikipedia.org/wiki/Media_(communication).

(d) Unauthorised disruption,

(e) Unauthorised modification, or

(f) Unauthorised destruction.

This definition has now added a new dimension to the concept of cyber security. This definition is also in *sync* with the current prevailing times, since mobiles and mobile devices are increasingly now being made as smart devices which can access the Internet and can store huge volumes of information. Already, as per information and trends available in the public domain more and more iPads, Tablets, Smart Phones and Smart Devices are being used for the purposes of accessing the internet. Consequently, keeping "communication devices" out of the purview of cyber security would not have been prudent. Therefore, section 2(1)(nb) has been drafted by lawmakers in futuristic terms, keeping in mind the developments that are likely to happen in the future.

It is pertinent to note that section 2(1)(nb) is a precursor to elaborate provisions pertaining to cyber security that have been detailed by various provisions of the amended Information Technology Act, 2000.

Section 2(1)(ta) of the Information Technology Act, 2000

"Section 2(1)(ta)—Electronic Signature

"electronic signature" means authentication of any electronic record by a subscriber by means of the electronic technique specified in the Second Schedule and includes digital signature.

Section 2(1)(ta) defines the term "electronic signature" to mean authentication of any electronic records by subscribers by means of electronic techniques specified in the Second Schedule and includes digital signatures. Since, communication devices including iPads, Tablets, Smart Phones and Smart Devices have electronic data and information resident therein; authentication of the said mobile electronic records would also qualify to come within the ambit of "electronic signatures".

(1) Mobile electronic signatures could also be brought within the ambit of "electronic signatures" by the Government at an appropriate time in the future.

(2) A mobile signature is a digital signature generated either on a mobile phone or on a SIM card[34].

(3) The mobile e-signature allows identifying the signatory and ensures authenticity of electronic documents thus signed.[35]

(4) Mobile signatures are electronic signatures which are created using a mobile device and rely on signature or certification services in a location independent telecommunication environment. They allow signatory mobility beyond fixed, secure desktop workstations with trusted, personal signing equipment. Although using mobile devices for signature creation has several shortcomings (*e.g.*, display size, communication costs, limited computing power), the high market penetration of cell phones and

34. www.wikipedia.org.

35. www.wikipedia.org.

the mobility gained make this effort potentially successful and promising.[36]

Section 2(1)(w) of the amended Information Technology Act, 2000

One of the most significant developments and contributions of the amended Indian Cyberlaw is that it has come up with an entirely new concept of "intermediary". The said concept is a very vast and elaborate concept and is pretty wide and comprehensive in its approach, applicability and ambit.

Section 2(1)(w) has, for the first time, defined the term "intermediary" under the amended Information Technology Act, 2000.

Section 2(1)(w) states as follows:

> *"intermediary" with respect to any particular electronic records, means any person who on behalf of another person receives, stores or transmits that record or provides any service with respect to that record and includes telecom service providers, network service providers, internet service providers, web-hosting service providers, search engines, online payment sites, online auction sites, online market places and cyber cafes.*

In the context of mobiles, iPads, Tablets, Smart Phones and Smart Devices, intermediary with respect to mobile electronic records, would mean any person who on behalf of another person receives, stores or transmits that record or provides any service with respect to that record. The said definition is both prescriptive as well as illustrative. The said definition includes, within its ambit, all kinds of telecom service providers. Thus, all kinds of mobile service providers of any nature whatsoever, who on behalf of another person receive, store or transmit any electronic record or provide any service with respect to that record, would qualify as an "intermediary". Thus, all mobile service providers including telecom service providers would be intermediaries. Further, all mobile value added service providers, which are providing different kinds of value added services, would also qualify as "intermediaries", within the meaning of section 2(1)(w) of the amended Information Technology Act, 2000.

Further, all kinds of mobile payments sites, which provide payment related service on mobiles, iPads, Tablets, Smart Phones and Smart Devices would also qualify as "intermediaries".

The definition of the term "intermediary" is very vast and huge and would incorporate within its ambit almost any service provider of any nature or description whatsoever, who is providing any services pertaining to iPads, Tablets, Smart Phones and Smart Devices as also data resident on, received at or transmitted by the said computers, computer systems, computer networks, computer resources and communication devices. Section 2(1)(w) has an added significance since that has to be read with the requirements of the section 79 of the amended Information Technology Act, 2000. These will be dealt with separately under a separate subsequent chapter.

While it is difficult to discuss the parameters of words in just the definition clauses, however the justice to the words have been done, by discussing it in a broader sense in the chapters ahead.

36. www.wikipedia.org.

Legalities

Section 3 of the Information Technology Act, 2000

The Indian Cyberlaw has dealt with the important issue pertaining to authentication of electronic records. Electronic records, by their very inherent nature, are of such a nature that they are capable of being duplicated or replicated with very minimal, additional cost. Further, the inherent nature of electronic records is such that the copy is almost exactly the same as the original. As such, in the context of the ecosystem pertaining to electronic records, authentication of electronic records assumes tremendous significance. Section 3 of the amended Information Technology Act, 2000 provides the legal framework that exists in India for authentication of electronic record. Section 3 of the amended Information Technology Act, 2000 provides as follows;

*"**Section 3. Authentication of Electronic Records.**—(1) Subject to the provisions of this section, any subscriber may authenticate an electronic record by affixing his digital signature.*

(2) The authentication of the electronic record shall be effected by the use of asymmetric crypto system and hash function which envelop and transform the initial electronic record into another electronic record.

Explanation.—For the purposes of this sub-section, "hash function" means an algorithm mapping or translation of one sequence of bits into another, generally smaller, set known as "hash result" such that an electronic record yields the same hash result every time the algorithm is executed with the same electronic record as its input making it computationally infeasible—

(a) to derive or reconstruct the original electronic record from the hash result produced by the algorithm;

(b) that two electronic records can produce the same hash result using the algorithm.

(3) Any person by the use of a public key of the subscriber can verify the electronic record.

(4) The private key and the public key are unique to the subscriber and constitute a functioning key pair."

Section 3 of the amended Information Technology Act, 2000 has provided for authentication of electronic records. Since the year 2000, this provision has provided for authentication of electronic records by affixing of digital signatures.

Section 3 talks about the process of authentication of an electronic record. Authentication is very important in order to ensure the veracity and authenticity of the electronic record. It also enables to determine whether a particular electronic record has originated from the source, which it says, is the source of its origin. Without authentication, the authenticity of an electronic record is very difficult to prove. It is also very difficult to prove whether an electronic record has been tampered with, without resorting to authentication.

The law provides that any subscriber can do the authentication of the electronic record by affixing his digital signature. Digital signatures have been defined in section 2(1)(p) to mean authentication of any electronic record by a subscriber by means of an electronic method or procedure in accordance with section 3.

Section 3(2) declares a technology, specifically mandated for digital signatures, to be legal and valid in India. The section states that the authentication of the electronic record by digital signatures shall be affected in India under the Information Technology Act, 2000 only by the use of asymmetric crypto system and hash function. The hash functions must envelop and transform the initial electronic record into another electronic record. This section is of particular relevance to the Information Technology Act, 2000 as for the first time, it specifies a technology standard for an electronic process, in this case for digital signatures, being asymmetric crypto system with hash function.

The *Explanation* to section 3(2) explains hash function to mean an algorithm mapping or translation of one sequence of bits into another generally smaller, set known as "hash result". The algorithm mapping or translation must be such that an electronic record yields the same hash result every time the algorithm is executed with the same electronic record as its input. This must be done so that it makes it computationally infeasible, to devise or reconstruct the original electronic record from the hash result produced by the algorithm and further, that the two electronic records can produce the same hash result using the algorithm.

The entire regime of digital signatures is based upon the concept of public key and private key. Both these keys are simultaneously generated by the algorithm; while the private key remains with the subscriber, the public key remains with the Certifying Authority and the public key is used by other members of the public to verify that the digital signature on a particular document has been affixed by using the private key of the concerned subscriber.

Section 3(3) further states that any person, by use of the public key of the subscriber, can verify the electronic record and the fact that a subscriber, who has affixed his digital signature using his private key, has authenticated the electronic record.

Section 3(4) states that the private key and the public key are unique to the subscriber. The two keys have to be unique, otherwise the said digital signature would not work. Also, both the public and private key must constitute a functioning key pair. The words "key pair" have been defined by section 2(1)(x) as a pair of private key and its mathematical related public key, which are generated at the same time by an algorithm. The two public and private keys are related to each other in such a manner that the public key alone can verify a digital signature, which is created by a private key. If the key pair is not functioning, then the digital signature shall not work and it will not be possible to authenticate an electronic record.

Of particular significance is the fact that section 3A has been inserted into the Information Technology Act, 2000 by the Information Technology (Amendment) Act, 2008.

Section 3A provides as follows:

*"**Section 3A. Electronic Signature.**—(1) Notwithstanding anything contained in section 3, but subject to the provisions of sub-section (2), a subscriber may authenticate*

any electronic record by such electronic signature or electronic authentication technique which—

(a) is considered reliable; and

(b) may be specified in the Second Schedule.

(2) For the purposes of this section any electronic signature or electronic authentication technique shall be considered reliable if—

(a) the signature creation data or the authentication data are, within the context in which they are used, linked to the signatory or, as the case may be, the authenticator and to no other person;

(b) the signature creation data or the authentication data were, at the time of signing, under the control of the signatory or, as the case may be, the authenticator and of no other person;

(c) any alteration to the electronic signature made after affixing such signature is detectable;

(d) any alteration to the information made after its authentication by electronic signature is detectable; and

(e) it fulfils such other conditions which may be prescribed.

(3) The Central Government may prescribe the procedure for the purpose of ascertaining whether electronic signature is that of the person by whom it is purported to have been affixed or authenticated.

(4) The Central Government may, by notification in the Official Gazette, add to or omit any electronic signature or electronic authentication technique and the procedure for affixing such signature from the Second Schedule:

Provided that no electronic signature or authentication technique shall be specified in the Second Schedule unless such signature or technique is reliable.

(5) Every notification issued under sub-section (4) shall be laid before each House of Parliament."

A perusal of section 3A would clearly show that it is very broad and incorporates within its ambit, all kinds of electronic authentication, including mobile authentication. The provisions of section 3A are so wide enough to incorporate therein, mobile electronic signatures or electronic authentication mechanisms which could be used on iPads, Tablets, Smart Phones and Smart Devices. The mandatory requirement for the said mobile electronic signatures or mobile authentication techniques is that it is considered reliable and which may be specified in the Second Schedule.

The Government of India has bestowed upon itself, the ability to prescribe any electronic signature or electronic authentication technique and the procedure for affixing such signature in the Second Schedule.

At a time when Unique Identification Project (UID)/Aadhaar Project in India is beginning to take roots, it is very relevant to recognise the significance of biometrics and other forms of electronic authentication. Herein lies a wonderful opportunity for the Government to seize thought leadership in this direction by specifying a variety of electronic signatures. It will be interesting to see how the

Government seizes the wonderful opportunity provided to it by virtue of section 3A of the amended Information Technology Act, 2000. One of the biggest drawbacks of the Information Technology Act, 2000 was that it was a technology specific legislation and that it did not respect technological neutrality. The Information Technology (Amendment) Act, 2008, inserted an era of technological neutrality by introducing the concept of "electronic signatures".

A perusal of section 3A(2) clearly shows that any mobile electronic signature or mobile authentication technique shall be considered reliable if and only if all the five conditions stipulated under section 3A(2) (a) to (e) are fulfilled.

Thus, the *first* important legal requirement for mobile signatures to be considered reliable is that the signature creation date or authentication date, are, within the context in which they are used, linked to the signatory or as the case may be the authenticator and to no other person. This condition is mandatory as it goes to the root of the principles of electronic authentication. There can be no compromise to this basic principle.

The *second* legal requirement that mobile signatures need to fulfil are that the signature creation data or the authentication data were, at the time of signing, under the control of the signatory or, as the case may be, the authenticator and of no other person. The control of signatory or the authenticator over the signature creation data or authentication data, is key for any kinds of electronic authentication and mobile authentication is no exception to the said fundamental premise.

The *third* important requirement of reliability for mobile signatures is that any alteration to the said mobile signatures, made after affixing such signatures, is detectable. Such an exercise is absolutely essential for ensuring the authenticity and veracity of the concerned mobile electronic records, on which the said mobile signatures are affixed.

The *fourth* important mandatory condition of reliability for mobile signatures is that any alteration to the information made, after its authentication, by the concerned electronic signature or mobile signature is detectable.

The *fifth* important condition of reliability for any mobile signature is that it must fulfil such other conditions which may be prescribed. These conditions would be prescribed by the Central Government from time-to-time, keeping in mind the requirements of the times, business and society. Further, the Central Government has retained upon itself the power to prescribe the procedure for the purpose of ascertaining, whether electronic signature or mobile signature is that of the person, by whom it is purported to have been affixed or authenticated. Further, under section 3A of the amended Information Technology Act, 2000, the Central Government has retained upon itself, the discretion to notify in the Official Gazette, any changes to any electronic signatures or electronic authentication techniques. The Central Government may add to or omit any electronic signature or electronic authentication technique and the procedure for affixing such signatures, from the Second Schedule. The proviso to section 3A(4) clearly shows that no electronic signatures or authentication techniques, including mobile signatures or mobile authentication techniques, shall be specified in the Second Schedule unless such signatures or technique is reliable.

It is pertinent to point out that though the amended Information Technology Act, 2000 has provided for the concept of electronic signatures, yet for the purposes of section 3, the only specific signatures that have been stipulated by law, for the purposes of authentication of electronic records, are digital signatures. No other kinds of electronic signatures have, at the time of writing, being yet prescribed for the purposes of authentication of electronic records. As such, the digital signatures, as issued by the duly licensed Certifying Authority, as licensed by the Controller of Certifying Authorities, in India are the only legal method, by means of which a subscriber can authenticate any electronic records.

Section 4 of the Information Technology Act, 2000

*"**Section 4. Legal recognition of electronic records.**—Where any law provides that information or any other matter shall be in writing or in the typewritten or printed form, then, notwithstanding anything contained in such law, such requirement shall be deemed to have been satisfied if such information or matter is—*

(a) rendered or made available in an electronic form; and

(b) accessible so as to be usable for a subsequent reference".

Section 4, provides for the legal recognition to all records, documentation and information in the electronic form. Prior to the coming into force of the Information Technology Act, 2000, the electronic form was not universally recognized as a legal form. This was so due to the absence of any specific enactment to that effect. Section 4 seeks to address the vacuum existing in this regard earlier.

Section 4 provides that wherever there is requirement of any specific law that information or any other matter has to be in writing or in typewritten or in printed form, then such requirement of any law shall be deemed to have been satisfied in case the following two conditions exist:

1. If the concerned information or matter is rendered or made available in the electronic form; and
2. That the information or matter is in the electronic form so that the same can be accessed and is capable of being used for a subsequent reference.

This provision has been made, notwithstanding anything contained in any other law for the time being in force. As such, the provisions of section 4 have been given overriding effect and are made universally applicable to all laws prevailing in our country, which require any information or matter to be in writing or in typewritten or in printed form.

Merely making information available or running the same in an electronic form is not sufficient. The information, that is referred to, has also to be made readable and usable for subsequent references. If the electronic forms were not capable of being accessed so that the same can be used for the subsequent reference, then the requirement of section 4 would not be satisfied. Such an electronic record will not have legal validity and sanction or recognition inasmuch as the provisions of section 4 are not satisfied.

Thus, section 4 envisages the existence of an electronic record which is not a one-time e-record but which is capable of being used again and again. Only such an electronic record would be a valid and legal electronic record, within the meaning of section 4 of the Information Technology Act, 2000.

By a single stroke, section 4 has achieved what no other law had achieved earlier. It has made all electronic information, electronic records, electronic documents, and electronic databases as legal electronic records, which can be duly proved and produced in a court of law.

Section 4 gives legality to the electronic format. The logical consequence of this is that e-mail or electronic mail also becomes legal.

It is pertinent to note that all communication devices including mobile phones, iPads, Tablets, Smart Phones, Smart Devices, personal cell phones, personal digital assistants or combination of both or any other device which is used to communicate, send or transmit any text, message, video, audio or image or use data or information in electronic form, all ultimately deal with mobile electronic or digital data. As such, all mobile records are electronic records. This is although more so mobile data is "data" within the meaning of section 2(1)(o) of the amended Information Technology Act, 2000. Further, all information on iPads, Tablets, Smart Phones and Smart Devices would classify as "information" within the meaning of section 2(1)(v) of the amended Information Technology Act, 2000. Further, such information is in electronic form as defined under section 2(1)(r) of the amended Information Technology Act, 2000 as such information is information that is generated, sent, received or stored in media, magnetic, optical, computer memory or similar device. As such, mobile records are purely electronic records and are fully covered by the terms of section 4 of the amended Information Technology Act, 2000.

Thus, if any law provides that information or any other matter shall be in writing or either in typewritten or printed form, then notwithstanding anything contained in such law, such requirement shall be deemed to be satisfied if the said information or matter is rendered or made available in an electronic form in any iPads, Tablets, Smart Phones and Smart Devices and also that the same is accessible so as to be usable for subsequent reference in the said communication device. Thus, all mobile records have now also been given complete legal recognition, acceptability and acceptance in the eyes of law.

An interesting point that arises is whether anonymous emails including those sent through iPads, Tablets, Smart Phones and Smart Devices and communication devices have also been granted legal validity. *Firstly*, there is no direct reference of the same either under section 4 of the Information Technology Act or in any specific provision. A perusal of this section and the existing jurisprudence would conclude that anonymous emails are not barred under the present law.

Section 4 is only an enabling provision. It only states that where any law provides any information or matter to be in writing, type written or printed format, then that requirement of law shall be satisfied by use of an electronic format.

Thus, seen from one angle, section 4 could be interpreted to automatically grant legality to anonymous e-mails. At the same time, it is pertinent to note that there is no specific provision in the Information Technology Act, 2000, which debars the same. In the United States, anonymity is seen as an integral part of basic freedom of speech and expression guaranteed by the United States Constitution and as such, has been given legal validity and sanction. But a majority of Indian law requires the document of any person to be signed or authenticated by his mark or signature in order to be duly proved in a court of law and as such, it can be interpreted that Indian law does not grant legal sanction and validity to anonymous e-mails, as they are not signed as per law. Also there are dangers in making anonymous e-mails legal, especially when the source of the email, let alone of the sender, is not known. The law on the issue is still to develop.

An important question that comes up for consideration is whether a contract can come into existence without affixation of Digital Signatures.

Contracts are governed by the Indian Contract Act, 1872. It is pertinent to note that the Information Technology Act, 2000 has not amended the Indian Contract Act, 1872.

The definition of "contract" under section 2(h) and the definition of "agreement" under section 2(e) of the Indian Contract Act, 1872, have not clarified the mode of agreements. But after the enactment of Information Technology Act, 2000, agreement includes mobile agreement and other sorts of electronic agreements. Mobile agreements/contracts concluded by using the electronic means and/or communication device, will be valid agreement/contracts.

But such contracts must satisfy all the essential conditions prescribed under section 10 of the Indian Contract Act, 1872 which are as under;

Section 10 of the Indian Contract Act, 1872 states as follows:

> *"All agreements are contracts if they are made by the free consent of parties competent to contract, for a lawful consideration and with a lawful object, and are not hereby expressly declared to be void.*
>
> *Nothing herein contained shall affect any law in force in India and not hereby expressly repealed by which any contract is required to be made in or in the presence of witnesses, or any law relating to the registration of documents".*

Under the Indian Contract Law, a contract can be both written and oral. Oral contracts can be duly proved under law. In the context of the electronic medium, it is possible for two persons sitting at different places to enter into a valid agreement, merely by exchanging e-mails/SMSs without signing the same with their digital signatures. In that case, it can be proved that both the persons have agreed upon their agreed terms, by exchanging e-mails/SMSs and have decided not to sign the same. In that case, such an agreement, even though not digitally signed, would be valid in a court of law, provided the parties concerned can prove the same.

However, if the parties want to sign their electronic agreement, they can do so by way of affixing their digital signatures and in such a case, the said digitally signed contract would be valid and legal in the eyes of law.

Similarly, it can also be shown that a contract, the terms of which are reduced in writing in the electronic format, has come into effect. Thus, an e-contract can come into existence without affixing Digital Signatures.

In fact, there is no specific provision under the Information Technology Act, 2000, which bars an e-contract, which is not digitally signed. Of course, there would be a need to prove the same in a court of law, as per the requirements of the amended Indian Evidence Act, 1872.

Section 5 of the amended Information Technology Act, 2000

Since authentication is an important element of ensuring the non-tampering of the electronic records, it is, therefore, very essential for the legislation to grant legal recognition to manner of electronic authentication. We have already seen in section 3 of the amended Information Technology Act, 2000 that authentication of electronic records have been dealt with in detail. Section 3 primarily talks about authentication of electronic records by affixation of digital signatures by a subscriber. However, electronic authentication is not dependent upon digital signatures alone. Electronic authentication can be done through a variety of means such as, section 3A has provided for the concept of electronic signatures. Having so provided for the concept of electronic authentication and electronic signatures, it was essential that the legislation should provide a legal provision for legal recognition of electronic signatures. The said provision is now specifically provided for under section 5 of the Information Technology Act, 2000. Section 5 of the Information Technology Act, 2000 states as follows:

> ***"Section 5. Legal recognition of electronic signature.***—*Where any law provides that information or any other matter shall be authenticated by affixing the signature or any document shall be signed or bear the signature of any person, then, notwithstanding anything contained in such law, such requirement shall be deemed to have been satisfied, if such information or matter is authenticated by means of electronic signature affixed in such manner as may be prescribed by the Central Government.*
>
> *Explanation.—For the purposes of this section, 'signed', with its grammatical variations and cognate expressions, shall, with reference to a person, mean affixing of his hand written signature or any mark on any document and the expression 'signature' shall be construed accordingly."*

Section 5 provides for the legal recognition of electronic signatures. Under the existing law, signatures of persons are used as a means of authenticating any information or matter. Therefore, signatures assume immense significance in the eyes of law.

In *Hindustan Construction Company Ltd.* v. *Union of India*, AIR 1967 SC 526 the Supreme Court held the following important observation on signatures and signing:—

> "...In Webster's New World Dictionary the word "sign" means to write one's name on, as in acknowledging authorship, authorizing action, etc." To write one's name is signature.
>
> ....Signing means writing one's name on some document or paper. The document must be signed in such a way as to make it appear that the person signing it is the author of it, and if that appears, it does not matter what the form of the instrument is, or in what part of it the signature occurs.
>
> ...."So long as there is the signature of the arbitrator or umpire on copy of the award filed in court and it shows that the person signing has

authenticated the accuracy or correctness of the copy the document would be a signed copy of the award."

Section 5 has a sweepingly wide applicability. It provides that wherever any law stipulates any particular information to be authenticated by affixing the signature of any person, then that requirement shall also be deemed to be satisfied if such information or matter is authenticated by means of affixing electronic signatures in a manner prescribed by the Government. Further, if any law requires any documents to be signed or bearing the signature of any person, then such requirement of law shall also be deemed to have been met if the document is affixed with electronic signatures of the subscriber. Of course, the affixation of electronic signatures has to be in such a manner, as may be prescribed by the Central Government. This is notwithstanding anything contained in any other law for the time being in force in the country. Thus, section 5 has been given immensely wide amplitude and scope, and overrides anything inconsistent therewith contained in any other law for the time being in force in India.

The term "electronic signatures" have already been defined under section 2(1)(ta) to mean authentication of any electronic record by a subscriber by means of the electronic technique specified in the Second Schedule and includes digital signature. Section 3(2) specifies that the authentication of electronic record shall be effected by the use of asymmetric crypto system and hash function, which envelop and transform the initial electronic record into another electronic record. The explanation to section 5 states that for the purposes of section 5, the "signed", shall mean affixing of the handwritten signature or any mark on any document by any person. The explanation further explains that the word "signature" shall also be construed accordingly in the same terms. The legal effect of section 5 is that now not only digital signatures but all other future kinds of electronic signatures, as may be specified by the Government, shall be legal and valid in the eyes of law.

Section 6A of the Information Technology Act, 2000

"Section 6A. Delivery of Services by Service Provider.—*(1) The appropriate Government may, for the purposes of this Chapter and for efficient delivery of services to the public through electronic means authorise, by order, any service provider to set up, maintain and upgrade the computerised facilities and perform such other services as it may specify by notification in the Official Gazette.*

Explanation.—For the purposes of this section, service provider so authorised includes any individual, private agency, private company, partnership firm, sole proprietor firm or any such other body or agency which has been granted permission by the appropriate Government to offer services through electronic means in accordance with the policy governing such service sector.

(2) The appropriate Government may also authorise any service provider authorised under sub-section (1) to collect, retain and appropriate such service charges, as may be prescribed by the appropriate Government for the purpose of providing such services, from the person availing such service.

(3) Subject to the provisions of sub-section (2), the appropriate Government may authorise the service providers to collect, retain and appropriate service charges under

this section notwithstanding the fact that there is no express provision under the Act, rule, regulation or notification under which the service is provided to collect, retain and appropriate e-service charges by the service providers.

(4) The appropriate Government shall, by notification in the Official Gazette, specify the scale of service charges which may be charged and collected by the service providers under this section:

Provided that the appropriate Government may specify different scale of service charges for different types of services."

Section 6A has been added into the Information Technology Act, 2000 by the provisions of the Information Technology (Amendment) Act, 2008.

Section 6A is a provision that has been enacted, keeping in mind the benevolent interests of the Republic of India as a sovereign, socialist, secular, democratic republic. Section 6A provides the Government with the ability to reach out its electronic governance services to the common citizens of India, using the private sector. In fact, section 6A provides the legal basis and structure for a long era of private public partnership in electronic governance in India.

For that particular purpose, the Central Government has identified service providers as the relevant vehicles, through which, the electronic governance services could be provided on a mass scale to the people at large.

Section 6A provides the discretion to the appropriate Government to do certain acts pertaining to service providers. The said discretion can be exercised either by the Central Government or by the State Government. Further, the said discretion has to be exercised for the purposes of Chapter III of the Information Technology Act, 2000 and also for the purposes of efficient delivery of services to the public, through electronic means. Keeping the aforesaid objectives in mind, the appropriate Government may authorise, by order, any service provider to do any of the following activities:

(a) Set up the computerised facilities.

(b) Maintain the computerised facilities

(c) Upgrade the computerised facilities.

(d) Perform such other services as the appropriate Government may specify by notification in the Official Gazette.

The main objectives of section 6A are to ensure that the reach of electronic governance services is expanded to the maximum extent possible, to the common man of India. The *Explanation* to section 6A(1) clearly shows that the Legislature has defined the term "service provider" to include all kinds of legal entities. The said service provider could either be an individual, private agency, private company, partnership firm, sole proprietorship firm or any other body or agency. All the aforesaid legal entities must have been granted permission by the appropriate Government to offer services through electronic means, in accordance with the policy underlined in the service sector. The Government could utilize the said service providers for the purposes of churning out relevant electronic governance services, which could then be reached out at the mass scale, to the common people of India.

Apart from ordering service providers to do the aforesaid activities, the appropriate Government has also been given the discretion to authorise any of such service providers to collect, retain and appropriate such service charges as may be prescribed by the appropriate Government. The said charges would be prescribed, for the purposes of providing such services to the persons availing such services.

Given the special nature of the Information Technology Act, 2000 as a special legislation, section 6A(3) makes it clear that the Government has the discretion to authorise any service providers to collect, retain and appropriate service charges under this provision. This has been done, notwithstanding the fact that there is no express provision under the Act, legislation, rule, regulation and notification under which the services are provided, to collect, retain and appropriate e-service charges by the said service providers. Thus, by enacting this provision, the Legislature has strengthened the hands of the appropriate Governments in making sure that absence of any provisions under any prevailing laws pertaining to collection, retention or appropriation of service charges, does not come in the way of the efficient delivery of electronic governance services to the public, by electronic means. Section 6A, when read with section 81 of the Information Technology Act, 2000, clearly shows that the provisions of this legislation and section 6A shall prevail over anything inconsistent therewith contained in any other law for the time being in force. This would also be applicable to all kinds of services made available, using iPads, Tablets, Smart Phones and Smart Devices platforms as also mobile communication devices.

Further, the Legislature has given appropriate powers to the appropriate Government to specify by notification in the Official Gazette as follows:—

(a) The scale of service charges as may be charged.

(b) The scale of service charges which may be collected by the service providers under section 6A.

However, the proviso to section 6A(4) clearly provides that the appropriate Government, both Central and State Government, has been given the discretion to specify different scales of service charges for different kinds of services. This is but natural and reasonable since the inputs and technicalities required for efficient delivery of any specific service would be inherently different from any other service, and hence, differentiation of charges to be charged for making available such services has been provided for.

All in all, section 6A paves the way for the Government to utilize private service providers including mobile service providers, to make available efficient delivery of services to the public through, electronic means. In the coming times, as more and more mobile users are increasing in India, the Government of India and the appropriate State Governments are likely to take the route of mobile, iPads, Tablets, Smart Phones and Smart Devices and mobile networks to reach out efficient delivery of electronic services to iPads, Tablets, Smart Phones and Smart Devices users in India. Such an exercise would be prudent and expedient, given the widespread network and coverage of mobile revolution in India. This would not just to help further strengthen the cause of electronic governance in India but would also pave the way forward for mobile electronic governance or mobile governance in the times to come.

Section 7 of the Information Technology Act, 2000

> "***Section 7. Retention of electronic records.***—*(1) Where any law provides that documents, records or information shall be retained for any specific period, then, that requirement shall be deemed to have been satisfied if such documents, records or information are retained in the electronic form, if—*
>
> *(a) the information contained therein remains accessible so as to be usable for a subsequent reference;*
>
> *(b) the electronic record is retained in the format in which it was originally generated, sent or received or in a format which can be demonstrated to represent accurately the information originally generated, sent or received;*
>
> *(c) the details which will facilitate the identification of the origin, destination, date and time of dispatch or receipt of such electronic record are available in the electronic record:*
>
> *Provided that this clause does not apply to any information which is automatically generated solely for the purpose of enabling an electronic record to be dispatched or received.*
>
> *(2) Nothing in this section shall apply to any law that expressly provides for the retention of documents, records or information in the form of electronic records.*"

Section 7 stipulates the principle of law for retention of electronic records in those cases where the existing laws do not expressly provide for the retention of documents, records or information in the form of electronic records. Many existing laws in our country require and mandate that certain documents, records or information be retained for a specified period in a specified form. Section 7 states that wherever any law provides that certain documentation, information or records shall be retained for any specific period, then that requirement shall be deemed to have been satisfied if such documentation, records or information are retained in the electronic form.

However, it is important that three conditions must be satisfied, before any documents, records or/and information are retained in the electronic form. The absence of any one of the following three conditions would not give legal status to the retained electronic records.

Firstly, it is important that the information contained in such electronic record must remain accessible so that the same can be used for a subsequent reference. This is imperative inasmuch as the idea of electronic retention of records is to increase the longevity of their life and to facilitate more frequent and convenient reference and accessibility to the same.

Secondly, it is also mandated that the concerned electronic record must be retained in the form in which it was originally generated, sent or received or in any form which can be demonstrated to represent accurately and without any deviation, the information originally generated, sent or received. This is essential so as to ensure that there is no tampering with the form and contents of the electronic record, since the time of its creation. Thus, this condition ensures that the authenticity of the electronic document is preserved.

Thirdly, the retained electronic record must contain the details that will facilitate the identification of the origin, destination, date and time of dispatch or receipt of such electronic record. This is also essential for preserving authenticity of electronic record.

Computers, computer systems, computer networks, and other computer resources for the purpose of enabling an electronic record to be dispatched or received, generate a lot of information in the electronic form automatically. Such information is excluded from the parameters and ambit of section 7(1) of the Information Technology Act, 2000, by means of the proviso to the sub-section.

Section 7(2) states that where any law expressly provides for the retention of documents, records or information in the form of electronic records, section 7 would not apply to such situations. Section 7 only applies if any concerned law is silent on the issue of retention of electronic records.

Backup electronic information would come within the ambit of Section 7 of the Information Technology Act, 2000. Of course, it shall be necessary that the electronic backup information should also satisfy the mandatory conditions detailed under section 65B of the amended Indian Evidence Act, 1872, as amended by the Information Technology Act, 2000.

Section 7A of the Information Technology Act, 2000

> ***"Section 7A. Audit of Documents, etc. Maintained in Electronic Form.—*** *Where in any law for the time being in force, there is a provision for audit of documents, records or information, that provision shall also be applicable for audit of documents, records or information processed and maintained in the electronic form."*

Section 7A has brought forward the concept of electronic audit. Where any law prevailing for the time being in force, has provided for the provision of audit of documents, records and information, the said provision has now been extended to the electronic and digital platform as well. Section 7A now paves a way for audit of electronic records and documents. The law has now provided that wherever any existing provision provides for audit of documents, records or information, the said provision shall also be applicable for audit of documents, records and information, processed and maintained in the electronic form. This is a new area and as time passes by, electronic audit will become a matter of tremendous significance. As time passes by, even electronic records pertaining to the mobile networks and communication devices would also need to be appropriately audited and would come within the ambit of the audit specified under section 7A. More and more service providers and mobile operators need to ensure that their mobile electronic records are appropriately audited, wherever there is a specific requirement of law to the said effect.

Section 10A of the Information Technology Act, 2000

Section 10A has been enacted for the purposes of adequate clarification of jurisprudence around electronic contracts. The contracts in the actual world are governed by the Indian Contract Act, 1872.

The term "Contract" has been defined under section 2 (h) of the Indian Contract Act, 1872 which reads as under;

"An agreement enforceable by law is a contract".

Section 10 of the Indian Contract Act, 1872 provides the essential conditions of valid contract which are as follows:

> *"All agreements are contracts if they are made by the free consent of parties competent to contract, for a lawful consideration and with a lawful object, and are not hereby expressly declared to be void.*
>
> *Nothing herein contained shall affect any law in force in India and not hereby expressly repealed, by which any contract is required to be made in or in the presence of witnesses, or any law relating to the registration of documents."*

Thus, for the purpose of valid contracts, an agreement must satisfy all the essential ingredients prescribed under section 10 of the Indian Contract Act.

It is important to note that the Indian Contract Act, 1872 was enacted in the year 1872. At the said time, the British legislative draftsman could not be faulted,. for not having a very futuristic vision of how technology would evolve.

However, with the advent of electronic format, more and more contracts and agreements are being concluded in the electronic form. E-mail contracts are becoming the norm of the day. If any e-mail agreement satisfies the aforesaid conditions, the same would also become a contract within the meaning of section 10 of the Indian Contract Act.

Normally speaking, there is first on offer, and then there is acceptance of an offer which leads into the resulting of a binding contract. In today's world, more and more people are using electronic format and the electronic means for the purposes of communication of proposals, acceptance of proposals as also the revocation of proposals and acceptances. These are done using computers, computer systems, computer networks, computer resources and communication devices. A lot of contracts are also done using iPads, Tablets, Smart Phones and Smart Devices, because iPads, Tablets, Smart Phones and Smart Devices are very convenient devices for the purposes of communication of proposals, the acceptance of proposals as well as the revocation of proposals and acceptances.

Section 10A of the Information Technology (Amendment) Act, 2008 provides for the validity of contracts formed through electronic means which reads as follows:

> *"Where in a contract formation, the communication of proposals, the acceptance of proposals, the revocation of proposals and acceptances, as the case may be, are expressed in electronic form or by means of an electronic record, such contract shall not be deemed to be unenforceable solely on the ground that such electronic form or means was used for that purpose".*

Section 10A clarifies the conditions that where in a contract formation:

(a) The communication of proposals are expressed in electronic form or by means of an electronic record.

(b) The acceptance of proposal is expressed in the electronic form or by means of an electronic record.

(c) The revocation of proposals and acceptances, as the case may be are expressed in electronic form or by means of electronic record.

Such electronic records are deemed to be legal and valid.

Section 10A categorically specifies that such contract shall not be mandatorily deemed to be unenforceable solely on the ground that such electronic form or means was used for that purpose. The net effect of this is that all iPads, Tablets, Smart Phones and Smart Devices contracts which are contracted using iPads, Tablets, Smart Phones and Smart Devices as well as communication devices also become legal and valid, in the eyes of law in India. Further, all iPads, Tablets, Smart Phones and Smart Devices contracts cannot be and shall not be deemed to be unenforceable solely on the ground that such iPads, Tablets, Smart Phones and Smart Devices contracts have been executed or finalised, using electronic form or means for the same.

For example, a manufacturer of dolls sends an SMS quotation to his potential buyer where he says that he is willing to sell cartons of 10 dolls for Rs.10,000. In response to the said SMS, the potential buyer sends another SMS by reply to the manufacturer stating that he is willing to buy the said carton of 10 dolls for Rs. 10, 000 and the manufacturer should send the said carton of 10 dolls. This is a typical illustration of mobile contract and in the event of any dispute tomorrow in a court of law between the manufacturer and the buyer, this mobile contract cannot be discriminated against, only on the grounds that the electronic form or means was used for the purposes of contract formation. In the said *Illustration*, the communication of proposal, the acceptance of a proposal was expressed in the electronic form, by means of electronic record, being SMS which could be transmitted through iPads, Tablets, Smart Phones and Smart Devices. As such, the said contract shall not be deemed to be unenforceable solely on the ground that such electronic form or means was used for that purpose.

Let us take a second *Illustration*. The owner of a dry-cleaning shop sends an SMS to his existing customer wherein he says that on the occasion of Diwali, his dry-cleaning shop shall dry-clean two carpets for the cost of one carpet. The said SMS further states that the said offer is only valid for three days. The existing customer of the dry cleaning shop responds within three days on SMS from his smart phone stating that he is willing to accept the offer of dry cleaning of two carpets at the cost of one carpet and asks the dry cleaning shop to collect the carpet from his residence. This is yet another *Illustration* of iPads, Tablets, Smart Phones and Smart Devices contract, wherein the for the purposes of contract formation, the communication or proposal and the acceptance of proposal has been expressed in the electronic form as also by means of electronic record, being SMSs sent and transmitted through communication devices. By virtue of section 10A of the amended Information Technology Act, 2000, such contract shall not be deemed to be unenforceable, solely on the ground that such electronic form or means was used for the said purpose.

Thus, section 10A provides legality to all kinds of electronic contracts and iPads, Tablets, Smart Phones and Smart Devices as well as mobile contracts.

This paves a way for huge growth in mobile commerce in India. More and more companies, legal entities and individuals would be using iPads, Tablets, Smart Phones and Smart Devices for the purposes of entering into various transactions. With the mobile economy coming in a big way, mobile phones, iPads, Tablets, Smart Phones and Smart Devices will be the preferred way of communicating the communication of proposals, acceptance of proposals as also the revocation of proposals or acceptances, as the case may be.

Section 10A is likely to pave the way for huge growth and spurt in iPads, Tablets, Smart Phones and Smart Devices and mobile contracts and their legal validity in India. Such provision would also be enabling in nature and will help the courts of the country to grant legal validity, sanction and recognition to various kinds of electronic and iPads, Tablets, Smart Phones and Smart Devices and mobile contracts. Section 10A is the foundation on which the pyramid of mobile commerce, mobile contracts and electronic contracts are going to be based, as time passes by.

Section 14 of the Information Technology Act, 2000

> ***"Section 14. Secure electronic record***—*Where any security procedure has been applied to an electronic record at a specific point of time, then such record shall be deemed to be a secure electronic record from such point of time to the time of verification."*

Section 14 has given detailed definition of a secure electronic record. It has stipulated that where any security procedure has been applied to an electronic record at any point of time, such an electronic record shall be deemed to be a secure electronic record, from the point of application of the security procedure till the time the electronic record is verified.

It may be pertinent to mention that section 2(1)(zf) defines the words "security procedure" to mean the security procedure prescribed under section 16 by the Central Government. Thus, only the prescribed security procedure as stipulated by the Government is the relevant security procedure mentioned in section 14. If parties apply any security procedure other than the procedure prescribed by section 16, then though practically, the electronic record may be a secure electronic record, yet in the eyes of law, it would still not qualify to be a secure electronic record as the conditions of section 16 are not met.

Section 16 describes the powers of the Central Government to prescribe the security procedure. The security procedure has to be prescribed keeping in mind the existing commercial practices prevailing at the relevant time. However, section 16 has stipulated certain guiding factors, which have to be kept in mind by the Central Government at the time of prescribing the security procedure. Thus, the prescribed security procedure may include the following:

(1) the nature of the transaction;

(2) the level of sophistication of the parties with reference to their technological capacity;

(3) the volume of similar transactions engaged in by other parties;

(4) the availability of alternatives offered to but rejected by any party;

(5) the cost of alternative procedures; and

(6) the procedures in general use for similar types of transactions or communications.

The Central Government has already implemented the Information Technology (Certifying Authorities) Rules, 2000 and the Information Technology Security Guidelines.

It is important to remember that section 14 talks about secure electronic records, which is a wider term than a Secure Digital Signature. There can be other electronic records, which may be independent of Digital Signature.

Section 14 has direct applicability in the context of iPads, Tablets, Smart Phones and Smart Devices. This is so because iPads, Tablets, Smart Phones and Smart Devices all use electronic records. However, these records are not deemed to be secure electronic records. In case where a person applies any security procedure to the said electronic record resident on iPads, Tablets, Smart Phones and Smart Devices at a specific point of time, then the said mobile record shall be deemed to be secure electronic records, from such point of time to the time of its verification. At the time of writing, there is not much clarity on what kind of security procedures could be applied to electronic records resident on communication devices. However as technology and time passes by, we are likely to see the emergence of security procedures, specifically applicable to iPads, Tablets, Smart Phones and Smart Devices.

Section 15 of the Information Technology Act, 2000

*"**Section 15. Secure Electronic Signature**—An electronic signature shall be deemed to be a secure electronic signature if—*

(i) the signature creation data, at the time of affixing signature, was under the exclusive control of signatory and no other person; and

(ii) the signature creation data was stored and affixed in such exclusive manner as may be prescribed

Explanation.—In case of digital signature, the "signature creation data" means the private key of the subscriber"

Section 15 has been inserted into the Information Technology Act, 2000 by the Information Technology (Amendment) Act, 2008. Section 15 has provided for the first time, the concept of secure electronic signatures. Thus, the law has made a distinction between a normal electronic signature as well as secure electronic signatures. Electronic signatures are defined under section 2(1)(ta) to mean authentication of any electronic record by a subscriber by using electronic technique specified in the Second Schedule and includes digital signatures. It is pertinent to note that at the time of writing, the Second Schedule to the Information Technology Act, 2000 is blank and does not contain any entry. As such, at the time of writing, digital signatures alone are the valid electronic signatures in the country. As and when the Government specifies any other electronic technique in the Second Schedule, the said authentication of electronic records, using the said specified and prescribed electronic technique, as specified in the Second Schedule, to the Information Technology Act, 2000 would also be deemed to be an electronic signature.

Section 15 has provided for the concept of secure electronic signatures. Two conditions have to be satisfied by any electronic signature before the same is deemed to be a secure electronic signature. The said two conditions are as follows:—

(a) The signature creation data, at the time of affixing signature, was under the exclusive control of the signatory and no other person; and

(b) The signature creation data was stored and affixed in such exclusive manner as may be specified.

The *Explanation* to section 15 clearly states that in the case of digital signatures, the private key of the subscriber is his signature creation data.

The said conditions have been stipulated so as to further enhance the level of security of electronic signatures. It is absolutely paramount that the signature creation data at the time of affixing signature, must be under the exclusive control of the signatory and no one else, in order for the said electronic signatures to be secure. Further, the said signature creation data has to be stored and affixed in such exclusive manner which may be specified. At the time of writing, no such manner has been specified. As such, in the context of electronic signatures, secure electronic signatures are not yet a reality.

This is so since the Government has yet to specify the exclusive manner in which the signature creation data, being the private key of the subscriber, in the context of digital signatures, has to be stored and affixed. Clearly, the concept of secure electronic signatures is a futuristic concept and is likely to provide for far more secure electronic records and secure electronic authentication of electronic records, as time passes by.

At the time of writing, mobile electronic signatures have not yet become a part of the mainstream usage. The concept of mobile electronic signatures is developing. Once the said concept becomes fully developed, would users start looking at the options of secure mobile electronic signatures. At the time of writing, this area is a virgin area; a lot of work is expected to be done on this subject as time passes by.

Section 16 of the Information Technology Act, 2000

*"**Section16. Security procedures and Practices.**—The Central Government may, for the purposes of sections 14 and 15, prescribe the security procedures and practices:*

Provided that in prescribing such security procedures and practices, the Central Government shall have regard to the commercial circumstances, nature of transactions and such other related factors as it may consider appropriate."

Section 16 has been amended by means of the Information Technology (Amendment) Act, 2008. Section 16 deals with security procedures and practices. Section 16 grants the discretion to the Central Government that it may, for the purposes of section 14 of the Information Technology Act, 2000 dealing with secure electronic records and section 15 of the Information Technology Act, dealing with secure electronic signatures, prescribe the security practices and procedures.

The proviso to section 16 clearly provides that while prescribing such security practices and procedures, the Central Government shall mandatorily have regard to the following factors:

(a) The commercial circumstances,

(b) Nature of transactions, and

(c) Such other related factors as it may consider appropriate.

At the time of writing, no such security practices and procedures have yet been specified by the Central Government under section 16 of the amended Information Technology Act, 2000, in the context of computers, computer systems and computer networks. Further at the time of writing, it is pertinent to point out that no specific security procedures and practices have been prescribed by the Central Government with reference to iPads, Tablets, Smart Phones and Smart Devices for the purposes of sections 14 and 15 of the amended Information Technology Act, 2000. The Central Government, while prescribing such security procedures and practices, shall have regard to the overall commercial circumstances that would exist in the mobile ecosystem, the nature of the mobile transactions and such other relevant factors pertaining to the iPads, Tablets, Smart Phones and Smart Devices environment as the Central Government may consider appropriate.

Liability

Section 43 of the Information Technology Act, 2000

Initially, the Information Technology Act, 2000 was made applicable only for computers, computer systems and computer networks but with the passage of time, these provisions of the Information Technology Act, 2000 have been made applicable to the iPads, Tablets, Smart Phones and Smart Devices, mobile phones and other communication devices. In the early stage of Information Technology Act, 2000 there were no specific provisions for iPads, Tablets, Smart Phones and Smart Devices. Later, the Information Technology (Amendment) Act, 2008 specifically includes the term "communication device" under section 2(1)ha) of the Information Technology Act, 2000. Communication device includes mobile phones, cell phones, personal digital assistants, smart phones, iPhones, iPads, Tablets and Smart Devices etc. Section 43 of the Information Technology Act, 2000 deals with the penalties in case of damage to the computer, computer system etc., without the permission of the concerned owner. Section 43 of the Information Technology Act, 2000 reads as follows:

"Section 43. Penalty and Compensation for damage to computer, computer system, etc.—*If any person without permission of the owner or any other person who is in-charge of a computer, computer system or computer network,*

(a) accesses or secures access to such computer, computer system or computer network or computer resource;

(b) downloads, copies or extracts any data, computer data base or information from such computer, computer system or computer network including information or data held or stored in any removable storage medium;

(c) introduces or causes to be introduced any computer contaminant or computer virus into any computer, computer system or computer network;

(d) damages or causes to be damaged any computer, computer system or computer network, data, computer data base or any other programmes residing in such computer, computer system or computer network;

(e) disrupts or causes disruption of any computer, computer system or computer network;

(f) denies or causes the denial of access to any person authorised to access any computer, computer system or computer network by any means;

(g) provides any assistance to any person to facilitate access to a computer, computer system or computer network in contravention of the provisions of this Act, rules or regulations made thereunder;

(h) charges the services availed of by a person to the account of another person by tampering with or manipulating any computer, computer system, or computer network;

(i) destroys, deletes or alters any information residing in a computer resource or diminishes its value or utility or affects it injuriously by any means;

(j) Steals, conceals, destroys or alters or causes any person to steal, conceal, destroy or alter any computer source code used for a computer resource with an intention to cause damage;

he shall be liable to pay damages by way of compensation to the person so affected.

Explanation.—For the purposes of this section,—

(i) "computer contaminant" means any set of computer instructions that are designed—

(a) to modify, destroy, record, transmit data or programme residing within a computer, computer system or computer network; or

(b) by any means to usurp the normal operation of the computer, computer system, or computer network;

(ii) "computer database" means a representation of information, knowledge, facts, concepts or instructions in text, image, audio, video that are being prepared or have been prepared in a formalised manner or have been produced by a computer, computer system or computer network and are intended for use in a computer, computer system or computer network;

(iii) "computer virus" means any computer instruction, information, data or programme that destroys, damages, degrades or adversely affects the performance of a computer resource or attaches itself to another computer resource and operates when a programme, data or instruction is executed or some other event takes place in that computer resource;

(iv) "damage" means to destroy, alter, delete, add, modify or re-arrange any computer resource by any means;

(v) "computer source code" means the listing of programmes, computer commands, design and layout and programme analysis of computer resource in any form.'

Section 43 is one of the most dominant provisions under the Indian Information Technology Act, 2000. Section 43 appears in Chapter IX entitled "Penalties, Compensation and Adjudication". Section 43 for the first time in the legislative history of independent India, has provided for statutory damages by way of compensation for illegal or undesirable acts pertaining to use of computers, computer systems and computer networks. The said section initially had eight grounds on which damages by way of compensation could be awarded. By virtue of the amendments brought by the Information Technology (Amendment) Act, 2008, two more new grounds have been added for seeking damages by way of compensation.

A perusal of said provision clearly shows that it is talking about activities concerning use of computers, computer systems and computer networks. It is pertinent to note that the term "communication device" *per say* has not been mentioned directly or specifically under section 43 of the Information Technology Act, 2000. However, the way the definitions of the terms "computer", "computer system" or "computer network" have been couched in such wide ambit language, there is little doubt that "communication devices" would also be covered within the ambit of section 43 of the amended Information Technology Act, 2000.

Before we proceed forward it is important once again to examine the definition of the term computer, computer systems and computer network.

Section 2(1)(i) defines the term "computer" in the following terms:

"computer means any electronic magnetic, optical or other high-speed data processing device or system which performs logical, arithmetic, and memory functions by manipulations of electronic, magnetic or optical impulses, and includes all input, output, processing, storage, computer software, or communication facilities which are connected or related to the computer in a computer system or computer network."

The definition of the term "computer" is vast enough to include all kinds of iPads, Tablets, Smart Phones and Smart Devices to the extent that such iPads, Tablets, Smart Phones and Smart Devices or communication devices are high-speed data processing devices or systems which perform logical, arithmetic and memory functions by manipulations of electronic, magnetic or optical impulses. Further, the term "computer" includes all input, output, processing, storage, computer software or communication facilities which are connected or related to the computer in a computer system or computer network. Thus, any iPad, Tablet, Smart Phone and Smart Device , which is a high-speed data processing device which performs logical, arithmetic and memory functions, also comes within the ambit of the term computer. Further, iPads, Tablets, Smart Phones and Smart Devices invariably perform functions by manipulations of electronic impulses.

Further, all iPads, Tablets, Smart Phones and Smart Devices still are both input and output facilities or even communication facilities which are connected or related to the computer network being the mobile communication network. As such, iPads, Tablets, Smart Phones and Smart Devices, cell phones, personal digital assistants as well as any other kind of communication devices would qualify to come within the ambit of the term "computer", as defined under the Information Technology Act, 2000.

Further, the term "computer system" has also been very widely defined in the following manner under section 2(1)(l):

> *"computer system" means a device or collection of devices, including input and output support devices and excluding calculators which are not programmable and capable of being used in conjunction with external files, which contain computer programmes, electronic instructions, input data and output data, that performs logic, arithmetic, data storage and retrieval, communication control and other functions."*

A computer system must fulfil the following criteria:

(a) It must either be a device or collection of devices.

(a) It could include input and output support devices.

(b) It excludes calculators which are not programmable.

(c) It is capable of being used in conjunction with external files, which contain computer programmes, electronic instructions, input data and output data that performs logical, arithmetic, data storage and retrieval, communication control and other functions.

Thus, cell phone is also a device which is capable of being used in conjunction with external files which contain computer programmes, electronic instructions, input data and output data. Further, the said cell phone performs logic, arithmetic, data storage and retrieval, communication control and other functions.

At this juncture, it is also relevant for us to examine the very comprehensive definition given to the term "computer network". "Computer network" is defined under section 2(1)(j) of the amended Information Technology Act, 2000 in the following terms;

> *"computer network" means the inter-connection of one or more computers or computer systems or communication device through—*
>
> *(i) the use of satellite, microwave, terrestrial line, wire, wireless or other communication media; and*
>
> *(ii) terminals or a complex consisting of two or more inter-connected computers or communication device whether or not the inter-connection is continuously maintained.*

A perusal of section 2(1)(j) clearly shows that the term "computer network" means the interconnection of one or more computers or computer systems or communication devices. Thus, all kinds of interconnection between one or more communication devices also come within the ambit of the term "computer networks". Clearly, in this regard, all mobile networks in the country qualify as computer networks.

Further, it is important that the interconnection of the aforesaid must be through either the use of satellite, microwave, terrestrial line, wire, wireless or other communication media. Further the interconnection of one or more computers could be through terminals or complex consisting of two or more interconnected computers or communication devices, whether or not the interconnection is continuously maintained or not. Thus, computer network also includes interconnection of communication devices through terminals or complex consisting of two or more interconnected communication devices. Thus, all mobile communications in the country fully qualify within the ambit of the term "computer network".

Thus, if any of the grounds stipulated under section 43 are done with reference to iPads, Tablets, Smart Phones and Smart Devices or any other communication devices which are used to communicate, send or transmit text, video, audio and image, the provisions of section 43 of the Information Technology Act, 2000 could be invoked.

Section 43 basically provides that if any person without permission of the owner or any other person who is in-charge of computer, computer system or computer network does any of the ten activities or acts so specified, he would be liable to pay damages by way of compensation to the person so affected. It is pertinent to point out that earlier section 43 had provided for the maximum limit of damages by way of compensation not exceeding one crore rupees to the person so affected. However, by virtue of addition of section 46(1A), it is now been provided that Adjudicating Officers shall exercise jurisdiction to adjudicate matters in which claim for injury or damage does not exceed rupees five crores. That doesn't mean that the damages beyond rupees five crores cannot be sought. The law has now specifically provided that the jurisdiction in respect of the claim for injury or damage exceeding rupees five crores shall vest in the court of competent jurisdiction.

Thus, the law has two kinds of damages. The first kind of damages by way of compensation are up to the tune of rupees five crores, which could be granted under Chapter IX of the Information Technology Act, 2000 by the Adjudicating Officer. These are done by means of the summary procedures as stipulated under Chapter IX of the amended Information Technology Act, 2000. However, the second categories of damages are by way of compensation beyond five crores which can only be claimed in the court of competent jurisdiction.

It is important to now examine each ground for seeking damages by way of compensation:

Section 43(a)

Section 43(a) provides the first ground for damages by way of compensation:

"if any person, without permission of the owner or any other person who is in-charge of the computer, computer system or computer network, accesses or secures access to such computer, computer system or computer network or computer resource."

The word "access" has been defined in section 2(1)(a) of the IT Act, 2000 with its grammatical variations and cognate expressions means gaining entry into, instructing or communicating with the logical, arithmetical or memory function resources of a computer, computer system or computer network. The words used in section 2(1)(a) are "gaining entry instructing or communicating with the logical, arithmetical or memory function resources of a computer, computer system or computer network".

The entry can be actually made physically by opening up a computer and gaining physical access of the same or the entry can be made online by means of gaining access through internet, intranet or other related networks. This would actually mean that if anyone, without the permission of the owner or in-charge, gains entry into or instructs or communicates with the logical, arithmetical or memory function resources of a computer, computer system or computer network, he would be liable to pay damages under section 43(a) of the Information Technology Act, 2000.

The actual quantum of damages would depend upon the various peculiar factors of the case including the amount of gain or unfair advantage made as a result of the default, the amount of loss caused or the repetitive nature of the default act (as specified in section 47 of the Information Technology Act, 2000). Of course, it would depend upon the relevant facts and circumstances of each case as to how much quantum of damages needs to be awarded by the statutory authority namely, the Adjudicating Officer. If somebody accesses a protected system, then the quantum of damages is likely to be higher than the quantum of damages to be awarded in the case of gaining access into a normal network.

Section 43(b)

Section 43(b) lays down the second alternative condition for grant of damages by way of compensation. The sub-section states that:

> *"if anyone, without permission of the owner or any other person who is in-charge of a computer, computer system or computer network, downloads, copies or extracts any data, computer database or information from such computer, computer system or computer network, including information or data held or stored in any removable storage medium" he shall be liable to pay compensation to the person so affected."*

This sub-section further clarifies that downloading, copying or extracting any information or data held or stored in any removable storage medium like floppy, CD, Zip Drive, Pen Drive, Removable hard disks etc., would also be violation of section 43(b) which should attract awarding of damages.

Section 43(b) uses the words "downloads, copies or extracts any data". The word "data" has been defined in section 2(1)(o) to mean a representation of information, knowledge, facts, concepts or instructions which are being prepared or have been prepared in any formalised manner, and is intended to be processed, is being processed or has been processed in a computer system or computer network, and may be in any form (including computer printouts, magnetic or optical storage media, punched cards, punched tapes) or stored internally in the memory of the computer. The definition of data under section 2(1)(o) talks about the same as a representation of information. The word "information" is defined under section 2(1)(v) to include data, message, text, images, sound, voice, codes, computer programmes, software and databases or micro film or computer generated microfiche.

The *Explanation* (ii) to section 43 states that the phrase "computer database" means a representation of information, knowledge, facts, concepts or instructions in text, image, audio, video that are being prepared or have been prepared in a formalized manner or have been produced by a computer, computer system or computer network and are intended for use in a computer, computer system or computer network. *Explanation* (ii) has defined "computer database" in very broad terms and rightly so, to strengthen the hands of the law and to act as a deterrent for other people trying to download, copy or extract the computer database of any computer without due and authorized permission.

Section 43(b) has effectively covered almost all perceivable ingredients of data, computer database or information and in case anyone downloads, copies or extracts the same from a computer, computer system or computer network without permission of the owner or in-charge thereof, he is liable to pay damages by way of compensation to the person so affected.

Section 43(b) also includes within its broad ambit, even that information or data which have been held or stored in any removable storage medium like floppy, CD, Zip Drive, Pen Drive, removable hard disks or any other media. Thus, the message is loud and clear. If anyone downloads, copies or extracts data, computer database or information from any computer, computer system or computer network, he is doing so purely at his own risk and is liable to pay damages. The quantum of damages would depend upon the peculiar facts and circumstances of each case.

Section 43(c)

Section 43(c) defines the third alternate condition, which is made a ground to file an action for damages. As per sub-section (c):—

> *"if anyone, without permission of the owner or any other person who is in-charge of a computer, computer system or computer network, introduces or causes to be introduced any computer contaminant or computer virus into such computer, computer system or computer network", he shall be liable to pay damages by way of compensation.*

This clause assumes immense significance in view of the growth of Internet, cyberspace and computers where computer contaminants or viruses are being utilized to launch attacks and offences in order to cause monetary damage. In the first part of 2000, the "I Love You" virus, which had spread all across the world through e-mail, caused damage worth approximately 1.2 billion US dollars.

Explanation (i) to section 43 has defined computer contaminant to mean any set of computer instructions that are designed to modify, destroy, record, transmit data or programme residing within a computer, computer system or computer network; or any set of computer instructions that are designed by any means to usurp the normal operation of the computer, computer system or computer network.

Also the words "computer virus" have been defined by *Explanation* (iii) to section 43 to mean any computer instruction, information, data or programme that destroys, damages, degrades or adversely affects the performance of a computer resource or attaches itself to another computer resource and operates when a programme or data or instruction is executed or some other event takes place in that computer resource.

Further, *Explanation* (iv) to section 43 defines the word "damage" as meaning to destroy, alter, delete, add, modify or rearrange any computer resource by any means. Section 2(1)(K) defines "computer resource" to mean computer, computer system, computer network, data, computer database or software.

A cumulative reading of the aforementioned provisions makes it absolutely clear that the ambit of section 43(c) is wide and almost any conceivable situation relating to any computer contamination or virus could be brought within its scope. It is also important to note that under section 43(c), mere introduction or causing to introduce any computer contaminant or virus is sufficient to attract damages. It is immaterial whether the computer virus or contaminant has caused any financial loss or any security lapses.

Another question that comes up for consideration is what happens if someone sends an e-mail to my computer containing a virus and my computer automatically sends e-mails infected with the same virus to other computers? The important point is whether I would be liable to pay damages under section 43 of the Information Technology Act, 2000? In my opinion, it would really depend upon the peculiar facts and circumstances of each case. It will be necessary for me to immediately inform the concerned persons to whom infected e-mails have been sent from my computer, about the contaminated nature of the e-mails sent to them. This is likely to mitigate the damage to some extent but, technically speaking, the person who receives the contaminated e-mails from my computer, can sue me for damages if my e-mail introduces or causes to be introduced any computer contaminant or computer virus into his computer, computer system or computer network. In such a case, I would be liable to pay damages to the person so affected.

It is important to note that section 43 does not talk about intention or knowledge of the respondent. Whether a particular action of introducing a computer contaminant or virus is done intentionally or unintentionally, with or without any knowledge, the legal liability for damages by way of compensation remains the same.

The practical side of section 43(c) is that given the rampant use and prevalence of computer virii on the Internet, section 43(c) is likely to open the floodgates of litigation as opportunistic vested elements won't think a second time before commencing proceedings under section 43(c) of the Information Technology Act, 2000. A perusal of section 61 of the Information Technology Act, 2000 shows that the civil courts have no jurisdiction to entertain any suit or proceeding in respect of any matter which an Adjudicating Officer is empowered to determine.

Section 43(d)

Section 43(d) refers to the fourth alternative condition, the existence of which is imperative for the grant of damages:

> *"If any person, without the permission of the owner or any other person who is in-charge of a computer, computer system or computer network, damages or causes to be damaged any computer, computer system or computer network, data, computer database or any other programms residing in such computer, computer system or computer network," then that person is liable to pay damages.*

Explanation (iv) to section 43 read with section 2(1)(k) defines "damage" to mean destroying, altering, deleting, adding, modifying or rearranging by any means, any computer, computer system or computer network, data, computer database or software. It is not necessary that a person has to physically secure access to a computer, computer system or computer network in order to damage it. The law is only concerned with damage or causing of damage by an unauthorized person. The usage of the words "by any means" in *Explanation* (iv) to section 43 read with section 43(d) makes it clear that the damage or causing to be damaged may be done in any way whatsoever.

The damage may be caused to not only a computer, computer system or computer network, but also to any data, computer database or any other programme residing therein. Section 2(1)(o) has defined the word "data" to mean a representation of information, knowledge, facts, concepts or instructions which are being prepared or have been prepared in any formalised manner, and is intended to be processed, is being processed or has been processed in a computer system or computer network, and may be in any form (including computer printouts, magnetic or optical storage media, punched cards , punched tapes) or stored internally in the memory of the computer. The definition of data under section 2(1)(o) talks about the same as a representation of information. Section 2(1)(v) defines the word "information" to include data, message, text, images, sound, voice, codes, computer programmes, software and data bases or micro film or computer generated microfiche.

The *Explanation* (ii) to section 43 states that the phrase "computer database" means a representation of information, knowledge, facts, concepts or instructions in text, image, audio, video that are being prepared or have been prepared in a formalized manner or have been produced by a computer, computer system or computer network and are intended for use in a computer, computer system or computer network.

The perusal of the aforesaid provisions leaves no doubt in my mind that the wordings of section 43(d) are far more wide in their ambit and scope than what it appears on a plain reading of the sub-section. In fact, the language of section 43(d) is sufficient to cover almost a majority of the cases of damage and mischief that takes place in the context of the electronic environment in today's context.

To give a typical example, the virus "I Love You" damaged computer systems and networks throughout the world. If such kind of damage takes place after coming into the effect of Information Technology Act, 2000, people now have a remedy to ask for damages provided the identity of the person who has done the damage is known.

Section 43(e)

The fifth alternate condition for bringing an action for damages is stipulated in section 43(e), in the following language:—

> *"If any person, without permission of the owner or any other person who is in-charge of a computer, computer system or computer network, disrupts or causes disruption of any computer, computer system or computer network", he shall be liable to pay damages to the person so affected.*

The Information Technology Act, 2000 does not define the words "disrupt" or "causes disruption." However, Webster's New World Dictionary defines the word "disrupt" to mean to break apart, to interrupt the orderly course of a particular thing. The usage of the word "disrupt" or "disruption" in section 43(e) is of immense significance as it covers almost all the possible things which are likely to cause a stoppage or obstacle in the normal smooth running and operations of a computer, computer system or computer network. In a sense, section 43(e) covers all those cases, which are not covered by section 43(b), (c) and (d). However, what would amount to disruption of any computer, computer system or computer network, in a particular case would depend upon the peculiar facts and circumstances of that case. In the context of rapid growth of cyberspace, this provision is likely to be of immense value for the Information Technology industry as a whole.

Section 43(f)

Section 43(f) stipulates the sixth alternate condition, the existence of which attracts the liability of damages in the following language:—

> *"If any person without permission of the owner or any other person who is in-charge of a computer, computer system or computer network, denies or causes the denial of access to any person authorised to access any computer, computer system or computer network by any means", he shall be liable to pay damages by way of compensation to the person so affected.*

If any person, by any means, denies or causes the denial of gaining entry into, or instructing or communicating with the logical, arithmetical or memory function resources of a computer, computer system or computer network to a person who is duly authorised to access the same, that has been made a ground for seeking damages. The denial of service attacks against popular websites like yahoo and amazon.com in the new millennium were typical examples of this sub- section. If such a denial of service attack takes place in India after the Information Technology Act, 2000 has come into force, the action for damages could be initiated against the person who is responsible for the denial of service attacks. Similarly, if somebody causes obstacles in the legal access of authorized persons to any computer, computer system or computer network, that also would be covered by section 43(f) of the Information Technology Act, 2000.

Section 43(g)

Section 43(g) stipulates the seventh condition, the existence of which is required to attract the liability of damages. Section 43(g) is concerned with the alleged role of abettors or facilitators or accomplices in illegal or unauthorized acts. The sub-section states as under:—

> *"If any person without permission of the owner or any other person who is in-charge of a computer, computer system or computer network, provides any assistance to any person to facilitate access to a computer, computer system or computer network in contravention of the provisions of this Act rules or regulations made thereunder", he shall be liable to pay damages by way of compensation to the person so affected.*

The critical words used in section 43(g) are "any assistance". Any and every kind of perceivable help, aid, helping hand, or contribution to facilitate unauthorized access would come within the scope of the terms "any assistance".

Also, the words "any assistance" in section 43(g) are very wide to include any acts or omissions which have a direct nexus with or which can be related to any facilitation of unauthorized access to any computer, computer system or computer network, in contravention of the provisions of the Indian Cyberlaw.

If anybody gives help to any other person or aids that person in facilitating access and gaining entry into or instructing or communicating with the logical, arithmetical or memory function resources of a computer, computer system and computer network in contravention of the provisions of the Indian Cyberlaw and the rules, regulations and orders made thereunder, that person can be sued for damages. Of course, the exact damages to be awarded against the concerned person would depend upon the gravity of assistance provided or facilitation of such unauthorized access, the amount of loss caused by such an unauthorized access and the quantum of illegal or unlawful gain that has been attained by the unauthorized access.

Section 43(g) seeks to take care of all those people who abet in the illegal designs of others in gaining illegal and unauthorized access to a computer, computer system or computer network. Also, it is imperative to note that under section 43(g), the facilitation of access to a computer, computer system or computer network must be in contravention of the provisions of the Information Technology Act, 2000, IT Rules or regulations made thereunder. If there is no violation of either the provisions of the Information Technology Act, 2000, IT Rules or regulations, then section 43(g) would not be attracted and as such, there would be no question of awarding damages.

Section 43(h)

The eighth alternative condition necessary for attracting the liability of damages is stipulated in section 43(h) in the following terms:—

> *"If any person , without permission of the owner or any other person who is in-charge of a computer, computer system or computer network, charges the services availed of by a person to the account of another person by tampering with or manipulating any computer, computer system or computer network,", he is liable to pay the damages by way of compensation to the person so affected.*

The critical words used in section 43(h) are "tampering" or "manipulating". Again, the Information Technology Act, 2000 is silent in defining the terms "tampering" or "manipulating". Webster's New Word Dictionary states that the word "tampering" means to make illegal arrangements, to meddle with, especially so as to damage. Similarly, the word "manipulating" has been defined by the Dictionary to mean to manage or control artfully, often in unfair and fraudulent manner, to change or falsify figures, accounts etc., for one's own purposes.

This sub-section has more bearing on changing and manipulating of credit card numbers resident in a computer, computer system or computer network. These days, we are seeing a lot of credit card frauds taking place where mischief mongers tamper with valuable information concerning credit cards, often to misuse the same to the detriment and financial loss of the actual owner of the credit card. This sub-section aims to look at that particular aspect and to award appropriate damages.

For example, if any person steals the credit card details of another person which is stored in any computer, computer system or computer network, and uses the same to charge the services used by him to the account of the real owner of the credit card, then such a case would come within the ambit of section 43(h) of the Information Technology Act, 2000.

Similarly, if one person illegally and unauthorizedly comes to know about the credit card number and details of another person in the actual world, and uses the said information on any computer, computer system or computer network, to charge the services used by him to the account of the owner of the credit card, that action would come within the scope of the terms "manipulating any computer, computer system or computer network," and as such, would attract the liability to pay damages under section 43(h) of the Information Technology Act, 2000.

Section 43(i) of the Information Technology Act, 2000

The ninth alternative condition necessary for attracting the liability of damages is stipulated in section 43(i) in the following terms:—

> *"If any person , without permission of the owner or any other person who is in-charge of a computer, computer system or computer network destroys, deletes, or alters any information residing in a computer resource or diminishes its value or utility or affects it injuriously by any means", he shall be liable to pay damages by way of compensation to the person so affected.*

Section 43(i) has been added for the first time in the Information Technology Act, 2000 by the Information Technology (Amendment) Act, 2008. This provision seeks to incorporate the elements of the earlier section 66 of the Information Technology Act, 2000.

Thus, if any person does any of the following acts, he is liable to pay damages by way of compensation:

(a) The person destroys any information residing in a computer resource.

(b) The person deletes any information residing in a computer resource.

(c) The person alters any information residing in a computer resource.

(d) The person diminishes the value of any information residing in a computer resource or;

(e) The person diminishes the utility of information residing in a computer resource or;

(f) The person affects any information residing in a computer resource injuriously by any means.

If any of the aforesaid grounds are made out, the same has been made the basis for seeking damages by way of compensation. All the above acts are done without the permission of the owner or any other person, who is in-charge of a computer, computer system or computer network.

Destroys or Deletes or Alters

For the purposes of seeking damages under this ground, it must be shown that the person concerned, without the permission of the owner or any other person in charge of a computer, computer system, and computer network or computer resource has done so. Under section 2(1)(k), computer resource has been defined to include computer, computer system, computer network, data, computer database or software.

The Information Technology Act, 2000 unfortunately does not define the expression "destroys or deletes any information." *Explanation* (iv) to section 43 defines the word "damage" to mean to destroy, alter, delete, add, modify or rearrange any computer resource by any means. However the words "destroy or delete" have not been defined.

According to Webster's New World Dictionary, the word "destroy" means to tear down; demolish, to spoil completely; ruin, to put an end to, to kill, to neutralize the effect of, to make useless. The word "delete" has been defined therein as to take out, to cross out. Thus, this ground, by reasonable interpretation, has to be given the same meaning as is attributable to the destruction of information in the context of the electronic world and computers.

The law uses two different expressions "destroy" and "delete", thereby distinguishing deletion from destruction. In practice, both words, destruction and deletion, are used interchangeably by people without any effort to really understand or find nuances or differences between both the terms. Normally, deletion of data is on a lower level than destruction of data. A person could delete an electronic file in the computer but that does not necessarily mean that the electronic file would have been destroyed.

To give an example, the moment you empty the Recycle Bin, the deleted file is gone, but would such an act come within the meaning of destruction, moreso when it is possible to recover large chunks of the deleted file by computer forensic methods?

Also, the person concerned may alter any information residing in a computer resource. *Webster's New World Dictionary* defines the word "alter" to mean to make different in details; modify, to become different, to change. Information residing in a computer resource can be altered in numerous ways.

So, the moment any person, is actually deleting or destroying or altering any information that is either resident, an integral part or is a component of any computer, computer system, computer network, data, computer database or software, without permission of owner or in-charge thereof, the concerned person is liable to pay damages by way of compensation to the affected person.

Diminishes Value or Utility

Section 43(i) of the Information Technology Act, 2000 has included two more distinct clauses, both of them being alternative in application.

As per the first clause, the person may diminish the value or utility of any information resident in a computer resource. "Diminishing of value or utility of any information residing in a computer resource" is a vast phrase. Many matters can come within the ambit of this phrase. Unfortunately, the Information Technology Act, 2000 is silent on defining the words "diminishes its value and utility". Normally if things are tangible, appropriate valuations can be assigned to the same and the diminishing of valuation becomes a process that can be easily calculated.

However, the Information Technology Act, 2000 is silent on how to calculate the valuation of the electronic information that resides in any computer, computer system, computer network, data, computer database or software. The Act also does not give us any form or prescribed standards, by means of which, we can ascertain the valuation of electronic information that resides in a computer resource.

How does one prove the diminishing of value of information? Information *per se* is invaluable. In any case, the Information Technology Act, 2000 does not give any standards as to how monetary value can be imputed to information. There are also no standards available to show the diminishing of value of information residing in a computer resource. Similarly, the use of the word "utility" is a clause, which is going to be difficult to prove in a court of law. What standards can be applied to show the utility of any information residing in a computer resource and then to show it has been diminished? Since, no formula or parameter concerning diminishing of value or utility is given in the Information Technology Act, 2000, it becomes a very dangerous and difficult exercise to actually try to determine whether there has been a diminishing of value or utility of an information residing in a computer resource.

There are also other subsequent problems in this section. In the actual world, if physical products are replicated, the duplicates are invariably slightly different from the originals and can be so duly proved. The very nature of the electronic environment makes the distinction between the original and the copy, of no consequence. This is so because an electronic copy of an electronic record is just the same as the original electronic record. Also, there are no ways by which one can determine whether the concerned electronic record is the original electronic record or is a copy thereof.

It is important to note that section 43(i) refers to diminishing of value or utility of electronic information. Seen from one angle, a denial of service attack causes diminishing of value and utility and thus, a denial of service attack is also coverable within the provisions of section 43(i) of the Information Technology Act, 2000. Similarly, if someone sends a virus or a computer contaminant, which corrupts data, then interpreted broadly, even that can come within the four corners of section 43(i) provided it is proved that someone has sent the email containing the virus, to the computer without the permission of the owner or in-charge of the relevant computer. However, the law on the subject is still to develop and it would be interesting to see how section 43(i) is interpreted in the coming times.

Affecting Information Injuriously By Any Means

Section 43(i) states an alternative ingredient *i.e.*, any person may affect the information residing in a computer resource injuriously by any means, without the permission of the owner or the person in-charge thereof.

There is a major difficulty in legally defining how someone affects any information residing in any computer, computer system, computer network, data, computer database or software injuriously. It is of critical importance to note that the law is silent in defining the word "injuriously" in the context of the electronic environment. The Information Technology Act, 2000 does not give us any parameters or standards to determine what can tantamount to affecting any information residing in a computer resource injuriously by any means.

The use of the expression "by any means" provides a power of discretion to the adjudicating authorities to interpret the nature of the means. The expression "by any means" is wide enough to include all perceivable means of affecting information within the knowledge of mankind, from the beginning of history till now.

Further, there are no formulae given under the Information Technology Act, 2000 which would actually guide the adjudicating authorities in determining how any information residing in a computer resource has been affected and that how such affection is injurious in nature. What is the difference between affection and injurious affection, how to determine the essential ingredients of injurious affection, what all affections would not come within the ambit of injurious affection, what would be the level of injury to the information in order to qualify as an injurious affection, how to determine the kind and nature of the injury to the information, what methods and standards to adopt to determine the injurious affection and how to distinguish between injurious infection as distinguished from deletion or destruction – these are various questions to which the Information Technology Act, 2000 holds out no answers. Thus, this leaves things completely at the sweet will and discretion of the adjudicating authorities. Also, it will be an uphill task for the complainant to prove under section 43 of the Information Technology Act, 2000 as to how information residing in a computer resource has been affected injuriously.

Another important issue for consideration is whether diminishing of goodwill or reputation over a network would come within the word diminishing of value or utility of electronic information. On a clear reading, it would seem that such diminishing of goodwill or reputation is a consequence of diminishing of value or utility of electronic information residing in a computer resource, and as such, is not likely to be included within the ambit of section 43(i) of the amended Information Technology Act, 2000.

It is pertinent to point out that destruction, deletion and alteration are concepts that are well-known in the context of information or data residing in a computer resource. However, the law has introduced the element of diminishing the value or utility of information residing in a computer resource. This is a very wide concept and incorporates within its ambit, all kinds of acts, deeds or things which have an effect of diminishing the inherent value and utility of any information residing in a computer resource. The said information could either be confidential information, trade secrets, personal information, business information, professional information, social information or any other information which could be of value or utility. Unauthorised access into such information by any person, would tend to diminish the value and utility of such information. Hence, a wide variety of activities, hereinbefore not envisaged, could be brought within the ambit of diminishing of value or utility of any information residing in a computer resource. Thus, activities like unauthorised access into somebody's iPad, Tablet, Smart Phone and/or Smart Device for the purposes of accessing the contents therein, including the contacts, SMSs, MMSs would constitute acts which diminished the value and utility of information residing in a computer resource. Further, the act of deliberately sending mobile infections or virii to iPads, Tablets, Smart Phones and Smart Devices clearly is aimed at diminishing the value and utility of information resident or saved in the said mobile devices.

The list in this regard could be endless. The law has taken the best course by only stipulating broad generic principles without evolving any specific formula for the application thereof.

In addition, the phrase "affecting any information residing in a computer resource injuriously by any means" is very wide, comprehensive and futuristic in nature. It incorporates, within its comprehensive ambit, all kinds of affecting acts which intend to affect injuriously, negatively, prejudicially, in any manner whatsoever any information residing in a computer resource. This clause has really been added by the Legislature to cover all kinds of futuristic circumstances that could arise in the times to come, pertaining to or impacting any information injuriously by any means. As such, this is one of the widest possible grounds for seeking damages by way of compensation and is expected to be widely used ground in the times to come.

Section 43(j) of the Information Technology Act, 2000

The tenth alternative condition necessary for attracting the liability of damages is stipulated in section 43(i) in the following terms:—

> *"If any person without permission of the owner or any other person who is in-charge of a computer, computer system or computer network, steals, conceals, destroys or alters or causes any person to steal, conceal, destroy or alter any computer source code used for a computer resource with the intention to cause damage, he shall be liable to pay damages by way of compensation to the person so affected."*

Section 43(j) has been added for the first time under the Information Technology Act, 2000 by the provisions of the Information Technology (Amendment) Act, 2008. Section 43(j) seeks to add some of the salient features of section 65 of the Information Technology Act, 2000 which has made the stipulated activities as a cyber crime punishable with three years' imprisonment and fine which could extend to rupees two lakh or with both.

If any person without the permission of the owner or any other person who is in-charge of a computer, computer system or computer network does any of the following activities, he is liable to pay compensation under section 43(j):

(a) The person steals any computer source code used in a computer resource with an intention to cause damage;

(b) The person conceals any computer source code used for a computer resource with an intention to cause damage;

(c) The person destroys any computer source code used for a computer resource with an intention to cause damage;

(d) The person alters any computer source code used for a computer resource with an intention to cause damage;

(e) The person causes any other person to steal any computer source code used for a computer resource with an intention to cause damage;

(f) The person causes any person to conceal any computer source code used for a computer resource with an intention to cause damage;

(g) The person causes any person to destroy any computer source code used for a computer resource with an intention to cause damage;

(h) The person causes any person to alter any computer source code used for a computer resource with an intention to cause damage.

It is pertinent to note that *Explanation* (v) has been added in section 43 which provides the definition of the term "computer source code" to mean the listing of programmes, computer commands, design and layout and programme analysis of computer resource in any form. The term "steal" has not been defined, not under the Information Technology Act, 2000. The *Illustrated Oxford Dictionary* defines the term "steal" to mean "take illegally, take without right or permission, especially in secret with the intention of not returning it".

Similarly, the word "conceal" has not been defined under section 43(j) of the Information Technology Act, 2000. *Webster's New World Dictionary* defines the word "conceal" to mean to put out of sight, hide, to keep secret. The word "conceal", used in section 43(j) of the Information Technology Act, 2000, has a direct nexus with a computer source code. What would tantamount to concealment in the context of a computer source code cannot be defined exhaustively and has to be determined on a case to case basis or on the peculiar facts and circumstances of each case.

Also the word "alter" has also not been defined. According to Webster's New World Dictionary, the word "alter" means to make different in details, modify, to become different, to change. The usage of the word 'alter' is likely to throw up numerous challenges in the coming times. Would just superficial altering attract the exposure to damages by way of compensation or has it to be material altering that would be covered by section 43(j) of the Information Technology Act? The law on section 43(j) of the Information Technology Act, 2000 is likely to develop over a period of time.

Thus, the perusal of the aforesaid provisions of section 43 shows that section 43 is in itself a complete code. Section 43 is one of the salient foundations on which the edifice of the amended Information Technology Act, 2000 is based. Section 43 is a tremendous movement and advancement in the Indian jurisprudence inasmuch as it is for the first time in the context of digital environment that the Legislature has provided for statutory damages by way of compensation.

Section 43 represents a revolutionary step forward in the context of the Legislature providing for distinct remedy of damages by way of compensation.

However, while in theory section 43 presents a very attractive proposition, in reality the practical experience under the Information Technology Act, 2000 has shown that section 43 is at best only an evolutionary remedy. This is primarily so because of the extremely shabby manner in which section 43 has been implemented. Right from the time of enactment of the Information Technology Act, 2000, till the time of writing, as per information based in the public domain, there are very few cases in which any damages by way of compensation has been awarded. This is primarily so, because of the extremely tardy manner of implementation of section 43 of the Information Technology Act, 2000.

It is not only very important to have good provisions of law. It is equally important to have built oriented infrastructure, implement effectively and successfully the spirit and principles of law. Unfortunately, section 43 has been a failed experiment in India till at the time of writing. This is primarily so, because of the move of the Government not to go in for highly qualified judicial officers to be the Adjudicating Officers. Instead, the Central Government has chosen to bend in the direction of the bureaucracy. The Central Government notified that all Information Technology Secretaries of different States shall be the Adjudicating Officers of the relevant States. The said Information Technology Secretary is a part of bureaucracy. The said person is neither a judicial officer nor is fully qualified in techno-legal terms as also in the nuances and legalities of the use of computers, computer systems, computer networks, computer resources and communication devices. Further, it is a practical fact that all Information Technology Secretaries of different State Governments are burdened with lot of work. Because of them being burdened with so much responsibilities and work, the work of adjudication under the Information Technology Act, 2000 looks like an additional burden that has been imposed upon the already busy schedule of the Information Technology Secretary. That being so, invariably it has been found that the Adjudicating Officers have not had the time, despite having inclination to deal with the adjudication proceedings under the Information Technology Act, 2000 in a manner that they would best want to do so.

It is pertinent to note that the Central Government notified the Information Technology (Qualification and Experience of Adjudicating Officers and Manner of Holding Enquiry) Rules, 2003. The said rules clearly stipulated under rule 4 (k) of the said rules that asfaras possible, every application shall be heard and decided in four months and the whole matter in six months.

However, adjudication proceedings were never finished in a period of six months anywhere in the country. On the contrary, adjournments are granted regularly and routinely on one ground or the other. With the result, adjudication of the claims under section 43 of the Information Technology Act, 2000 are often becoming a big challenge.

Despite the aforesaid challenges, section 43 still represents an extremely innovative platform for the Adjudicating Officers to innovate the provisions of law and hand over speedy effective and real justice to the affected parties.

Section 43 is an extremely important provision under the Information Technology Act, 2000 as it deals with the remedy of damages by way of compensation. The law of tort in the country is not well developed and even after more than 60 years of independence, not much progress has been made in this discipline of law. Even courts in India have been hesitant to grant big quantum of damages by way of compensation.

In this scenario, section 43 assumes importance and comes across as a breath of fresh air. This is the first instance, where by means of legislation, statutory damages by way of compensation have been provided for and the quantum of statutory damages is also the single largest quantum of damages made available under the Indian law. The idea behind enacting section 43 was that if anyone enters into any computer, computer system or computer network without due permission of its owner or in-charge, and does various unauthorized activities, then the actual damage caused to the affected person would be immense. This provision seeks to provide monetary redress to the victims of the aforesaid unauthorized acts. If implemented properly, section 43 promises to bring effective, real and substantial justice to the doors of common man.

Thus, section 43 details ten conditions, the existence and proof of any one of them, is sufficient to attract the liability to pay damages by way of compensation.

However, one question that comes up for consideration is how to enforce an order for damages by way of compensation passed under sections 43 and 46 by the Adjudicating Officer. Section 64 of the Information Technology Act states that a penalty including a penalty imposed under section 43 of the Information Technology Act, if it is not paid, shall be recovered as an arrear of land revenue. Since land revenue is a State subject under List II in the Seventh Schedule to the Constitution, different States have enacted different laws relating to land revenue and the recovery of its arrears.

By way of illustration, we can take the example of Delhi, which has enacted the Delhi Land Reforms Act, 1954.

Section 136 of the Delhi Land Reforms Act, 1954 provides the procedure for recovery of arrears of land revenue. Section 136 states as follows:—

"An arrear of land revenue may be recovered by any one or more of the following processes—

(a) by serving a writ of demand or a citation to appear on any defaulter,

(b) by arrest and detention of his person,

(c) by attachment or sale of his movable property including produce,

(d) by attachment of the holding in respect of which the arrear is due,

(e) by sale of the holding in respect of which the arrear is due, or

(f) by attachment or sale of other immoveable property of the defaulter."

The administrative machinery under the land revenue legislations of different States can recover the arrears of land revenue. In the context of the Information Technology Act, 2000, once the Adjudicating Officer awards penalty by way of damages, the party, against whom such damages are awarded, is duty bound to pay the penalty unless the same has been set aside in appeal. If that party fails to pay the penalty by way of damages, then the applicant/complainant can move an application before the Adjudicating Officer for recovery of the same. In that case, the Adjudicating Officer can direct the said penalty to be recovered as arrears of land revenue. The Adjudicating Officer can pass an order directing the Tehsildar/ Collector of the concerned area to recover the penalty as an arrear of land revenue.

An examination of section 43 and Chapter XI of the Information Technology Act, 2000 shows that there can be numerous cases where the provisions of damages and criminal liability would overlap. It seems that the Legislature was very clear in its mind inasmuch as it has only declared certain acts as penal offences under Chapter XI, which have been burdened with criminal liability. A number of other acts, which could have attracted criminal liability, have not been burdened with the same. Instead, they have been brought under the scope of civil liability in the form of damages by way of compensation under Chapter IX of the Information Technology Act, 2000. Due to this approach adopted by the Legislature, it is imperative that the intention of the Legislature be given full effect. It lies upon the law enforcement agencies and the Judiciary to ensure that the provisions of criminal and civil liability under the Information Technology Act, 2000 have to be strictly complied with.

All said and done, section 43 is a very important step taken towards granting the remedy of statutory damages to the people of our country. This provision is likely to go a long way in contributing towards the robust growth of law of tort in India, more so in the context of the electronic medium.

Section 43A of the Information Technology Act, 2000

Section 43A has been added for the first time under the Information Technology Act, 2000 by virtue of the Information Technology (Amendment) Act, 2008.

Section 43A is a provision of immense significance as it not only provides for the first time the fiduciary responsibility to protect data in a statutory manner but also makes the failure of the fulfilment of the statutory duty to protect data, as a ground for seeking damages by way of compensation, to the person so affected. Section 43A states as follows:

> *"**Section 43A. Compensation for failure to protect data.**—Where a body corporate, possessing, dealing or handling any sensitive personal data or information in a computer resource which it owns, controls or operates, is negligent in implementing and maintaining reasonable security practices and procedures and thereby causes wrongful loss or wrongful gain to any person, such body corporate shall be liable to pay damages by way of compensation to the person so affected.*
>
> *Explanation.—For the purposes of this section,—*
>
> *(i) 'body corporate' means any company and includes a firm, sole proprietorship or other association of individuals engaged in commercial or professional activities;*
>
> *(ii) 'reasonable security practices and procedures' means security practices and procedures designed to protect such information from unauthorised access, damage, use, modification, disclosure or impairment, as may be specified in an agreement between the parties or as may be specified in any law for the time being in force and in the absence of such agreement or any law, such reasonable security practices and procedures, as may be prescribed by the Central Government in consultation with such professional bodies or associations as it may deem fit;*
>
> *(iii) 'sensitive personal data or information' means such personal information as may be prescribed by the Central Government in consultation with such professional bodies or associations as it may deem fit."*

The salient features of section 43A are as follows:

(a) There has to be a body corporate.

(b) The said body corporate could either be any company or could be a firm, sole proprietorship or any association of individuals engaged in commercial or professional activities.

(c) The said body corporate must be handling any data or information in the electronic form.

(d) The said data must be sensitive personal data or information.

(e) The possessing, dealing or handling of sensitive personal data or information must be in a computer resource, whether it be a computer, computer system, computer network, data, computer data base or software.

(f) The said computer resource must be owned, controlled or operated by the said body corporate.

(g) The said body corporate must implement and maintain reasonable security practices and procedures pertaining to the said sensitive personal data or information

(h) The said body corporate is negligent in implementing and maintaining reasonable security practices and procedures.

(i) That by virtue of the said negligence, the said body corporate causes wrongful loss or wrongful gain to any person.

If all the aforesaid conditions are satisfied, the said body corporate is mandatorily liable to pay damages by way of compensation. A perusal of the inherent principles behind section 43A clearly shows that the focus of the Legislature is upon protecting and preserving sensitive personal data and information belonging to any legal entity. Any body corporate or service provider, who is possessing, dealing or handling with the sensitive personal data or information, is straggled with the statutory responsibility to protect and preserve the same. For the purposes of fulfilling such obligation, it is essential that the said body corporate must implement and maintain reasonable security practices and procedures.

It is important here to note that the *Explanation* (ii) to section 43A has given a very comprehensive definition of the term "reasonable security practices and procedures". As per the said *Explanation*, "reasonable security practices and procedures" mean the following:

(1) Security practices designed to protect information.

(2) Security procedures designed to protect information.

(3) The protection of information has to be from unauthorised access, damage, use, modification, disclosure or impairment.

(4) That the said specifications of information and its protection from the aforesaid acts by appropriate security practices and procedures may be specified in an agreement between the parties.

(5) The said protection of information from the aforesaid illegal acts may be specified in any law for the time being in force.

(6) In case, if there is any absence of any such agreement or any law, such reasonable security practices and procedures as may be prescribed by the Central Government.

The Central Government would only prescribe the reasonable security practices and procedures in consultation with such professional bodies or associations as it may deem fit.

That from the aforesaid, it is, thus, clear that there are three distinct scenarios in which reasonable security practices and procedures would be applicable. The said three scenarios are as follows:

The first scenario consists of the agreement between legal entities wherein the said agreement stipulates the security practices and procedures which must be followed by the possessor, dealer or handler of sensitive, personal data or information to protect sensitive, personal data or information from unauthorized access, damage, use, modification, disclosure or impairment. If any such reasonable security practices are mandated in the private agreement between the parties, the obligating party who is obliged to implement and maintain such reasonable security practices and procedures, must do so. Negligence in implementing and maintaining such reasonable security practices and procedures, would expose the obligating party to pay damages by way of compensation.

The second scenario would be when such reasonable security practices and procedures are specified in any law prevailing for the time being in force. It could be possible that any specific law at any point of time in the future, may specify specific security practices and procedures to be followed by concerned parties. In case, the defaulting party does not follow the said reasonable security practices and procedures as are stipulated by any specific law, then the said defaulting party has to face the music in the form of exposure to pay civil damages by way of compensation under the amended Information Technology Act, 2008.

The third scenario would be when no such reasonable security practices and procedures are stipulated in any agreement or any law. In that case, such reasonable security practices and procedures that may be prescribed by the Central Government would be the said reasonable security practices and procedures which the concerned parties are obligated to implement and maintain. If any party is negligent in implementing and maintaining reasonable security practices and procedures, then it is also exposed to damages by way of compensation.

As per the provisions of section 46(1A), these damages could be up to five crore before the Adjudicating Officer and beyond five crore, in a court of competent jurisdiction. Section 43A promises to be a provision of tremendous relevance and significance as time passes by. With more and more people using iPads, Tablets, Smart Phones and Smart Devices as default devices for storing, accessing, maintaining, sending and receiving sensitive personal data or information, it is but natural that with the passage of time, negligence in implementation and maintenance of reasonable security practices and procedures pertaining to the sensitive personal information residing in such communication devices, would become a basis for seeking damages by way of compensation.

At the time of writing, the Government has yet to specify the sensitive personal data as also reasonable security practices and procedures under section 43A of the amended Information Technology Act, 2000. The Government of India has notified the Information Technology (Reasonable Security Practices and Procedures and Sensitive Personal Data or Information) Rules, 2011, which have detailed the various kinds of sensitive personal data and the reasonable security practices and procedures, which need to be followed for protecting the same. Of course, the

Central Government is mandated to consult with such professional bodies or associations as it may deem fit and proper in this regard. Having said that, since the new amended Information Technology Act, 2000 has already come into effect from October 27, 2009, there is no denying the fact that parties can always specify the reasonable security practices and procedures within their private agreements which other stake-holders to the concerned agreement, are duty bound to comply with. Failure to comply with such reasonable security practices and procedures would also expose the said defaulting party to pay damages by way of compensation under the amended Information Technology Act, 2000.

This provision is also matter of tremendous significance from the perspective of corporate India. Corporate India today is plagued with issues pertaining to misuse of confidentiality and confidential data or trade secrets. People working in companies often today tend to take the company's data back home. The concept of company's data as its own data does not exist. Most of the employees today have no qualm or guilt of any kind whatsoever in taking corporate data back home. The problem is the mindset where people do not perceive the said act to be one which could be a foundation for potential legal claims, both civil and criminal.

In the context of strengthening the hands of corporate India for the purposes of protecting and preserving their confidential data and trade secrets, the provisions of section 43A is likely to come in more handy as time passes by. However, it is time that the Government needs to revise and revisit the practice of making the Information Technology Secretaries of different States as Adjudicating Officers. The Central Government has to clearly acknowledge the fact that section 43 has been a failed experiment in India from 2000 to 2009. It is important to note that with new amendments to the Information Technology Act, 2000 coming into effect from October 27, 2009; effective action must be taken by the Central Government to streamline adjudication proceedings and also to appoint highly qualified judicial officers for adjudication proceedings rather than appointing the current Information Technology Secretaries of different State Governments as Adjudicating Officers.

As time passes by, we are likely to see more enhanced significance of section 43A. However, section 43A and the remedy provided by it may still be illusionary in case effective action is not taken by the Central Government to improve the level and quantum of quality of adjudication proceedings before the Adjudicating Officers. Further, time is of essence in any Information Technology *paradigm*. Thus, if any proceedings for damages by way of compensation under the Information Technology Act, 2000 also take years, the people's expectations of trust and confidence in the efficacy and efficiency of the provisions of the Information Technology Act, 2000 to grant them access to speedier and effective justice are belied. The Government of India needs to ensure that such expectations of the people of India are not belied in the times to come.

Section 44 of the Information Technology Act, 2000

*"**Section 44. Penalty for failure to furnish information return, etc.**—If any person who is required under this Act or any rules or regulations made thereunder to—*

(a) *furnish any document, return or report to the Controller or the Certifying Authority fails to furnish the same, he shall be liable to a penalty not exceeding one lakh and fifty thousand rupees for each such failure;*

(b) *file any return or furnish any information, books or other documents within the time specified therefor in the regulations fails to file return or furnish the same within the time specified therefor in the regulations, he shall be liable to a penalty not exceeding five thousand rupees for every day during which such failure continues;*

(c) *maintain books of account or records, fails to maintain the same, he shall be liable to a penalty not exceeding ten thousand rupees for every day during which the failure continues."*

Various penalties have been provided under section 44 if there is non-compliance of certain specified conditions. Section 44(1) states that if any person fails to furnish any document, return or report to the Controller of Certifying Authorities which that person is required under the Information Technology Act, Rules or Regulations made thereunder, to furnish, that person shall be liable for a penalty not exceeding Rs. 1,50,000 for each such failure.

Further, if the Certifying Authority fails to furnish any documents, report or return to the Controller which the Certifying Authority is required under the Information Technology Act, Rules or regulations made thereunder, to furnish, the Certifying Authority shall be liable to pay penalty not exceeding Rs. 1,50,000 for each such failure. Penalties are liable to be recovered as an arrear of land revenue under section 64 of the Information Technology Act, 2000 and in case of failure of any party or the Certifying Authority to pay any penalty, the Digital Signature Certificate or the licence, as the case may be, can be suspended till the time the penalty is paid.

Further, if a person who is mandated by the Information Technology Act, Rules or Regulations made thereunder, to file any return or furnish any information, books or other documents within a specified time, and if the said person fails to file or furnish the same within the time specified, he shall be liable to pay penalty not exceeding Rs. 5,000 for each day, during which such failure continues.

Similarly, if any person is mandated by the Information Technology Act, 2000, Rules or Regulations made thereunder, to maintain books of account or records and if that person fails to maintain the same, that act attracts penalty. The penalty in such a case amounts to Rs. 10,000 for each day, during which the failure continues.

The rationale behind enacting section 44 is basically to ensure that people comply with the provisions of the Information Technology Act, Rules or regulations made thereunder. Any failure to comply with the provisions would meet with steep economic penalty and in many cases, penalty would be continuing on a day to day basis till the time such failure continues or subsists. The Adjudicating Officer under section 46 of the Information Technology Act, 2000, shall levy these penalties.

Section 45 of the Information Technology Act, 2000

*"**Section 45. Residuary penalty.**—Whoever contravenes any Rules or regulations made under this Act, for the contravention of which no penalty has been separately provided, shall be liable to pay a compensation not exceeding twenty-five thousand rupees to the person affected by such contravention or a penalty not exceeding twenty-five thousand rupees."*

Three kinds of penalties have been defined under section 44. The Act further envisages that there may be other residuary cases of contravention of the provisions of the Indian Cyberlaw where the Information Technology Act, 2000 has not specified any penalty. In such a case, section 45 comes into play. Section 45 specifically provides that where no penalty has been separately provided for the contravention of any Rules or regulations made under the Information Technology Act, 2000, if any person contravenes such Rules and regulations, then he shall be liable to pay compensation not exceeding Rs. 25,000 or a residuary penalty of a sum not exceeding Rs. 25,000. This penalty, by way of compensation, has been imposed to provide monetary relief that would go to the person affected by such contravention.

Section 45 is distinguished from section 44 inasmuch as section 44 imposes penalty, the amount of which would go only to the exchequer. Section 45 provides for penalty, both in the form of a levy accruing to the exchequer as also by way of compensation. In case of compensation, the amount of penalty in question would not go to the Government but to the person affected by such contravention, which may or may not necessarily be the Government.

Section 46—Power to adjudicate

Section 46 talks of a statutory authority called the Adjudicating Officer. In the Information Technology Act, 2000, the Adjudicating Officer is the third statutory authority that finds mention after the Controller of Certifying Authorities and the Certifying Authorities. Adjudicating Officers shall be appointed for the purpose of adjudication under Chapter IX of the Information Technology Act, 2000.

The Adjudicating Officers shall be appointed by the Central Government for the purpose of adjudging under Chapter IX whether any person has committed a contravention of any of the provisions of the Information Technology Act, 2000 or of any Rule, regulations, direction or order made thereunder. Thus, an Adjudicating Officer will adjudicate a contravention and violation of the provisions of the Information Technology Act, 2000, Information Technology Rules, 2000, Information Technology (Certifying Authority) Regulations, 2001, other directions or orders made thereunder. The Adjudicating Officer shall be an officer, not below the rank of a Director to the Government of India or an equivalent officer of the State Government. It may be pertinent to note that the Adjudicating Officer is the first level of redress under the Information Technology Act.

The main role of the Adjudicating Officer is to hold an inquiry in the manner, which may be prescribed by the Central Government. What is of importance is to note that the Adjudicating Officer has been given the power to adjudicate whether any person has committed a contravention of any of the provisions of the Information Technology Act, 2000, Information Technology Rules, 2000,

Information Technology (Certifying Authority) Regulations, 2001 or other directions or orders made thereunder. Therefore, the ambit and jurisdiction of the Adjudicating Officer is to adjudicate the contravention of provisions of the Information Technology Act, rules, regulations, directions or orders made thereunder only to the exclusion of any other authority. For the purpose of adjudging, the Adjudicating Officer has to hold an enquiry in the manner, as stipulated by the Central Government.

It is important to note that the Central Government has been mandated to appoint an Adjudicating Officer for adjudging the commission of any contravention of the provisions of the Indian Cyberlaw. The Central Government has no discretion in the matter of appointment of the Adjudicating Officer. The Central Government has not been granted the role of a filtering authority to filter the complaints for adjudication under Chapter IX and as such, it cannot, at any point of time, refuse to appoint an Adjudicating Officer, as the word used by section 46(1) is 'shall'.

Section 46(2) mandates that the Adjudicating Officer must follow the principles of natural justice and give opportunity of being heard to the concerned person whose contravention is being adjudged. The concerned person has to be given a reasonable opportunity for making representation in the matter. The Adjudicating Officer is also mandated to carry out the said inquiry and if, after the conclusion of such inquiry, the Adjudicating Officer is satisfied that the concerned person has committed the contravention, then the Adjudicating Officer has been given the discretion to impose penalty or award compensation. He may impose such penalty or award such compensation as he thinks fit in accordance with the provision of the section 46. This discretion has to be exercised according to well-established principles of law.

A perusal of section 46 shows that a lot of discretion has been given to the Adjudicating Officer. However, no standards or parameters have been laid down to guide the exercise of discretion of the Adjudicating Officer. It is expected that the discretion shall be exercised in accordance with the well-established principles of law. Further, the Act has not specified the manner in which the adjudication has to be conducted by the Adjudicating Officer. The Act has also not detailed the exhaustive scope of territorial jurisdiction of the Adjudicating Officer.

The qualifications of Adjudicating Officer are dealt with in section 46(3). It is stated that the Central Government would not appoint any person as an Adjudicating Officer unless he has such experience in the field of Information Technology and legal or judicial experience as may be prescribed.

The Information Technology Act stipulates that there would be many Adjudicating Officers. If more than one Adjudicating Officer is appointed, it has been mandated that the Central Government shall specify the subject-matters over which the Adjudicating Officers will have jurisdiction as also their territorial jurisdiction.

Under section 46(5) the Adjudicating Officers have been given the power of a Civil Court as conferred upon the Cyber Appellate Tribunal under section 58(2). It is important to note that section 61 of the Information Technology Act, 2000 bars the jurisdiction of civil courts. An Adjudicating Officer shall have the same powers as are vested in Civil Court under the Code of Civil Procedure, 1908, while trying a suit in respect of the following matters:—

(a) summoning and enforcing the attendance of any person and examining him on oath;

(b) requiring the discovery and production of documents or other electronic records;

(c) receiving evidence on affidavits;

(d) issuing commissions for the examination of witnesses or documents;

(e) reviewing its decisions;

(f) dismissing an application for default or deciding it *ex parte*;

(g) any other matter which may be prescribed.

Further, an Adjudicating Officer shall be deemed to be a civil court for the purposes of sections 345 and 346 of the Code of Criminal Procedure, 1973. The effect of this would be that when any such offence as is described in sections 175, 178, 179, 180 or 228 of the Indian Penal Code is committed in the view or presence of the Adjudicating Officer, the Adjudicating Officers shall be deemed to be a Civil Court. The Adjudicating Officer may cause the offender to be detained in custody and may, at any time before the rising of the Adjudicating Officer on the same day, take cognizance of the offence and, after giving the offender a reasonable opportunity to show cause why he should not be punished under section 345, sentence the offender to a fine not exceeding two hundred rupees, and, in default of payment of fine, to simple imprisonment for a term which may extend to one month, unless such fine be sooner paid.

In every such case, the Adjudicating Officer shall be deemed to be a Civil Court, which implies that it shall record the facts constituting the offence with the statement, if any, made by the offender, as well as impose a fine or sentence.

If any offence is under section 228 of the Indian Penal Code, the record shall show the nature and stage of the judicial proceeding in which, the Adjudicating Officer was interrupted or insulted, was sitting, and the nature of the interruption or insult.

Further, the Adjudicating Officer is deemed to be a Civil Court for the purposes of section 346, Cr. P.C. As such, the practical working of the same would possibly evolve in the manner detailed hereinbelow. If the Adjudicating Officer in any case considers that a person accused of any of the offences referred to in section 345, Cr. P.C. and committed in its view or presence should be imprisoned otherwise than in default of payment of fine, or that a fine exceeding two hundred rupees should be imposed upon him, or if such Adjudicating Officer is for any other reason of the opinion that the case should not be disposed of under section 345, such Adjudicating Officer, after recording the facts constituting the offence and the statement of the accused as hereinbefore provided, may forward the case to a Magistrate having jurisdiction to try the same, and he may further require security to be given for the appearance of such person before such Magistrate, or if such sufficient security is not given, shall forward such person in custody to such

Magistrate. Also, the Magistrate to whom any case is forwarded under the section, shall proceed to deal with, as far as may be, as if it were instituted on a police report.

Further, all proceedings before the Adjudicating Officer shall be deemed to be judicial proceedings within the meaning of sections 193 and 228 of Indian Penal Code. Thus, if any person, intentionally gives false evidence in any stage of the proceedings before the Adjudicating Officer, or fabricates false evidence for the purpose of being used in any stage of the proceedings before the Adjudicating Officer, he shall be punished, for the offence of false evidence, which shall be imprisonment of either description for a term which may extend to seven years and shall also be liable to fine. Further, whoever, intentionally offers any insult or causes any interruption to the Adjudicating Officer, while such adjudicating officer being a public servant is sitting, in any stage of the judicial proceedings, shall be punished with simple imprisonment for a term which may extend up to six months or with fine which may extend to one thousand rupees or with both.

The Adjudicating Officer has been given very comprehensive powers *i.e.* of a Civil Court, the proceedings before him shall be deemed to be judicial proceedings and he has been given the single most important job of adjudging the violations of the provisions of the Information Technology Act, 2000, Rules, Regulations, directions or orders made thereunder.

However, in the absence of specific parameters being stipulated by the Information Technology Act, 2000, there are numerous challenges that are likely to arise in the said scenario. It may be pertinent to note that the Controller of Certifying Authorities under section 28(1) or any officer authorized by him, shall take up for investigation any contravention of the provisions of this Act, Rules and regulations made thereunder. It may be submitted that the same powers have been conferred on an Adjudicating Officer under section 46 and there is likelihood of conflict that may arise between the two statutory authorities. The power of the Adjudicating Officer to adjudicate whether any person has committed a contravention of any of the provisions of the Information Technology Act, 2000 or any Rule, Regulation, direction or order made thereunder is very wide and includes not just power to investigate as is given to the Controller under section 28(1), but also the power to hold an inquiry under section 46(1). Such conflicting provisions are likely to create problems for the smooth functioning of the Information Technology Act, 2000.

The Information Technology Act, 2000 has been made applicable under section 1(2) not only to the whole of India, but also to any offence or contravention thereunder committed outside India by any person. It is not clear how the Adjudicating Officer shall adjudicate if any contravention of the provisions of the Information Technology Act, any Rule, regulation, direction or order made thereunder has been committed outside India. Further, cybercrimes and other illegal activities take place in cyberspace. In cyberspace, it is very difficult to come to a conclusion as to from what particular place does a particular act or violation or contravention takes place. In such a scenario, it is not clear how the Adjudicating Officer would decide as to where a particular contravention took place, and how he will adjudicate upon it. Such provisions are also likely to lead to conflict of jurisdiction with other authorities in other nations who are duly authorized to deal with such scenarios.

Section 46 is in the nature of an absolute statement without any clarification. The words "contravention of any of the provisions of this Act" makes it clear that any contravention of any section would attract the jurisdiction of the Adjudicating Officer.

However, the wordings of section 46 have to be harmoniously constructed and interpreted, keeping in mind the scheme and other provisions of the Information Technology Act, 2000.

A close scrutiny of the section reveals that the Adjudicating Officer has been empowered only to determine contraventions under sections 43, 44 and 45 of the Act. Chapter XI of the Act deals with "offences" and provides for punishment of fine and/or imprisonment for committing offences like tampering with computer source documents, hacking and other offences prescribed therein. The trial of these offences would not fall within the jurisdiction of Adjudicating Officer as the Adjudicating Officer has been conferred with the powers of a Civil Court under section 46(5) of the Information Technology Act, 2000. The trial of offences committed under Chapter XI of the Information Technology Act, 2000 would therefore still be within the jurisdiction of the relevant criminal courts, be it those of the Metropolitan Magistrate or the Additional Sessions Judge under the provisions of the Code of Criminal Procedure.

Section 46 has been amended by the Information Technology (Amendment) Act, 2008. In section 46(1), for the earlier words, direction or order made thereunder", the words "direction or order made thereunder which renders him liable to pay the penalty or compensation" have been substituted.

Further, Section 46(1A) has been added. As per section 46(1A), the Adjudicating Officer shall mandatorily exercise jurisdiction to adjudicate matters in which the claim for injury or damage does not exceed 5,00,000,00 INR. Thus, all claims for damages by way of compensation upto 5,00,000,00 INR can be filed with the Adjudicating Officer. The proviso to section 46(1A) clearly shows that, in case, if the claim for injury or damages exceed 5,00,000,00 INR, then the jurisdiction to entertain such agreement shall vest with the court of competent jurisdiction. Thus, the net result is that, if any person who is aggrieved by the various acts detailed under section 43 of the Information Technology Act, 2000, wants to file damages upto 5,00,000,00 INR, he can do so by filing it before the Adjudicating Officer. For claims beyond amount of 5,00,000,00 INR, the said claims will have to be filed in court of competent jurisdiction.

Further section 46(5c) has been added by the Information Technology (Amendment) Act, 2008. The net effect of this is that every Adjudicating Officer shall be deemed to be a Civil Court for the purposes of Order XXI CPC. Order XXI CPC deals with execution of decrees and orders. Thus, the net effect of section 46(5c) is that all the orders passed by the Adjudicating Officers shall be deemed to be decree which are liable to be executed and hence the Adjudicating Officer shall be deemed to be a Civil Court for the purposes of Order XXI CPC.

Section 66 of the Information Technology Act, 2000

One of the most significant and predominant provisions of the Indian Cyberlaw, is section 66 of the Information Technology Act, 2000. In its earlier avatar, it was one of the most significant provisions of India's first e-commerce legislation. The author had since the year 2000, referred to the said section, as the Mother India provision of the Indian Cyberlaw.

Section 66 has been dramatically amended by the Information Technology (Amendment) Act, 2008, which has completely replaced the language of the earlier section 66 of the Information Technology Act, 2000.

Earlier section 66 of the Information Technology Act, 2000 referred to the offence of hacking in the following terms:

"(1) Whoever with the intent to cause or knowing that he is likely to cause wrongful loss or damage to the public or any person destroys or deletes or alters any information residing in a computer resource or diminishes its value or utility or affects it injuriously by any means, commits hacking:

(2) Whoever commits hacking shall be punished with imprisonment up to three years, or with fine which may extend upto two lakh rupees, or with both."

The way, the offence of hacking was defined under the earlier section 66, was extremely wide as to incorporate a variety of acts, which did not amount to hacking, but it was still an offence under section 66 of the earlier Information Technology Act, 2000.

The Information Technology (Amendment) Act, 2008 has inserted a completely new language under section 66. Section 66 of the amended Information Technology Act, 2000 states as follows:

"***Section 66. Computer related offences.***—*If any person, dishonestly or fraudulently, does any act referred to in section 43, he shall be punishable with imprisonment for a term which may extend to three years or with fine which may extend to five lakh rupees or with both.*

Explanation.—For the purposes of this section,—

(a) the word 'dishonestly' shall have the meaning assigned to it in section 24 of the Indian Penal Code (45 of 1860);

(b) the word 'fraudulently' shall have the meaning assigned to it in section 25 of the Indian Penal Code (45 of 1860)."

The first important feature that appears from the perusal of section 66 is that the ambit and scope of section 66 of the amended Information Technology Act, 2000, has been expanded even much beyond the scope of the earlier section 66. As such, from a mere provision on hacking, section 66 is now addressing various computer-related offences. It is pertinent to point out, that Legislature has already defined various activities which tantamount to misuse of computers, computer systems and computer networks under section 43 of the amended Information Technology Act, 2000 on the basis of which damages by way of compensation can be awarded.

Section 66 stipulates that if any person dishonestly or fraudulently commits any act referred from section 43(a) to 43(j) of the amended Information Technology Act, 2000, the same has been declared as an offence. The said offence is punishable with imprisonment for a term which may extend to three years or with fine which may extend to five lakh rupees or with both.

For the purposes of understanding the scope, ambit and applicability of the relevant clauses of section 43 of the amended Information Technology Act, 2000, it is relevant to reproduce herein below section 43 of the amended Information Technology Act, 2000, which is as follows:

*"**Section 43. Penalty and Compensation for damage to computer, computer system, etc.**—If any person without permission of the owner or any other person who is in-charge of a computer, computer system or computer network,*

(a) accesses or secures access to such computer, computer system or computer network or computer resource;

(b) downloads, copies or extracts any data, computer data base or information from such computer, computer system or computer network including information or data held or stored in any removable storage medium;

(c) introduces or causes to be introduced any computer contaminant or computer virus into any computer, computer system or computer network;

(d) damages or causes to be damaged any computer, computer system or computer network, data, computer data base or any other programmes residing in such computer, computer system or computer network;

(e) disrupts or causes disruption of any computer, computer system or computer network;

(f) denies or causes the denial of access to any person authorised to access any computer, computer system or computer network by any means;

(g) provides any assistance to any person to facilitate access to a computer, computer system or computer network in contravention of the provisions of this Act, Rules or regulations made thereunder,

(h) charges the services availed of by a person to the account of another person by tampering with or manipulating any computer, computer system, or computer network,

(i) destroys, deletes or alters any information residing in a computer resource or diminishes its value or utility or affects it injuriously by any means

(j) Steals, conceals, destroys or alters or causes any person to steal, conceal, destroy or alter any computer source code used for a computer resource with an intention to cause damage,

he shall be liable to pay damages by way of compensation the person so affected.

Explanation.—For the purposes of this section—

(i) 'computer contaminant' means any set of computer instructions that are designed—

(a) to modify, destroy, record, transmit data or programme residing within a computer, computer system or computer network; or

(b) by any means to usurp the normal operation of the computer, computer system, or computer network;

(ii) 'Computer Database' means a representation of information, knowledge, facts, concepts or instructions in text, image, audio, video that are being prepared or have been prepared in a formalised manner or have been produced by a computer, computer system or computer network and are intended for use in a computer, computer system or computer network;

(iii) 'Computer Virus' means any computer instruction, information, data or programme that destroys, damages, degrades or adversely affects the performance of a computer resource or attaches itself to another computer resource and operates when a programme, data or instruction is executed or some other event takes place in that computer resource;

(iv) 'Damage' means to destroy, alter, delete, add, modify or re-arrange any computer resource by any means.

(v) 'Computer Source Code' means the listing of programmes, computer commands, design and layout and programme analysis of computer resource in any form."

For the detailed commentary on the ten grounds elaborated under section 43 of the amended Information Technology Act, 2000, kindly refer to the commentary under section 43 of the amended Information Technology Act, 2000 in the book.

It is pertinent to point out that the said activities and acts, as detailed from section 43(a) to 43(j) committed *per se* themselves, do not become offences. The acts done as detailed under section 43 only continue to be grounds for seeking damages by way of compensation. It is only when the said acts, are done, dishonestly or fraudulently, does the said acts transform themselves into various crimes, as detailed under section 66 of the amended Information Technology Act, 2000 .

It is pertinent to point out that the *Explanation* to section 66 of the amended Information Technology Act, 2000 explains that the words "dishonestly" and "fraudulently" shall have the same meanings assigned to them under section 24 and 25 of the Indian Penal Code, respectively.

Section 24 of the Indian Penal Code provides the legal definition of the term "dishonestly"

Section 24 of the Indian Penal Code provides as follows:

"Whoever does anything with the intention of causing wrongful gain to one person or wrongful loss to another person is said to do that thing "dishonestly".

Section 24 stipulates that if any person does anything with the intention of causing wrongful gain to one person or wrongful loss to another person, that person does, the said thing dishonestly. The entire definition of the term "dishonestly" is dependent upon causing wrongful gain or wrongful loss to another. It is pertinent to point out that section 23 of the Indian Penal Code, defines the terms "wrongful loss" and "wrongful gain" in the following manner:

Section 23

"Wrongful gain" is gain by unlawful means of property which the person gaining is not legally entitled.

"Wrongful loss" is the loss by unlawful means of property to which the person losing it is legally entitled.

A person is said to gain wrongfully when such person retains wrongfully, as well as when such person acquires wrongfully. A person is said to lose wrongfully when such person is wrongfully kept out of any property as well as when such person is wrongfully deprived of property".

In "*Kishan Kumar* v. *Union of India*"[39], the Supreme Court held that, the expression "wrongful gain includes wrongful retention and wrongful loss includes being kept out the property as well as being wrongfully deprived of property".

The judiciary has over the years evolved detailed case-law on the concept of "Dishonestly".

In "*Abdul Fazal Siddiqui* v. *Fatehchand Hirawat*",[40] the Hon'ble Supreme Court reiterated the, definitions of "dishonestly" and "fraudulently" as detailed in sections 24 and 25 of the Indian Penal Code respectively

In "*B. Suresh Yadav* v. *Sharifa Bee*[41]", the Hon'ble Supreme Court held that regarding the expression "dishonestly" as contained in section 24 thereof in terms whereof something must be done with an intention of causing wrongful gain to one person or wrongful loss to another.

In "*Charanjit Singh Chadha* v. *Sudhir Mehra*[42]", the Hon'ble Supreme Court held that the element of 'dishonest intention' which is an essential element to constitute the offence of theft, cannot be attributed to a person exercising his right under an agreement entered into between the parties as he may not have an intention of causing wrongful gain or to cause wrongful loss to the hirer.

In "*R.R. Diwakar* v. *V.B. Guttal*"[43], the Hon'ble Karnataka High Court held that, the word "dishonestly" is defined by section 24 of Penal Code. A person who does anything with the intention of causing wrongful gain to one person or wrongful loss to another person, is said to do that thing 'dishonestly'

In "*Raju Jha* v. *Emperor*",[44] the Hon'ble Patna High Court held that, the section does not say that the word "dishonestly" is applicable only when there is an intention of causing wrongful loss to another person but properly construed means that cases of intention of causing such wrongful gain to one person or wrongful loss to another person but properly coming with wider class of dishonest actions.

It is pertinent to note that the *Explanation* to section 66 of the amended Information Technology Act, 2000 stipulates that the term "fraudulently" for the purposes of section 66 of the amended Information Technology Act, 2000 shall have the meanings assigned to it under section 25 of Indian Penal Code.

---

39. AIR 1959 SC 1390.
40. (1996) 6 SCC 32.
41. AIR 2008 SC 210.
42. AIR 2001 SC 3721.
43. 1975 Cr LJ 90.
44. AIR 1943 Pat 60 (63).

Section 25 of the Indian Penal Code gives the legal definition of the term "fraudulently". Section 25 of the Indian Penal Code provides as follows:—

"A person is said to do a thing fraudulently if he does that thing with intent to defraud but not otherwise."

As per the provisions of section 25, if a person does a particular thing with intention to defraud but not otherwise, that person is set to do a thing fraudulently. The foundation of the legal definition of the term "fraudulently" is dependent on the phrase "intend to fraud".

It is important to note that the terms "fraud" and 'defraud" are not defined in the Indian Penal Code. The word "defraud" is of double meaning in the sense that it either may or may not, imply deprivation, and as it is not defined, its meaning must be sought by consideration of the context in which the word "fraudulently" is found.[45]

Over the years the Judiciary has evolved distinctive case-law on the aforesaid section.

In "*S.P. Chengalvaraya Naidu* v. *Jagannath*"[46] the Hon'ble Supreme Court held in the context of, non-disclosure of relevant material and material documents in the court in a partition suit with a view to obtain advantage, that the word "fraud" was defined as an act of deliberate deception with a design of securing something by taking unfair advantage of another.

In "*Dr. Vimla* v. *Delhi Administration*"[47] , the Hon'ble Supreme Court held that, the expression "defraud" involves two elements, namely, deceit and injury to the person deceived. The injury may even comprise a non-economic or non-pecuniary loss. Even in those rare cases where the benefit to the deceiver does not cause corresponding loss to the deceived, the second condition is satisfied.

In "*Abdul Fazal Siddiqui* v. *Fatehchand Hirawat*",[48] the Hon'ble Supreme Court reiterated the definition of "fraudulently" defined in section 25 of the Indian Penal Code.

Thus, a cumulative examination of section 66 of the amended Information Technology Act, 2000 that the acts referred to under section 43 of the amended Information Technology Act, 2000, must be done either dishonestly or fraudulently. If any of the two elements namely dishonestly or fraudulently is missing, the said acts do not become cybercrimes under section 66 of the amended Information Technology Act, 2000. Given the fact that section 66 provides for imprisonment for a term which may extend to three years, computer-related offences under section 66 of the amended Information Technology Act, 2000 are clearly bailable offences and hence, lack the teeth that the people and users of computer systems, expect the law to have. Consequently, despite the broad ambit, scope and applicability of section 66 of the amended Information Technology Act,

---

45. *Abas Ali,* supra.
46. (1994) 1 SCC 1.
47. AIR 1963 SC 1572.
48. (1996) 6 SCC 32.

2000, the said provision belies the expectations of the users and victims of computer-related offences as the same does not provide adequate deterrent quantum of punishment to cyber criminals, who perpetuate various kinds of computer-related offences.

Section 66A of the Information Technology Act, 2000

The Information Technology Act, 2000 has been amended to incorporate a new provision, being section 66A. This section provides for the offence of sending offensive messages through communication devices or computer resources. The Legislature has been alive to the fact that with increasing adoption and usage of iPads, Tablets, Smart Phones and Smart Devices in India, the misuse of iPads, Tablets, Smart Phones and Smart Devices has been happening at a very rampant pace. However, people utilize iPads, Tablets, Smart Phones and Smart Devices for a variety of purposes for expressing their opinions, frustrations, emotions, thought processes, perspectives and views.

Lot of times, the said expressions may not be in compliance with the requirements of public decency, morality or other standards existing in the contemporary society at the relevant time. This misuse of iPads, Tablets, Smart Phones and Smart Devices have resulted in targeting of individuals and therefore, causing a lot of anguish, harassment, anxiety to the victims. Earlier, the law did not have many teeth, with regard to misuse of iPads, Tablets, Smart Phones and Smart Devices. However, the Information Technology Act, 2000 has now been amended to incorporate section 66A. Section 66A applies to any information that is sent, either by means of a computer resource or a communication device.

Section 66A reads as follows:

*"**Section 66A. Punishment for sending offensive messages through communication service, etc.**—Any person who sends, by means of a computer resource or a communication device,—*

(a) any information that is grossly offensive or has menacing character; or

(b) any information which he knows to be false, but for the purpose of causing annoyance, inconvenience, danger, obstruction, insult, injury, criminal intimidation, enmity, hatred, or ill will, persistently by making use of such computer resource or a communication device; or

(c) any electronic mail or electronic mail message for the purpose of causing annoyance or inconvenience or to deceive or to mislead the addressee or recipient about the origin of such messages,

shall be punishable with imprisonment for a term which may extend to two three years and with fine.

Explanation:—For the purposes of this section, terms 'electronic mail' and 'electronic mail message' means a message or information created or transmitted or received on a computer, computer system, computer resource or communication device including attachments in text, image, audio, video and any other electronic record, which may be transmitted with the message."

The Government of India has been aware of the manner in which, iPads, Tablets, Smart Phones and Smart Devices have been continuously misused, not only for the purposes of causing harassment of the target but also generally creating lot of nuisance in that regard. Initially meant to be a means of communicating, today iPads, Tablets, Smart Phones and Smart Devices have become a source of nuisance. Invariably today companies use iPads, Tablets, Smart Phones and Smart Devices for the purposes of marketing as also unsolicited market and spam. Unsolicited calls today are the norm of the day. Irrespective of the standing of the person or his preference, almost every second or third person receives unsolicited calls, either for loan or some insurance or other related product. This is being primarily so because of the absence of any specific legislation pertaining to protection of privacy of people, in the context of use of iPads, Tablets, Smart Phones and Smart Devices. Companies have exploited in this drawback of existing provisions of law to the hilt. The Telecom Regulatory Authority of India (TRAI) had been seized of this matter and had come up with the idea of DO NOT CALL list. However, in the absence of any specific legislation to provide the enabling regulatory mechanism and teeth to the same, the DO NOT CALL experiment in India has met with more failure than success. Despite people registering with DO NOT CALL list, they continue to get calls from a variety of marketers. Further, these calls not only waste the productive time of productive persons but also land up in wasting national man-power, national productivity and national time. This is a part of nuisance which invades into the privacy of the people and trouble the people to the hilt. That is the reason, why the Government wanted to regulate the usage of communication devices and communication services. It has also been seen for more than a decade in India that mobile phones have been used for sending offensive messages. These messages are sent invariably in a fit of anger, rage, emotion, or any other stage. However, the net result of such offensive messages, sent by mobiles and other communication devices, is often devastating upon the receiver of the said offensive messages. These messages constitute not just violation of any senses of persons but also tend to disturb the addressees. That is why, the Parliament came up with a distinctive provision being section 66A. Initially, section 66A was perceived because of number of practical problems facing the Information Technology Act, 2000. The Information Technology Act, 2000 had been passed in the year 2000 primarily as a legislation meant for promoting e-commerce in India and providing a legal frame work in support thereof. However, a couple of newly emerged cyber crimes like cyber stalking were not at all covered. The Legislature, by enacting section 66A, has directly covered cyber stalking using computer sources as also mobile stalking.

If any person uses any mobile phone, smart phone, personal digital assistant or any devices used for communicating, sending or transmitting any text, video, audio or image, for the various activities listed under section 66A(a) to (c), he shall be guilty of an offence, which is punishable with imprisonment for a term which may extend to three years and with fine.

Any person who sends, by means of his iPad, Tablet, Smart Phone and/or Smart Device, any information that is grossly offensive or has menacing character commits an offence under section 66A of the amended Information Technology Act, 2000.

The words "grossly offensive" and "menacing character" has not yet been defined under the Information Technology Act, 2000 and the same has been left to the subjective interpretation of the law-enforcement agencies and the courts. For the reason of understanding, it is feasible to break the words and go by their dictionary meaning so that the usage of the words is clearer.

The following definitions give more clarity to the meaning of the following words:—

1. OFFENSIVE[49]

   Violating or tending to violate or offend against; "violative of the principles of liberty"; "considered such depravity offensive against all laws of humanity"

2. MENACING[50]

   Menace – a perceived threat or danger; the act of threatening; a dangerous person; to make threats (against someone); to intimidate; to endanger someone or something; to imperil or jeopardize.

Thus, any information of any nature which is transmitted using iPads, Tablets, Smart Phones and Smart Devices, which is grossly offensive would qualify as an offence. The said information could be offensive to person's moral standards, his privacy, his standing, stature, credibility, goodwill or even position in society. Further, if any information sent using iPads, Tablets, Smart Phones and Smart Devices has got a menacing character in the sense of it threatening to harm the character, personality, standing, stature of any person, which shall also be deemed to be an offence under section 66A of the amended Information Technology Act, 2000.

Today, a large number of people misuse the iPads, Tablets, Smart Phones and Smart Devices for the purposes of sending information, which they know is false, but which they send for vested interests. These vested interests can either be for the purposes of annoying someone, or causing inconvenience, danger or obstruction to them. A large number of times, these informations are sent by iPads, Tablets, Smart Phones and Smart Devices, with a purpose to insult the recipient, as also to cause injury and criminal intimidation to the concerned person. It is amazing how iPads, Tablets, Smart Phones and Smart Devices can be used to intimidate people and to bring them into submission. Further, if any person uses a iPad, Tablet, Smart Phone and Smart Device and sends information, which he knows to be false which is sent for the purposes of causing enmity, hatred or ill-will and the said acts are normally done persistently, by making use of the concerned mobile phones, personal digital assistants, blackberries, smart phones and other communication devices, then that those activities also come within the ambit of the offence defined under section 66A(b) of the amended Information Technology Act, 2000. The said offence will also be punishable with three years imprisonment and fine.

A lot of people use smart phones and communication devices for the purposes of accessing the internet as also sending, receiving, transmitting and forwarding e-mails and electronic mail messages. The law has today made it illegal for any

49. wordnetweb.princeton.edu/perl/webwn.

50. en.wiktionary.org/wiki/menace.

person to send, by means of using mobile phones, smart phones, blackberries, mobile devices, personal digital assistants and/or communication devices, any e-mail or electronic mail messages for the purposes of causing annoyance or inconvenience to the recipient. Such acts have been brought within the ambit of criminal penalty. In that sense, cyber stalking using electronic mail messages through iPads, Tablets, Smart Phones and Smart Devices, has been sought to be specifically covered by the provisions of the amended Section 66A of the Information Technology Act, 2000. Further, if any person sends, by means of mobile phones, smart phones, blackberries, mobile devices, iPads, Tablets, Smart Devices, personal digital assistants and/or communication devices, any electronic mail or electronic mail message to mislead the addressee or recipient about the origin of such message, that is also deemed to be an offence punishable with three years' imprisonment and fine.

It is important to note that section 66A(c) tries to cover slightly the phenomenon of spam including mobile spam. However, the entire issue of spam including mobile spam, cannot be effectively tackled only with just having one provision in place. This is all the more so, because the said provision only makes the said offence as a bailable offence. This provision lacks effective teeth and is a mere paper tiger provision. India has not come up with any dedicated anti-cyber spam legislation in this regard. However, limited level of protection has been sought to be given under section 66A of the amended Information Technology Act, 2000.

It is important to point out that the *Explanation* to section 66A of the amended Information Technology Act, 2000 defines the terms "electronic mail" and "electronic mail messages". These terms are defined to mean a message or information created, transmitted, or received on iPads, Tablets, Smart Phones and Smart Devices and/or communication devices. This definition is very wide and includes all attachments in text, image, audio, video or other electronic record, which may be transmitted with a message. This definition of the terms "electronic mail" and "electronic mail message" is indeed very broad and comprehensive and is likely to be used, in the cases of misuse of iPads, Tablets, Smart Phones and Smart Devices and/or communication devices by victims, as also the law-enforcement agencies. However, since section 66A is only bailable offence, it still does not put much deterrence in the minds of potential mobile criminals.

All iPads, Tablets, Smart Phones and Smart Devices users in India need to be aware of three broad categories of activities which have been declared as criminal act. Broadly three kinds of activities have been brought within the ambit of criminal penalty under the new amended section 66A of the amended Information Technology Act, 2000. If any person sent by means computer resource or communication device any information that is grossly offensive or has menacing character, then the same is an offence under the amended section 66A. This is a very broad section as it includes not just information sent through computers, computer systems, computer networks and computer resources but also all kinds of communication devices like mobiles, handsets, iPads, Tablets, Smart Phones and Smart Devices. Thus, if any person sent information to my mobile which is grossly offensive and has menacing character, he is exposed to potential punishment with imprisonment for a term which may extend to three years and with fine.

It also needs to be appreciated that what is offensive and menacing has to be understood in the context of the relevant society of India at the relevant time. Thus, something, which may not be offensive a decade ago or earlier, could now be deemed to be offensive. Thus, the Legislature has given the discretion to the law enforcement agencies and the court shall decide as to what is offensive or grossly offensive or has menacing character. Thus, when people use their iPads, Tablets, Smart Phones and Smart Devices for the purposes of threatening a person by SMS or MMS need to be now careful as the said activities have been brought within the ambit of criminal penalty.

In case if sexually explicit content is sent by iPads, Tablets, Smart Phones and Smart Devices to recipients on their mobile phones, the same could also be deemed to be grossly offensive and having menacing character. Everything will depend upon the facts and circumstances of each case and each case has to be tested on the strength of merits of the facts stated therein.

Further, if any person sends by means of a computer resource or communication device any information which he knows to be false but which is sent for the purposes of causing annoyance, inconvenience, danger, obstruction, insult, injury, criminal intimidation, enmity, hatred or ill-will persistently by making use of such computer resource or communication device, the same will also be deemed to be an offence punishable under section 66A of the amended Information Technology Act, 2000 with the term which may extend to three years and with fine. Thus, offences like cyber stalking, cyber nuisance, cyber harassment and cyber defamation are all brought within the ambit of section 66A of the amended Information Technology Act, 2000. However, the beauty of new section 66A is that it also incorporates within its ambit all the aforesaid activities done using mobile phones, cell phones, smart phones, blackberries, personal digital assistants, iPads, Tablets, and Smart Devices. Thus, spreading malicious defamation campaigns using mobile devices is specifically covered within the ambit of section 66A. Further, sending threatening information by SMS would also qualify within the ambit of the said provision. Mobile nuisance, mobile harassment or also related offences would be now covered within the ambit of section 66 of Information Technology Act, 2000. However, for this section to be applicable it is necessary to prove the persistent usage of a computer resource or communication device to do the aforesaid acts. The said acts must be done persistently by making use of such computer resource or communication device.

Another third category of activities brought within the ambit of criminal liability are when a person sends by means of a computer resource or communication device, any electronic mail or electronic mail message for the purpose of causing annoyance or inconvenience or to deceive or to mislead the addressee or recipient about the origin of such messages. If the aforesaid activities are done, the same are also punishable with imprisonment for a term which may extend to three years and also with fine. This is possibly a very wide section and incorporates therein almost a variety of offences. The Legislature intended to target in a limited manner computer spam by enacting the said section. This is so because, spam or unsolicited commercial e-mail are electronic mail messages which are sent either to create annoyance or inconvenience or to deceive or to mislead the addressee or the recipient about the origin of such messages. To some extent, the said section could also incorporate therein the phenomenon of the newly emerging mobile spam. However, it needs to be kept in mind that the *Explanation* to section 66A provides a detailed meaning of the terms electronic mail and electronic mail messages. *Explanation* to section 66A clearly says that electronic mail and electronic mail message for the purposes of the present section mail, message or information created or transmitted or received on computer, computer systems, computer resource or communication device including attachments in text, video, audio, image and any other electronic record which may be transmitted with the message. Thus, it is very clear that electronic mail message not only includes the message but also all attachments therein which are in text, audio, video, image or any other electronic form or record.

To some extent, this provision would also cover elements pertaining to mobile spam. However, when one examines in details the said provision, one realizes that the said provision is not at all adequate to deal with the menace of spam, whether on computers or in mobile phones, iPads, Tablets, Smart Phones and Smart Devices. This is so because, spammers today take extraordinary care and precaution to ensure that their steps cannot be traced and that they cannot be identified. Thus, in a majority of cases, the identity of spammers itself cannot be known since they are using a number of proxy servers and other devices and technologies so as to hide their real identities. Further, they deliberately create landmines on the way so that the law enforcement agencies cannot track up their spam related activities to them. Since, that is the accepted norm of the day, section 66A(c) does not provide an effective legal remedy in the practical terms. This is so because, in a number of cases, it is impossible to find out the real identity of the spammer.

Further, it needs to be appreciated that spam is such a complicated subject that it cannot be addressed very simplistic by section 66A(c). Countries across the world have applied their collective wisdom and have come to the conclusion that spam needs to be distinctly regulated by detailed legislations. That is why different countries have had different legislations aimed dedicatedly at spam. These spam-related legislations include the CAN Spam Act of the United States of America, Anti-Spam Law of Australia and the Anti-Spam Law of New Zealand of 2007.

Clearly, even in those countries, having these comprehensive legal provisions in the form of special dedicated legislations and statutes to spam, spam has still not yet been brought fully within the blanket of regulation. India cannot afford to achieve much by a singular provision being section 66A(c) which in any case has been limited applicability. To that extent, one does realize that Indian Legislature has failed the expectations of the nation in this regard. Today, India has emerged as one of the top ten originators of spam across the world. This has happened primarily because of the absence of regulation in this regard. Even, when the Government of India have legislated the amended Information Technology Act, 2000, it still has not given any detailed provisions relating to spam. India has missed a tremendous opportunity to regulate spam by providing for specific detailed legal provisions in this regard. Because of the severe limitations of section 66A which presupposes the identity of the spammer being known, even instances pertaining to mobile spam are not likely to be effectively covered under the new legislation.

While section 66A has made some advancement, it still does not provide any effective remedy in the event of spam or mobile spam emerging from unknown destinations. India has lost the window of opportunity in legislating a detailed legal regime to regulate spam and this is likely to be further assisting spammers who can continue to go ahead and indulge in spamming activities, without any fear of law or any deterrent effect upon them.

Another important feature for section 66A is that it has brought within its ambit all activities pertaining to smart phones, blackberries, iphones as well as personal digital assistants which are used for the purposes of sending and receiving e-mails and electronic mail messages. Thus, now e-mail does not need to be only sent by a computer system or laptop. It can even be sent by a blackberry, smart phone, iphone, personal digital assistants and all the activities pertaining to same are also now brought within the ambit of the legality, as stipulated under the amended Information Technology Act, 2000. It is expected that with the passage of time, more and more people are likely to adopt the usage of mobile technologies as well as iPads, Tablets, Smart Phones and Smart Devices. That being so, increasingly people would use iPads, Tablets, Smart Phones and Smart Devices and communication devices for accessing their electronic records as also electronic mail messages. The propensity to commit the crime using these digital communication devices are likely to increase with the passage of time. Section 66A is expected to be applicable to all such activities using any iPads, Tablets, Smart Phones and Smart Devices or communication devices pertaining to electronic mail messages.

Section 66B of the Information Technology Act, 2000

> ***"Section 66B. Punishment for dishonestly receiving stolen computer resource or communication device.****—Whoever dishonestly received or retains any stolen computer resource or communication device knowing or having reason to believe the same to be stolen computer resource or communication device, shall be punished with imprisonment of either description for a term which may extend to three years or with fine which may extend to rupees one lakh or with both."*

In today's world, people are using mobiles as a disposable item. Once mobile phone is used for a long period of time, it is either disposed off or just thrown in the wastepaper basket. However, because of the propensity to use mobiles very frequently a lot of cases have arisen pertaining to theft of iPads, Tablets, Smart Phones and Smart Devices. Traditionally an iPad, Tablet, Smart Phone and Smart Device is a movable property and the theft of iPads, Tablets, Smart Phones and Smart Devices is covered within the standard offence of theft defined under section 378 of the Indian Penal Code. However, Legislature also required that people should be further deterred from retaining stolen mobile phones, smart phones, Blackberries, mobile devices, personal digital assistants and/or communication devices.

Therefore, the Parliament has introduced section 66B of the amended Information Technology Act, 2000. Section 66B clearly makes dishonest receiving or retaining of any stolen mobile phones, smart phones, blackberries, mobile devices, personal digital assistants and/or communication devices knowing or having the reason to believe that same to be stolen mobile phones, iPads, Tablets, smart phones, blackberries, mobile devices, personal digital assistants and/or communication devices, as a punishable offence. This offence is punishable with imprisonment of either description for a term, which may extend to three years or fine, which may extend to rupees one lakh or with both. This is a bailable offence, by virtue of the provisions of the amended Information Technology Act, 2000. This provision is also particularly helpful for all corporate and legal entities, who give mobile phones, iPads, Tablets, smart phones, blackberries, mobile devices, personal digital assistants and/or communication devices to their employees for the purposes of efficiently and effectively performing their day to day official functions and operations These mobile phones, iPads, Tablets, smart phones, blackberries, mobile devices, personal digital assistants and/or communication devices have a large amount of confidential data and information belonging to the concerned companies. However, rogue employees often resign without giving notice and often do not return back these communication devices. Such kind of scenarios will also be covered within the ambit of section 66A of the amended Information Technology Act, 2000. Further, specifically the act of dishonestly receiving and retention of stolen computer resource or communication devices either with the knowledge that the same is stolen or having reason to believe the same to be stolen, has thus now been brought within the ambit of the criminal offence. This provision is likely to provide effective remedy to people, whose mobile phones often get stolen by different persons and who further continue to retain, use or sell the same, to the detriment of the original owner of the iPads, Tablets, Smart Phones and Smart Devices and/or communication devices. Such an exercise is now brought specifically within the ambit of section 66B of the amended Information Technology Act, 2000.

Section 66C of the Information Technology Act, 2000

> *"**Section 66C. Punishment for identity theft.**—Whoever, fraudulently or dishonestly make use of the electronic signature, password or any other unique identification feature of any other person, shall be punished with imprisonment of either description for a term which may extend to three years and shall also be liable to fine with may extend to rupees one lakh."*

Today identity theft has emerged as major headache for nations, especially in the western world. "Identity Theft", is common man's parlance, means the phenomenon of stealing another person's identity.

Wikipedia states that Identity theft is a form of fraud in which someone pretends to be someone else by assuming that person's identity, typically in order to access resources or obtain credit and other benefits in that person's name. The victim of identity theft (here meaning the person whose identity has been assumed by the identity thief) can suffer adverse consequences if he or she is held accountable for the perpetrator's actions. Organizations and individuals who are duped or defrauded by the identity thief can also suffer adverse consequences and losses, and to that extent are also victims. The term identity theft was coined in 1964 and is actually a misnomer, since it is not literally possible to steal an identity as such – more accurate terms would be identity fraud or impersonation or identity cloning but identity theft has become commonplace.

Section 66C has provided for the offence of identity theft. The said provision has been drafted in very generic and broad terms and incorporates therein the fraudulent or dishonest making use of the electronic signature, password or any other unique identification feature of any person. While, the said provision has not specifically mentioned communication devices therein yet the said provision is equally applicable in the context of communication devices. Today, there are a large number of smart phones use passwords for accessing the same. In case a person comes to know about a password of another and then misuses it on the mobile phones, iPads, Tablets, smart phones, blackberries, mobile devices, personal digital assistants and/or communication devices of other person, such an act would also come within the ambit of the section 66C of the amended Information Technology Act, 2000.

Further, if any person fraudulently or dishonestly, makes use of any other unique identification feature of any person on any mobile phones, iPads, Tablets, smart phones, blackberries, mobile devices, personal digital assistants and/or communication devices, that act is also brought within the ambit of criminal offence. Such an act is punishable under section 66C of the amended Information Technology Act, 2000.

It is pertinent to point out that section 66C does not give the definition of the term unique identification feature. Further, section 2 of the amended Information Technology Act, 2000 also does not give the definition of the term "unique identification feature".

Let us examine the individual definition of the term in the phrase "unique identification feature"

Illustrated Oxford Dictionary defines *"Unique as unequalled; having no like, equal or parallel".*

Illustrated Oxford Dictionary defines *"identification as the act or an instance of identifying."*

Illustrated Oxford Dictionary defines *"features as a distinctive or characteristic part of the thing"*

However, it is important to note that the words any other "unique identification feature" are very vast, comprehensive and futuristic in their approach and perspective. Thus, even though technology may change and continuously evolve, any unique identification feature of any person in any new technology could also come within the ambit of section 66C of the amended Information Technology Act, 2000. The said section makes the offence punishable with imprisonment of either description for a term, which may extend to 3 years and shall also be liable to fine, which may extend to rupees one lakh.

While, the Legislature has to be complimented for introducing section 66C, which has dealt with the offence of identity theft for the first time and has made it the basis for criminal punishment and fine, yet the disappointing feature is that the said section is only a bailable offence. The said offence is a bailable offence where the accused, even if arrested, would be entitled to bail as a matter of right. Such bailability of the offence of identity theft clearly makes the said provision a paper tiger provision and does not provide a effective deterrent effect on, people not to indulge in identity theft. Further, such a provision also fails to give effective remedy to victims of identity theft, perpetuated through any ambit or usage of technology. In that sense, the addition of section 66C is two steps forward and one step backward. The law needs to be made far more stringent in terms of its deterrent effect and in terms of it providing effective remedies to victims of identity theft.

Section 66D of the Information Technology Act, 2000

> ***"Section 66D. Punishment for cheating by personation by using computer resource.***—*Whoever, by means for any communication device or computer resource cheats by personating, shall be punished with imprisonment of either description for a term which may extend to three years and shall also be liable to fine which may extend to one lakh rupees."*

Another major advancement done by the amended Information Technology Act, 2000 is providing for the offence under section 66D therein. The said section provides for the offence of cheating by personation by using computer resource or communication device.

It is pertinent to point out that the offence of cheating by personation is defined under section 416 of the Indian Penal Code.

Section 416 of Indian Penal Code reads as under:

> *"A person is said to "cheat by personation" if he cheats by pretending to be some other person, or by knowingly substituting one person for another, or representing that he or any other person is a person other than he or such other person really is.*
>
> *Explanation.*—The offence is committed whether the individual personated is a real or imaginary person."

The punishment for cheating by personation is given under section 419 of the Indian Penal Code. In the following terms:—

> ***"Section 419. Punishment for cheating by personation.***—*Whoever cheats by personation shall be punished with imprisonment of either description for a term which may extend to three years, or with fine, or with both."*

The main essential ingredients of the offence of cheating by personation is when a person cheats by pretending to be some other person. The essential ingredients of section 416 are that a person is said to cheat by personation if he cheats:

(a) by pretending to be some other person, or
(b) by knowingly substituting one person from another person, or
(c) representing that he is a person other than he really is, or
(d) representing that any other person is a person other than such other person really is.

The *Explanation* to section 416 clearly provides that the offence of cheating by personation is committed whether the individual personated is a real or imaginary person.

It is pertinent to now refer to the *Illustrations* given under section 416 Indian Penal Code which are as detailed below:

Illustration

(a) *A* cheats by pretending to be a certain rich banker of the same name. *A* cheats by personation.

(b) *A* cheats by pretending to be *B*, a person who is deceased. *A* cheats by personation.

Having now examined the concept of the offence of cheating by personation we have noted that in today's world people are increasingly resorting to cheating by personation using technology and technology tools. Such cheating by personation is done by computers, computer systems, computer networks and computer resources. Further, such cheating by personation is also done by people using the mobile phones, iPads, Tablets, smart phones, blackberries, mobile devices, personal digital assistants and/or communication devices. The Legislature has now provided for section 66D which has stipulated that cheating by personation, by means of any communication device or computer resource, is an offence punishable with imprisonment of either description for a term, which may extend to three years and shall also be liable to fine which may extend to one lakh rupees. Thus, if any person cheats by pretending to be some other person, by using a computer, computer system, computer network, communication device or computer resource or mobile phones, iPads, Tablets, smart phones, blackberries, mobile devices, personal digital assistants and/or communication devices, he is deemed to have committed the offence under section 66D of the amended Information Technology Act, 2000.

Further, if a person cheats by pretending to the another person, who is already predeceased, by using any mobile phone, iPads, Tablets, smart phones, blackberry, mobile device, personal digital assistant and/or communication devices or computers, or computer systems, computer networks, or computer resources, he is also deemed to have committed the offence under section 66D of the amended Information Technology Act, 2000, as amended by the Information Technology (Amendment) Act, 2008.

Section 66D assumes significance as it incorporates all instances of cheating by personation, by using iPads, Tablets, Smart Phones and Smart Devices. Further, cheating done by personation by using computer resources including computers, computer systems, and computer networks as also data and information resident therein are also brought within the ambit of criminal penalty under section 66D of the amended Information Technology Act.

Section 66D is likely now to be utilized on a far wider scale since people are misusing the computer resources and communication devices and are indulging in cheating by personation using computer resources and iPads, Tablets, Smart-Phones and Smart Devices. However since the said section provides only for a bailable offence, the deterrent effect of the offence is missing.

Section 66E of the amended Information Technology Act, 2000

The Legislature has sought to protect the privacy of individuals in the electronic and mobile ecosystem. Section 66E has been added to provide for the offence of violation of privacy.

Section 66E of the amended Information Technology Act, 2000 provides as under:

> ***"Section 66E. Punishment for violation of privacy.***—*Whoever, intentionally or knowingly captures, publishes or transmits the image of a private area of any person without his or her consent, under circumstances violating the privacy of that person, shall be punished with imprisonment which may extend to three years or with fine not exceeding two lakh rupees, or with both.*
>
> *Explanation.—For the purposes of this section—*
>
> *(a) "transmit" means to electronically send a visual image with the intent that it be viewed by a person or persons;*
>
> *(b) "capture", with respect to an image, means a videotape, photograph, film or record by any means;*
>
> *(c) "private area" means the naked or undergarment clad genitals, pubic area, buttocks or female breast;*
>
> *(d) "publishes" means reproduction in the printed or electronic form and making it available for public;*
>
> *(e) "under circumstances violating privacy" means circumstances in which a person can have a reasonable expectation that—*
>
> *(i) he or she could disrobe in privacy, without being concerned that an image of his private area was being captured; or*
>
> *(ii) any part of his or her private area would not be visible to the public, regardless of whether that person is in a public or private place."*

The essential ingredients of section 66E is that a person has to intentionally or knowingly capture, publish or transmit the image of a private area of any person without his or her consent, under circumstances violating the privacy of that person.

It is important to point out that the following essential acts need to be performed:

(a) Capturing,

(b) Publishing, or

(c) Transmitting.

All the said three acts need to be done either intentionally or knowingly.

All these three acts must relate to the image of a private area of any person.

It is pertinent to point out that word "transmit" has been defined by the *Explanation* (a) to mean to electronically send a visual image with the intent that it be viewed by a person or persons. This incorporates, within its ambit, transmission done using computers, computer networks, computer systems, computer resources as well as transmission done using the iPads, Tablets, Smart

Devices, smart phones, blackberries, mobile devices, personal digital assistants and/or communication devices. This is so because transmission is done by computer resources and communication devices by electronically sending the concerned images over computer networks.

Further, the word "capture" has been explained by *Explanation* (b) to section 66E with respect to any image to mean a video tape, photograph, film or records by any means. Since, today a large number of mobile phones, iPads, Tablets, smart-phones, blackberries, and/or communication devices come with inbuilt cameras. It is today the given norm to capture images using mobile phones, iPads, Tablets, smart phones, blackberries, and communication devices. Hence, misuse of iPads, Tablets, Smart Phones and Smart Devices for the purpose of violating a person's privacy is on the rise.

It is further pertinent to note that *Explanation* (c) to section 66E defines the term "private area" to mean the naked or undergarment clad genitals, pubic area, buttocks or female breast. Thus, the law has only taken a very small restrictive definition of the term "private area of any person" to mean the aforesaid. Further, it is imperative that the said capturing, publishing or transmitting the image of a private area of any person has to be, without his or her consent. Further, it is essential that the said acts must be done under circumstances violating the privacy of that person. *Explanation* (e) to section 66E provides as under:

> *"(e) under circumstances violating privacy" means circumstances in which a person can have a reasonable expectation that—*
>
> *(i) he or she could disrobe in privacy, without being concerned that an image of his private area was being captured; or*
>
> *(ii) any part of his or her private area would not be visible to the public, regardless of whether that person is in a public or private place."*

The said *Explanation* states that "under circumstances violating privacy" refers to the reasonable expectation of a person of the circumstances within which he or she could disrobe in privacy, without ever being concerned that an image of his/her private area was being captured. Further, the said term also includes therein circumstances where a person could have a reasonable expectation that any part of his or her private area would not be visible to the public. This is regardless or whether, the said person is in a public or private place. The said provision is indeed broad to cover all aspects pertaining to the female and male organs. This provision also extremely relevant, given the huge number of MMS controversies that have happened in India, beginning with the reporting of the famous *DPS MMS* case or *Baazee.com* case. In this case, mobile phone was used for the purposes of creating or publishing an MMS wherein oral sex was being administered by a school girl to a school boy.

Thus, if any person now makes an MMS, of any person regarding his private areas under circumstances violating his or her privacy, such an act is an offence punishable with imprisonment which may extend to three years or with fine which may extend to two lakh rupees or with both. This provision would also aim to act as a deterrent against the peeping toms, spy-cameras and web-cameras which are installed without permission of concerned persons, so as to invade their privacy. Such an act would now be brought within the ambit of criminal penalty and would be punished under section 66E of the amended Information Technology Act, 2000.

While, the said advancement is indeed appreciable, it is indeed also disappointing to see that the law has itself not made much progress in the direction of protecting and preserving privacy. The concept of privacy is a very large, ever expanding concept. It does not just include the private areas of persons. People have a reasonable expectation of privacy pertaining to their persons as also relating to data privacy. Unfortunately, the law has not touched anything on the concept of data privacy. Further, such provision only takes a very restrictive narrow interpretation of the concept of privacy.

There is a need to amend the Indian Information Technology Act, 2000, to bring within its ambit, more instances of violations of data privacy of persons and legal entities using iPads, Tablets, Smart Devices, smart-phones, blackberries, mobile devices, personal digital assistants and/or communication devices. Thus, while some misuse by communication devices, which violate the privacy of others has been sought to be made criminally liable under section 66E of the amended Information Technology Act, 2000, there are still a large number of areas pertaining to violation of data privacy, which still have not been legislated upon by the amended Information Technology Act, 2000 and which require urgent immediate proactive attention of and action by the Government of India.

Section 66E has chosen to address certain limited aspects pertaining to individual's privacy and its violation. Over the last one decade, India has seen various instances where the privacy of individuals has been violated and the said acts have been reproduced in the digital format. A few years back, we had the Bangaru Lakshman spy camera scandal where the former chief of a political party was seen on camera accepting bribe. We also have instance where Trisha, a Tamil film actress suddenly discovered that her nude scenes showing her bathing in her bathroom was released on the Internet. This was thanks to a spy camera being installed in her bathroom. In the *DPS MMS* case, we also saw how the MMS making capabilities of the mobile phones had been misused to capture a girl giving oral sex to the boy a co-student in a prominent school in Delhi, India. We have also seen a number of cases being reported where mobile phones with cameras, have been used, without authorization to capture the private parts as well as private moments of individuals, thereby invading the privacy of that concerned individuals.

By and large the aforesaid instances have kept on happening in India because of the inherent defect under the existing law of India. One of the biggest tragedies as far as the legislations in independent India is concerned, is that India does not have dedicated law to protect privacy. Possibly a need for a same never arose earlier. However, the judge made law in India has made some advances in this regard.

The Supreme Court of India has held that the fundamental rights of life includes the right of privacy and thus if any State action contravenes the privacy of any individual, the same can be challenged in the writ jurisdiction of any relevant court. However, the biggest problem still continues to be that instances of violation of privacy of individuals by other private entities are not yet brought within the ambit of specific legislation. Further, in India, the concept of data privacy does not exist. To a large extent, the historical reasons in India need to be claimed responsible for this. This is so because India has emerged out of the joint family set up. As such children from the very beginning were encouraged to share their information and as such the concept of private space for individuals did not exist. Consequently, it was but natural to expect that there would be no dedicated legislation to protect privacy in India. However, as video voyeurism becoming more and more popular, the Government of India decided to enact a special provision being section 66E of the amended Information Technology Act, 2000.

It is important to note that the term "privacy" has still not been defined under the amended Information Technology Act, 2000. It is important now to consider the various judicial pronouncements by the Supreme Court on the subject of privacy:

In *R. Rajagopal* v. *State of Tamil Nadu*,[51] the Supreme Court held as follows:—

> "The right of privacy to be implicit in the right to life and liberty guaranteed to the citizens of India by article 21. "It is the right to be let alone". Every citizen has a right to safeguard the privacy of his own."

In *Sunkara Satyanarayana* v. *State of Andhra Pradesh, Home*,[52] the Andhra Pradesh High Court held as follows:

> "The right to privacy as an independent and distinctive concept originated in the field of Tort Law, under which a new cause of action for damages resulting from unlawful (invasion) of privacy was recognised. This right has two aspects which are but two faces of the same coin: (1) the General Law of Privacy which affords a tort action for damages resulting from an unlawful invasion of privacy, and (2) the constitutional recognition given to the right to privacy which protects personal privacy against unlawful governmental invasion. The first aspect of this right must be said to have been violated where, for example, a person's name or likeness is used, without his consent, for advertising or non-advertising purposes or for that matter, his life-story is written – whether laudatory or otherwise – and published without his consent as explained hereinafter. In recent times, however, this right has acquired a constitutional status."
>
> 44. Therefore, right to privacy though not an enumerated fundamental right, is constitutionally recognised enforceable right flowing from Article 21 of the Constitution. Invasion of this right gives cause of action for tortious liability besides right to enforce through Constitutional Courts. In this context the principle laid down by the Supreme Court in *Kharak Singh's* case (*supra*), *Govind's* case (*supra*) and *Malak Singh* v. *State of Punjab*, AIR 1981 SC 760 with reference to police surveillance and violation of right to privacy may be noticed.
>
> 45. In *Kharak Singh's* case (*supra*) the Supreme Court held that unless specifically authorized by law, it is constitutionally impermissible to invade

51. (1994) 6 SCC 632.
52. 2000 (1) Ald (Cri) 117: 2000 Cr LJ 1297.

the privacy of an individual violating Article 21 of the Constitution. The Supreme Court held as follows:

> "The position therefore is that if the action of the police which is the arm of Executive State is found to be infringed any of the freedoms guaranteed to the petitioner, the petitioner would be entitled to the relief of *mandamus* which he seeks to restrain the State from taking action under the regulations."

In *Directorate of Revenue* v. *Mohammed Nisar Holia,*[53] the Supreme Court held as follows:

> "An authority cannot be given an untrammeled power to infringe the right of privacy of any person. Even if a statute confers such power upon an authority to make search and seizure of a person at all hours and at all places, the same may be held to be *ultra vires* unless the restrictions imposed are reasonable ones."

In *Kharak Singh* v. *State of Uttar Pradesh,*[54] the Apex Court held as follows:

> "The appellant was being harassed by police under Regulation 236(b) of UP Police Regulation, which permits domiciliary visits at night. The Supreme Court held that the Regulation 236 is unconstitutional and violative of Article 21. It concluded that the Article 21 of the Constitution includes "right to privacy" as a part of the right to "protection of life and personal liberty". The Court equated 'personal liberty' with 'privacy', and observed, that "the concept of liberty in Article 21 was comprehensive enough to include privacy and that a person's house, where he lives with his family is his 'castle' and that nothing is more deleterious to a man's physical happiness and health than a calculated interference with his privacy".

In *People's Union for Civil Liberties (PUCL)* v. *Union of India,*[55] the Supreme Court held as follows:

> "The telephone tapping by Government under section 5(2) of Telegraph Act, 1885 amounts infraction of Article 21 of the Constitution of India. Right to privacy is a part of the right to "life" and "personal liberty" enshrined under Article 21 of the Constitution. The said right cannot be curtailed "except according to procedure established by law".

> *Gobind* v. *State of Madhya Pradesh,*[56] the Supreme Court laid down that "...........privacy-dignity claims deserve to be examined with care and to be denied only when an important countervailing interest is shown to be superior. If the Court does find that a claimed right is entitled to protection as a fundamental privacy right, a law infringing it must satisfy the compelling State interest test........."

The focus of the entire provision under discussion is upon the relevant circumstances, in which any person can have a reasonable expectation of privacy. Thus, for example, a person can have a reasonable expectation of privacy in his

53. (2008) 2 SCC 370: (2007) 12 SCR 906.
54. AIR 1963 SC 1295: (1963) 2 Cr LJ 329.
55. (1997) 1 SCC 301.
56. (1975) 2 SCC 148.

or her own bathroom or her own bedroom, without ever being concerned that an image of his or her private area was being captured. Further, wherever a person has a reasonable expectation that any part of his or her private area would not be visible to the public, regardless of whether that person is in the public or private place, that expectation is now sought to be protected by the provisions of the amended section 66E of the Information Technology Act, 2000 as amended.

Further, examination and analysis of the *Explanations* (a) to (e) given to section 66E of the amended Information Technology Act, 2000 clearly show that the focus of the section is on video voyeurism.

Explanation (a) to section 66E explains the term "transmit" to mean to electronically send the visual image with the intent that it will be viewed by person or persons, all kinds of transmissions of images of the private areas of any person, would be brought within the ambit of section 66E of the amended Information Technology Act, 2000. It is pertinent to point out that *Explanation* (b) to section 66E explains the word "capture" with respect to any image to mean to videotape, photograph, film or record by any means. Thus, whether the videotaping is being done by a video camera recorder, digital recorder, cell phone with camera, or any other similar device or any other communication device, all such activities will now be covered within the ambit of the amended Information Technology Act, 2000. Thus, if any person captures a photograph or films or videos the private area of any other person, without that person's knowledge and under circumstances violating the privacy of a person, his actions come within the ambit of section 66E of the amended Information Technology Act, 2000.

It is important to now analyze as to what is the legal definition of the term "private areas". *Explanation* (c) to section 66E defines the term "private area" to mean the naked or undergarment clad genitals, pubic area, buttocks or female breast. The perusal of the said provision clearly shows that the same is primarily meant to target the private areas of individuals, both, males and females. However, particular significant are the words "undergarment clad genitals". This is one area that is likely to provide confusion as we go long. Can it be said that the model, modelling for the bikini when being recorded by another person, the said act could also be brought within the ambit of section 66E of the amended Information Technology Act, 2000? I think there will be problems in overall applicability of the aforesaid provisions of law.

Further, *Explanation* (d) to section 66E defines the term "publishes" to mean the reproduction in the printed or electronic form and making it available to public. Thus, all kinds of electronic publishing are also brought within the ambit of the section 66E of the amended Information Technology Act, 2000.

It is pertinent to point out that section 66E does not specify the mode by means of which the said violation of privacy takes place. Thus, whether the said acts were done either using a computer, computer systems, computer network, computer resources as also any other form of communication device including mobile phones, cell phones, personal digital assistants, iPads, Tablets, Smart Devices, smart-phones, blackberries and other communication devices, which are used to send, receive or transmit in any form, audio, video, text or image all have been brought within the ambit of section 66E of the Information Technology Act, 2000.

Thus, if any person uses the camera in his iPad, Tablet, Smart-Phone and/or Smart Device for the purposes of violating the privacy of individual under the parameters detailed under section 66E of the amended Information Technology Act, 2000, such an act also comes within the ambit of criminal penalty as described under section 66E of the Information Technology Act, 2000. The sending of an MMS capturing the private area of any person thereby violating of his privacy under the parameters detailed under section 66E of the amended Information Technology Act, 2000, would also now be brought within the ambit of penalty and be punished with imprisonment for a term which may extend to three years or with fine which may extend to two lakh rupees or with both. Thus, it is expected that instances pertaining to video voyeurism, especially mobile video voyeurism, are likely to be specifically covered within the ambit of section 66E of the amended Information Technology Act, 2000.

Section 66F of the Information Technology Act, 2000

*"**Section 66F. Punishment for cyber terrorism.**—(1) Whoever,—*

(A) with intent to threaten the unity, integrity, security or sovereignty of India or to strike terror in the people or any section of the people by—

(i) denying or cause the denial of access to any person authorized to access computer resource; or

(ii) attempting to penetrate or access a computer resource without authorisation or exceeding authorised access; or

(iii) introducing or causing to introduce any computer contaminant;

and by means of such conduct causes or is likely to cause death or injuries to persons or damage to or destruction of property or disrupts or knowing that it is likely to cause damage or disruption of supplies or services essential to the life of the community or adversely affect the critical information infrastructure specified under section 70, or

(B) knowingly or intentionally penetrates or accesses a computer resource without authorisation or exceeding authorised access, and by means of such conduct obtains access to information, data or computer database that is restricted for reasons of the security of the State or foreign relations; or any restricted information, data or computer database, with reasons to believe that such information, data or computer database so obtained may be used to cause or likely to cause injury to the interests of the sovereignty and integrity of India, the security of the State, friendly relations with foreign States, public order, decency or morality, or in relation to contempt of court, defamation or incitement to an offence, or to the advantage of any foreign nation, group of individuals or otherwise,

commits the offence of cyber terrorism.

(2) Whoever commits or conspires to commit cyber terrorism shall be punishable with imprisonment which may extend to imprisonment for life."

The offence of cyber terrorism has been introduced for the first time in the history of independent India in the form of the amendment to the Information Technology Act, 2000. India, for the last few years, has been seeing the tremendous increase in the amount of activities that tantamount to terrorism. India has also discovered on the way that terrorists are extremely technology savvy and are invariably a couple of steps ahead of the law enforcement agencies. Further, the advent of the Internet and new tools including tools for encryption, data masking, proxy server hopping and other related tools, have made sure that terrorists are indeed using cyber space in a big way. That is the reason, why in repeated terrorist attacks in India, there was increasingly more and more evidence that was being discovered of tremendous reliance on technology by terrorists. That is the reason, why the Government of India had been thinking of the need for amending the law to put up a provision for cyber terrorism.

The author himself testified before the Parliamentary Standing Committee of the Indian Parliament and underlined and stressed the need for incorporating cyber terrorism as an offence under the amendments to the Information Technology Act, 2000. The catalyst in this direction happened to be the 26/11 Mumbai attacks. The Mumbai attacks left no doubt in anybody's mind that cyber terrorism was here to stay and unless the same is handled by a strong hand, it is likely to go out of control and impact India prejudicially as time passes by. Therefore, the new offence of cyber terrorism was incorporated under the amended Information Technology Act, 2000.

This provision is incorporated under section 66F of the amended Information Technology Act, 2000. A perusal of the entire section clearly shows that it is talking about computer resources as also data, information and computer databases.

The term "computer" has been defined in a very vast term under section 2(1)(i) as under:

> *"computer" means any electronic magnetic, optical or other high-speed data processing device or system which performs logical, arithmetic, and memory functions by manipulations of electronic, magnetic or optical impulses, and includes all input, output, processing, storage, computer software, or communication facilities which are connected or related to the computer in a computer system or computer network."*

A perusal of the said definition would clearly show that this is so vast enough to include any kind of high-speed data processing device or system which performs logical, arithmetic and memory functions, by manipulations of electric, magnetic or optical impulses and includes all input, output, processing, storage, computer software or communication facilities which are connected or related to a computer in a computer system or computer network. The said definition is so vast so as to specifically include all communication devices as well.

A broad analysis of the offence of cyber terrorism defined under section 66F(1) shows that it is broadly classified into two major categories of activities. The first thing that strikes any person about the said definition is the huge, comprehensive and extremely wide ambit, scope, applicability and nature as also character of the offence of cyber terrorism. It is possibly been defined in the widest possible terms as known across the world and to that extent, the Indian Legislature needs to be duly complemented for its thought leadership in this direction. The first major category of activities covered by cyber terrorism would include the following essential ingredients:

A person must have an intention to threaten the following:

- The unity of India,
- Integrity of India,
- Security of India,
- Sovereignty of India,
- To strike terror in the people,
- To strike terror in any section of the people.

The aforesaid intention must be followed by doing the following acts:

- Denying or causing the denial of access to any person authorised to access computer resource; or
- Attempting to penetrate or access a computer resource without authorization or exceeding authorised access; or
- Introducing or causing to be introduced any computer contaminant.
- Thereafter by means of such conduct;
- The person either causes or is likely to cause death or injuries to persons; or
- The person concerned causes damage to or the destruction of property; or
- The said person disrupts or knowing that it is likely to cause damage or disruption of supplies or services essential to the life of the community; or
- It adversely affects the critical information infrastructure specified under section 70 of the Information Technology Act, 2000.
- Commits the offence of cyber terrorism.

A broad analysis of the aforesaid section would therefore show that there has to be an intention to threaten the unity, integrity, security or sovereignty of India or to strike terror in the people or any section of the people.

The second essential ingredient is that there must be a cogent act of either denying or causing the denial of access to any person authorised to access the computer resource or attempting to penetrate or access a computer resource without authorization or exceeding unauthorised access.

Or introducing or causing to be introduced any computer contaminant.

The third essential element is that the aforesaid intention and acts must either cause or are likely to cause death or injuries to persons. Further, the said acts must either cause damage or destruction of property or disruption of the same or disruption of supplies essential to the life of the community or either result in the adversely affecting the critical information infrastructure specified under the Information Technology Act, 2000. The net result is that any act, which has got any connection, association, nexus or relationship with terror, is covered under this section. Thus, a perusal of the said section would show that this is possibly widest possible characterization of the offence of cyber terrorism. However, a perusal of section 66F shows that this is only the first sub-set of the offence of cyber terrorism.

We now proceed to examine the second category of activities which are classified as cyber terrorism. The second set of activities postulate that any person must knowingly or intentionally penetrate or access a computer resource without authorization or exceeding authorised access. Further, by means of doing such an act the said person obtains access to information and data or computer database, that is restricted. The said restrictions can be for any of the reasons including the following:

- Security of the State,
- Foreign relations, or
- The said information could be any restricted information, data or computer database. The aforesaid acts must be done with reasons to believe that such information, data or computer database so obtained may be used to cause or likely to cause an injury. The said injury could be caused to any of the following:
- Interests of sovereignty and integrity of India,
- Security of State,
- Friendly relations with foreign States,
- Public order,
- Decency,
- Morality,
- In relation to contempt of court, defamation or incitement to an offence, or
- To the advantage of any foreign nation, group of individuals or otherwise.

If the acts fulfil the aforesaid parameters, they fall within the ambit of the offence of "cyber terrorism".

The said offence is indeed very broad and includes not just people who directly use computers, computer resources, data and information as also computer databases in the electronic form to cause detriment to the cause of the sovereignty and integrity of India but also all those people who assist such people in their various illegal activities aimed to strike terror in the hearts of people at large.

As per section 66F(2) it is been categorically provided that whoever commits or conspires to commit cyber terrorism shall be punishable with imprisonment, which may extend to imprisonment for life.

Thus, clearly the ambit of such offence is very wide and includes within itself, all offences of cyber terrorism committed using computers resources including communication devices, ceil phones, smart-phones, personal digital assistants, and any other device which is used to communicate any text, video, audio or image. Thus, the usage of iPads, Tablets, Smart-Phones and Smart Devices for the purposes of either planning, discussing, analyzing, executing terror attacks or other terror plans itself comes within the ambit of the offence of cyber terrorism. Almost any and every technological device that terrorists use today can be brought within the ambit of a computer since the same are invariably electronic, magnetic, optical or other high-speed data processing devices or systems which perform logical, arithmetic and memory functions by manipulations of electronic, magnetic or optical impulses. The said addition of section 66F into the law book has clearly strengthened the hands of the law enforcement and the Indian nation at large in its fight against cyber terrorism. Apart from the applicability of existing laws pertaining to terror and terrorism, section 66F now becomes an immensely valuable weapon added in the arsenal of the nation, in its fight against cyber terrorism.

At the time of writing, the section has not been very extensively utilised. However, as time passes by, it is but natural to expect that this provision is likely to be used more and more, not only in cases pertaining to committing acts of terror using computer systems and computer networks but also in the context of usage of mobiles, mobile devices, iPads, Tablets, Smart Devices, smart-phones, personal digital assistants and other communication devices.

Section 66F clearly represents one of the crowning glories of the amended Information Technology Act, 2000. Its relevance in the fight against terrorism in cyber space as also mobile terrorism and terrorism executed using mobile phones and iPads, Tablets, Smart-Phones and Smart Devices is immense. However, what is currently required is a far more proactive and flexible interpretation of the said provision.

While India needs to be duly complemented for coming up with its detailed provisions pertaining to cyber terrorism, on a more objective analysis, one realizes that the fight against cyber terrorism by any nation cannot be won by one single provision alone. Clearly, India requires far more detailed legal provisions to assist the effective implementation and the applicability of section 66F of the amended Information Technology Act, 2000. Further, comprehensive procedures, processes and presumptions in relation to cyber terrorism need to be more elaborately detailed, whether in the Information Technology Act, 2000 or by means of secondary legislation which can help provide the platform for expeditious trial of cyber terror-related cases.

Because of the application of section 81 of the amended Information Technology Act, 2000, the provisions of section 66F related to cyber terrorism shall prevail notwithstanding anything contrary contained therewith in any other law for the time being in force. The Information Technology Act, 2000 being a special legislation, its provisions pertaining to cyber terrorism prevail over anything inconsistent therewith in any other law including the existing anti-terror laws of India.

The author believes that there need to be certain presumptions that need to be drawn up in cyber terrorism-related cases. There is need for further coming up with appropriate secondary legislation with regard to practices and procedures to be followed, in the context of cyber terrorism. This is although more so, as in the times to come, terrorism is gone to be shifting completely to iPads, Tablets, Smart-Phones and Smart Devices and communication devices and the hands of law enforcements agencies need to be duly strengthened in their fight against cyber terrorists. The author personally believes that the sovereignty and integrity of India is paramount and no forces or terrorist groups can ever be allowed to subvert the sovereignty and integrity of India or the security of the State, friendly relations with other nations, public order decency or morality. As time passes by, as more and more cases pertaining to cyber terrorism are likely to occur, there would be a need for distinct cyber terror courts who would need to be duly trained in this regard and who can provide far more effective expeditious platform for expeditious trial of cyber terror-related cases.

Section 67 of the amended Information Technology Act, 2000

Section 67 of the Information Technology Act, 2000 has been amended by the Information Technology Amendment Act, 2008. The net effects of the amendments has been that the quantum of punishment for the offence under section 67 has been reduced from the earlier specified quantum of punishment. Under the earlier provision, the said offence was punishable on first conviction with imprisonment of either description for a term which may extend to five years and with fine which may extend to one lakh rupees and in the event of a second or subsequent conviction, with imprisonment of either description for term which may extend to ten years and also with fine, which may extend to two lakh rupees.

Section 67—Publishing of information which is obscene in electronic form states as follows:

> *"Whoever publishes or transmits or causes to be published or transmitted in the electronic form, any material which is lascivious or appeals to the prurient interest or if its effect is such as to tend to deprave and corrupt persons who are likely, having regard to all relevant circumstances, to read, see or hear the matter contained or embodied in it, shall be punished on first conviction with imprisonment of either description for a term which may extend to three years and with fine which may extend to five lakh rupees and in the event of second or subsequent conviction with imprisonment of either description for a term which may extend to five years and also with fine which may extend to ten lakh rupees".*

Sex has always been an inspiring subject for mankind from the very beginning. This is one subject that has generated immense debate, discussion and controversy during each succeeding period of history in all civilizations of the world. The obsession for sex and its related acts have resulted in the origin of pornography. According to *Webster's New World Dictionary*, "pornography" means writings, pictures etc., intended primarily to arouse sexual desire.

Pornography has been a subject of contentious and controversial legal regulation in history. Lawmakers all across the world have always felt the need to curtail the exhibition, display and impact of pornographic materials, pornography and obscenity on the minds of the public at large in different societies. However, laws of different nations have adopted various methods to regulate pornography especially child pornography.

Section 67 deals with the penal offence of publishing of information, which is obscene in the electronic form. Section 67 of the Information Technology Act, 2000 is modelled on the basis of section 292 IPC. As such, before examining section 67 of the Information Technology Act, 2000, it would be prudent to examine briefly section 292 IPC.

In India, the offence of obscenity is dealt with under the Indian Penal Code. Section 292 IPC deals with the offence of obscenity.

Section 292 IPC states as follows:—

"292. *(1) For the purposes of sub-section (2), a book, pamphlet, paper, writing, drawing, painting, representation, figure or any other object, shall be deemed to be obscene if it is lascivious or appeals to the prurient interest or if its effect, or (where it comprises two or more distinct items) the effect of any one of its items, is, if taken as a whole, such as to tend to deprave and corrupt person, who are likely, having regard to all relevant circumstances, to read, see or hear the matter contained or embodied in it.*

(2) Whoever—

(a) sells, lets to hire, distributes, publicly exhibits or in any manner puts into circulation, or for purposes of sale, hire, distribution, public exhibition or circulation, makes, produces or has in his possession any obscene book, pamphlet, paper, drawing, painting, representation or figure or any other obscene object whatsoever, or

(b) imports, exports or conveys any obscene object for any of the purposes aforesaid, or knowing or having reason to believe that such object will be sold, let to hire, distributed or publicly exhibited or in any manner put into circulation, or

(c) takes part in or receives profits from any business in the course of which he knows or has reason to believe that any such obscene objects are, for any of the purposes aforesaid, made, produced, purchased, kept, imported, exported, conveyed, publicly exhibited or in any manner put into circulation, or

(d) advertises or makes known by any means whatsoever that any person is engaged or is ready to engage in any act which is an offence under this section, or that any such obscene object can be procured from or through any person, or

(e) offers or attempts to do any act which is an offence under this section, shall be punished on first conviction with imprisonment of either description for a term which may extend to two years, and with fine which may extend to two thousand rupees, and, in the event of a second or subsequent conviction, with imprisonment of either description for a term which may extend to five years, and also with fine which may extend to five thousand rupees.

Exception.—This section does not extend to—

(a) any book, pamphlet, paper, writing, drawing, painting, representation or figure—

(i) the publication of which is proved to be justified as being for the public good on the ground that such book, pamphlet, paper, writing, drawing, painting, representation or figure is in the interest of science, literature, art or learning or other objects of general concern, or

(ii) which is kept or used bona fide *for religious purposes;*

(b) any representation sculptured, engraved, painted or otherwise represented on or in—

(i) *any ancient monument within the meaning of the Ancient Monuments and Archaeological Sites and Remains Act, 1958, or*

(ii) *any temple, or on any car used for the conveyance of idols, or kept or used for any religious purpose."*

Interestingly the Indian Penal Code, 1860 does not define the word "obscene" or "porn". Section 292 IPC basically states that a book, pamphlet, paper, writing, drawing, painting, representation, figure on any other object shall be deemed to be obscene if:—

1. it is lascivious, or
2. it appeals to the prurient interest, or
3. its effects, or (where it comprises two or more distinct items) the effect of any one of its items, is, if taken as a whole, such as to tend to deprave and corrupt persons who are likely, having regard to all relevant circumstances, to read, see or hear the matter contained or embodied in it.

Coming specifically to the Information Technology Act, section 67 of the Information Technology Act defines an offence substantially similar to section 292 IPC, the only material difference being that section 67 of the Information Technology Act has made the offence of obscenity applicable to any material in the electronic form and in the electronic world. Thus, each and every electronic information, which is obscene, would come within the rigours of section 67 of the Information Technology Act, 2000.

Section 67 uses the same tests for determining obscenity as are defined under section 292 IPC. Thus, section 67 of the Information Technology Act, 2000 refers to "any material which is lascivious or appeals to the prurient interest or if its effect is such as to tend to deprave and corrupt persons who are likely, having regard to all relevant circumstances, to read, see or hear the matter contained or embodied in it..." These are the same expressions, which are used in section 292 IPC.

Neither the Information Technology Act, 2000 nor the Indian Penal Code, 1860 give any definitions of the terms "lascivious" or "prurient". The *Webster's New World Dictionary* defines the term "lascivious" as characterized by or expressing lust or lewdness, wanton, tending to excite lust. Similarly, the term "prurient" has been defined as having lustful ideas or desires, full of or causing lust; lascivious; lewd. It is further important to note that the Dictionary defines the term "lust" as a desire to satisfy one's sexual needs; especially strong sexual desire, excessive desire, great zest, to feel an intense desire, especially sexual desire.

Neither are there any uniform standards for determining what is lascivious or prurient nor there can be. By its very inherent nature, lust, as a feeling, differs from person to person and from situation to situation. Recognizing the same, the Hon'ble Supreme Court of India has held that the concept of obscenity differs from country to country and the same is dependant on the standards in contemporary society. The idea as to what is to be deemed to be obscene has varied from age to age, from region to region and even from person to person, depending upon the particular social conditions and there cannot be an immutable standard of moral values.

Another challenge that arises for consideration is what would be the standards that are likely to be kept in mind by the authorities in determining whether any information or material in the electronic form is lascivious or appeals to the prurient interest.

For this, it would be interesting to examine the trends of judicial pronouncements made by the Supreme Court and various High Courts on various occasions to dwell more upon the ingredients of section 292 IPC.

It may be pertinent to mention that the landmark judgment that the Supreme Court delivered on section 292 IPC, on which section 67 of the Information Technology Act, 2000 is based, was in the case entitled *Ranjeet Udeshi* v. *State of Maharashtra,* AIR 1965 SC 881: (1965) 2 Cr LJ 8: (1965) 1 SCR 65. In that judgment, the Supreme Court held as under:—

> "The word, as the dictionaries tell us, denotes the quality of being obscene which means offensive to modesty or decency: lewd, filthy and repulsive. It cannot be denied that it is an important interest of society to suppress obscenity. There is, of course, some difference between obscenity and pornography in that the latter denotes writings, pictures, etc., intended to arouse sexual desire while the former may include writings etc. not intended to do so but which have that tendency. Both, of course, offend against public decency and morals but pornography is obscenity in a more aggravated form.
>
> ... Condemnation of obscenity depends as much upon the morals of the people as upon the individual. It is always a question of degree or as the lawyers are accustomed to say, of where the line is to be drawn. It is, however, clear that obscenity by itself has extremely poor value in the propagation of ideas, opinions and informations of public interest or profit. When there is propagation of ideas, opinions and informations of public interest or profit, the approach to the problem may become different because then the interest of society may tilt the scales in favour of free speech and expression. It is thus that books on medical science with intimate illustrations and photographs, though in a sense immodest, are not considered to be obscene but the same illustrations and photographs collected in book form without the medical text would certainly be considered to be obscene. Section 292, Penal Code deals with obscenity in this sense and cannot thus be said to be invalid in view of the second clause of Article 19."

In this case, Justice M. Hidayatullah held that in order to determine whether any material is obscene or not, the test laid down in *Regina* v. *Hicklin* should not be discarded. The *Hicklin* case lays emphasis on the potentiality of the mentioned object or material to deprave and corrupt by immoral influences as the critical factor to determine obscenity. In 1868, in the landmark case entitled *Regina* v. *Hicklin*, (1868) 3 QB 360 the test of obscenity was defined as follows:

> "...the test of obscenity is this, whether the tendency of the matter charged as obscenity is to deprave and corrupt those, whose minds are open to such immoral influences, and into whose hands a publication of this sort may fall..."

The Supreme Court further held in *Ranjeet Udeshi* v. *State of Maharashtra,* AIR 1965 SC 881: (1965) 2 Cr LJ 8: (1965) 1 SCR 65 that what is obscene would always remain a question to be decided in each case. However, the apex court advocated that it was the duty of the court to consider the alleged obscene matter by taking an overall view of the entire work. It was further held that an overall view of the obscene matter in the setting of the whole work would, of course, be necessary, but the obscene matter must be considered by itself and separately to find out whether it is so gross and its obscenity is so decided, that it is likely to deprave and corrupt those whose minds are open to influences of this sort and into whose hands the book is likely to fall.

Further, in the case entitled *C.K. Karodkar* v. *State of Maharashtra*, AIR 1970 SC 1390: 1970 Cr LJ 1273: (1970) 2 SCR 80 the Supreme Court held that the standards of obscenity would differ from country to country depending on the standards of morals of contemporary society. "What is considered as a piece of literature in France may be obscene in England and what is considered in both countries as not harmful to public order and morals may be obscene in our country". It was further held that, "what we have to see is whether a class, and not an isolated case, into whose hands, the book, article or story falls suffer in their moral outlook or become depraved by reading it or might have impure and lecherous thoughts aroused in their minds. The charge of obscenity must, therefore, be judged from this aspect."

It is the duty of the Court to consider the obscene matter by taking an overall view of the entire work and to determine whether the obscene passages are so likely to deprave and corrupt those whose minds are open to such influences and in whose hands the book is likely to fall and in doing so, one must not overlook the influence of the book on the social morality of our contemporary society.

The use of the term "obscenity" is restricted to sexual immorality. The true test is thus not to find out what depraves the morals in any way whatsoever but what leads to deprave in only one way, *viz.*, by exciting sexual desires and lascivious thoughts.

The question regarding "obscenity" is one of fact and depends upon various circumstances and no hard and fast rule can be laid down. It does not depend altogether on oral evidence but must be judged by the Court.

The effect produced by the publication on an ordinary members of the society has to be ascertained. Such ordinary persons are expected to be of normal temperament. The standard of the reader is neither one of exceptional sensibility nor one without any sensibility whatsoever.

A vulgar writing is not necessarily obscene. Vulgarity arouses a feeling of disgust and revulsion and also boredom but does not have the effect of depraving, debasing and corrupting the morals of any reader of the novel whereas obscenity has the tendency to deprave and corrupt those, whose minds are open to such immoral influences.

If a publication has the tendency to deprave and corrupt the minds of people reading it, it is within the mischief of the section (292 IPC) though the author or the publisher has an ulterior object, which is innocent and laudable.

Whether the publication is obscene or not depends upon the material itself and not upon the motive.

In determining whether or not a publication is obscene regard must be had to that publication alone; other books not the subject of charges cannot be considered.

A picture of a woman in the nude is not *per se* obscene. For the purpose of deciding whether such picture is obscene, one has to consider to a great extent the surrounding circumstances, the pose of the posture, the suggestive element in the picture and the person or persons in whose hands it is likely to fall.

The scope of the expression "any material which is lascivious or appeals to the prurient interest or if its effect is such as to tend to deprave and corrupt persons who are likely, having regard to all relevant circumstances, to read, see or hear the matter contained or embodied in it" has to be interpreted in the light of the various principles and tests laid down by the aforesaid judicial pronouncements.

The perusal of the aforesaid authorities and judicial pronouncements make it clear that the Supreme Court and various High Courts have relied more upon the element of the impact on the public at large rather than pure nudity standards. This has been a more balanced approach, as nudity *per se* cannot be said to be obscene or lascivious or prurient. If that were so, then our entire ancient cultural heritage involving nudity like Khajuraho and *Kamasutra* would have been made illegal. Surely this is not the case.

The next consideration that engages one's mind is whether the principles of law laid down by the different pronouncements detailed above under section 292 IPC could fairly and materially be made applicable to the offence under section 67 Information Technology Act, 2000. I am of the opinion that this indeed would be the logical approach.

However, I would like to add a note of caution to the effect that the said judicial pronouncements under section 292 IPC cannot be fully applied to section 67, Information Technology Act, 2000. This is so as the abovenoted judgments have been delivered in the context of the actual world and the specific requirements of section 292 IPC which relate to a book, pamphlet, paper, writing, drawing, painting, representation, figure or any other object, in the real world. None of the aforesaid judgments have been delivered in the context of the electronic environment and the Internet.

Section 67 of the Information Technology Act has created a bit of confusion by merely copying the material phrases from section 292 IPC and by not taking into consideration the changed standards of society and human behaviour in modern India. The Indian Penal Code was enacted in 1860, at a time when India was under the colonial rule of the British and the Indian society was highly conservative.

With the passage of each succeeding decade and with our independence, standards of perceptions and morals have changed substantially. The passage of time has led to further liberalization of ideas relating to nudity and pornography. The 1990's saw the liberalization of the Indian economy, and the influx of Western inputs, television channels and the coming of the Internet have all radically changed perspectives relating to morals, pornography and obscenity in India.

It would have been better if the Legislature had taken the changed societal standards in consideration while enacting section 67 of the Information Technology Act. The Information Technology Act has not really defined standards to ascertain what is obscene, lascivious or prurient in the context of the electronic medium at a time when Internet is flooded with pornography. It has been left to the subjective interpretation of the relevant law-enforcement agency to define what exactly is obscene, in the context of the peculiar facts and circumstances of each case.

No doubt, the pronouncements made under section 292 IPC would act, as guiding principles for courts but the courts would be required to act proactively and interpret section 67 of Information Technology Act, 2000 in the context of Internet, cyberspace and the electronic form. This is all the more required, especially at a time when the world at large is struggling to cope up with the challenges of controlling the menace of online pornography.

There is no doubt that pornographic and blue films and pictures are indeed lascivious in nature and they appeal to the prurient interest as well. I am of the opinion that the *Hicklin* test would still be applicable in the context of the electronic form, though the Judiciary would now be required to suitably modify and adapt the *Hicklin* test in the context of the online environment and the Internet.

Another basic concern relating to section 67, Information Technology Act, 2000 would be as to how the same would be implemented outside the territorial boundaries of India. At the time of writing, as per one estimate, more than half of the total content available on the net is pornographic. A majority of the pornographic content of the Internet has been hosted on websites, which are in turn hosted on web servers, which are outside the territorial jurisdiction of India, though available here. How would law enforcement agencies in India check the offence of online pornography emanating outside the country? Technically speaking, the Information Technology Act, 2000 states in sections 1(2) and 75 that it shall be applicable not only to the whole of India but also to any offence or violation of the provisions of this Act done by any person of any nationality anywhere in the world. This approach is clearly not practical under the norms of existing international law. No country can assume jurisdiction over the citizens of other countries. Enacting a law like the Information Technology Act with transnational jurisdiction is likely to create a lot of challenges and problems, more-so in the context of regulating online obscenity and pornography.

Another point to note is the tremendous disparity of punishment between section 292 IPC and section 67 of the Information Technology Act, 2000. Under section 292 IPC, a person convicted of the offence can be punished with imprisonment upto 2 years and fine upto two thousand rupees in the first conviction and with imprisonment upto 5 years and fine upto five thousand rupees in subsequent convictions.

The quantum of punishment in section 67 is much higher. Under section 67, Information Technology Act, 2000, a person convicted of the offence can be punished with imprisonment which may extend to three years and fine which may extend to five lakh rupees on first conviction and with imprisonment which may extend to five years and fine which may extend to ten lakh rupees on second or subsequent convictions.

The only material difference that section 67 makes to the offence defined under section 292 IPC is that it has extended the same offence to the electronic format.

Thus, a peculiar situation is likely to emerge in the practical working and implementation of the Information Technology Act, 2000.

For example, a person may publish a pornographic book and he is liable to be punished with imprisonment up to two years under section 292 IPC. But at the same time, if the same person publishes the pornographic book in the electronic form, then he becomes liable to a much higher imprisonment of five years and fine up to one lakh rupees under section 67, Information Technology Act, 2000.

It is important to note that publishing a pornographic book in the real world and in the electronic world is not substantially different in any way. Only the procedures are different. While in the real world, a person would get a pornographic book published by means of the printing press over actual paper, in the electronic medium, he would publish the same book by converting it into the electronic form by means of an electronic process and which may be stored in a computer, computer system, computer network or floppy, disk, CD etc.

It is equally important to note that the pornographic content of the book in question does not change, whether it is published upon paper in the actual world or whether it is published in the electronic form in a computer file. Similarly, the intention to publish the pornographic content in the form of the pornographic book does not change at all in the two instances.

It can be argued that since all things are the same in the two different scenarios of publishing in the actual world and in the electronic form, there is no rationale in giving a higher quantum of punishment for the publication in the electronic form as compared to publication in the real world. It can be further argued that the delivery mechanism of a particular process or the procedure adopted for arriving at any product has never been held any importance or relevance in criminal jurisprudence of our country and more so in the context of granting of penal punishment. This erroneous approach by law-makers in adopting penal standards for granting the quantum of punishment for the same offence under the Information Technology Act is likely to lead to immense complications and weird results. It can also be argued that not only is this approach likely to lead to miscarriage of justice but it is also likely to violate the fundamental rights guaranteed to the citizens under Chapter III of the Constitution of India.

However, I am of the opinion that due to the inherent nature of the electronic medium and the electronic format, any information is capable of being transmitted at a far greater speed to a much larger number of people than a similar exercise in the real world with available procedures. This is so because of the very character of the electronic media and its potential capabilities of instantaneously spreading pornographic content to innumerable people.

Thus, the impact of publishing, transmitting or causing to be published any obscene material in the electronic form, can have a far more impact on innumerable people, and as such, the Legislature has adopted a correct approach in granting an enhanced quantum of punishment for an offender under section 67 of the Information Technology Act, 2000.

Another contentious issue raised by the Information Technology Act, 2000 is that it metes out differential treatment with regard to quantum of punishment of different offences. This has been done without any ostensible reason. Thus, for example, if a person hacks into a computer, computer system or computer network of a big multinational company causing billions of US dollars as damages, he can only be punished under section 66 of the Information Technology Act, 2000 with imprisonment upto three years and fine upto two lakh rupees. In contrast, if a person publishes an obscene electronic material, then, under section 67 of the Information Technology Act, 2000, he can, on first conviction, be punished with imprisonment which may extend upto three years and fine which may extend upto five lakh rupees.

There is actually no comparison between a hacking causing damage worth billions of dollars and a mere publication of an obscene electronic material. Thus, severe cyber crimes have been awarded less punishment in comparison with others.

Section 292 IPC uses the words "any other object". This is a very wide term and can be argued to be including any material or object in an electronic form. However, since section 67 of the Information Technology Act, 2000 specifically deals with obscene materials in the electronic form, section 292 IPC shall not be applicable in case of obscene electronic materials. It may be stated here that the Information Technology Act, 2000 is a special legislation, which overrides the inconsistent provisions of the existing legislations. Section 81 of the Information Technology Act, 2000 specifically states as under:

> "The provisions of this Act shall have effect notwithstanding anything inconsistent therewith contained in any other law for the time being in force."

Thus, this really means that section 292 IPC shall not be applicable to any material or information in the electronic form and in the context of the electronic form, the provisions of section 292 IPC shall be overridden by section 67 of the Information Technology Act, 2000.

It is pertinent to point out that section 67 refers to material in the electronic form. Section 67 does not *per se* referred to any specific medium by means of which such material is published, transmitted or caused to be published. As such all kinds of medium are included therein. Thus any kind of publication, transmission or causing to be published or transmitted of any material in the electronic form including such material as is published, transmitted as well as caused to be published or transmitted in iPads, Tablets, Smart-Phones and Smart Devices would also qualify to be fully covered under the ambit of section 67 of the Information Technology Act, 2000. This is so because the iPads, Tablets, Smart-Phones and Smart Devices are communication devices which use the electronic form for the purposes of generating, preserving, transmitting and storing data and information. As such section 67 has direct applicability to any kind of publishing, transmission as well as causing to be published to or transmitted in the electronic form of any obscene content which is so done using a communication device, cell phone or personal digital assistant. For example, when a person sends another person an obscene SMS it would still qualify to be an offence under section 67 of the amended Information Technology Act, 2000. For example, somebody takes a picture of the private parts of another person on his iPad, Tablet, Smart Phone and/or Smart Device using the inbuilt camera he not only publishes but also causes to be published the said obscene electronic material in the electronic form and as such the said act also qualifies to be an offence under section 67 of the amended Information Technology Act, 2000. Further more forwarding of obscene or lascivious SMSs or MMSs would also come within the ambit of the offence under section 67 of the amended Information Technology Act, 2000.

At this stage, it would be relevant to refer to some of the cases which have been reported in India in the context of obscenity in the electronic medium.

Arjika Case

Prior to the coming into effect of the Information Technology Act, 2000, the *Arjika* case had emerged. As reported, in this case, the police registered a case under section 292 of the Indian Penal Code after being alerted by Interpol. The crux of the case is that there was a site called *www.sweeties.arjika.com,* which was hosting child pornography material. The concerned website showed customized videos of three hours' duration, where children were depicted in sexual orgies. The videos showed pictures of naked children between the ages of 6 and 15. However, all this pornographic material was camouflaged beautifully. The site on its home page featured the famous cartoon character Pokeman. On clicking the same, there was hard-core child pornographic material available on the site.

Interpol, who has a detection wing against online child pornography, alerted the CBI who registered the case under section 292 IPC. Thereafter, CBI arrested one Arvind K Shyam Jagdam of Arjika Impex Pvt. Ltd., a Hyderabad-based computer engineer on the ground that he owned the domain, which was hosting the pedophile site. Investigations further revealed that Jagdam allegedly set up a free website with free web space to be taken by anyone in cyberspace after due registration at the site. Consequently, someone in Peru registered on this free website and created a pedophilic site under the camouflage of cartoon character Pokeman on the home page. Another interesting element of the case was that the naked children shown on the site were missing from their respective homes. It is also important to note that in this case, Jagdam had offered a free website with free web space to anyone on the Internet so long as he registered on the site. As such, Jagdam had no physical control over the contents of the website and could not be said to be the author of the contents. The authorities basically alleged Jagdam to be guilty of negligence on the ground that when he got the free space through North Sky, he had signed an agreement promising that no pornographic site would be hosted by *www.arjika.com.*

This case also raises complicated issues relating to jurisdiction, since the domain name in question is owned by an Indian, the creator of the pedophilic site is based in Peru while the server of the website is based in America. This case raises tremendously complicated issues concerning various aspects relating to online pornography. It would be interesting to see how this pre-Information Technology Act cyber porn matter proceeds towards its logical conclusion.

Air Force Bal Bharati School Case

In the first case of its kind, the Delhi Police Cyber Crime Cell registered a case under section 67 of the Information Technology Act, 2000. In this case, a 16-year-old boy of Air Force Bal Bharti School, a prominent school of Delhi, created a website at the URL www.amazing-gents.8m.net. The website was hosted by the schoolboy on free web space. It was dedicated to Air Force Bal Bharti School and contained text material. On this site, lucid, explicit, sexual details were given about various "sexy" girls and teachers of the school. Girls and teachers of the school were also classified under the basis of their physical attributes and perceived sexual preferences. The website was going on as a part of an adult boys joke amongst a students peer group.

This continued for some time till one day, the beans were spilt when one of the boys told a girl "featured" on the site about it. The father of the girl, being an Air Force officer, registered a case under section 67 of the Information Technology Act, 2000 with the Delhi Police Cyber Crime Cell. The police picked up the concerned student and kept him at Timarpur juvenile home. It was almost after one week that the Juvenile Board granted bail to the 16-year-old student. It is pertinent to note that the website did not contain any photographic material but only had text material which was allegedly obscene in nature. The matter is subjudice.

State of Tamil Nadu v. *Dr. L. Prakash*

In the last week of December 2001, India saw the registration of yet another case under section 67 of the Information Technology Act, 2000. The case was registered against Dr. L. Prakash of Chennai on the complaint of one Ganesh, a young man from Pondicherry.

Ganesh filed a criminal complaint at the Vadapalani police station at Chennai, alleging that Dr. L. Prakash was blackmailing him to have sex with women for featuring in pornographic videos and pictures. Ganesh, an SSLC student, alleged that Dr. L. Prakash threatened him with a revolver and forced him into sex. It is also alleged that Ganesh escaped to Pondicherry once but the doctor again blackmailed Ganesh into the sex racket.

Dr. L. Prakash is alleged to have lured college girls and working women for his pornographic videos and pictures with offers of big money. Even the women working at his clinic were reportedly not spared. Dr Prakash allegedly preyed on women to keep his porn websites *www.realindianporn.com* and *www.tamilsex.com* thriving. The doctor allegedly circulated blue films and nude pictures through e-mails from his home. It was also alleged that the doctor's brother Laxmanan, who resides in the United States, helped him to sell pornographic videos in the West from which, the earnings reportedly ran into thousands of US dollars.

Consequently, a case was registered under section 67 of the Information Technology Act, 2000, section 4 read with section 6 of the Indecent Representation of Women Act and section 27 of the Arms Act and sections 120-B and 506(2), IPC. In this case, the accused was convicted and awarded life imprisonment.

Baazee.com case

This case related to an obscene MMS, wherein a school girl was giving a schoolboy oral sex. This case has been discussed in the chapter entitled "Liability of Mobile Service Providers".

Another fear that is looming large is whether section 67 of the Information Technology Act, 2000 would be effective or would it just remain a paper tiger. Clearly there are numerous lacunae in section 67 of Information Technology Act, 2000 and its practical implementation is likely to lead to numerous problems, complications and challenges. The biggest challenge is that section 67 of the Information Technology Act only makes publishing or causing to be published any lascivious or prurient material in the electronic form, a penal offence. Accessing or viewing any pornographic or obscene electronic information has not been made a penal offence. This issue is a matter of immense debate in the international Cyberlaw circles.

With the passage of time, it is hoped that the various issues raised by section 67 of the Information Technology Act, 2000 would be properly resolved.

Section 67A of the amended Information Technology Act, 2000

> ***"Section 67A. Punishment for publishing or transmitting of material containing sexually explicit act, etc., in electronic form.***—*Whoever publishes or transmits or causes to be published or transmitted in the electronic form any material which contains sexually explicit act or conduct shall be punished on first conviction with imprisonment of either description for a term which may extend to five years and with fine which may extend to ten lakh rupees and in the event of second or subsequent conviction with imprisonment of either description for a term which may extend to seven years and also with fine which may extend to ten lakh rupees."*

Section 67A has been introduced for the first time in the Information Technology Act, 2000 by the Information Technology (Amendment) Act, 2008. This new section seeks to penalize the acts of publishing of material containing sexually explicit act or conduct.

The Legislature has quite some time ever since the Information Technology Act, 2000 is passed, being bothered that while section 67 of the Information Technology Act, 2000 specifically had provided for punishing publication, transmission or causing to be published or transmitted lascivious electronic information, there were no direct provisions for explicit sexual act or conduct.

Thus, there was felt a need for providing a specific provision which could bring such an act within the ambit of penalty.

Section 67A covers the following activities in the electronic form pertaining to any material which contain sexually explicit act or conduct:

(a) Publication of such material in the electronic form.

(b) Transmission of such material in the electronic form.

(c) Causing of publishing or transmission of the said material in the electronic form.

It is pertinent to point out that the legislation does not specifically define as to what is sexually explicit act or conduct. In such a scenario, the common parlance meaning of the same would prevail. Any act of publishing, transmitting or causing to be published and transmitted any electronic information containing sexually explicit act or conduct has now been made a penal offence. Such an offence is punishable on first conviction with imprisonment of either description for a term which may extend to five years and with fine which may extend to ten lakh rupees. In case, a person is convicted the second or subsequent time under section 67A, the law has provided for imprisonment of either description for a term which may extend to seven years and also with fine which may extend to ten lakh rupees.

In this sense, section 67A has been brought on a higher pedestal than section 67. Thus, the Legislature has now sought to distinguish between publication and transmission of minor pornography and sexually explicit acts or conduct. Thus, instances pertaining to electronic information which is lascivious or which appeals to the prurient interests or the effect of which is to tend to deprave and corrupt the minds of those who are likely to see, read or hear the same, are specifically covered within the ambit of section 67 of the Information Technology Act, 2000. However, the law has appreciated that publishing, transmission or causing to be published and transmitted electronic content containing sexually explicit act or conduct, may have a much more negative and prejudicial impact upon the not only the tender minds of children but also would have an undesirable impact upon the society at large. As such, the Legislature has provided for much higher punishment under section 67A rather than the limited quantum of punishment that is now provided for under section 67 of the amended Information Technology Act, 2000.

Section 67A is also concerned with material in the electronic form. As such any material which is published, transmitted or caused to be published or transmitted using a cell phone, iPad, Tablet, Smart Device, smart-phone, personal digital assistant or any other kind of communication device would also be fully covered within the ambit of offence under section 67A of the amended Information Technology Act, 2000.

This is so because today iPads, Tablets, Smart Phones and Smart Devices use the digital format. Further iPads, Tablets, Smart Phones and Smart Devices come with a variety of gadgets including cameras, audio voice recorder etc. As such any kind of misuse of iPads, Tablets, Smart Phones and Smart Devices for the purposes of publishing or transmitting any material which contains sexually explicit act or conduct of any other person, comes fully within the mischief of section 67A of the amended Information Technology Act, 2000.

For example, when a person using his mobile phone camera, captures two people having a sexual intercourse, the said material becomes material in the electronic form which contains sexually explicit act or conduct and as such, this act of mere capturing or publication of the said sexually explicit material on the iPads, Tablets, Smart Phones and Smart Devices or other communication device would completely fall within the ambit of section 67A of the amended Information Technology Act, 2000. To take another illustration, if a person records through his iPad, Tablet, Smart Phone and/or Smart Device, mobile phone camera, sexually explicit conduct of two persons, irrespective of their sex, the same would also qualified to be an offence under section 67A of the amended Information Technology Act, 2000. To take yet another illustration, if a person captures two males engaging into sexually explicit conduct, the said material would also fall within the mischief of section 67A of the amended Information Technology Act,

2000 and is liable to be so punished accordingly. Taking a further illustration if a person receives an MMS of sexually explicit act of two persons on his iPad, Tablet, Smart Phone and/or Smart Device and further forwards the same to his friends, he also commits an offence under section 67A of the amended Information Technology Act, 2000.

Section 67 is a non-bailable cognizable offence. There can be no given formula of what would constitute sexually explicit act or conduct. Every case would be dependent upon peculiar facts and circumstances.

However, instances like capturing people having intercourse or fondling of private parts or display of private parts or other sexual acts or conduct would qualify to be covered within the ambit of this section. Given instances like men sucking breasts of women would also constitute sexually explicit act or conduct to be covered within the ambit of section 67A of the amended Information Technology Act, 2000.

Thus, making a blue film or transmitting or publishing a blue film on the Internet would then invoke the requirements of section 67A of the amended Information Technology Act, 2000.

There can be no comprehensive list of what would constitute explicit sexual act or conduct. However, such list would be dependant upon the peculiar facts and circumstances of each case. At the end of the day it will be upon the discretion of the concerned court to decide whether the information in electronic form so published and transmitted or caused to be published or transmitted, is of such a nature which would constitute depicting sexually explicit act or conduct. Section 67A presents yet another important weapon in the arsenal of the law enforcement agencies in their fight against cyber pornography and cyber sex.

Section 67B of the amended Information Technology Act, 2000

"Section 67B. Punishment for publishing or transmitting of material depicting children in sexually explicit act, etc., in electronic form.—*Whoever,*—

(a) publishes or transmits or causes to be published or transmitted material in any electronic form which depicts children engaged in sexually explicit act or conduct; or

(b) creates text or digital images, collects, seeks, browses, downloads, advertises, promotes, exchanges or distributes material in any electronic form depicting children in obscene or indecent or sexually explicit manner; or

(c) cultivates, entices or induces children to online relationship with one or more children for and on sexually explicit act or in a manner that may offend a reasonable adult on the computer resource; or

(d) facilitates abusing children online, or

(e) records in any electronic form own abuse or that of others pertaining to sexually explicit act with children,

shall be punished on first conviction with imprisonment of either description for a term which may extend to five years and with fine which may extend to ten lakh rupees and in the event of second or subsequent conviction with imprisonment of either description for a term which may extend to seven years and also with fine which may extend to ten lakh rupees:

Provided that provisions of section 67, section 67A and this section does not extend to any book, pamphlet, paper, writing, drawing, painting representation or figure in electronic form—

(i) *the publication of which is proved to be justified as being for the public good on the ground that such book, pamphlet, paper, writing drawing, painting representation or figure is in the interest of science, literature, art or learning or other objects of general concern; or*

(ii) *which is kept or used for* bona fide *heritage or religious purposes.*

Explanation.—For the purposes of this section "children" means a person who has not completed the age of 18 years."

Section 67B is yet another provision that has been specifically added under the Information Technology Act, 2000 by the Information Technology (Amendment) Act, 2008. Section 67B has tried to address a crying need of the hour which had been repeatedly stressed over the last few years from various stakeholders. Today, we realize that children are massively exploited on the Internet. Child-pornography does play a very important role within the overall context of cyber pornography and cyber sex. Countries across the world have realized that fighting the entire battle against pornography is a huge task and the same would take far more resources, time, effort and energies. Hence, some countries have started to concentrate their efforts in the direction of targeting child-pornography, which is a smaller subset of the overall online pornography. In this regard, nations have enacted various stringent regulations, rules and procedures to effectively tackle child-pornography. The United States of America is a leading example in that regard.

When, the Information Technology Act, 2000 was implemented in the year 2000, it only had one general provision on online pornography being section 67 of the Information Technology Act, 2000. Section 67 only penalized publishing, transmitting or causing to be published information in electronic form which is lascivious or which appeals to the prurient interests or the effect of which is to tend to deprave and corrupt the minds of those who are likely to see, read or hear the same. These were very broad parameters that were enacted, keeping in mind the broad requirements of targeting at cyber pornography. However, as time passed by, there were doubts that were raised as to whether the same would be applicable to child-pornography. Though there was no doubt in the mind of the academicians and the Judiciary that the said provisions would apply to child-pornography, yet there was distinctly a hesitancy to not invoke section 67 of the Information Technology Act, 2000 in matters pertaining to child-pornography. In fact, in the year 2000, child-pornography was not even a matter of priority for the Legislature or the government. However as time passed by, we realized that focus shifted on targeting child-pornography. For the said focus thanks to various international initiatives and awareness programmes. Different countries started enacting different legislations against child pornography and child abuse. Consequently, India took a leaf out of the international experience pertaining to child-pornography and decided not to go for a separate legislation targeting child-pornography but to insert a distinct new provision in the Information Technology Act, 2000, by virtue of the Information Technology (Amendment) Act, 2008.

A perusal of the provisions of section 67B shows that the law has now brought within the ambit of criminal exposure and penalty, various kinds of acts pertaining to child abuse and child-pornography and related information in electronic form pertaining thereto.

Five broad kinds of acts have been brought within the ambit of criminal penalty. Section 67B(a) criminalizes the acts of publishing, transmitting or causing to be published or transmitted material in any electronic form which depicts children engaged in sexually explicit act or conduct. Clearly, the target of section 67A is to prevent publishing, transmitting as well as causing to be published or transmitted electronic information showing children engaged in sexually explicit act or conduct. This is rightly done so, because such conduct, apart from encouraging pedophiles, also has a very negative debilitating impact upon the tender minds of the society. It is pertinent to note that section 67B(a) talks about material in any electronic form. Thus, all kinds of materials including materials on mobile phones, cell phones, personal digital assistants, iPads, Tablets, Smart Phones and Smart Devices or any other communication device which is used to communicate audio, video, image or text would qualify within the ambit of section 67B(a) of the amended Information Technology Act, 2000. Section 67B(a) reproduces the same parameters which are made the foundation under sections 67 and 67A of the Information Technology Act, 2000. These golden parameters are the following:

(a) Publishing,

(b) Transmitting, or

(c) Causing to be published or transmitted material in electronic form.

The only distinction under section 67B(a) is that the same is only applicable to electronic material, which depicts children engaged in sexually explicit act or conduct. In India, the age of the teenager majority is 18 years and as such any person below the age of 18 years, is deemed to be a minor and hence a child. As such, Section 67B(a) is applicable to any teenager as would also come within the ambit of " a child". The *Explanation* to section 67B clearly defined that for the purposes of section 67B, children means a person who has not completed the age of 18 years. Thus, section 67B(a) could also be made applicable to publishing, transmitting or causing to be published or transmitted information in the electronic form which depicts teenagers below the age of 18 years engaged in sexually explicit act or conduct. Typically speaking, a case of *DPS MMS* would be capable of being registered under section 67(B)(a) of the Amended Information Technology Act, 2000

Thus, section 67B(a) provides for preventing, publishing or transmission of electronic information, depicting children and teenagers below 18 years engaged in sexually explicit act or conduct.

Section 67B(b) is of far greater significance, impact and import. This is because of the vast parameters that are used under section 67B(b). Section 67B(b) changes the fundamental premise on which, Indian law on pornography has been based till date. Earlier prior to the Information Technology (Amendment) Act, 2008 coming into force on October 27, 2009, there was no law passed by the Parliament of India which prevented people from viewing pornography. The focus of the law was on preventing publishing and transmission of pornography or pornography-related materials. However, section 67B(b) has now sought to criminalize the following acts pertaining to material in any electronic form depicting children in obscene or indecent or sexually explicit manner:—

- ✓ Creation of text or digital images of the same
- ✓ Collection of the same
- ✓ Seeking of the same
- ✓ Browsing of the same
- ✓ Downloading of the same
- ✓ Advertising of the same
- ✓ Promoting the same
- ✓ Extending the same
- ✓ Distributing the same.

Thus, not just creation of text or digital images pertaining to child-pornography but also its collection, seeking, advertising, promotion, exchanging or distribution has been brought within the ambit of the Indian Cyberlaw. In addition, what is of particular significance is the fact that even mere browsing of child-pornography content has been brought within the ambit of criminal penalty under section 67B(b).

Further even downloading child-pornography has also been made as an offence under section 67B(b) of the amended Information Technology Act, 2000.

This is possibly for the first time where the law has made a fundamental radical change in its premises and has even criminalized the browsing or downloading of child-pornographic material.

This provision seems assumes tremendous significance, given the fact of the unknown nature of the internet and its architecture. A large number of times, people are browsing through various websites and they often would click on some provided clicks. At the time when they click on some click, they have no clue of what would be featuring on the said website. Considering the fact that there are a large number of deceptive websites and web links available, the browsing individual has virtually no control of what kind of website would he be transported to, on the clicking of unknown click. The law has now been made so much strict and stringent that even if one accidentally or unintentionally lands up on to webpage which contains child-pornography, that will tantamount to browsing child-pornography and hence would be covered within the offence, defined under section 67B(b) of the amended Indian Information Technology Act, 2000.

Further, a large number of times, softwares are available with different misleading descriptions for download. Lot of people view pornography and would often like to download the same on their computers. At the time of downloading any particular file, users would invariably have little idea or inkling of what exactly would be contained in the said file that he is downloading as the contents of the file being downloaded, would not be known to the concerned user. If such downloading file contains child pornographic material, the same also becomes an act which comes within the ambit of the offence defined under section 67B(b) of the amended Information Technology Act, 2000.

Ever since Internet was commercially introduced in our country, we have come across various cases where adults have either posed as children or pedophiles have become active on chat groups and other lists, so as to cultivate false relationships with children, all aimed at enticing or inducing the children for online relationships, culminating in sexual acts. Unfortunately, the law earlier did not have any specific provisions in this regard. Consequently, the perpetuators of such crime would invariably be let off. However, the Information Technology (Amendment) Act, 2008 has now specifically provided the provisions of section 67B(c) of the said law. Section 67B(c) criminalizes the following activities:—

- ✓ Cultivating children to online relationships with one or more children for and on sexually explicit act,
- ✓ Enticing children to online relationships with one or more children, for and on sexually explicit act,
- ✓ Inducing children to online relationship with one or more children, for and on sexually explicit act,
- ✓ Cultivating children to online relationship with one or more children, in a manner that may offend a reasonable adult on a computer resource,
- ✓ Enticing children to online relationship with one or more children in a manner that may offend a reasonable adult on a computer resource, or
- ✓ Inducing children to online relationship with one or more children in a manner that may offend a reasonable adult on a computer resource.

The gamut of all the aforesaid activities has been brought within the ambit of criminal penalty. Section 67B(c) tends to target all pedophiles and their various undesirable online activities, which are targeted at children for or on sexually explicit acts. Further, another important aspect of section 67B(c) is that the activities of the said pedophile could be such or be in a manner that may offend a reasonable adult on a computer resource.

The law has not really defined what would be the parameters for "offending a reasonable adult on a computer resource". However, if one looks at the prevailing jurisprudence one would realize that in this case also, the test of the reasonable man would be applicable. The test of a reasonable man postulates all that a reasonable man would do under reasonable circumstances. Thus, a reasonable man of reasonable prudence, being a reasonable adult, if he gets offended by any activity of cultivating, enticing or inducing children to online relationships with one or more children, that alone would be sufficient to bring the said acts within the ambit of criminal penalty. This would be notwithstanding the fact as to whether the person doing the act did it with any particular intention or knowledge of the fact as to whether he is or not a pedophile. Thus, the offence under section 67B(c) is of a very wide nature, ambit and canvas and is likely to be so interpreted in the times to come in that particular manner.

Section 67B(d) makes it an offence of any person facilitating abusing children online. The offence has been defined in very less number of words yet the potential applicability, ambit and scope of the said offence is indeed huge and highly comprehensive. First and foremost, it is important to note that the law does not define what is meant by the terms of abusing children. Abusing children could be done in a variety of manners.

Child abuse[57] *is the physical, sexual or emotional mistreatment of children.*

Childhood is the era of the golden days of a child. There is an evergreen need of nurturing children in such a way that their childhood memories always remain a good memory for them. Keeping this thought process in mind, the law and the Judiciary have already bent in the direction of protecting children and their innocent childhood.

The Supreme Court of India in *Rosy Jacob* v. *Jacob A. Chakramakkal*, AIR 1973 SC 2090: (1973) 3 SCR 918 observed as follows:

> "The children are not mere chattels nor are they mere playthings for their parents. Absolute right of parents over the destinies and the lives of their children has, in the modern changed social conditions, yielded to the considerations of their welfare as human beings so that they may grow up in a normal balanced manner to be useful members of the society...".

Further, the law also does not define what exactly is meant by facilitation but from the overall perspective it can definitely be stated that any act, deed or thing done in furtherance of or towards the direction of or contributing to or having a connection, association, nexus, relationship of any kind whatsoever, to abusing children online, would be classified as coming within the ambit of the scope of the term facilitation "as indicated under section 67B (d) of the amended Information Technology Act, 2000."

The term "facilitates" has been defined by law lexicon in the following terms:

Facilitate[58] means to make easier; assist the progress of

Facilitate[59] something (FORMAL) to make an action or a process possible or easier

The word 'online' means all forms of information and communication technologies like the internet, iPads, Tablets, Smart Phones and Smart Devices etc. Three types of abuse of sexual nature that occur against children online are identified to be solicitation, providing access to sexually explicit content by minors and exploitation of children for child pornography.

Term 'Online Child Sexual Abuse' should include the following:

(1) Online sexual grooming of minors, which means enticing and soliciting the child for further offline abuse.

---

57. http://en.wikipedia.org/wiki/Child_abuse.
58. http://www.thefreedictionary.com/facilitates.
59. http://www.oxfordadvancedlearnersdictionary.com/dictionary/facilitates#facilitate.

(2) Access to sexually-explicit content by minors, which means the child accessing obscene and harmful content including child sex abuse images, both intentionally and otherwise.

(3) Production or reception of online child sex abuse images, which means producing or receiving any online sexually abusive representation of a child. Here, 'child' means a person under eighteen years of age and would include both real as well as virtual children, as well as adults who appear to be children

India Department of Child Services conducted survey from July, 2008 to December, 2009, 47571 children were reported as possible victims of abuse and 33405 of neglect.[60]

Thus, the scope and ambit of offence under section 67B(d) is tremendous and massive and would incorporate therein any act, deed, thing done which has connection, association, nexus or relationship of any kind whatsoever pertaining to abusing of children online. This assumes tremendous significance, given the overall voices that have been raised across the world for protecting the children.

Section 67B(e) makes it an offence for any person to record in any electronic form, his own abuse or that of others pertaining to sexually explicit act with children. The law has been deliberately drafted in vague and broad terms. It is not clear as to what would alone constitute own abuse and that of others pertaining to sexually explicit act with "children". However, it can reasonably be stated that all acts, deeds and things pertaining to abuse of the human body and its relationship to sexually explicit act with children would come within the ambit of the parameters of section 67B(e) of the amended Information Technology Act, 2000.

Section 67B(e) pertains to a miscellaneous repository clause that has been handed by the law primarily to bring within its ambit, all kinds of acts pertaining to child pornography or sexually explicit acts with children, which may not come within the ambit of the parameters as defined under section 67B(a) to 67B(e) of the amended Information Technology Act, 2000.

If any person does any of the acts stipulated under section 67B(a) to (e), he shall be punished on first conviction with imprisonment of either description for a term which may extend to five years and with fine which may extend to ten lakh rupees. In the case of a second or subsequent conviction, the person concerned would be punishable with imprisonment of either description for a term, which may extend to seven years and also with fine which may extend to ten lakh rupees. Thus, the offence under section 67B of the amended Information Technology Act, 2000 is a non-bailable and cognizable offence and is thus on a much more serious pedestal and footing than section 67 of the Information Technology Act, 2000.

Section 67B is of very wide amplitude and includes within its ambit, all kinds of acts done using communication devices, iPads, Tablets, Smart Phones and Smart Devices for the purposes of publishing or transmission of material depicting children in sexually explicit acts. Thus the use of iPads, Tablets, Smart Phones and

60. http://www.articlebase.com/computers-articles/statistics-and-cell-phones-538109.html.

Smart Devices for the purposes of publication of electronic content, which depicts children engaged in sexually explicit act or conduct, would qualify as an offence under section 67B of the amended Information Technology Act, 2000.

If somebody takes pictures through his iPad, Tablet, Smart Phone and Smart Device of children engaging into sexually explicit acts which depicts children in obscene or indecent manner, the same also becomes an offence under section 67B of the amended Information Technology Act, 2000. The scope of section 67B is so wide enough so as to also include within its ambit, all kinds of pedophiles, as also the case of iPads, Tablets, Smart Phones and Smart Devices for the purposes of cultivating, inducing or enticing children to online relationships for sexually explicit act. Such kind of an action also becomes an offence under section 67B of the amended Information Technology Act, 2000.

The law is not only concerned about publication of electronic content which depicts children engaged in sexually explicit act; the law has even gone further to bringing, within its ambit, those people who record their own abuse pertaining to sexually explicit acts with children. Thus if a person uses an iPad, Tablet, Smart Phone and Smart Device for the purposes of recording his own sexually explicit acts with children, the said act itself becomes an offence and is punishable under section 67B of the amended Information Technology Act, 2000.

Of particular significance is the proviso to section 67B of the amended Information Technology Act, 2000. The proviso to section 67B provides that the provisions of section 67, 67A and 67B of the amended Information Technology Act, 2000 does not extend to certain excepted categories. These categories include any book, pamphlet, paper, writing, drawing, painting, representation or figure in the electronic form. However for the purposes of the said book, pamphlet, paper, writing, drawing, painting, representation or figure to come within the ambit of exception, it is important that the publication of the said book, pamphlet, paper, writing, drawing, painting, representation or figure in electronic form is proved to be justified as being for the public good on the ground that such book, pamphlet, paper, writing, drawing, painting, representation of figure is in the interests of the following:

(a) Science,

(b) Literature,

(c) Art,

(d) Learning, or

(e) Other objects of general concern.

The proviso further provides that for this exemption to be applicable, the said book, pamphlet, paper, writing, drawing, painting, representation or figure in electronic form is kept or used for *bona fide* heritage or religious purposes.

The net effect of the said proviso is that thus it would not be an offence for publishing, transmitting or causing to be published or transmitted any information in the electronic form, which is either lascivious or which appeals to the prurient interests or which contains the sexually explicit conduct or act or which pertains to children in sexually explicit acts or conduct if the same is justified as being for the public good and that the same is in the interest of science, literature, art, learning or other objects of general concern or which is kept or used for *bona fide* heritage or religious purposes.

To give a categorical illustration of the said proviso the act of publishing, transmitting or causing to be published or transmitted any information in electronic form which potentially shows some child abuse or pornography or sexually explicit act or conduct which is either in the interest of science, literature, art, learning or other objects of general concern or which is kept or use for *bona fide* heritage or religious purposes, would not be constituting a crime under section 67, 67A and 67B of the amended Information Technology Act, 2000.

The net effect of the said proviso is to exclude from the applicability of the criminal penalty, electronic information which may be lascivious or which would appeal to the prurient interests or the effect of which would be to tend to deprave and corrupt the minds of people who are likely to see, read or hear the same or which may contain child abuse or sexually explicit conduct or act, if the same can be proved to be of public good or in the interest of science, literature, art or learning or other subjects of general concern or which is kept or use for *bona fide* heritage or religious purposes.

The net effect of the proviso is that it seeks to exempt objects of science, literature, art, learning or other objects of general concern or objects connected with *bona fide* heritage or religious purposes, which may contain pornographic, lascivious content or sexually explicit content or may have connection with depicting children engaged in sexually explicit act or conduct in the electronic form, but which is necessary for the purposes of public good.

Seen from a holistic perspective, the law has now been tremendously strengthened with the addition of section 67A and 67B of the amended Information Technology Act, 2000. Together, section 67, 67A and 67B of the amended Information Technology Act, 2000 form a trilogy which would be highly handy and relevant in the fight of India against cyber pornography and child-pornography and its efforts to contain and prevent such kind of illegal content, been published or transmitted within the territorial boundaries of India or on the Internet.

It is pertinent to note that the provisions of section 67, 67A and 67B of the amended Information Technology Act, 2000 are all applicable to the context of mobile data as also all electronic records resident on iPads, Tablets, Smart Phones and Smart Devices and any other communication devices, which are used to transmit audio, video, text or images. Thus, all kinds of data resident on iPads, Tablets, Smart Phones and Smart Devices, which is lascivious or mobile electronic records or which appeals to the prurient interests or interest or publishing or transmitting mobile electronic records in the electronic form containing sexually explicit acts or conduct or depicting children in sexually explicit act or conduct or other acts of child abuse or child-pornography would now be specifically brought within the ambit of section 67, 67A and 67B of the amended Information Technology Act, 2000.

These provisions would also be extremely handy for India in fighting its war against mobile pornography and mobile child-pornography.

Section 67C of the amended Information Technology Act, 2000

> ***"Section 67C. Preservation and retention of information by intermediaries.—***
> *(1) Intermediary shall preserve and retain such information as may be specified for such duration and in such manner and format as the Central Government may prescribe.*
>
> *(2) any intermediary who intentionally or knowingly contravenes the provisions of sub-section (1) shall be punished with an imprisonment for a term which may extend to three years and also be liable to fine."*

Section 67C has been added in the Information Technology Act, 2000 by the Information Technology (Amendment) Act, 2008.

This provision deals with the most important aspect relating to electronic retention by intermediaries. The said provision is couched in a mandatory language as it uses the word 'shall'. Intermediaries have been straddled with the mandatory responsibility of preserving and retaining such information in electronic form, as may be specified for such duration and in such manner and format, as may be prescribed by the Central Government. This is primarily been done so as to ensure that intermediaries do not tamper, alter or manipulate, in any manner whatsoever, with concerned electronic logs pertaining to the various services provided by them. Today, service providers increasingly are becoming repositories of information in the electronic form. This is although more relevant, in respect of not just electronic information about the personal details of their subscribers but also pertaining to electronic logs of various transactions done by various persons on their electronic and mobile platforms. These log information become of critical significance, moreso not only in the context of tracking and investigating cyber crimes and mobile crimes, but also for the purposes of relying upon the same as the impartial evidence provided by service providers, in respect of various contentious issues and disputes between the parties. Today, increasingly courts are relying upon the data provided by the logs within the service provider's records to come to conclusions and settlement of various disputes. As such, it is important that the service providers and intermediaries must not only retain the said data and information in the electronic form, but also must do it for a minimum period of time and in such manner and format, as may be prescribed by the Central Government. At the time of writing, no prescription has yet been made by the Central Government for the exact duration of electronic retention as also the manner and format of electronic retention. However, these are matters of crucial significance, for the entire sustenance of the e-economy and also for regulating undesirable and criminal activities in cyber space.

An intermediary thus cannot now take the stand that he had failed or omitted to save certain portions of his electronic records. At the time of writing, there is currently ambiguity about the period, for which such electronic logs and records need to be established and retained. However, that does not mean that there is no obligation upon the service provider of any kind whatsoever, not to retain the said information in the electronic form.

This import and interpretation takes further support from section 67C(2). Section 67C(2) makes the intentional or knowingly contravention of section 67C(1) as a penal offence. The said offence is made punishable with imprisonment for a term which may extend to 3 years and shall also be liable to fine.

This section 67C(2) has to be read in conjunction with section 85 of the Information Technology Act, 2000 which provides that when the offences are committed by intermediaries as companies, every person, who at the time the contravention was committed, was in-charge of and was responsible to the company for the conduct of the business of the company as also the company shall be guilty of the said contravention and shall further be liable to be proceeded against and punished accordingly.

Everything depends on what kind of information may be specified for what duration and in what format and manner by the Central Government. At the time of writing, the Central Governme7nt has not yet prescribed any such requirements under section 67C of the amended Information Technology Act, 2000. For example, the Central Government could specify that the intermediaries shall preserve and retain the logs pertaining to all activities done on their electronic platforms or services by all users for a period of two years. In case, if such direction is prescribed in the Central Government, or intermediaries who fall in the respective definitions of the term "intermediary" shall be mandated to retain the said logs pertaining to activities on the electronic platforms for the stipulated period of two years. To take yet another illustration, the Central Government could also specify and prescribe the intermediaries to maintain the contents of information being dealt with by them, which contain reference to specific terms which could cause prejudicial impact upon the security and stability or integrity of India for a period of seven years. For example, the government could specify the intermediaries to keep a record of all communications and data that is dealt with, or processed by the intermediaries in their capacity as an intermediary, which have reference to certain words like bomb, combat, terrorism, terror etc. In case if the said prescription is so made, each and every intermediary is required and mandated under law to preserve and retain such information for a period of seven years. If the said retention is not done by the intermediary intentionally or knowingly, the intermediary effectively plays with fire as the said act becomes an offence punishable with imprisonment for a term which may extend to 3 years and shall also be liable for fine.

At the time of writing, it is thus amply clear that service providers and intermediaries need to be doubly careful of ensuring that they retain and preserve the information pertaining to the kind, category, manner and format specified by the Central Government but specifically all records pertaining to their logs and all transaction records which will help identify the nature of the transaction, the identity of the user, the details of the activities done by the user on the electronic or mobile platform of the intermediary and the complete factum of initiation, processing and conclusion of the relevant transactions on the electronic and mobile networks of the intermediaries. This provision is the first categorical provision pertaining to electronic retention and is likely to help almost all stakeholders.

From the perspective of the intermediaries, the said section may be seen as an economic burden on their business. However, it needs to be appreciated that all businesses have various kinds of compliance requirements. The business of being an intermediary, involves within itself the inherent exposure to the legal liability to preserve and maintain the concerned electronic records, including log records for potential access by the Government, in the times to come.

Section 69 of the amended Information Technology Act, 2000

> ***"Section 69. Power to issue directions for interception or monitoring or decryption of any information through any computer resource.***—*(1) Where the Central Government or a State Government or any of its officer specially authorised by the Central Government or the State Government, as the case may be, in this behalf may, if satisfied that it is necessary or expedient to do in the interest of the sovereignty or integrity of India, defence of India, security of the State, friendly relations with foreign States or public order or for preventing incitement to the commission of any cognizable offence relating to above or for investigation of any offence, it may subject to the provisions of sub-section (2), for reasons to be recorded in writing, by order, direct any agency of the appropriate Government to intercept, monitor or decrypt or cause to be intercepted or monitored or decrypted any information generated, transmitted, received or stored in any computer resource.*
>
> *(2) The procedure and safeguards subject to which such interception or monitoring or decryption may be carried out, shall be such as may be prescribed.*
>
> *(3) The subscriber or intermediary or any person in-charge of the computer resource shall, when called upon by any agency referred to in sub-section (1), extend all facilities and technical assistance to—*
>
> *(a) provide access to or secure access to the computer resource generating, transmitting, receiving or storing such information; or*
>
> *(b) intercept, monitor, or decrypt the information, as the case may be; or*
>
> *(c) provide information stored in computer resource.*
>
> *(4) The subscriber or intermediary or any person who fails to assist the agency referred to in sub-section (3) shall be punished with imprisonment for a term which may extend to seven years and shall also be liable to fine."*

Section 69 has been amended by the Information Technology (Amendment) Act, 2008. Section 69, after amendment, becomes one of the most important tools in the hands of sovereign India to protect its sovereign rights from various illegal, criminal and terrorist activities that have been targeted against India.

The 26/11 Mumbai attacks have demonstrated in no uncertain terms that not just mobile communication but also electronic networks and Internet are being used in a very dangerous manner so as to execute attempts to undermine the sovereignty and integrity of India.

The 26/11 Mumbai attacks have demonstrated how the mobile networks as also the computer resources as also the Internet are being and can be potentially misused in a manner so as to detrimentally impact the sovereignty and integrity of India.

As such in today's world when there are various security challenges that the Indian nation is facing, it becomes although more necessary for the sovereign Indian Government to try to know about the various designs and efforts that have been made against the sovereign interests of India. In that context, section 69 assumes paramount significance. Section 69 provides for the power to issue directions for interception, monitoring or decryption of any information through any computer resource.

The significance of section 69 is brought forward by the fact that it talks about "computer resources". The term "computer resource" is defined under section 2(1)(k) to mean computer, computer systems, computer network, data, computer database or software. However, when one examines the definition of the term "computer network" defined under section 2(1)(j) of the Information Technology Act, 2000 it clearly means the interconnection of one or more computers, computer systems or communication devices through the use of satellite, microwave, terrestrial line, wire, wireless or other communication media as also through terminals or a complex consisting of two or more interconnected computers or communication devices, whether or not the interconnection is continuously maintained. Thus all kinds of mobile networks as also communication devices as also computers, computer systems and computer networks come within the ambit of the terms computer resource, as referred to under section 69 of the Information Technology Act, 2000. The coverage of section 69 is thus comprehensive for all kinds of computers, computer systems, computer networks, computer resources, communication and electronic devices.

Section 69 provides the discretion to direct interception, monitoring or decryption of information through any computer resource.

The earlier section 69 of the Information Technology Act, 2000 had vested in the hands of the Controller of Certifying Authorities, the discretion so as to direct interception of any information transmitted to any computer resource.

However, as time passed by, potentially it was realized that the said exercise was not a convenient nor expedient exercise since the earlier law had only provided for the Controller of Certifying Authorities to be satisfied for interception and then the Controller could direct any agency of the Government to intercept any information transmitted through any computer resource. The Legislature realized that given the speed in which activities are being done and the manner, in which India's mobile and computer networks are being targeted, it is only necessary and expedient that the time delay in getting the appropriate directions for interception of electronic evidence, be minimized to the barest extent possible. As such, the Legislature decided that instead of the Controller of Certifying Authorities, it shall now be the appropriate government who will have the power to direct interception, monitoring or decryption of information through any computer resource. The said appropriate government could either be the Central Government or it could be a State Government or it could be any of its officers who are specially authorized by the Central Government or the State Government in this behalf.

Section 69 requires that the appropriate government or its officers needs to be satisfied that it is necessary or expedient to direct interception, monitoring or decryption in the following circumstances:

- ✓ In the interests of sovereignty or integrity of India,
- ✓ In the interests of defence of India,
- ✓ In the interests of security of the State,
- ✓ In the interests of friendly relations with foreign States,
- ✓ In the interests of public order,
- ✓ In the interests of preventing incitement to the commission of any cognizable offence relating to the above or in the interests or for investigating of any offence.

If the appropriate government or any of its authorized officers are satisfied about any of the following parameters, the appropriate government or its authorized representative or officers, may, direct interception, monitoring or decryption. However, the said direction has to be for reasons to be recorded in writing. Further, if the aforesaid parameters are satisfied, the appropriate government or its officers may direct any agency of the appropriate government to do any of the following:

- ✓ To intercept any information generated, transmitted, received or stored in any computer resource,
- ✓ To monitor any information generated, transmitted, received or stored in any computer resource,
- ✓ To decrypt any information generated, transmitted, received or stored in any computer resource,
- ✓ Cause to be intercepted any information generated, transmitted, received or stored in any computer resource,
- ✓ Cause to be monitored any information generated, transmitted, received or stored in any computer resource,
- ✓ Cause to be decrypted any information generated, transmitted, received or stored in any computer source.

Thus, the scope of the powers that have been granted, are indeed huge, wide and comprehensive. The only caveat is that the said powers have to be exercised subject to the provisions of section 69(2) of the amended Information Technology Act. Section 69(2) stipulates that the procedural safeguards subject to which such interception, monitoring or decryption may be carried out shall be such as may be specified. These would be specified by appropriate notification in the Official Gazette which is yet to be specified at the time of writing. However, all procedures, safeguards, checks and balances as may be prescribed by the appropriate government from time to time regarding to interception, monitoring or decryption, shall need to be carried out.

It is pertinent to note that earlier section 69 only talked about interception of information transmitted through any computer resource in India. However, the ambit, scope and applicability of the amended section 69 has been tremendously widened and made far more comprehensive. Section 69 now deals not just with interception but also with monitoring and decryption of information which is generated, transmitted, received or stored in a computer resource. Thus, the current section 69 is far more wider in its applicability and is of tremendous relevance from the perspective of protecting and preserving the sovereign interests of India.

The said agency of the appropriate government which has been directed to intercept, monitor or decrypt or cause to be intercepted, monitored or decrypt any information generated, transmitted, received or stored in any computer resource, has been giving the mandatory responsibility to call upon any subscriber or intermediary or person in-charge of the computer resource to co-operate in such an exercise. It is also been made mandatory responsibility of the said subscriber or intermediary or any person in-charge of the computer resource, to extend all facilities and technical assistance to the said specified agency, for the purposes of interception, monitoring or decryption. Further, whenever such an agency calls for any assistance facilities or technical assistance the subscriber, intermediary or any other person in-charge of the computer resource has the mandatory duty to extend all technical facilities and technical assistance with respect to the following:

- ✓ Providing access to or securing access to the computer resource generating, transmitting, receiving or storing such information,
- ✓ To intercept, monitor or decrypt the information as the case may be,
- ✓ To provide information stored in the computer resource.

Thus, each subscriber or intermediary or person in-charge of a computer resource, has to be mentally prepared that whenever he or she is called upon by any specified agency, which has been authorized to intercept monitor or decrypt information, he/she would be required to extend mandatorily all possible facilities and technical assistance for the aforesaid activities. This would include technically extending facilities and technical assistance to provide access or to secure access to the relevant computer resource which is generating, transmitting and receiving or storing such information. Thus, not only the physical access to the said computer resource would have to be provided but even access to all data and information resident therein or transmitted there from, shall also be required to be provided.

Further, the said subscriber, intermediary or other person has to be prepared to extend all facilities and technical assistance to intercept, monitor or decrypt information, as the case may be. It is clear that there are lot of potential problems regarding the actual implementation of the section as we go along. This is so because it is possible that the subscriber, intermediary or person in-charge of the computer resource, may or may not have all facilities and technical assistance to intercept monitor or decrypt information. Further, the said subscriber intermediary or person in-charge of computer resources is further mandated to extend all facilities and technical assistance to provide information in the computer resource.

The Legislature has been very comprehensive in elaborating all detailed obligations that it requires the subscribers, intermediaries or persons in-charge of computer resources to perform, when they are called upon so to do, by an agency which is directed to intercept, monitor or decrypt information under section 69 of the amended Information Technology Act, 2000. However, while legislating such provision, the Legislature seems to have forgotten that it may not be possible at all times for the said subscriber, intermediary or other person in-charge of computer resource to provide or extend all facilities and technical assistance to intercept, monitor or decrypt information, as the case may be. While, in theory it is good to stradle the said subscriber, intermediary or person in-charge of its computer resource, with all obligations to extend facilities and technical assistance for the said operations, the practical situation may be completely different. This assumes all the more significance, given the specific provisions that are provided under section 69(4) of the Information Technology Act, 2000.

Section 69(4) categorically says that if the subscriber, intermediary or any person in-charge of a computer resource fails to assist the agency in the manner as referred to under section 69(3), he commits an offence. The said offence shall be punishable with imprisonment for a term which may extend to 7 years and shall also be liable to fine. Thus, section 69(4) creates a very serious and complex offence. The danger of section 69(4), is that large number of subscribers, intermediaries and persons in-charge of computer resources may come within the ambit of the mischief under section 69(4), inadvertently or unintentionally. The way section 69(4) is worded, there is no need to show the existence of any intention or knowledge. A mere failure to assist the agency has been made a crime punishable with imprisonment for a term which may extend to 7 years, apart from fine. It is very much possible that lot of unsuspecting and *bona fide* subscribers, intermediaries and persons in-charge of computer resources may be sucked in the whirlpool of the offence created under section 69(4) of the amended Information Technology Act, 2000. The Legislature has overlooked the practical realities that at the relevant time, the subscriber, intermediary or persons in-charge of computer resources may not have all facilities and technical assistance for the purposes of interception, monitoring or decrypting information of any computer resource. This is so because, the facilities of interception, monitoring or decryption of information would involve not just specialized software and tools but also various new kinds of hardware. Non-purchasing of the said hardware as also the softwares for interception, monitoring or decryption of information, could come within the ambit of failure to assist the agency. Hence, it is very much possible that the law enforcement agencies may book up a large number of subscribers, intermediaries or persons in-charge of computer resources on the ground that they have failed to assist the designated agency for interception, monitoring or decryption. Section 69(4) is a provision which is likely to be potentially misused, as time passes by. This becomes all the more relevant, in the context of communications through iPads, Tablets, Smart Phones and Smart Devices, mobile communications as also mobile servers and mobile computing. A large number of subscribers, intermediaries and persons in-charge of computer resources do not retain with them the facilities and technical assistance to intercept, monitor or decrypt information, passing through the said mobile hardware, mobile handset, personal digital assistance, or any other communication devices or computer networks. In the event of the said subscribers, intermediaries or persons in-charge of computer resources being called upon by the designated agency to extend all facilities and technical assistance to intercept, monitor or decrypt information there are chances that such group of subscribers, intermediaries or persons in-charge of computer resources may not be in a position to extend the said facilities and technical assistance. Penalizing the said failure to do so is a very harsh step and is likely to become a contentious bed of issues, as time passes by.

Further, such a provision under the law is likely to be potentially far more misused than any other specific provisions detailed under section 69 of the amended Information Technology Act, 2000.

It will be very important that the procedures and safeguards, subject to which such interception, monitoring or decryption may be carried out as referred to under section 69(2), be made, as far as possible, most comprehensive and detailed so as to potentially rule out any potential misuses of section 69 of the Information Technology Act, 2000. Further, the said procedures and safeguards need to be detailed, keeping in mind not just the requirements of national security and sovereignty of India but also of the capacity and capability of these subscribers, intermediaries or persons in-charge of computer resources to extend all facilities and technical assistance to intercept, monitor or decrypt information, as the case may be.

The problem arises because of the usage of the word "all facilities and technical assistance" as detailed under section 69(3). The word "all facilities and technical assistance" is an absolute and all encompassing phrase, which does not fall in the admit of any exceptions.

Had the law talked about all available or reasonable facilities or technical assistance then the situation may have been different. However, with the current law stipulating the need for the subscriber, intermediary or person in-charge of computer resources to extend all facilities and technical assistance to intercept, monitor or decrypt information, there are going to be a lot of challenges, as one examines the practical implementation of section 69 in the times to come.

Section 69A of the Information Technology Act, 2000

> ***"Section 69A. Power to issue directions for blocking for public access of any information through any computer resource.***—*(1) Where the Central Government or any of its officer specially authorised by it in this behalf is satisfied that it is necessary or expedient so to do in the interest of sovereignty and integrity of India, defence of India, security of the State, friendly relations with foreign States or public order or for preventing incitement to the commission of any cognizable offence relating to above, it may subject to the provisions of sub-section (2), for reasons to be recorded in writing, by order, direct any agency of the Government or intermediary to block for access by the public or cause to be blocked for access by the public any information generated, transmitted, received, stored or hosted in any computer resource.*
>
> *(2) The procedure and safeguards subject to which such blocking for access by the public may be carried out, shall be such as may be prescribed.*
>
> *(3) The intermediary who fails to comply with the direction issued under sub-section (1) shall be punished with an imprisonment for a term which may extend to seven years and also be liable to fine."*

Section 69A has been added in the Information Technology Act, 2000 by the Information Technology (Amendment) Act, 2008. Section 69A is dedicated to this subject of issuing directions for blocking for public access of any information through any computer resource.

This is for the first time that blocking as a phenomenon has been addressed under the Information Technology Act, 2000. It may be pertinent to point out that in the Information Technology Act, 2000, blocking was not specifically mentioned. Consequently the Ministry of Information Technology, Department of Information Technology issued the Gazette Notification (Extra-ordinary) number G. S. R. 181(E) dated 27th February, 2003. By means of the said notification, Computer Emergency Response Team of India (CERT-IN) had been designated as the single authority for issuance of instructions in the context of blocking of websites.

Thereafter, the Ministry of Communication and Information Technology, Department of Information Technology, Government of India also published another Gazette Notification bearing number G. S. R. 529(E), dated 7 July, 2003 with the subject "Procedure for Blocking of Websites". By means of the said gazette notification, the detailed procedure for blocking of website was detailed.

The said procedure of blocking of websites was resorted to from 2003 onwards for a variety of purposes and circumstances. However, the Legislature felt that there was a need for providing for specific legislative provisions on blocking. Consequently, section 69A was inserted in the Information Technology Act, 2000.

By virtue of section 69A, the power to issue directions for blocking for public access of any information through any computer resource has now been specifically stipulated in the hands of the Central Government or any of its officers specially authorized by it in this behalf. Thus, by virtue of section 69 A, the provisions of this section have precedence over the notifications dated 27th February, 2003 and 7th July, 2003.

Before directing blocking of access by the public of any information generated, transmitted, received, stored or hosted in any computer resource, the Central Government or its officer has to be satisfied that the said blocking is necessary or expedient so to do. Further, the satisfaction has to be to the effect that the blocking is necessary or expedient so to do in the interest of the following:

- ✓ Sovereignty and integrity of India,
- ✓ Defence of India,
- ✓ Security of the State,
- ✓ Friendly relations with foreign States,
- ✓ Public order,
- ✓ For preventing incitement to the commission of any cognizable offence relating to the above.

If the Central Government is satisfied that it is necessary to block in the interest of any of the aforesaid parameters, it has been granted the discretion to order to direct any agency of the government or intermediary to block for access by the public any information generated, transmitted, received, stored or hosted in any computer resource. Needless to state, the said blocking must be in writing and it must record reasons why blocking is being permitted. Further, the order of blocking has to be subject to the provisions of section 69A(2) of the Information Technology Act, 2000. The order of blocking could also direct any agency of the government or intermediary not only to block for access granted by the public or even caused to be blocked for access by the public, any information generated, transmitted, received, stored or hosted in any computer resource.

Section 69A(2) provides that the procedures and safeguards, subject to which such blocking for access by the public may be carried out, shall be such as may be specified by the Central Government. At the time of writing, no such procedures or safeguards relating to the subject at hand have yet been specified. Needless to state, the said procedures and safeguards must be elaborately detailed and reduced on paper and further must be stringently implemented. This is absolutely essential not just to limit the potential misuse of this provision and power of blocking but also to enhance the confidence of the people and the users at large, with the proposed regime of blocking. It will go well if the Central Government consults with all relevant stake-holders before detailing and specifying the procedures and safeguards that need to be adopted, subject to which such blocking for access by the public may be carried out.

Section 69A(3) creates a new offence. The intermediary who fails to comply with the directions of blocking as given under section 69A of the Information Technology Act, 2000 commits an offence. The said offence is punishable with imprisonment for a term which may extend to 7 years and shall also be liable to fine. Thus, a very serious, heinous crime has been created by section 69A(3). It will be the mandatory responsibility of the intermediary, once directed to block for access by the public or cause to be blocked for access by the public, any information, to ensure that the said information be blocked forthwith. Failure to comply with the direction of blocking will invite imprisonment for a term which would extend to 7 years as also to fine. Needless to say, if the intermediary is a company, the provisions of section 85 of the Information Technology Act, 2000 shall come into force. If the offences under section 69A(3) is committed by a company, every person, who at the time the contravention was committed, was in-charge of and was responsible to the intermediary company for the conduct of the business of the company as well as the intermediary company, shall be guilty of the said contravention and shall be liable to be proceeded against and punished accordingly.

Section 69A provides an important tool in the arsenal of the government to deal with undesirable information which is generated, transmitted, received, stored and hosted in any computer resource in India. The said power shall be an important power for assisting the Government of India in meeting various challenges, as time passes. History has shown that blocking has not necessarily always been effective or successful. In the past, in various instances, whenever the government would block or direct the blocking of particular website, the said website would find that its traffic has dramatically increased because of the curiosity of the people to know why the said blocking is ordered and what specific content lies on the said website. Further, given the inherent nature, architecture and character of the Internet, it is always possible to go and access the said information or website that is blocked from indirect means. Further, it needs to be appreciated that blocking of any website at best is only a phenomenon that is effective within the territorial boundaries of India. The same does not apply to any Internet Service Providers or Intermediaries which are located outside the physical boundaries of India.

As such, the efficacy of blocking any specific information needs to be reassessed and re-examined. However, nonetheless it can still be stated that the power to block and the consequent blocking of information generated, transmitted, received, stored or hosted in any computer resource, still is an important significant, power in the weaponry of any sovereign nation in its fight against the challenges raised by undesirable information generated, transmitted, received, stored or hosted in any computer resource.

Section 69B of the amended Information Technology Act, 2000

"Section 69B. Power to authorise to monitor and collect traffic data or information through any computer resource for cyber security.—*(1) The Central Government may, to enhance cyber security and for identification, analysis and prevention of intrusion or spread of computer contaminant in the country, by notification in the Official Gazette, authorise any agency of the Government to monitor and collect traffic data or information generated, transmitted, received or stored in any computer resource.*

(2) The intermediary or any person in-charge or the computer resource shall, when called upon by the agency which has been authorised under sub-section (1), provide technical assistance and extend all facilities to such agency to enable online access or to secure and provide online access to the computer resource generating, transmitting, receiving or storing such traffic data or information.

(3) The procedure and safeguards for monitoring and collecting traffic data or information, shall be such as may be prescribed.

(4) Any intermediary who intentionally or knowingly contravenes the provisions of sub-section (2) shall be punished with an imprisonment for a term which may extend to three years and shall also be liable to fine.

Explanation.—For the purposes of this section,—

(i) "computer contaminant" shall have the meaning assigned to it in section 43;

(ii) "traffic data" means any data identifying or purporting to identify any person, computer system or computer network or location to or from which the communication is or may be transmitted and includes communications origin, destination, route, time, data, size, duration or type of underlying service and any other information."

Section 69B has been added in the Information Technology Act, 2000 by the Information Technology (Amendment) Act, 2008. Section 69B has been added for the purposes of enhancing cyber security of India and for the purposes of identification, analysis and prevention of intrusion or spread of computer contaminants in the country. Section 69B refers to the concept of "traffic data" and its monitoring and collection.

At the very outset, it is important to see and examine the concept of "traffic data".

Explanation to section 69B clearly gives a definition of the term "traffic data". As per the said *Explanation*, "traffic data" basically means any data identifying any data which:

(a) Is identifying any person, computer system or computer network or location to or from which the communication is or may be transmitted;

(b) Any data which is purporting to identify any person, computer system or computer network or location to or from which the communication is or may be transmitted.

Further, as per the said definition the term "traffic data" includes the following:

- ✓ Communication origin,
- ✓ Destination,
- ✓ Route,
- ✓ Time,
- ✓ Data/date,
- ✓ Size,
- ✓ Duration of underlying service,
- ✓ Type of underlying service, or
- ✓ Any other information.

Thus, the concept of "traffic data" is all encompassing and includes all kinds of data which is used either for identifying or to identify any specific person, computer system or computer network. Such traffic data is further used to identify any location to or from which, the communication is or may be transmitted. The significance of traffic data for protecting the sovereignty and integrity of any nation, can hardly be overestimated. Traffic data gives the vital signals and information to the law enforcement agencies, who are investigating various contraventions and challenges to national security and cyber security of any nation. In the context of India, traffic data assumes tremendous significance, given the huge challenges to national security and cyber security that India is currently facing. Over the last few years, India has seen various amounts of criminal activities and attacks which are targeted at not just undermining the sovereignty and integrity of India as also the security of the State and friendly relations with other nations. Further, such attacks on Indian national security and cyber security are aimed to destabilize the nation and further negatively impact public order.

Thus, in order to meet with the challenges raised by cyber criminals and cyber terrorists, law enforcement agencies require traffic data for the purposes of not just proactively taking steps to protect the national security and cyber security of India but also to specifically rely upon them in instances where cyber crimes and crimes against nation are being investigated against cyber criminals and cyber terrorists.

In that particular scenario, traffic data assumes tremendous significance since that is the crucial and relevant link through which, the concerned cyber criminal/cyber terrorist is linked to the crime.

It is pertinent to note that the earlier Information Technology Act, 2000 did not talk anything about traffic data. However, the concept of traffic data has been taken by India from the Council of Europe's Convention on Cybercrime where such concept has been more elaborately detailed.

Council of Europe's Convention on Cybercrime has underlined its treaty position relating to traffic data in the following term:

"Article 1(d) – Traffic data

28. For the purposes of this Convention traffic data as defined in article 1, under sub-paragraph (d), is a category of computer data that is subject to a specific legal regime. This data is generated by computers in the chain of communication in order to route a communication from its origin to its destination. It is therefore auxiliary to the communication itself.

29. In case of an investigation of a criminal offence committed in relation to a computer system, traffic data is needed to trace the source of a communication as a starting point for collecting further evidence or as part of the evidence of the offence. Traffic data might last only ephemerally, which makes it necessary to order its expeditious preservation. Consequently, its rapid disclosure may be necessary to discern the communication's route in order to collect further evidence before it is deleted or to identify a suspect. The ordinary procedure for the collection and disclosure of computer data might therefore be insufficient. Moreover, the collection of this data is regarded in principle to be less intrusive since as such it doesn't reveal the content of the communication which is regarded to be more sensitive.

30. The definition lists exhaustively the categories of traffic data that are treated by a specific regime in this Convention: the origin of a communication, its destination, route, time (GMT), date, size, duration and type of underlying service. Not all of these categories will always be technically available, capable of being produced by a service provider, or necessary for a particular criminal investigation. The "origin" refers to a telephone number, Internet Protocol (IP) address, or similar identification of a communications facility to which a service provider renders services. The "destination" refers to a comparable indication of a communications facility to which communications are transmitted. The term "type of underlying service" refers to the type of service that is being used within the network, *e.g.*, file transfer, electronic mail, or instant messaging.

31. The definition leaves to national Legislatures the ability to introduce differentiation in the legal protection of traffic data in accordance with its sensitivity. In this context, article 15 obliges the parties to provide for conditions and safeguards that are adequate for protection of human rights and liberties. This implies, *inter alia*, that the substantive criteria and the procedure to apply an investigative power may vary according to the sensitivity of the data."

The aforesaid treaty position, as detailed in Council of Europe's Convention on Cybercrimes, elaborates the concept of "traffic data" and how the same may be dealt with, by national legislations, of nations who are signatories of the said Convention on Cybercrimes.

Section 69B of the amended Information Technology Act, 2000 gives the discretion to Central Government to notify in the Official Gazette and authorize any agency of the Government, to monitor and collect traffic data or information generated, transmitted, received or stored in any computer resource. The said discretion can be exercised to enhance cyber security of India as also for identification, analysis and prevention of intrusion or spread of computer contaminants in the country. Any agency of the Government could be authorized by notification in the Official Gazette by the Central Government to monitor and collect traffic data or information generated, transmitted, received or stored in any computer resource.

The said agency of the Government, which is so authorized by the Central Government has been given the powers to call upon any legal entity in India to provide technical assistance pertaining to monitoring and collection of traffic data or information generated, transmitted, received or stored in a computer resource. Further, the said agency has been given the powers to call upon any person in-charge of a computer resource or any intermediary to extend all facilities to such agency for the following purposes:

(a) To enable online access, or

(b) To secure and provide online access to the computer resource generating, transmitting, receiving or storing such traffic data or information.

Once, the authorized agency of the Government so directs the intermediary or any other person in-charge of a computer resource to provide the aforesaid technical assistance and extend all facilities to enable the aforesaid functions, the said intermediary or any person in-charge of a computer resource is duty-bound to provide all technical assistance and extend all facilities to such agency for the aforesaid purposes. Providing technical assistance and extending all facilities to such authorized agency for the aforesaid purposes is the mandatory duty of an intermediary or any person in-charge of a computer resource. Further, duty is of very stringent nature. Any intermediary who intentionally and knowingly contravenes such a duty gets exposed to criminal liability. Such intermediary, who intentionally or knowingly contravenes such a duty, shall be punished with imprisonment for a term which may extend to 3 years and shall also be liable to fine.

Further, the procedure and safeguards for monitoring and collecting traffic data or information shall be such as may be prescribed by the Central Government.

At the time of writing no such safeguards or procedures for monitoring and collecting the traffic data or information have been prescribed. Section 69B becomes an important ammunition in the arsenal of the Republic of India to fight potential challenges to its national security, integrity and sovereignty. Section 69 becomes an important foundation through which the Central Government aims to enhance cyber security of India and further aims to identify, analyze and prevent intrusion or spread of computer contaminants in the country.

The *Explanation* to section 69B defines the term "computer contaminant" to the effect that the said term shall have the same meaning as assigned to it under section 43 of the Information Technology Act, 2000.

Explanation I to section 43 states that the term "computer contaminant" means any set of computer instructions that are designed—

(a) To modify, destroy, record, transmit data or programme residing within a computer, computer system or computer network; or

(b) By any means to usurp the normal operations of the computer, computer system or computer network.

The definition of the term "computer contaminant" under section 43 of the Information Technology Act, 2000 is very vast and includes all kinds of computer malware, spyware and other computer contaminants which may evolve with the passage of time. The said definition of the term "computer contaminant" is indeed of a futuristic nature and is likely to be of tremendous assistance to India as it proceeds ahead in its fight against computer contaminants and to further protect and preserve the cyber security of India as also the sovereignty, integrity and security of India.

Given the huge growth in the adoption of iPads, Tablets, Smart Phones and Smart Devices in India, mobile traffic data assumes tremendous significance as per one study, India Mobile Data Traffic Growing Fastest in the World[61]. As per this study, it is projected that India has the highest country mobile data traffic growth rate of any country, with a CAGR of 222% from 2009 to 2014. The study says that annual global mobile data traffic will reach 3.6 exabytes per month or an annual run rate of 40 exabytes by 2014. Such a figure equates to a 39-fold increase from 2009 to 2014, or a CAGR of 108%.

All the aforedetailed mobile traffic data would be fully covered within the ambit of section 69B of the amended Information Technology Act, 2000.

Section 70A of the amended Information Technology Act, 2000

> *"**Section 70A. National nodal agency.**—(1) The Central Government may, by notification published in the Official Gazette, designate any organisation of the Government as the national nodal agency in respect of Critical Information Infrastructure Protection.*
>
> *(2) The national nodal agency designated under sub-section (1) shall be responsible for all measures including Research and Development relating to protection of Critical Information Infrastructure.*
>
> *(3) The manner of performing functions and duties of the agency referred to in sub-section (1) shall be such as may be prescribed."*

Since, mobile infrastructure including mobile networks are important critical aspects for not just the security and stability of India but also for the purposes of Indian economy and all sectors and communication, the Central Government has decided to come up with the concept of a National Nodal Agency. By means of the amendments to the Information Technology Act, 2000 as amended by the

61. http://www.secondrepublic.in/StoryDescription.aspx?mainid=1&storyid=762.

Information Technology (Amendment) Act, 2008, the Central Government has created the concept of a National Nodal Agency. The said Nodal Agency shall be with respect to critical information infrastructure protection. Under section 70A, the Central Government has reserved upon itself, the discretion to notify, by publishing in the Official Gazette, any organization of the Government to be the National Nodal Agency in respect of critical information infrastructure protection.

The said agency shall be responsible for all aspects for the protection, preservation and security of the national critical information infrastructure. This will be such critical information infrastructure, which is critical for the country as a whole and also for its various sovereign functions. The said National Nodal Agency shall be responsible for all steps, measures and acts that need to be done or taken relating to protection of critical information infrastructure of India. The said Nodal Agency has also been burdened with the responsibility of ensuring research and development in respect of critical information infrastructure. The Central Government has further reserved upon itself, the power to prescribe the manner of performing, functions and duties of the said National Nodal Agency.

Considering the fact that today mobile networks are extremely relevant for the purposes of communication and also form the lifeline of Indian economy, protecting mobile networks and related infrastructure pertaining to the same would be a bigger priority for any Government and India is no exception. As such, the concept of National Nodal Agency in the perspective of the mobile networks as critical information infrastructure of India, becomes all the more relevant.

Section 72A of the amended Information Technology Act, 2000

> *"Section 72A. **Punishment for disclosure of information in breach of lawful contract.**—Save as otherwise provided in this Act or any other law for the time being in force, any person including an intermediary who, while providing services under the terms of lawful contract, has secured access to any material containing personal information about another person, with the intent to cause or knowing that he is likely to cause wrongful loss or wrongful gain discloses, without the consent of the person concerned, or in breach of a lawful contract, such material to any other person, shall be punished with imprisonment for a term which may extend to three years, or with fine which may extend to five lakh rupees, or with both."*

Since the last one decade, India has seen tremendous growth in the area of outsourcing. Though outsourcing in India began in the form transcription in call centers, it soon transformed itself to higher levels of Business Process Outsourcing, Legal Process Outsourcing and Medical Process Outsourcing. The said outsourcing industry has acted as a boost for the Indian economy. However, the said outsourcing sectors have also seen various outages of third party data belonging to foreign clients. Hence, there has been a tremendous need to protect third party data and also misuse of information in breach of a lawful contract. As such, the Indian Legislature has been alive to the said issue and have therefore included section 72A under the Information Technology Act, 2000. The said section 72A has been added by virtue of the Information Technology (Amendment) Act, 2008.

The said provision makes an offence for the act of disclosing information in breach of a lawful contract. Today, a large number of service providers and intermediaries have access to material containing personal information about other persons, clients and customers access to material is achieved during the course of providing services, under the terms of the lawful contract. We have also seen various instances where service providers and intermediaries have gone ahead and misused the said personal information about other persons. This is often done in breach of a lawful contract that would exist between the said intermediary and its customers. In order to prevent such action happening, the law has now stipulated a crime as detailed under section 72A. If any person, including an intermediary, is providing services under the terms of a lawful contract, he is obligated to abide with the terms of the lawful contract. Further, if during the factum of providing services under the said lawful contract, any person, including the intermediary, has secured access to any material which contains personal information about other person and the said access has been done with the intention to cause or knowing that is likely to cause wrongful loss or gain and further thereto, the said person, including the intermediary, discloses such material to any other person without the consent of the person concerned or in breach of a lawful contract, then the said act has been made an offence punishable. The said offence is punishable with imprisonment for a term, which may extend to 3 years or with fine which may extend to 5 lakh rupees or with both. The purpose of section 72A is to provide deterrence for all persons including intermediaries who have, while providing services under the terms of a lawful contraet, secured access to material containing personal information about third parties. The said persons, including intermediaries, are duty bound to protect and preserve the authenticity and veracity of the said personal information about third parties. If the said persons do not choose to protect and preserve the said information but with an intention to cause or knowing that there are likely to cause wrongful loss or gain further disclose such personal information to any other person, without the consent of the person concerned or in breach of the lawful contract, then the said act comes within the ambit of criminal penalty.

The said provision shall be extremely relevant for the purposes of the Indian outsourcing industry. It will also be relevant for checking the misuse of personal data done by service providers who invariably, while collecting personal data for the purposes of providing services for the customers, land up sharing the said personal data with other business partners. Today invariably, typically are bombarded with various phone calls on our iPads, Tablets, Smart Phones and Smart Devices asking us to buy certain insurance policies or take certain loans. The said acts are primarily done as our data, including personal information pertaining to our iPads, Tablets, Smart Phones and Smart Devices, is shared by our service provider with other third party business partners with or without consideration.

However, by the mere sharing of the said third party information and by further making such calls, there is an intention to cause and knowing that the said service provider is likely to cause wrongful loss to customers. Further, the service providers do share the said data with their business partners and that they do so for the purposes of causing wrongful gain. Section 72A promises to be a huge potent weapon in the hands of the lay consumers, who can use it against erring service providers and other legal entities who disclose information about them without their permission, to other third parties with an intention to cause or knowing that the same is likely to cause wrongful loss or wrongful gain.

At the time of writing, section 72A has not been invoked in the context of the mobile ecosystem in India. However, it is only a question of time when the said provision becomes fully enforceable in the context of the iPads, Tablets, Smart Phones and Smart Devices and connected mobile ecosystem. I distinctly believe that if section 72A is interpreted properly and is effectively implemented, the misuse of personal information by any persons including intermediaries and its disclosure to unauthorized third parties is likely to be substantially reduced. It is interesting to see how the actual working of section 72A of the amended Information Technology Act, 2000 will pan out in the coming times.

Section 77A of the amended Information Technology Act, 2000

*"**Section 77A. Compounding of Offences.**—A court of competent jurisdiction may compound offences, other than offences for which the punishment for life or imprisonment for a term exceeding three years has been provided, under this Act:*

Provided that the court shall not compound such offence where the accused is, by reason of his previous conviction, liable to either enhanced punishment or to a punishment of a different kind:

Provided further that the court shall not compound any offence where such offence affects the socio-economic conditions of the country or has been committed against a child below the age of 18 years or a woman.

(2) The person accused of an offence under this Act may file an application for compounding in the court in which offence is pending for trial and the provisions of sections 265B and 265C of the Code of Criminal Procedure, 1973 shall apply."

Section 77A has been added by virtue of the Information Technology (Amendment) Act, 2008. This section has provided for exit from potential legal consequences for the concerned stake-holders. It also provides an important remedy for closure of legal cases where the main dispute between the parties has been long compromised.

It has been seen as a practice experience amongst criminal courts that criminal cases, after registration goes on for trial for years and years and a lot of inconvenience and harassment is caused to the persons who are involved in the same, even if the said persons are involved in the same either erroneously or wrongfully.

As such, section 77A has now provided for the concept of compounding of offences. The power for compounding offences has been given to court of competent jurisdiction. Of course, the limitation is that only such offences can be compounded which are punishable only with imprisonment for a term upto three years. This effectively means that all offences which are punishable with imprisonment for a term exceeding three years have been specifically exempted and brought outside the ambit of compounding of offences.

It is important to note that the discretion that has been given to the court of competent jurisdiction for compounding is complete, absolute and unfettered. However, the proviso to section 77A clearly says that the said court shall not compound any such offence where the accused has already been convicted earlier and is liable to be punished with enhanced management or to a punishment of a different kind.

The second proviso to section 77A clearly shows that the court shall also not compound any offences, which affect the social, economic conditions of the country. Further, the offences, ,which have been committed against a child below the age of 18 years or women, have also been exempted from the ambit of compounding of offences and hence the said offences cannot be compounded.

No automatic compounding of offences can take place under the amended Information Technology Act, 2000. Any person who is accused of an offence under the Information Technology Act, 2000 has been given the option to file an application for compounding of offence. The application for compounding the offence has to be filed in the same court, in which the offence is pending for trial. In that regard, once the said application is filed, the Information Technology Act, 2000 has provided that the provisions of section 265B and 265C of the Code of Criminal Procedure, 1973 shall apply.

It is pertinent to note that by virtue of operation of section 81 of the Information Technology Act, 2000, the provisions of the Information Technology Act, 2000 shall have overriding effect notwithstanding anything inconsistent therewith contained in any other law for the time being in force.

Thus, seen from a holistic perspective, section 77A does provide a very effective remedy for closure of criminal cases, being registered under the Information Technology Act, 2000 to the extent that the same are only punishable with imprisonment for a term which does not exceed three years. It is pertinent to note that a majority of cybercrimes including those that have been inserted into the Information Technology Act, 2000 by the Information Technology (Amendment) Act, 2008 have been made punishable with three years' imprisonment. These crimes include the following:

(a) Tampering of computer source documents under section 65B of the Information Technology Act, 2000.

(b) Computer-related offences under section 66 of the Information Technology Act, 2000.

(c) The offences of sending offensive messages through communication devices under section 66A of the Information Technology Act, 2000.

(d) The offence of dishonestly receiving stolen computer resource or communication device under section 66B of the Information Technology Act, 2000.

(e) The offence of identity theft under section 66C of the Information Technology Act, 2000.

(f) The offence of cheating by personation by using computer resource under section 66D of the Information Technology Act, 2000.

(g) The offence for violation of privacy under section 66E of the Information Technology Act, 2000.

(h) The first conviction for the offence of publishing or transmitting of obscene electronic information under section 67 of the Information Technology Act, 2000.

(i) The offence of the failure of the intermediary to preserve and retain such information under section 67C (1) of the Information Technology Act, 2000.

(j) The offence of intermediary in knowingly or intentionally not providing technical assistance to the concerned agency for cyber security under section 69B of the Information Technology Act, 2000.

(k) The offence under section 70B(7) for the failure of the service provider and intermediary to provide the information as required by CERT-IN.

(l) The offence of making misrepresentation to the Controller of Certifying Authorities under section 71 of the Information Technology Act, 2000.

(m) The offence of breach of confidentiality of privacy under section 72 of the Information Technology Act, 2000.

(n) The offence for disclosure of information and breach of lawful contract under section 72A of the Information Technology Act, 2000.

(o) The offence of publishing electronic signature certificate false in certain particulars under section 73 of the Information Technology Act, 2000.

(p) The publication of electronic signature certificates for fraudulent purposes under section 74 of the Information Technology Act, 2000.

Thus, almost a majority of cybercrimes covered under the amended Information Technology Act, 2000, have been brought within the ambit and applicability of compounding of offences. The only major offences which cannot be compounded relate to direct offences as defined under the amended Information Technology Act, 2000, including the following:

(a) The second conviction for publishing or transmission of obscene electronic information under section 67 of the Information Technology Act, 2000.

(b) The offence of publishing or transmitting of material containing sexually explicit act or conduct in electronic form, under section 67E of the Information Technology Act, 2000.

(c) The offence of publishing or transmission of material depicting children in sexually explicit act or conduct in the electronic form, under section 67B of the Information Technology Act, 2000.

(d) The offence of the subscriber or the intermediary failing to assist the agency in interception monitoring or decryption of information under section 69(4) of the Information Technology Act, 2000.

(e) The offence of intermediary failing to comply with the directions for blocking for public access under section 69A of the Information Technology Act, 2000.

(f) The offence of breach of protected system under section 72(3) of the Information Technology Act, 2000.

(g) The offence of Cyber terrorism under section 66F of the Information Technology Act, 2000.

Thus, from the aforesaid lists, it is very clear that a majority of the cybercrimes under the amended Information Technology Act, 2000 including all kinds of mobile crimes, have been brought within the ambit of compounding of offences. The author distinctly believes that with the passage of time, such kinds of provisions will help far more people to come out of the rigours of such cyber crimes and mobilecrimes, as time passes by.

Section 77B of the amended Information Technology Act, 2000

"Section 77B. Offences with three years' imprisonment to be bailable.—*Notwithstanding anything contained in the Code of Criminal Procedure, 1973, (2 of 1974) the offence punishable with imprisonment of three years and above shall be cognizable and the offence punishable with imprisonment of three years shall be bailable."*

The Indian Information Technology Act, 2000 as amended, has provided for a departure in terms of its approach pertaining to various cybercrimes and mobile crimes. Section 77B specifically provides that all offences and cyber crimes including mobilecrimes, which are made punishable with three years' imprisonment under the Information Technology Act, 2000, shall be bailable offences. This has been so prescribed, notwithstanding anything contained in the Code of Criminal Procedure, 1973. Further, it has been provided that only the offence which is punishable with imprisonment of three years and above, shall become cognizable. This effectively means that for all offences punishable with three years' imprisonment, the accused shall be entitled to bail as a matter of right. Such a scenario is not necessarily conducive for the effective deterrence of cyber crimes and mobile crimes. This is invariably so because the moment the accused is let out on bail in a bailable offence, the propensity of the accused to go ahead and destroy the concerned incriminating electronic evidence which is not yet been recovered, is extremely high and as such an exercise invariably tends to impede the effective investigation of any cyber crimes and mobile crimes. This further ultimately impacts the conviction rate of the prosecution in terms of prosecuting the said cyber crimes and mobile crimes. There are demerits in the approach adopted by section 77B of the amendment Information Technology Act, 2000. This becomes all the more highlighted when one considers that at the time of writing, there are only couple of cyber crime convictions under the Information Technology Act, 2000 in India, even after the decade of the operation of the Indian Cyberlaw.

Section 78 of the amended Information Technology Act, 2000

"Section 78. Power to investigate offences.—*Notwithstanding anything contained in the Code of Criminal Procedure, 1973 (2 of 1974), a police officer not below the rank of an Inspector shall investigate any offence under this Act."*

Section 78 has been amended by the Information Technology (Amendment) Act, 2008. Earlier, the power to investigate all offences under the Information Technology Act, 2000 were granted to a police officer, not below the rank of Deputy Superintendent of Police. However, over a period of time, it was found that the police officers of the rank of Deputy Superintendent of Police did not invariably have the time or the bandwidth to investigate various offences as detailed under the Information Technology Act, 2000. Consequently, by virtue of the 2008 amendments, section 78 has been amended to provide that the police officer not below the rank of an Inspector shall investigate any offence under the Information Technology Act, 2000. This has been done, notwithstanding anything contained in the Code of Criminal Procedure, 1973. The net effect of this is that all kinds of mobile crimes which are stipulated and specifically covered under the amended Information Technology Act, 2000 can only be investigated by an Inspector and no one else. The efficacy of such a step is doubtful considering the fact that majority of inspectors are not very well conversant with the nuances and technical details pertaining to the working of mobiles, iPads, Tablets, Smart Phones and Smart Devices as also mobile networks and mobile data. Further, the said Inspectors also do not have the wherewithal, knowledge, awareness and tools so as to effectively detect, investigate and prosecute mobile crimes including seizing appropriate mobile evidence resident on communication devices. Clearly, the said step is not likely to contribute to the efficient detection, investigation and prosecution of mobile crimes and cyber crimes under the amended Information Technology Act, 2000.

Service providers & their liability

Section 79 of the Information Technology Act, 2000

"Section 79. Exemption from liability of intermediary in certain cases.— *(1) Notwithstanding anything contained in any law for the time being in force but subject to the provisions of sub-sections (2) and (3), an intermediary shall not be liable for any third party information, data, or communication link made available or hosted by him.*

(2) The provisions of sub-section (1) shall apply if—

(a) the function of the intermediary is limited to providing access to a communication system over which information made available by third parties is transmitted or temporarily stored or hosted; or

(b) the intermediary does not—

(i) initiate the transmission,

(ii) select the receiver of the transmission, and

(iii) select or modify the information contained in the transmission;

(c) the intermediary observes due diligence while discharging his duties under this Act and also observes such other guidelines as the Central Government may prescribe in this behalf.

(3) The provisions of sub-section (1) shall not apply if—

(a) *the intermediary has conspired or abetted or aided or induced, whether by threats or promise or otherwise in the commission of the unlawful act;*

(b) *upon receiving actual knowledge, or on being notified by the appropriate Government or its agency that any information, data or communication link residing in or connected to a computer resource controlled by the intermediary is being used to commit the unlawful act, the intermediary fails to expeditiously remove or disable access to that material on that resource without vitiating the evidence in any manner.*

Explanation.—For the purpose of this section, the expression "third party information" means any information dealt with by an intermediary in his capacity as an intermediary."

Section 79 is the solitary Section that appears in the Chapter-XII entitled *"Intermediaries Not To Be Liable In Certain Cases."* The said section deals with the exemption from liability of intermediaries in certain cases.

Section 79 is the solitary section, which stipulates the exposure of liability of intermediaries. These intermediaries would also include mobile service providers and mobile value added service providers. These intermediaries further have been made liable for third party data.

Section 79 states the liability of all intermediaries including mobile service providers and mobile value added service providers as well telecom service providers. This provision is an absolute provision and overrides anything inconsistent therewith, contained in any other law for the time being in force. However, section 79(1) is subject to the provisions of section 79(2) & (3). By and large, the Legislature has made legal proposition that a mobile intermediary or telecom service provider or mobile value added service provider shall not be liable for any third party information, data or communication link made available or hosted by him.

It is pertinent to point out that the term "third party information" has been defined in the *Explanation* to section 79, which states "third party information" means any information dealt with by an intermediary in his capacity as an intermediary.

It is pertinent to note that the term "information" has been defined under section 2(1)(v) of the amended Information Technology Act, 2000.

Section 79 of the amended Information Technology Act, 2000 is also applicable in the context of all kinds of mobile operators. This is specifically so, given definition of the term "intermediary". It may be submitted that section 2(1)(w) of the amended Information Technology Act, 2000 have defined the term "intermediary", with respect to any particular electronic records, to mean any person who, on behalf of another person receives, stores or transmits that record or to provide any service with respect to that record and includes specifically telecom service providers. Thus, all kinds of mobile service providers, mobile value added service providers, telecom service providers and telecom operators would clearly qualify within the ambit of the definition of the term "intermediary". Thus, any service provider of any kind whatsoever, whether direct or indirect, whose services are provided on a mobile platform or which is available using communication devices or mobile network would also qualify to be an "intermediary" within the meaning of section 2(1)(w) of the amended Information Technology Act, 2000. It may be submitted that today, a large number of value added services are being provided by various service providers as also by content service providers. The value-added services are providing various value additions for effective and more productive use of communication devices. All the service providers of the said mobile, iPad, Tablet, Smart Phone and Smart Device services will also be covered within the ambit of the term "intermediary".

Mobile service provider, being an intermediary, shall, as a principle, not be liable for any third party information, data or communication link made available or hosted by him. This, of course, subject to the provisions that are contained under section 79(2) & (3) of the amended Information Technology Act, 2000.

Of particular significance for mobile service providers and telecom service providers is a need for them to ensure compliance with the requirements of section 79(2) & (3) of the amended Information Technology Act, 2000. The said intermediary will not be liable if the three conditions stipulated under section 79(2) of the amended Information Technology Act, 2000 are fulfilled.

The following conditions must be complied with, by the mobile service providers, including telecom service providers and telecom operators, before they can think of complete exemption from liability for any third party information, data or communication link made available or hosted by them. These conditions are as follows:

(1) The first important condition is that the functional role of the mobile service provider, telecom service provider and telecom operator, in its capacity as an intermediary, is only limited to providing access to a communication system, over which information made available by third party is transmitted or temporarily stored or hosted. In the context of iPads, Tablets, Smart Phones and Smart Devices, the said communication systems would be the mobile networks as also the mobile platforms and mobile internet over which the information made available by third parties is transmitted or temporally stored, or hosted. The said communication system could also include mobile servers and mobile servers farms, over which information made available by third parties, is transmitted or temporally stored or hosted.

    Thus, the only focus that the mobile intermediary has to ensure is that its function is limited to providing access communication systems. The law does not stipulate that it needs to own or have any proprietary rights over the said communication system. The law does not even talk about the various licensing requirements in this regard. How the access is provided to the communication system by the intermediary is also not the concern of the law. The intermediary must only limit its role solely to providing access to communication system over which information made available by third parties is transmitted or temporally stored or hosted.

(2) The second important condition is that the mobile service provider, telecom service provider and telecom operator, does not have any control over the transmission. Thus, the said mobile service provider should not:

(a) Initiate the transmission,

(b) Select the receiver of the transmission, and

(c) Select or modify the information contained in the transmission.

(3) The third condition that needs to be complied with by any mobile service provider, telecom service provider and telecom operator is the fact that they, in their capacity, as an intermediary, observe due diligence, while discharging their duties, under the Information Technology Act, 2000 as also observes such other guidelines as the Central Government may prescribe in this regard.

The law still does not define what specifically is "due diligence". The Supreme Court has determined the test of due diligence from the perspective of a reasonable man. The test of a reasonable man does assume tremendous significance. What a reasonable man does in reasonable circumstances could be the relevant test to be applied, when examining and analyzing the scope of "due diligence" done by the mobile service provider, telecom service provider and telecom operator.

(4) The fourth important condition that needs to be complied with by the mobile service provider is the fact that it has, in its capacity as an intermediary, not conspired or abetted or aided or induced, whether by threats or promise or otherwise, in the commission of any unlawful act. Thus, any direct involvement by the mobile service provider in any illegal and unlawful act, is a direct guarantee for the exposure to liability under the Information Technology Act, 2000 for all third party data or information made available by it.

(5) The fifth important condition that needs to be complied with by the mobile service provider is that, upon receiving actual knowledge or upon being notified by the appropriate government or its agency that any information, data or communication link residing in or connected to a computer resource, controlled by the mobile service provider, is being used to commit the unlawful act, the mobile service provider as the intermediary, expeditiously removes or disables access to that material on that resource without vitiating the evidence in any manner whatsoever.

A perusal of the aforesaid conditions primarily show that most of these conditions would be part of the broader due diligence that would be expected to be done by any mobile service provider. Any direct involvement of any kind whatsoever, in the commission of any unlawful act or an offence, would itself be a ground for exposure to liability, both civil and criminal under the provisions of the amended Information Technology Act, 2000. Further, taking proactive action, upon being notified of any contravention, in terms of expeditiously removing or disabling access to the concerned offending material on the mobile networks would be a good ground and methodology, by means of which, mobile service providers can exit from liability from potential legal consequences, both civil and criminal, for various illegal and unlawful acts done using their computer networks and mobile networks.

It is important to note that section 79 of the amended Information Technology Act, 2000 has only become directly applicable to mobile service providers and telecom service operators, specifically ever since the concept of intermediary was introduced and implemented with effect from October 27, 2009. At the time of writing, there have been no reported cases pertaining to the liability of mobile service operators and mobile service providers. This is one area that is likely to be very interesting as time passes by.

Whatever parameters are applicable to the services of the mobile intermediary, have to be duly complied with. In case, if the mobile intermediary does not comply with anyone of the stipulated conditions and terms of the amended Information Technology Act, 2000, it shall be deemed to have not done "due diligence" while discharging his duties under this Act.

It is important to point out that the word "due diligence" has not been defined under the Information Technology Act, 2000.

Due diligence as a concept has been engaging the attention of jurisprudence for a long period of time. However, it is pertinent to note that the law relating to due diligence has developed basically in the context of the actual world and not in relation to the electronic environment or Internet. It goes without saying that a mobile service provider would be providing its services, which are connected with or somehow related to the mobile network, electronic environment and all kinds of perceivable electronic networks. The standards and parameters that are expected of due diligence in the electronic world concerning the e-format, are entirely different in their nature, scope and perspective than the perspectives relating to due diligence in the real world.

At the time of writing, there are no well developed universally recognized standards of due diligence in the mobile, iPads, Tablets, Smart Phones and Smart Devices environment. Another problem is how and in what particular way, would due diligence be judged? Would due diligence be judged in terms of money? For example, would due diligence mean spending of a specified amount of money by an intermediary, in direct proportion to the total volume of business? Or is due diligence going to be judged from standards of technology, as for example requiring a mobile service provider to adopt and use the technological standards as specified by regulation to be an indication of it being duly diligent? Or is due diligence going to be measured in terms of the test of a reasonable man? In the actual world, the test of a reasonable man with reasonable intelligence is a good deciding factor for establishing due diligence. However, we will have difficulties in applying the concept of a reasonable man in context of online/mobile environment. Should the test of a reasonable man be made the touchstone for deciding due diligence of a mobile service provider?

In the actual world, established community behaviour over a number of years and universally accepted standards have refined the test of a reasonable man to mean what a reasonable man with a reasonable mind would do in a particular situation. However, with the coming of the electronic age and environment, we would have difficulties in hand, given the inherent nature of the electronic and mobile, iPads, Tablets, Smart Phones and Smart Devices environments.

For example, a reasonable man would look left and right to ensure that no vehicle is coming, before crossing a road. However, the situations raised by electronic networks are far more complex. Any one situation over the mobile network can result in a number of logical and reasonable responses. As such, it would be difficult to apply the test of a reasonable man in the context of mobile networks.

As such, we are in the shifting sands of emerging technologies and standards. Mobile Law would be called upon to decide what could be "due diligence" that could be expected of a mobile service provider to prevent the commission of any offence or contravention.

Thus, due diligence is a mandatory requirement and essential obligation for the mobile intermediary can seek exemption from liability for third party data and information under the provisions of the amended Information Technology Act.

Pavan Duggal Associates does due diligence for all kinds of mobile service providers and mobile intermediaries.

In addition, the mobile intermediary is also burdened with the responsibility of observing such other guidelines as the Central Government may prescribe in this behalf. If the aforesaid conditions are complied with and subject to the provisions of section 79(3) of the amended Information Technology Act, 2000, the mobile intermediary is not liable for third party information data, or communication link made available by or hosted by him.

Section 79(3) further stipulates the conditions in which the exemption from liability for any third party information, data or communication link made available or hosted by a mobile intermediary would not be applicable. Section 79(3) states that the provision of the section 79(1) shall not apply if any of the two conditions stipulated therein are met. Mobile intermediaries shall continue to be liable for third party information, data or communication link made available or hosted by him if the intermediary has conspired, abetted, aided, induced or whether by threats or promise or otherwise, in the commission of unlawful act. Thus, the moment the intermediary has participated directly or indirectly in the commission of unlawful act, where actively or passively, the exemption from liability for third party information, data or communication link made available or hosted by the mobile intermediary shall not be applicable.

Further, if upon receiving actual knowledge or being notified by the appropriate government or its agencies that any information, data or communication link residing in or connected to computer resource controlled by the intermediary is being used to commit the unlawful act, the mobile intermediary fails to either expeditiously remove or disable access to that material on that the computer resource/mobile network without vitiating the evidence in any manner, the mobile intermediary including mobile service provider, telecom service provider and mobile value added service provider shall continue to be liable for all third party data or information made available by them.

The actual knowledge of the mobile intermediary begins, when any concerned user, subscriber or other person sends a communication in writing or a legal notice of any commission of unlawful act or that any information, data or communication link residing in or connected to computer resource controlled by intermediary is being used to commit the unlawful act. Further, the mobile intermediary can also be notified by the appropriate Government, Central government or State Government or any of its agencies, including law enforcement agencies, of committing of any unlawful act using the information, data or communication link residing in or connected to computer resource controlled by the mobile intermediary. Once, the mobile intermediary has received actual knowledge or have been notified of any provision of an unlawful act, using any data, information or communication link, residing in or connected to computer resource controlled by the intermediary, the intermediary has been mandated to expeditiously act and remove or disable access to the said material on its computer resource. Further, the mobile intermediary has been cast with the mandatory duty of ensuring that while it removes or disables access expeditiously to the offending material on its computer resources and/or mobile networks it does not vitiate the evidence in any manner. In case, if the mobile intermediary is not able to do these mandatory duties, it shall continue to be liable for all third party information, data or communication link made available or hosted by him.

Section 79 is one of those broad sections, which clarifies the law pertaining to exemption from liability of intermediaries in certain cases. In case, if the intermediary is liable, as it fails to comply with the mandatory requirements of the section 79(2) & (3) of the amended Information Technology Act, 2000, it could have exposure to legal consequences, both civil and criminal. The civil consequences could involve being sued for and paying damages by way of compensation up to rupees five crore per contravention as per the summary procedure providing under section 43 of the Information Technology Act, 2000. In addition, if the said contraventions deals with sensitive personal data, and due to the breach of the security of the same, loss is caused to some person, damages by way of compensation could also be awarded against the mobile intermediary under section 43A of the amended Information Technology Act, 2000.

The criminal liability could consist of imprisonment for the top management of the mobile intermediary, which could extent to three years imprisonment and five lakh rupees fine. Further, in case, if the computer resources of the mobile intermediary are being used to commit cyber terrorist act, then the top management of the mobile intermediary could also be exposed to criminal liability under section 66F which consist for life imprisonment and also fine. This is so by virtue of the operation of section 85 of the Information Technology Act, 2000, which stipulates the offence by companies. Normally speaking, mobile service providers, mobile value added service providers and telecom service providers are invariably companies. Whenever offences are done by companies, section 85 of the amended Information Technology Act, 2000 comes into play.

The net effect of section 85 is that where any offence is committed by a company, every person who, at the time of the contravention is committed, was in-charge of and was responsible to the company for the conduct of the business of the company as well as the company shall also be guilty of the said contravention and shall be liable to be proceeded against and punished accordingly. However, the law further provides the exit route for the top management from such exposure to criminal liability in case if every person who, at the time the contravention is committed, was in-charge of and was responsible to the company for the conduct of the business of the company, can prove two things:—

(a) That the contravention took place without his knowledge, or

(b) That he exercised "all due diligence" to prevent such contravention. Here again, the concept of due diligence has been invoked. Of course, under section 85 of the amended Information Technology Act, 2000, the *onus* upon the top management of the mobile intermediary company, is even much more heavier and bigger as the words used are "all due diligence" in section 85 as compared to the words "due diligence" under section 79 of the amended Information Technology Act, 2000.

It is also pertinent to refer to the judgment passed by the Delhi High Court in the case entitled *"Avnish Bajaj* v. *State of Delhi"*. In the said case, the Delhi High Court had held that Baazee.com in its capacity as the intermediary had failed to exercise diligence since its filters were faulty and allowed content that was pornographic in nature to pass through despite the listing itself having of same content and further the said website in its capacity as the intermediary did not account for any changes in its policy to tackle with the possibility of such content being listed on its website in the future. The Court held as follows:—

> "Investigation proves that the MD of Baazee.com[62], who exercised control over the day to day functioning of the organization did not exercise due diligence to prevent the listing of the said obscene and lascivious clipping. The investigation reveals that the policies and conduct of Baazee.com its MD was designed to increase sale and maximize profits. The investigations found that the policy-makers of the company were negligent in dealing with the matter and failed to exercise due diligence."

In the said judgment, the focus was on employing content filters by online auction portal, as held by the court. However that may or may not be directly applicable in the context of mobile service providers.

Thus, it is essential to point out that it is very important for a mobile service provider to perform its due diligence to escape the liability.

Section 79 is the solitary provision under the Indian Cyberlaw, which has defined the liability of mobile service providers and mobile intermediaries. The interplay of section 79 of the Information Technology Act, 2000 with other provision of law, demonstrates how the entire issue of mobile intermediaries' liability is going to develop.

Section 85 of the Information Technology Act, 2000

Today, a large number of companies are providing iPads, Tablets, Smart Phones and Smart Devices to their employees. This is being done for the purposes of enabling the employees to be far more efficient and mobile, apart from being available to their customers and clients on a 24x7 basis. A lot of companies are also hiring services from other third party mobile platforms, for the purposes of

---

62. Cri M.C. 3066/2006 Page 37 of 53 decided by Delhi High Court.

doing their day to day businesses. A lot of these iPads, Tablets, Smart Phones and Smart Devices are issued in the name of companies in the form of corporate accounts, though the user is specified as the concerned individual who is allocated the said mobile number. However, in case if there is a misuse or potential abuse of the iPads, Tablets, Smart Phones and Smart Devices, and if pursuant thereof offences are committed under the Information Technology Act, 2000, as amended, then the company cannot escape responsibility for the same. This is so because the said mobile phone number would be deemed to be that of the company and that being so, the offence would also be deemed to having been committed by the company. Hence, the subject of corporate liability in the context of misuse of iPads, Tablets, Smart Phones and Smart Devices assumes tremendous significance.

Section 85 of the Information Technology Act, 2000 deals with issue pertaining to liability for crimes committed by companies. Section 85 of the Information Technology Act, 2000 provides as follows:

> ***"Section 85. Offences by companies.***—(1) Where a person committing a contravention of any of the provisions of this Act or of any rule, direction or order made thereunder is a company, every person who, at the time the contravention was committed, was in-charge of, and was responsible to, the company for the conduct of business of the company as well as the company, shall be guilty of the contravention and shall be liable to be proceeded against and punished accordingly:
>
> Provided that nothing contained in this sub-section shall render any such person liable to punishment if he proves that the contravention took place without his knowledge or that he exercised all due diligence to prevent such contravention.
>
> (2) Notwithstanding anything contained in sub-section (1), where a contravention of any of the provisions of this Act or of any rule, direction or order made thereunder has been committed by a company and it is proved that the contravention has taken place with the consent or connivance of, or is attributable to any neglect on the part of, any director, manager, secretary or other officer of the company, such director, manager, secretary or other officer shall also be deemed to be guilty of the contravention and shall be liable to be proceeded against and punished accordingly.
>
> *Explanation.—For the purposes of this section,—*
>
> *(i) "company" means any body corporate and includes a firm or other association of individuals; and*
>
> *(ii) "director", in relation to a firm, means a partner in the firm."*

Section 85 details the procedure to be followed where corporate entities or companies commit offences or violations. Section 85(1) states that where a company commits a contravention of any provisions of the Information Technology Act, 2000 or any rules, directions or orders made thereunder, the company as well as every person who, at the time of contravention was in-charge of the company, shall be responsible and guilty of the contravention.

Similarly, any person who, at the time of relevant contravention, was responsible to the company for the conduct of the business of the company shall also be guilty of the contravention along with the company. Persons in-charge should be responsible to the company for the conduct of the business of the company. Such persons shall be liable to be proceeded against as an accused along with the company and shall also be liable to be punished, according to the nature of the offence. The proviso to section 85(1) provides some relief in the mechanism proposed in the section. Every person, who is at the time of relevant contravention by the company, was in charge of and responsible to the company for the conduct of the business of the company, shall not be liable for punishment in two cases:—

(1) If the relevant person in-charge of or responsible to the company for the conduct of the business of the company proves that the contravention by the company took place without his knowledge. The *onus* of proof has been placed upon the person who was in-charge of or responsible to the company. However, this is a very hard *onus* to discharge. The *onus* must be discharged by means of all available documentary and oral evidence. In case, the concerned person is able to prove that he had no knowledge of any contravention by the company, he shall not be liable for punishment.

(2) If the concerned person proves that he exercised all due diligence to prevent the contravention, by the company, of any of the provisions of the Information Technology Act, 2000 or any rules, directions or orders made thereunder. This clause also lays a very heavy *onus* to be proved. Due diligence *per se* has not been defined under the Information Technology Act, 2000. However, the principles of law relating to due diligence as held by the Supreme Court in the context of the Companies Act, 1956, shall be applicable in such cases. The due diligence will also have to be proved by means of all available documents and oral testimonies to the satisfaction of the court of law. The idea of enacting the proviso to section 85(1) is to prevent innocent and duly diligent officers of the company from being unduly punished for the offences committed by the company without their knowledge and also, despite their due diligence.

While section 85(1) attempts to protect duly diligent and *bona fide* officers of the erring company from punishment, Section 85(2) spells out another related provision. Section 85(2) seeks to punish the guilty or conspiring officers of the offending companies with a heavy hand. This provision has been drafted notwithstanding anything contained in section 85(1).

Where a company violates or contravenes any of the provisions of the Information Technology Act, 2000 or any rules, directions or orders made thereunder and it is proved that the contravention took place with the consent or connivance of any officer of the company whether it be the Director, Manager, Secretary or any officer of the company, such officer shall also be deemed to be guilty of the offence committed by the company. Consequently, the officer shall also be liable to be proceeded against and punished according to the nature of the contravention as stipulated in the Information Technology Act, 2000 or any rules, directions or orders made thereunder.

In addition, if it is also proved that the contravention by the company is attributable to any neglect on the part of any officer of the company, the negligent officer, whether a Director, Manager, Secretary or other officer of the company, shall be deemed to be guilty of the offence committed by the company and is liable to be proceeded against and punished against for the offence.

However, section 85(2) uses the words "and it is proved that the contravention has taken place". The *onus* of proof lies upon the complainant or the prosecution. The standards of neglect on the part of the officer of the company have not been defined under section 85(2). However, the neglect must be substantial and not superficial. Further, the neglect by the officer of the company must have a direct bearing upon the contravention of any of the provisions of the Information Technology Act, 2000 or any rules, directions or orders made thereunder, by the concerned company. If the contravention by the company is not attributable to any negligent officer of the company, no action against the concerned officer of the company would be legally maintainable under section 85. The language of section 85 is basically meant only for offences or contraventions committed by companies which means that the legal entity must be a company duly incorporated under the Companies Act, 1956. The *Explanation* to section 85 explains the scope of this provision and its applicability not only to companies, which are body corporates but also to all partnership firms and other associations of individuals.

Thus, any partnership firm under the Indian Partnership Act, 1932 would also be included within the definition of the term "company" as has been defined by the *Explanation* (i) to section 85. This is a welcome clause, as violations of the Information Technology Act, 2000 or any rules, directions or orders made thereunder, are not just limited to individuals or companies but even done by partnership firms or groups or association of individuals.

Similarly, *Explanation* (ii) to section 85 states that the word "director" in relation to firm means a partner in the firm. In case of a contravention of the provisions of the Information Technology Act, 2000 or any rules, directions or orders made thereunder by a firm, the partners of the firm shall also be deemed to be guilty of the same offence and shall be liable to be proceeded against and punished accordingly, provided that if a partner proves that the contravention by the partnership firm took place without his knowledge or that he, as a partner, exercised due diligence to prevent commission of any such contravention, in that case, the partner shall not be liable to be punished.

Further, if it is found that a partnership firm has made a contravention of the provisions of this Act or any rules, directions or orders made thereunder, with the consent or connivance of any partner, the same partner shall also be deemed to be guilty of the offence or the contravention and is liable to be proceeded against and punished accordingly.

Similarly, if a contravention by a firm is attributable to and neglect by any partner then the neglecting partner shall also be deemed to be guilty of the same contravention and is liable to be proceeded against and punished accordingly. Thus, with the enactment of section 85, the Indian Cyberlaw covers the contraventions of its provisions or any rules, directions or orders made thereunder, by all individuals, companies and partnership firms.

It is pertinent to note that proviso to section 85(1) to refers to the term "all due diligence."

The word "all due diligence" is very comprehensive word and does not include any such exception to the same.

Thus, companies and their top managements need to ensure that they exercised due diligence to prevent the commission of any contravention under the law, in order to escape any potential exposure to criminal consequences, in the event of misuse of iPads, Tablets, Smart Phones and Smart Devices , owned by the said companies.

Miscellaneous

Section 80 of the amended Information Technology Act, 2000

"Section 80. Power of police officer and other officers to enter, search, etc.— *(1) Notwithstanding anything contained in the Code of Criminal Procedure, 1973, (2 of 1974) any police officer, not below the rank of a Inspector, or any other officer of the Central Government or a State Government authorised by the Central Government in this behalf may enter any public place and search and arrest without warrant any person found therein who is reasonably suspected of having committed or of committing or of being about to commit any offence under this Act.*

Explanation.—For the purposes of this sub-section, the expression "public place" includes any public conveyance, any hotel, any shop or any other place intended for use by, or accessible to the public.

(2) Where any person is arrested under sub-section (1) by an officer other than a police officer, such officer shall, without unnecessary delay, take or send the person arrested before a Magistrate having jurisdiction in the case or before the officer-in-charge of a police station.

(3) The provisions of the Code of Criminal Procedure, 1973 (2 of 1974) shall, subject to the provisions of this section, apply, so far as may be, in relation to any entry, search or arrest, made under this section."

Section 80 relates to the power of police and other officers to enter, search any premises and take appropriate actions. Section 80 of the Information Technology Act, 2000 had granted powers of entry, search and arrest to a police officer, not below the rank of a Deputy Superintendent of Police. However, by virtue of the Information Technology (Amendment) Act, 2008, these powers have been now conferred upon police officers, not below the rank of an Inspector.

Section 80 of the amended Information Technology Act, 2000 is the first section that comes under Chapter XIII with a title "Miscellaneous". The significance of this section is that it gives a large amount of powers to the police officer not below the rank of an Inspector to do various activities as are detailed in the present section.

The said activities can be done by any police officer, not below the rank of an Inspector who is investigating any offence under the Information Technology Act, 2000.

Since, the offences under the Information Technology Act, 2000 have been amended to incorporate various mobile, iPad, Tablet, Smart Phone and Smart

Device related offences, any police Inspector or officer of an above rank has been given the discretion to enter any public place and conduct any search without warrant at the said public place. Further, the said police Inspector has also been given the power to arrest, without warrant, any person who is found at the said public place who is reasonably suspected of having committed or of committing or even of being about to commit any offence under the Information Technology Act, 2000. Thus, if any person is reasonably suspected of having committed any of the cyber and mobile crimes that are detailed under Chapter XI of the Information Technology Act, 2000, he could be searched, arrested without warrant. Further, if any person is in the process of committing an offence under the Information Technology Act, 2000, he could be arrested without warrant.

It is essential to point out here that if any crime is committed by use of iPads, Tablets, Smart Phones and Smart Devices, then police officer may take into custody the said iPads, Tablets, Smart Phones and Smart Devices, which is a hot/ primary evidence pertaining to reported mobile crime.

However, the most difficult aspect of section 80 is that it has given the power to any police Inspector to search and arrest without warrant any person who is reasonably suspected of being about to commit any offence under the Information Technology Act, 2000. This is a very wide discretion that has been granted and is likely to be misused a lot, as time passes by. The misuse of this provision, in the context of mobile crimes, becomes even more relevant since any kind of iPad, Tablet, Smart Phone and Smart Device, which is in the custody of any person, could be thought to be connected with any offence and hence any person could be reasonably suspected of being about to commit any offence under the Information Technology Act, 2000 as amended.

Explanation to section 80 of the Information Technology Act, 2000 clearly shows that the expression public place includes the following:

(a) Any public conveyance,

(b) Any hotel,

(c) Any shop,

(d) Any other place intended for use by or accessible to the public.

The said definition is indeed very wide and also incorporates within its ambit any public office of any company, since that office would be a place which is accessible to the public. For example, a hotel has been considered as a public place. It has not been specified which part of the hotel is a public place and thus by implication, every portion of the hotel including the rooms taken on hire by clients would come within the definition of public place. In addition, the Legislature has used the words "any other place intended for use by, or accessible to the public." This is the very wide definition of the word "public place" and would include almost any place, which is accessible to the public including offices, banks, chambers, hospitals and many others. The net effect of section 80 of the amended Information Technology Act, 2000 is that any police Inspector could walk in the public office of any company and could potentially create mischief. In that sense, the potential of misuse of the provisions of section 80 can hardly be overestimated.

Section 80(2) provides that where any person is arrested under section 80(1) by an officer other than the police officer, he shall, without unnecessary delay, take or send the person arrested to him before a Magistrate having jurisdiction in the case or before the officer in-charge of police station.

Of particular significance is section 80(3) which provides that provisions of section 80 shall have precedence over the provisions of Code of Criminal Procedure, 1973. This also finds corroboration from the language used under section 81 of the Information Technology Act, 2000 which says that the provisions of the Information Technology Act, 2000 shall have effect, notwithstanding anything inconsistent therewith contained in any other law for the time being in force. Clearly, the provisions of the Information Technology Act, 2000, being a special legislation, have overriding impact and effect. Subject to the provisions of section 80 of the Information Technology Act, 2000, the provisions of Code of Criminal Procedure, 1973 shall apply, so far as it may be, in relation to any entry, search or arrest made under section 80 of the Information Technology Act, 2000.

Thus, given the special significance and the special status of the Information Technology Act, 2000 as a special legislation, the powers granted to the police Inspector under section 80 of the Information Technology Act, 2000 are clearly of wide-ranging significance and import. Given the fact that the Information Technology (Amendment) Act, 2008 has given the powers of section 80 of the Information Technology Act to police officer not below the rank of an Inspector, a lot of material changes have been made to the earlier section 80. Earlier section 80 had given such powers only to Deputy Superintendent of Police. However, now with these powers been given to a police officer not below the rank of an Inspector, who may or may not be conversant with the technical aspects pertaining to usage of communication devices, such powers are likely to be potentially misused in the context of the widespread adoption and usage of iPads, Tablets, Smart Phones and Smart Devices in India.

However, seen from the perspective of investigation of any mobile crime, the powers granted under section 80 of the amended Information Technology Act, 2000 are of tremendous value and utility to an Inspector, as it helps to proactively investigate any mobile-related crime or other crimes as detailed under the Information Technology Act, 2000 and further go ahead and enter and search any public place without warrant and arrest a person who is reasonably suspected of having committed, committing or being about to commit a cyber and mobile crime. As such, the paramount significance of the powers granted under section 80 of the amended Information Technology Act, 2000 can hardly be emphasized.

Section 81 of the amended Information Technology Act, 2000

*"**Section 81. Act to have overriding effect.**—The provisions of this Act shall have effect notwithstanding anything inconsistent therewith contained in any other law for the time being in force:*

Provided that nothing contained in this Act shall restrict any person from exercising any right conferred under the Copyright Act, 1957 (14 of 1957) or the Patents Act, 1970 (39 of 1970)"

The Information Technology Act, 2000 is a special legislation as it is dealing with special issues. Section 81 outlines the status of the Information Technology Act, 2000 *viz.* other laws. It is a cardinal principle of law that wherever there is a special law, the same shall prevail over any general law, whenever any dispute arises between the two.

By means of section 81, it has been categorically provided that the provisions of the Information Technology Act, 2000 shall have effect and predominance over anything inconsistent contained in any existing law or regulation that is in force in the country. Thus, in case of a conflict between the Information Technology Act, 2000 and the general law, the provisions of the Information Technology Act, 2000 shall apply over and above the inconsistent provisions of the general law.

This special status has been granted to the Information Technology Act, 2000 as the said law seeks to impact the electronic format. Several Indian laws have been passed and implemented, prior to the coming of the electronic information age. As such, many of these old laws do not incorporate within them the capability of embracing and incorporating changes that the electronic form has brought about. In fact, in a number of cases, some of the existing laws in India have been passed even before the electronic format could be visualized. Consequently, such legislations are in danger of being in conflict with the new law. By enacting section 81, Parliament has reiterated its intention to give credence and prominence to the electronic format.

Section 81 only states that in case of any inconsistency between an existing law and the Information Technology Act, 2000, the provisions of the Indian Cyberlaw shall prevail. It does not say that the provisions of the Information Technology Act, 2000 shall apply notwithstanding anything contained in any law for the time being in force. Thus, those provisions of existing laws which are complementary to or which do not conflict with, the provisions of the Information Technology Act, 2000 shall continue to be applicable so as to supplement the provisions of the Information Technology Act, 2000. Further, it is important to note that section 81 uses the word "shall" which makes it a mandatory provision rather than a mere directory provision. All this helps in giving teeth to the procedure of law and machinery established under the Information Technology Act, 2000. The Information Technology Act, 2000 is a special law and prevails over anything inconsistent with the provisions of the same.

An interesting issue that arises for consideration is what happens in case of conflict between two special laws. It is likely that many special legislations are passed, after the coming into effect of the Information Technology Act, 2000. Such legislations may also have similar provisions, regarding having effect notwithstanding anything inconsistent therewith contained in any other law in the time being in force, including the Information Technology Act, 2000. In a scenario of conflict, the Judiciary will be called upon to harmoniously interpret both the special laws and establish a balance between the two special laws in such a manner so as to best serve the objectives of both the legislations.

This special Act can be directly interpreted in the iPads, Tablets, Smart Phones and Smart Devices ecosystem as it is the only special legislation passed by the

Parliament of India, which specifically deals with mobile phones and communication devices. This special law when interpreted in the context of the iPads, Tablets, Smart Phones and Smart Devices environment would have the same effect as it has on cyberspace environment.

Section 84A of the amended Information Technology Act, 2000

> ***"Section 84A. Modes or methods for encryption.****—The Central Government may, for secure use of the electronic medium and for promotion of e-governance and e-commerce, prescribe the modes or methods for encryption."*

In cryptography[63], encryption is the process of transforming information (referred to as plaintext) using an algorithm (called cipher) to make it unreadable to anyone except those possessing special knowledge usually referred to as a key. The result of the process is encrypted information (in cryptography, referred to as ciphertext). In many contexts, the word encryption also implicitly refers to the reverse process, decryption (e.g., "software for encryption" can typically also perform decryption), to make the encrypted information readable again (*i.e.*, to make unencrypted).

The Legislature has, for the first time, directly dealt with the important issue pertaining to encryption. It is pertinent to point out that earlier the subject of encryption had not been dealt within the Information Technology Act, 2000. In fact, the word "encryption" or "encrypt" did not appear anywhere within the text of the Information Technology Act, 2000. It only had one reference to one word namely "decrypt" and that too was in the context of the duty of any person to decrypt information, should he be directed to do so, once any information has been directed by the Controller of Certifying Authorities to be intercepted. Barring that, there was no such reference to encryption.

It was never clear as to what was the policy of the government and what exactly are the acceptable governmental levels of encryption.

It is but natural to expect that in today's world, more and more governments are inclined to strictly regulate the issue of encryption. This is so because, encryption as a technology, while is a tremendous boom for general authentication purposes, also can be used for criminal purposes as well. The potential misuse of encryption as a technology is a very important phenomenon that has emerged in the last one decade. In fact, cyber criminals and cyber terrorists today openly go ahead and use encryption, knowing fully well that breaking the levels of encryption could take lot of time, for the law enforcement agencies, which will be far more than enough for them to go ahead and achieve their various illegal designs.

It is pertinent to note that under the Internet Service Providers which is issued by the Department of Telecommunications, Government of India, only 40 bit encryption is as legally permitted. As time passed by, it purely became a matter of ridicule that when the officially permissible level for encryption in India was 40 bit, banks and other institutions in the country were openly using much higher

63. http://en.wikipedia.org/wiki/Encryption.

levels of encryption. Therefore, there was a tremendous pressure on the government to get some clarity on what was its documented stand on encryption.

It was in this regard that section 84 of the amended Information Technology Act, 2000 was put in place.

Section 84A clearly gives the discretion to the Central Government that it may for secure use of the electronic medium and for promoting e-governance and e-commerce, m-commerce prescribe the modes or methods of encryption. What the current modes and methods of encryption are or would be in the times to come, is clearly not defined. The same have been left to the discretion of the Central Government, to prescribe such modes or methods of encryption, as time passes by.

Such modes or methods of encryption would also be directly applicable for all communication devices as also mobile networks, apart from being applicable for computers, computer systems and computer networks as well as computer resources.

Section 84B of the amended Information Technology Act, 2000

> ***"Section 84B. Punishment for abetment of offences.***—*Whoever abets any offence shall, if the act abetted is committed in consequence of the abetment, and no express provision is made by this Act for the punishment of such abetment, be punished with the punishment provided for the offence under this Act.*
>
> *Explanation.—An act or offence is said to be committed in consequence of abetment, when it is committed in consequence of the instigation, or in pursuance of the conspiracy, or with the aid which constitutes the abetment."*

Section 84B has been added in the Information Technology Act, 2000 by the Information Technology (Amendment) Act, 2008. Earlier, there was no punishment for abetment of offences, as defined under the Information Technology Act, 2000. Section 84B provides that whoever abets any offence and further ensures that the act is committed in consequence of the abetment, he himself commits an offence under section 84B of the amended Information Technology Act, 2000. As per the *Explanation*, the term "an act or offence committed in consequence of abetment" is said to be committed when the same is committed in consequence of the instigation of the conspiracy or in pursuance of, the said act or with the aid which constitutes abetment.

Thus, any person who abets and further does acts which are committed in consequence of abetment, commits an offence under section 84B of the amended Information Technology Act, 2000. Such an offence is punishable, where no express provision is made by the Information Technology Act, 2000, with imprisonment which is provided for the said offence under the Information Technology Act, 2000. Thus, for example if a person who abets the offence of cyber terrorism under section 66F of the Information Technology Act, 2000, and ensure that the act abetted is committed in consequence of the abetment, then he shall also be punished for cyber terrorism under section 66F with imprisonment which may extend to imprisonment for life.

The *Explanation* to section 84B of the Information Technology Act, 2000 clearly defines when can an act or offence be said to be committed in consequence of abetment. The said act is so said to be committed in consequence of abetment if any of the following three conditions are met:

(a) The act is committed in consequence of the instigation.

(b) The act is committed in pursuance of the conspiracy.

(c) The act is committed with the aid which constitutes the abetment.

Thus, all kinds of aiding and abetting exercises have been brought within the ambit of the specific offences defined under section 84B of the amended Information Technology Act, 2000. This provision can be directly applicable and interpreted in the context of the iPads, Tablets, Smart Phones and Smart Devices ecosystem. Any person who abets any offence committed using a communication device and mobile networks or which is targeted at communication devices and mobile networks can be fully covered under section 84B of the amended Information Technology Act, 2000.

Section 84C of the amended Information Technology Act, 2000

*"**Section 84C. Punishment for attempt to commit offences.**—Whoever attempts to commit an offence punishable by this Act or causes such an offence to be committed, and in such an attempt does any act towards the commission of the offence, shall, where no express provision is made for the punishment of such attempt, be punished with imprisonment of any description provided for the offence, for a term which may extend to one-half of the longest term of imprisonment provided for that offence, or with such fine as is provided for the offence, or with both."*

Section 84C has been added in the Information Technology Act, 2000 by the Information Technology (Amendment) Act, 2008. This section is indeed significant as it makes the attempt to commit offences also an offence and stipulates punishment thereof.

Section 84C provides the following conditions must be specified:

(a) There must be a person who attempts to commit an offence which is punishable under the Information Technology Act, 2000, or

(b) The person causes such an offence to be committed which is punishable under the Information Technology Act, 2000, and

(c) In such an attempt, does any act towards for commission of the offence.

If any of the conditions (a) or (b) as well as condition (c) are satisfied, the said act constitutes an offence under section 84C of the amended Information Technology Act, 2000. The said provision provides for the punishment of such an offence. The said provision says that such an offence, where no express provision is made for the punishment of such attempt, is punishable with imprisonment and fine. The quantum of imprisonment and fine shall depend upon the exact offence that is attempted to be committed. The punishment consists of imprisonment of any description provided for the said offence under the Information Technology Act, 2000 for a term which may extend to one-half of the longest term of imprisonment provided for that offence, or with such fine as is provided for the offence, or with both.

Just for example, if a person attempts to commit an offence for publishing child pornography, the said offence of publishing child pornography under section 67B of the amended Information Technology Act, 2000 and is punishable with imprisonment for a term which may extend to five years and with fine which may extend to ten lakhs rupees on first conviction. As such, the attempt to commit such an offence punishable under section 67B would be punishable with imprisonment of either description for a term which may extend to two and half years and with fine which may extend to ten lakhs rupees or with both.

Section 84C is likely to be an effective tool in the hands of the law enforcement while booking and prosecuting the offences pertaining to attempt to commit various offences defined under the Information Technology Act, 2000.

The aforesaid is the detailed analysis of the various provisions of the Indian Information Technology Act, 2000 as amended, which impact the use of iPads, Tablets, Smart Phones and Smart Devices in India as also data and information in the electronic form, resident therein.

So in case you are using iPads, Tablets, Smart Phones and Smart Devices in India, you have to be alive to the fact that your device is fully covered under the Indian law being the Information Technology Act, 2000. You could often argue that my iPad, Tablet, Smart Phone and Smart Device is not my computer and why should this law cover my iPad, Tablet, Smart Phone and Smart Device? This could be a valid question except the fact that the reality is completely different. It is indeed correct that the Indian Cyberlaw, at the time when it was first drafted, was only drafted keeping in mind the specific requirements to regulate activities of computers, computer systems and computer networks. However, over the period of time, as time passed by, it became more and more prudent that the applicability of the law was bit little and there was a need for making it far more comprehensive and also its scope, application and applicability. That is the reason why the Information Technology Act, 2000 was amended by the Information Technology (Amendment) Act, 2008. The said amendments broadened the scope and applicability of the Information Technology Act, 2000 and made it applicable, apart from computers, computer systems and computer networks, to also computer resources and communication devices. This completely changes the landscape. These new amendments which came into effect from 27th October, 2009, clearly brought within its ambit all iPads, Tablets, Smart Phones, Smart Devices and communication devices of any scope, nature, description or characteristics whatsoever.

All communication devices, cell phones, personal digital assistance or combination of both or any other device used to communicate, send or transmit any text, video, audio or image are covered under the Indian Cyberlaw. All Computers including all electronic, magnetic, optical or other high-speed data processing devices or systems which perform logical, arithmetic, and memory functions by manipulations of electronic, magnetic or optical impulses image are also covered under the Indian Cyberlaw.

The law has now given a legal recognition not just to all these iPads, Tablets, Smart Phones and Smart Devices, but has further provided legal recognition for data and information that is residing therein, that is generated, transmitted, stored, retained or hosted in any manner whatsoever in the said iPads, Tablets, Smart Phones and Smart Devices. Consequently, data and information in the electronic form, which is in your iPads, Tablets, Smart Phones and Smart Devices, has been granted legality by virtue of section 4 of the Information Technology Act, 2000. A lot of people use lot of authentication mechanisms on these iPads, Tablets, Smart Phones and Smart Devices. These iPads, Tablets, Smart Phones and Smart Devices are used for authentication purposes for the purposes of authenticating electronic data and information that is generated, stored or transmitted on the said iPads, Tablets, Smart Phones and Smart Devices.

The aforesaid is the legal position in India pertaining to use of iPads, Tablets, Smart Phones and Smart Devices as also data and information residing therein. All stakeholders who use these iPads, Tablets, Smart Phones and Smart Devices will have to be increasingly very careful about the way they make use of these iPads, Tablets, Smart Phones and Smart Devices. These iPads, Tablets, Smart Phones and Smart Devices are not just the gateway of convenience and increasing efficiency, these are also gateway to potential legal exposure. As such, as a user of iPads, Tablets, Smart Phones and Smart Devices, it will always be beneficial if you have the aforesaid legal nuances in mind. If you are a company *i.e.*, providing iPads, Tablets, Smart Phones and Smart Devices to your employees, make sure that you as a legal entity comply with the relevant provisions of the relevant law that impacts the use of iPads, Tablets, Smart Phones and Smart Devices as also data and information residing thereon, being the Information Technology Act, 2000 as amended and rules and regulations made thereunder.

CHAPTER 3
LEGAL ISSUES PERTAINING TO BRING YOUR OWN DEVICE (BYOD)

BYOD is the new hottest trend emerging on the horizon. As the world is moving towards the converged environment and as people are getting more and more connected on 24x7 basis on the digital networks, BYOD is becoming the preferred method of communication and existence on digital networks.

The first question that comes to one's mind is, what exactly is BYOD? The term "BYOD" stands for Bring Your Own Device. BYOD as a concept has emerged couple of years back.

BYOD is short for *bring your own device*. In the consumerization of IT, BYOD is a phrase that has become widely adopted to refer to employees who bring their own computing devices – such as smart phones, laptops and PDAs – to the workplace for use and connectivity on the corporate network.[64]

Bring Your Own Device (BYOD) identifies the recent trend of employees bringing personally-owned mobile devices to their place of work, and using those devices to access privileged company resources such as email, file servers and databases as well as their personal applications and data.[65]

The popular perception is that the BYOD revolution was sparked by the advent of Apple's iPhone. The iPhone, and subsequently the iPad, are certainly catalysts that have contributed to the accelerated adoption of BYOD policies in many organizations, but the concept of users wanting to choose their own devices, or use their own PCs to get work done predates these devices – it is just that, recently, the percentage of these types of devices in use has grown significantly. Corporate philosophy has had much to do with driving BYOD as well.

Companies' IT support policies have been pushing employees to be more independent and autonomous for decades.

Even in organizations where the IT department still mandates specific operating systems, hardware platforms, and mobile devices, rogue employees have worked around those requirements to get the job done. Nomadic employees embrace the concept of being independent and autonomous, and manifest it by sometimes ignoring company policy and choosing the tools that help them be more effective, and work more efficiently.[66]

64. http://www.webopedia.com/TERM/B/BYOD.html
65. http://en.wikipedia.org/wiki/Bring_your_own_device
66. http://blogs.technet.com/b/security/archive/2012/07/18/beginner-s-guide-to-byod-bring-your-own-device.aspx

BYOD as a trend, is gaining increasingly more adoption. This is borne by the following figures concerning BYOD that are emerging across the world[67].

- 53% of organizations officially condone BYOD in some way, but less than half of them provide any financial subsidy for users who supply their own equipment.
- 22% of organizations allow personal devices to be used, but require that they be managed by the company IT personnel.
- Cost savings resulting from employees using their own PCs and mobile devices may be offset by increased IT support and security costs.
- A majority of companies are somewhat or very concerned about the risk of data breaches or intellectual property leaks

A survey published by the pinterest infographics about BYOD (Bring Your Own Device) demonstrates the rise of BYOD as below:[68]

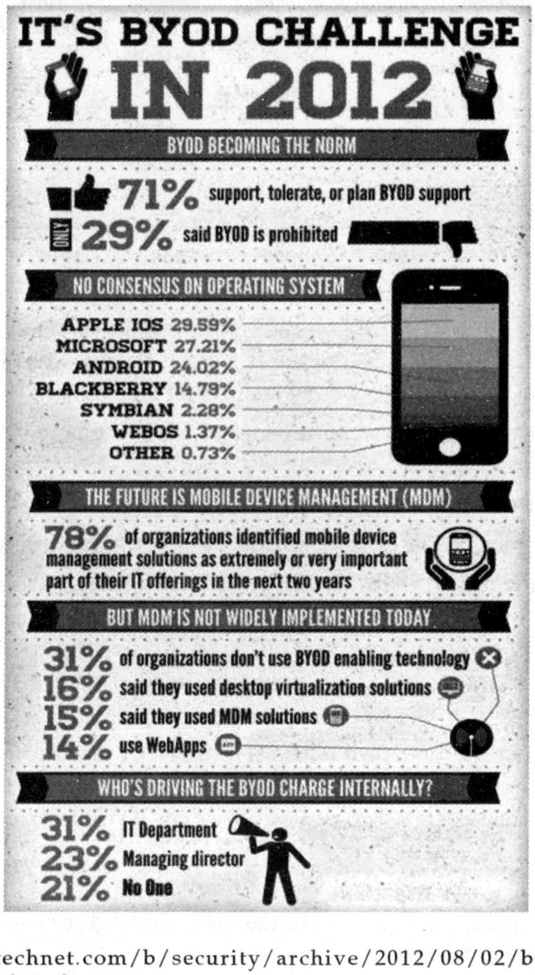

67. http://blogs.technet.com/b/security/archive/2012/08/02/byod-organizations-question-risk-vs-benefit.aspx
68. http://pinterest.com/pin/129830401728313023

Further, according to the study of Information Law Group, they have presented the following BYOD statistics graph where they have demonstrated that mobile web will rule by 2015.[69]

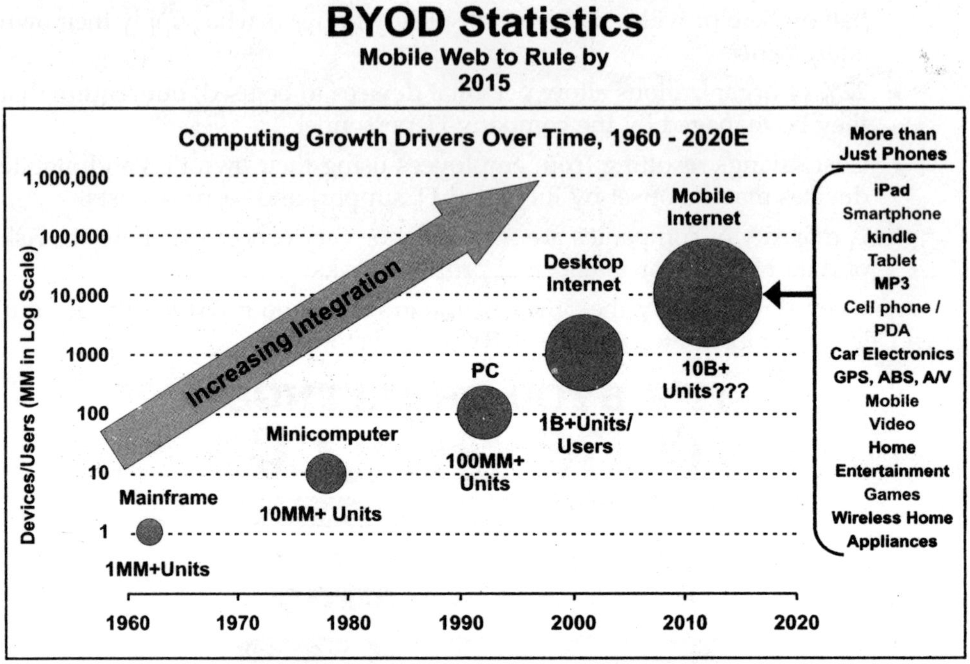

Bring your own device (BYOD) versus company purchased device is a burning debate within the CIO ranks. Some say it's over, that it's too late to stop BYOD. But the statistics so far point to a less secure BYOD world.[70]

- 74% of companies allow some sort of BYOD usage.
- Less than 10% of organizations are "fully aware" of the devices accessing their network.
- 81% of employees use at least one device for business use.

An IDC survey found that in 2011, 40% of devices used by information workers to access business applications were personal devices, compared with 30% in 2010, a 33% increase in just one year. According to the survey, 30% of information workers used their PCs, and 10% used their tablets for work-related tasks.[71]

Recently, Cognizant has published a paper on the topic entitled "Making BYOD Work for Your Organization" wherein it has been demonstrated through facts and graphs that the demand and adoption of BYOD varies by industry, with

69. http://www.isaca-denver.org/Conferences/RMISC/Presentations/301-Legal_Implications_ of_BYOD.pdf
70. http://www.forbes.com/sites/markfidelman/2012/05/02/the-latest-infographics-mobile-business-statistics-for-2012
71. http://www.cognizant.com/RecentHighlights/Making-BYOD-Work-for-Your-Organization.pdf

financial services, insurance, healthcare and professional services leading the way.[72]

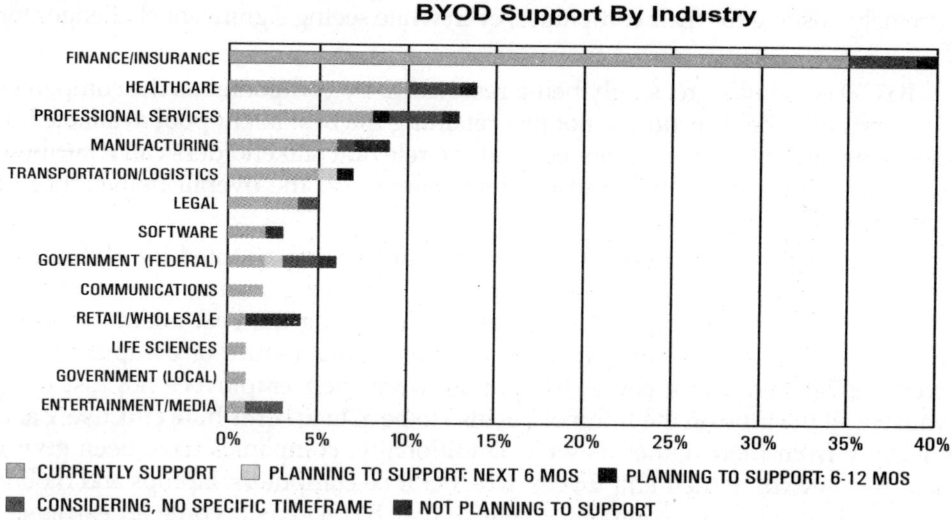

As far as India is concerned, there are not much scientifically obtained figures/surveys available pertaining to penetration of BYOD. However, there are some sketchy figures available.

BT Study[73]: A study report released in April, 2012, by British Telecommunications plc (BT) found that BYOD is making progress within the corporate environment, with 60 per cent. of employees using personal devices for work. India is one of the countries with some of the highest usage – 80 per cent., second only to China with 92 per cent. The BT research also shows that 82 per cent. of companies say they already allow BYOD or will do so, within the next 24 months. BYOD is a relatively recent trend where employees are allowed and even encouraged to bring personally-owned devices to work place and use them to access company resources like e-mail, file servers, and databases. The study was based on survey of more than 2,000 users and decision-makers across 11 countries, including India.

CISCO Study[74]: Another study, whose results were released in mid-May, 2012 by Cisco, seemed to strengthen the BT results, finding that most organizations world-wide are now enabling "Bring Your Own Device" in the enterprise, with a staggering 95% of respondents saying their organizations permit employee-owned devices in some way, shape or form in the workplace. This study also concluded that the average number of connected devices per knowledge worker is expected to reach 3.3 by 2014, up from an average of 2.8 in 2012. Cisco says BYOD is

72. http://www.cognizant.com/RecentHighlights/Making-BYOD-Work-for-Your-Organization.pdf
73. http://efytimes.com/e1/84591/Survey-Reveals—Usage-Of-Bring-Your-Own-Device-BOYD-In-India
74. http://efytimes.com/e1/84591/Survey-Reveals—Usage-Of-Bring-Your-Own-Device-BOYD-In-India

perceived by most respondents to be a gateway to greater business benefits. Over three-fourths (76%) of IT leaders surveyed, categorized BYOD as somewhat or extremely positive for their companies, even while seeing significant challenges for IT.

BYOD is today increasingly being resorted to by companies as the companies are working in the direction of not just retaining the best talent pool available but also for ensuring that the employees and the relevant stakeholders can contribute in a more better productive and efficient manner, to the overall deliverance of services or business offerings.

In India, the concept of BYOD is increasingly being adopted by companies. Companies argue that this is essential not just for giving a sense of continuity to their employees but also for the purposes of retaining the best talent available. Further, companies believe that given the ubiquitous nature of computing and given the 24x7 nature of connectivity, they want their employees not just to be available all the time on the Internet but also to be able to contribute effectively and efficiently from their homes as well. Traditionally, companies have been giving their own devices to their employees, whether it be computers, laptops and mobile phones. However, now companies believe that BYOD has become an extremely important economical option to exercise.

BYOD brings with it, various advantages as compared to the traditional capital expenditure that the company has to invariably expend on its computers, computer systems and computer networks. By a single stroke, if a company allows BYOD, it reduces dramatically its expenses on capital infrastructure. Thus, this links to tremendous savings as far as companies are concerned. This is also borne by the figures in this regard.

While there is no argument with the basic proposition that BYOD brings extremely economic results for the companies, the fact remains that there are various legal, policy and regulatory challenges pertaining to BYOD.

If a company is using or is contemplating to use BYOD within India, then it has to be alive of various legal, policy and regulatory challenges that it is likely to face in this regard. This chapter aims to examine some of these legal challenges that legal entities could face in the event they adopt or are planning to adopt BYOD, as a corporate culture exercise.

The first thing that companies in India need to be aware of, when they adopt BYOD is the factum pertaining to limitation of liability. The moment, an employee brings his own smart device to work, he gets to have the company's corporate information on his own device. This is so because whenever you bring your own device to work, you will need to connect to the corporate network for the purposes of accessing your device and also for the purposes of communication and doing their day to day duties. The moment an outside device gets connected to the corporate network, there are inherent challenges pertaining to security of the corporate networks as also the confidentiality of data and information residing on corporate networks. Invariably, companies would have to take steps so as to protect the security of their networks as also to ensure that infected outside devices are not connected to the corporate networks or that they do not really introduce a computer contaminant or virus which negatively and prejudicially impacts the value and utility of electronic information residing on the corporate networks.

Thus, one of the foremost challenges that the company is likely to face, in the context of BYOD, is when an employee gets a device to the work which is infected or which has malicious program, malware or spyware installed therein which is primarily aimed for the purposes of doing unauthorized activities on corporate networks. Thus, the company needs to ensure that it has implemented and maintained reasonable security practices and procedures, when it is actually allowing BYOD culture on corporate networks.

Another major challenge that companies are likely to face pertains to the confidentiality of information. Large amount of confidential data resides on corporate networks and once the company allows BYOD, it allows its users and employees to get their own devices connected on to the corporate network and also download corporate confidential data residing on corporate networks.

Today, given the high rate of attrition that is existing in various industries, invariably employees are moving in between jobs. Because of lot of attrition, people land up in resigning or leaving their jobs for better avenues. Most of the times, they take their own devices with them. The net effect of this is that large amounts of corporate data including confidential data and information of the companies often tend to go alongwith the said devices, alongwith the said employees, when they leave the said companies. This effectively means that the said confidential data is getting outside the corporate's control. In such a scenario, the companies have actually no control of how the said information is likely to be used or misused, once the employee leaves its employment. There are also no guarantees as to how the said employee is going to use or misuse or abuse the said corporate information, even while in employment, once he takes his own device back to home. There are tremendous chances of unauthorized access of corporate data by entities and persons, who are not legally authorized to access the said information. This is likely to bring forward various complicated challenges not only for the purposes of protecting the security and confidentiality of confidential information and data of companies, but also for ensuring that the same are not unauthorizedly distributed, transmitted or in any other manner shared or hosted on any other unauthorized computer resource. Thus, protection of corporate data and its confidentiality becomes an extremely important legal challenge facing the companies, before they can think of allowing BYOD.

Another major challenge that could potentially arise in the context of BYOD is that, in case if the device which the employee brings to the company, has got obscene or pornographic content thereon, which the employee would have downloaded, stored or viewed at home, the same is likely to have potential legal ramifications for the company. The law in this regard is pretty clear, as has been clarified by the provisions of the Information Technology Act, 2000. The moment, the said device brought under the BYOD banner, is connected to the corporate networks, the said device shall be deemed to be an extension of the corporate network and that being so, any activities done on the said device or any data stored on the said device, once connected to the corporate network, is likely to have potential legal ramifications for the company.

Once the employee's device is connected to corporate network which has pornographic content, the legal effect would be that the said pornographic content is not only published but is also caused to be published on the corporate network and is available for access. That being so, the company could itself face potential criminal exposure. This is so, because under section 67 of the Information Technology Act, 2000, publishing, transmitting or causing to be published or transmitted in the electronic format, any information which is lascivious or which appeals to the prurient interest or the effect of which is to tend to deprave and corrupt the minds of those, who having regard to the relevant circumstances, are likely to see, read or hear the same, is a penal offence punishable with 3 years' imprisonment and 5,00,000 INR.

Lots of times, it can also happen that an employee would have stored certain specific content on his own device which is of explicit sexual nature or which pertains to child pornography. The moment that employee's device is connected to corporate networks under the BYOD banner, the said content of explicit sexual activity and also child pornography shall also be deemed to be published as well as caused to be published by the said corporate network, thereby straight away attracting criminal liability for the company and its top management. It is pertinent to note that under section 67A of the amended Information Technology Act, 2000, it has been made an offence when a person publishes, transmits or causes to be published or transmitted any information in the electronic form, which contains information of explicit sexual nature and the said offence is punishable with 3 years' imprisonment and 5,000,00 INR. Further under section 67B of the amended Information Technology Act, 2000, if any person:

(a) publishes or transmits or causes to be published or transmitted material in any electronic form which depicts children engaged in sexually explicit act or conduct, or

(b) creates text or digital images, collects, seeks, browses, downloads, advertises, promotes, exchanges or distributes material in any electronic form depicting children in obscene or indecent or sexually explicit manner, or

(c) cultivates, entices or induces children to online relationship with one or more children for and on sexually explicit act or in a manner that may offend a reasonable adult on the computer resource, or

(d) facilitates abusing children online, or

(e) records in any electronic form own abuse or that of others pertaining to sexually explicit act with children, the said acts also have been declared as a heinous offence punishable with 5 years' imprisonment and fine of 10,000,00 INR.

Another major challenge that companies need to be careful about is when the smart device that the employee brings to the company under BYOD, contains illegal copies or infringing copies of software belonging to legitimate copyright-holders. The moment that the said device is connected to corporate networks, it will be presumed that the said device is a part of the corporate network and once it has infringing software thereon, there could be potential legal consequences for the said acts. Apart from employee bringing the said device to corporate network, the company also could be held responsible for the offence of infringing the copyright of the said relevant copyright-holders in their original literary works and computer software, thereby adding further legal exposure to the concerned company.

Seen from a purely legal angle, companies have to realize that they are legal entities which are governed by Indian law. The moment an Indian company uses computers, computer systems, computer networks, computer resources as also communication devices, it is fully covered by the Indian mother legislation pertaining to the same being the Information Technology Act, 2000. Thus, the said companies have to be alive to the fact that if the employee brings his own device and that some unauthorized activity on corporate network happens, the ultimate responsibility of such unauthorized activity is going to rest with the company. In such a scenario, it is possible for the company to face potential legal exposure and consequences for illegal or unauthorized activities done using devices, brought from their own home by the employees or by other outsiders.

Needless to say, if any loss is caused by any unauthorized activity done by any outside device which is brought under the BYOD banner, the company shall be deemed to be the legal entity that would be responsible for the said unauthorized activity or criminal activity and would face various consequences connected therewith.

The Information Technology Act, 2000 really provides for two kinds of legal liabilities for companies. There could be a civil liability to pay damages by way of compensation upto 50,000,000 INR, which can be provided against companies by Adjudicating Officers under section 46 of the Information Technology Act, 2000. That does not mean that the companies cannot be sued for compensation beyond 5,00,000,00 INR. Any affected person can sue any company for damages beyond 50,000,000 INR in a court of competent jurisdiction under the Information Technology Act, 2000 for any unauthorized activities done by devices brought under the BYOD banner. In addition, there could also be potential criminal consequences that the company's top management could be exposed to, for various cybercrimes committed by the outside devices which have been brought or connected to the company's premises and networks, under the BYOD banner. Various cybercrimes could be committed using the said outside devices which are made punishable with imprisonment ranging from 3 years to life imprisonment and fine ranging from 1,00,000 INR to 10,000,000 INR, under various provisions of Chapter XI of the amended Information Technology Act, 2000.

Complicating the scenario is the fact that the Information Technology Act, 2000 is a special legislation and the provisions of this law prevail over anything inconsistent therewith, contained in any other law for the time being in force. Further complicating the scenario is yet another provision being section 85 of the Information Technology Act, 2000 which clearly says that if an offence or criminal activity is committed by a company, then every person responsible for running the affairs and business of the company shall also be deemed to be guilty of the same offence and are liable to be punished accordingly.

The law in India fortunately provides an exit route for the top management of companies to exit from their potential criminal liability. Top management of companies can demonstrate that they either did not have any knowledge of the offence or contravention or that they had exercised all due diligence to prevent the commission of any offence or contravention under the law. If the top management of the company is able to prove any of the two conditions, then they could escape from the criminal consequences for such acts.

Further, companies which allow BYOD on their corporate networks, need to appreciate that the moment a device under the BYOD banner, is connected to the corporate network, the company in question becomes an intermediary under the Information Technology Act, 2000. This is so because the said company then becomes a legal entity who on behalf of another person receives, stores or transmits any particular electronic record or provides service with respect to that record. The very fact that the company provides connectivity to corporate networks as also to the Internet to employees coming with devices under the BYOD banner, the said companies become network service providers and hence also intermediaries under section 2 (1)(w) of the Information Technology Act, 2000.

The moment these companies become intermediaries, they are straddled with various obligations by the parameters of the Information Technology Act, 2000. As a principle, the Information Technology Act, 2000 provides that intermediaries shall not be held liable or responsible for any third party data, information or communication link made available or hosted by them, provided certain parameters of the law are met.

The following conditions must be complied with, by the intermediaries/ service providers, before they can think of complete exemption from liability for any third party information, data or communication link made available or hosted by them. These conditions are as follows:

(1) The first important condition is that the functional role of the service provider, in its capacity as an intermediary, is only limited to providing access to a communication system, over which information made available by third party is transmitted or temporarily stored or hosted. In the context of computers/mobiles, the said communication systems would be the computer/mobile networks as also the computer/mobile platforms and internet over which the information made available by third parties is transmitted or temporally stored, or hosted. The said communication system could also include computer servers and computer server farms, over which information made available by third parties, is transmitted or temporally stored or hosted.

    Thus, the only focus is that the intermediary has to ensure that its function is limited to providing access to communication systems. The law does not stipulate that it needs to own or have any proprietary rights over the said communication system. The law does not even talk about the various licensing requirements in this regard. How the access is provided to the communication system by the intermediary is also not the concern of the law. The intermediary must only limit its role solely to providing access to communication system over which information made available by third parties is transmitted or temporally stored or hosted.

(2) The second important condition is that the intermediary/service provider, does not have any control over the transmission. Thus, the said intermediary/service provider should not:

a. Initiate the transmission,

b. Select the receiver of the transmission, and

c. Select or modify the information contained in the transmission.

(3) The third condition that needs to be complied with by any intermediary/service provider is the fact that it, in its capacity, as an intermediary, observes due diligence, while discharging its duties, under the Information Technology Act, 2000 as also observe such other guidelines as the Central Government may prescribe in this regard.

The law still does not define what specifically is "due diligence". The Supreme Court has determined the test of due diligence from the perspective of a reasonable man. The test of a reasonable man does assume tremendous significance. What a reasonable man does in reasonable circumstances could be the relevant test to be applied, when examining and analyzing the scope of "due diligence" done by the mobile service provider, telecom service provider and telecom operator. Further, the due diligence parameters detailed in the Information Technology (Intermediary Guidelines) Rules, 2011 need to be complied with, in order to demonstrate the exercise of due diligence under the Information Technology Act, 2000 as amended.

(4) The fourth important condition that needs to be complied with by the intermediary/service provider is the fact that it has, in its capacity as an intermediary, not conspired or abetted or aided or induced, whether by threats or promises or otherwise, in the commission of any unlawful act. Thus, any direct involvement by the service provider in any illegal and unlawful act is a direct guarantee for the exposure to liability under the Information Technology Act, 2000 for all third party data or information made available by it.

(5) The fifth important condition that needs to be complied with by the service provider is that, upon receiving actual knowledge or upon being notified by the appropriate government or its agency that any information, data or communication link residing in or connected to a computer resource, controlled by the mobile service provider, is being used to commit the unlawful act, the service provider as the intermediary, expeditiously removes or disables access to that material on that resource without vitiating the evidence in any manner whatsoever.

As per section 79 of the Information Technology Act, 2000, the said intermediaries are obligated to exercise due diligence while discharging their obligations under the Information Technology Act, 2000. Under the Information Technology Act, 2000 as amended, the Central Government has notified various rules including the Information Technology Rules, 2011 and the Information Technology (Intermediary Guidelines) Rules, 2011, which really specify various parameters for due diligence. As such , companies concerned have to ensure that they comply with the provisions of due diligence and also comply with other parameters as indicated above before they can be exempt from potential liability under the Information Technology law, both civil and criminal.

One of the inherent dangers under BYOD is that companies have actually no control on the manner in which the devices belonging to their employees will be used for the purposes of activities concerning data and information in the electronic form. As such, companies are required to have in place stringent policies and documentation which can not only help protect the legal interests of the company but also help ensure that in the event of potential legal challenge emerging in future, the company could be able to demonstrate that it had exercised due diligence, while discharging its obligations under the Information Technology Act, 2000. Further, companies, who want to provide the BYOD banner, need to also take into consideration, various other steps so as to protect their legal interests.

At the time of writing, legal issues pertaining to BYOD are beginning to emerge. There is hardly any litigation that is being reported in the public domain pertaining to BYOD in India. However, it is only a question of time before such litigation becomes the norm of the day. Given the high attrition of employees and given their propensity to misuse corporate network, the chances of misuse of devices brought to corporate network under the BYOD banner, are going to dramatically increase as time passes by. Companies would be required proactively not only to protect their own corporate network, but also protect their own corporate entities from potential legal exposure, both civil and criminal under the law prevailing for the time being in force.

As such, there is need for having in place stringent policies and documentation which can help protect the companies in India from potential legal exposure, once they adopt BYOD.

It is always nice to travel on the road on a two-wheeler but the law mandates that the two-wheelers drivers must have helmets put on their heads, in order to safeguard their physical safety. Companies in India, who want to adopt and embrace the BYOD culture, need to ensure that they wear this particular helmet which is in the form of compliances of the applicable laws, rules and regulations, so that in the event there is a potential legal bump or difficult situation ahead, the said companies is not taken by surprise and have done their appropriate documented due diligence compliances in this regard.

Thus, in conclusion, it can be stated that there are various legal challenges that a company needs to be aware of, when it is currently looking at addressing the BYOD culture. Of course, lot of things will actually depend upon the peculiar nature of business of the company and its activities and the manner in which it does its business. The law has only provided general parameters. It is dependant upon the peculiar facts and circumstances of each case as to how the parameters would apply, moreso in the context of the evolving jurisprudence pertaining to BYOD in India. Companies would further be well advised that they must have in place appropriate policies and documents that help them to minimize their risks for potential legal exposure, in the event they are either engaging or planning to engage in BYOD as a corporate culture exercise.

CHAPTER 4

LEGAL ISSUES PERTAINING TO CLOUD COMPUTING IN INDIA

Cloud Computing is one of the latest buzz words that has hit the Information Technology ecosystem in the last one decade. Cloud initially had different meanings for different people. But as technology has developed, cloud computing has emerged as a very important component of the digital ecosystem.

The first thing that comes to one's mind is what exactly is Cloud Computing. There are various definitions of Cloud Computing.

Cloud Computing[75] is the use of computing resources (hardware and software) that are delivered as a service over a network (typically the Internet). The name comes from the use of a cloud-shaped symbol as an abstraction for the complex infrastructure it contains in system diagrams. Cloud Computing entrusts remote services with a user's data, software and computation.

There are various salient features of Cloud Computing.[76]

(a) Ease of use

Cloud Computing is very simple to use. The customer need not have any idea of the underlying technologies involved in the working of the application. With careful planning, every Cloud Computing application can be made user-friendly with a high degree of accessibility.

(b) Scalability

One of the most exciting features of Cloud Computing is the scalability. Applications running in Cloud Computing environments should be in a position to scale from a handful of users to thousands of user distributed geographically across the globe. All this can be done dynamically in a Cloud Computing environment.

(c) Risk

Cloud Computing helps in minimizing the risks of an organization to a very large extent. As Cloud Computing applications run on an "On-Demand" basis, a customer can utilize the application as per his requirements and pay only for the services used. This is almost 100% risk-free as a customer can move out of the application, once his requirements have been satisfied. Most importantly, there is no vendor lock-in lock-out in Cloud Computing applications.

---

75. http://en.wikipedia.org/wiki/Cloud Computing

76. http://cloud-smes.appspot.com/Introduction/DomainIntroduction/features.html

(d) Reliability

Cloud Computing applications rely heavily on their environment. These environments should have the capability to support the applications even under failures. This is known as High Availability. Models like Cluster Computing help in achieving this requirement.

(e) Cost

Cloud Computing applications follow a "Pay as per usage" policy, similar to that of Utility Computing. This policy is very beneficial to the users as they pay for resources they use, when and where required. Further, there isn't a question of investments which make Cloud Computing a low cost, risk free model for enterprises.

(f) Security

Cloud Computing builds on several secure protocols and security measures. However, security always remains a big apprehension in Cloud Computing applications. This is because the storage models in these services are vendor dependent and the vendor creditability is what determines the security of data.

High availability and reliability[77]**:** Availability of servers is high and more reliable as the chances of infrastructure failure are minimal.

Multi-sharing[78]: With the cloud working in a distributed and shared mode, multiple users and applications can work more efficiently with cost reductions by sharing common infrastructure.

Today, increasingly iPads, Tablets, Smart Phones and Smart Devices are getting connected to cloud computing for the purposes of saving data, because cloud computing brings with it tremendous and enormous benefits.

Cloud Computing brings with it many benefits to the end user. These include:[79]

- Access to a huge range of applications without having to download or install anything,
- Applications can be accessed from any computer, anywhere in the world,
- Users can avoid expenditure on hardware and software; only using what they need,
- Companies can share resources in one place,
- Consumption is billed as a utility with minimal upfront costs,
- Scalability *via* on-demand resources.

There are several differences from traditional hosting to cloud hosting. The main differences are:

- Cloud Computing is sold on demand
- The service is managed by the provider

---

77. http://www.jatit.org/volumes/research-papers/Vol9No1/10Vol9No1.pdf
78. http://www.jatit.org/volumes/research-papers/Vol9No1/10Vol9No1.pdf
79. http://www.itgovernance.co.uk/cloud-computing.aspx

- Users can determine the amount of services they take,
- Users can log on to the network from any computer in the world.

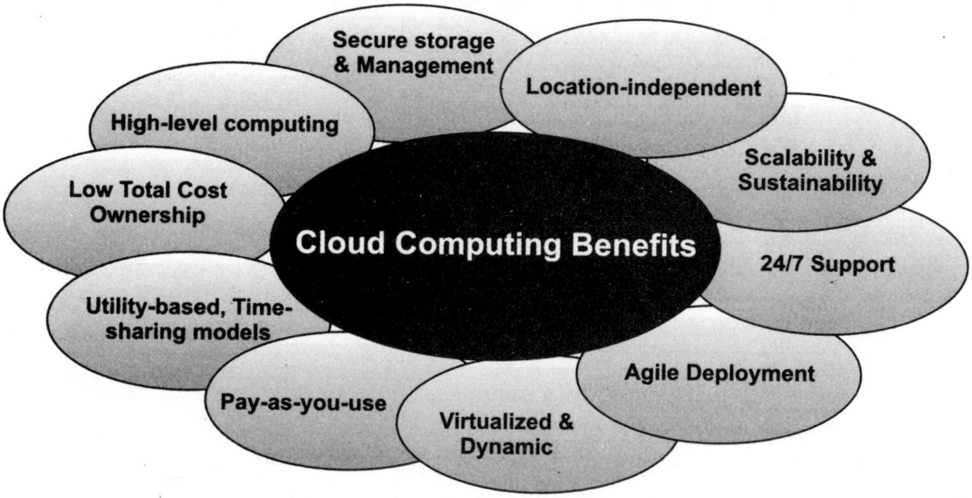

80

In the context of iPads, Tablets, Smart Phones and Smart Devices, Cloud Computing has become an integral aspect of offerings. Let's take the example of Apple. Apple has come up with various smart devices including iPhone, iPad and to supplement the efficacy of such devices, Apple has also come up with iCloud. **iCloud**[81] is a cloud storage and cloud computing service from Apple Inc. launched on October 12, 2011. As of July, 2012, the service has more than 150 million users. The service allows users to store data such as music and iOS applications on remote computer servers for download to multiple devices such as iOS-based devices running iOS 5 or later, and personal computers running OS X 10.7.2 "Lion" or later, or Microsoft Windows (Windows Vista service pack 2 or later). It also replaces Apple's MobileMe service, acting as a data syncing center for e-mail, contacts, calendars, bookmarks, notes, reminders (to-do lists), iWork documents, and other data. The service also allows users to wirelessly back-up their iOS devices to iCloud instead of manually doing so using iTunes. The cloud-based system allows users to store music, photos, applications, documents, bookmarks, reminders, backups, notes, iBooks, and contacts, and provides a platform for Apple's e-mail servers and calendars. Third-party iOS and OS X app developers are able to implement iCloud functionality in their apps through the iCloud API.

---

80. http://www.google.co.in/imgres?hl=en&sa=X&biw=1024&bih=677&tbm=isch&prmd=imvnsb&tbnid=EYSVnTOlWXDvzM:&imgrefurl=http://www.vt2me.com/it-services/cloud-virtualization-microsoft-hyper-v-vmware-vsphere-citrix-xenserver/benefits-of-cloud-computing/&docid=qOMA60iPdrSXMM&imgurl=http://www.vt2me.com/wp-content/uploads/2012/09/cloud_computing.jpg&w=553&h=296&ei=MfiRUNz5MZCHrAekp4CQBw & zoom = 1 & iact = rc & dur = 4 & sig=100487755140654612808&page=1&tbnh=164&tbnw=307&start=0&ndsp=10&ved=1t:429,i:69&tx=194&ty=65
81. http://en.wikipedia.org/wiki/iCloud

Cloud Computing has many benefits, however there are also some associated risks with using cloud computing. These include the following:[82]

- Users do not physically possess storage of their own data, which leaves the responsibility and control of data storage with the provider,
- Users could become dependent upon the cloud computing provider,
- With data held externally, business continuity and disaster recovery are in the hands of the provider,
- Data migration issues when changing cloud provider.

There are various legal ramifications for providing cloud services in the context of use of smart devices in India. All cloud operators become intermediaries under section 2(1)(w) of the Information Technology Act, 2000. This is so because the moment these cloud services are provided in the context of smart devices, the said service providers are providing various services with respect to particular electronic records. Further, the said service providers, with respect to particular electronic records, store, transmit or retain the said particular electronic records on their cloud networks, and hence, such service providers are intermediaries.

Under the law prevailing for the time being in force, the good news is that intermediaries are not responsible for any third party data, information or communication link made available by them. This is by virtue of section 79 of the Information Technology Act, 2000. However, the law has been very cleverly drafted in the sense that this principle is of course subject to the fact that the service provider, as an intermediary, complies with various other parameters defined under the Information Technology Act, 2000 as amended.

The following conditions must be complied with, by the Cloud Computing service providers, before they can think of complete exemption from liability for any third party information, data or communication link made available or hosted by them. These conditions are as follows:

(1) The first important condition is that the functional role of the Cloud Computing service provider, in its capacity as an intermediary, is only limited to providing access to a communication system, over which information made available by third party is transmitted or temporarily stored or hosted. In the context of computers/mobiles, the said communication systems would be the computer/mobile networks as also the computer/mobile platforms and internet over which the information made available by third parties is transmitted or temporally stored, or hosted. The said communication system could also include computer servers and computer server's farms, over which information made available by third parties, is transmitted or temporally stored or hosted. Thus, the only focus that the intermediary has to ensure is that its function is limited to providing access communication systems. The law does not stipulate that it needs to own or have any proprietary rights over the said communication system. The law does not even talk about the various

82. http://www.itgovernance.co.uk/cloud-computing.aspx

licensing requirements in this regard. How the access is provided to the communication system by the intermediary is also not the concern of the law. The intermediary must only limit its role solely to providing access to communication system over which information made available by third parties is transmitted or temporally stored or hosted.

(2) The second important condition is that the Cloud Computing service provider does not have any control over the transmission. Thus, the said Cloud Computing service provider should not:

(a) Initiate the transmission,

(b) Select the receiver of the transmission, and

(c) Select or modify the information contained in the transmission.

(3) The third condition that needs to be complied with by any cloud computing service provider is the fact that it, in its capacity, as an intermediary, observes due diligence, while discharging its duties, under the Information Technology Act, 2000 as also observes such other guidelines as the Central Government may prescribe in this regard. The law still does not define what specifically is "due diligence". The Supreme Court has determined the test of due diligence from the perspective of a reasonable man. The test of a reasonable man does assume tremendous significance. What a reasonable man does in reasonable circumstances could be the relevant test to be applied, when examining and analyzing the scope of "due diligence" done by the mobile service provider, telecom service provider and telecom operator. One of the most important significant parameters in this regard is that the relevant cloud service providers need to ensure that they exercise due diligence while discharging their obligations under the Information Technology Act, 2000. These obligations of due diligence have been stipulated under the Information Technology Rules, 2011 specifically Information Technology (Intermediary Guidelines) Rules, 2011.

(4) The fourth important condition that needs to be complied with by the Cloud Computing service provider is the fact that it has, in its capacity as an intermediary, not conspired or abetted or aided or induced, whether by threats or promise or otherwise, in the commission of any unlawful act. Thus, any direct involvement by the Cloud Computing service provider, in any illegal and unlawful act is a direct guarantee for the exposure to liability under the Information Technology Act, 2000 for all third party data or information made available by it.

(5) The fifth important condition that needs to be complied with by the Cloud Computing service provider is that, upon receiving actual knowledge or upon being notified by the appropriate government or its agency that any information, data or communication link residing in or connected to a computer resource, controlled by the mobile service provider, is being used to commit the unlawful act, the Cloud Computing service provider as the intermediary, expeditiously removes or disables access to that material on that resource without vitiating the evidence in any manner whatsoever.

Of course, in the context of providing cloud-based services in connection with iPads, Tablets, Smart Phones and other Smart Devices, it is relevant that various nuances have to be kept into mind by the relevant service providers. This becomes all the more relevant, given the advent of social media, thanks to which, every user has become a broadcaster and publisher. As the speed of broadcasting and publishing is very fast, it becomes a big challenge for all relevant service providers in the context of iPads, Tablets, Smart Phones and other Smart Devices, who are providing cloud-based services, to ensure compliance with the provisions of the amended Information Technology Act, 2000.

Further, providing of these cloud services could also be slightly problematic, in case if the said cloud services are misused by the users of the smart devices for the purposes of committing various crimes. It is pertinent to point out that various cybercrimes have been defined under the Information Technology Act, 2000. If any of the said crimes are committed on the cloud infrastructure/facilities of the service providers, then *prima facie* the person who has committed the offence, is going to be responsible. However, that does not mean that the cloud service provider is free from all exposure. The said cloud service provider would only be free from potential exposure for the said criminal activities in case the service provider is able to demonstrate that it had exercised all due diligence while discharging its obligations under the Information Technology Act, 2000 and further it had actually gone ahead and fulfilled all the parameters of the law prevailing for the time being in force.

One of the interesting features that one needs to appreciate in this regard is that the law in India in the context of providing cloud-based service has become dramatically different, in the context of *onus* of proof. Normally speaking, in the event of any contravention or any offence, the *onus* of proof clearly lies on the prosecution. The prosecution has to prove the accused as being involved in the said incriminating activity before he can be pronounced guilty by court of law. However in the context of cloud-based services provided by companies, the law has been drafted so as to put the *onus of proof* on the said companies/service providers. Once called upon to show as to how the contravening activity took place on the said Cloud Computing networks of the said service provider, the *onus* of proof will be upon the service provider to prove that it had exercised all due diligence while discharging its obligations under the Act and had further complied with the parameters of the law and had further also not abetted or conspired in the commission of any offence. It is only when the said corporate entity is able to discharge its *onus* of proof that it is going to be not facing potential legal exposure.

As such, in the context of Cloud Computing, it is therefore significant to note that various service providers have to put up various documentations, practices, policies and procedures in place which helps them to ensure compliance with law and further helps them to document their due diligence. In case if such an activity is not done, the said companies, which are providing Cloud Computing services in the context of smart devices, are likely to face various legal challenges in this regard.

In the context of providing Cloud Computing related services in connection with iPads, Tablets, Smart Phones and Smart Devices, the service providers also need to be aware that they could potentially be called upon to provide the relevant computer logs and hence retention of electronic logs in accordance with the law becomes an important parameter. The relevant service provider has to ensure not just compliance with the law prevailing for the time being in force including the Information Technology Act, 2000 but also various rules and regulations made thereunder, before it commences providing cloud computing related services in the context of use of iPads, Tablets, Smart Phones and Smart Devices.

Given the advent of huge storage that is happening on Cloud Computing, Cloud Computing service providers could also be called upon by the relevant law enforcement agencies in India so as to provide the relevant information for the purposes of dealing with any cyber security incident or for investigation of any cybercrime activity. In case, the said service provider is not able to provide any of the information, then it exposes itself to potential legal liability. In fact, the Information Technology Act, 2000 clearly stipulates that the government has, after 26/11 Mumbai attacks, been given huge amount of powers of interception, blocking, decryption and monitoring of electronic information. These powers have been conferred under the provisions of the Information Technology (Amendment) Act, 2008. For the purposes of effectively carrying out its obligations, the Government is further required to ensure that it gets the relevant inputs and information from the service provider.

The Cloud Computing service providers are mandated to retain the concerned electronic records in the exact manner in which they have been generated under the law. Once the law enforcement agency calls upon the service provider for information and the service provider is not able to provide the said information in the context of Cloud Computing and iPads, Tablets, Smart Phones and Smart Devices, then the service provider could have a serious problem at hand. Because such non-providing of services itself would tantamount to criminal activity and offence punishable with imprisonment and fine under the Information Technology Act, 2000. As such, various documentations and practices, procedures and policies need to be put in place by the relevant Cloud Computing service providers in India before they go about providing Cloud Computing-related services, in the context of use of iPads, Tablets, Smart Phones and Smart Devices.

Thus in conclusion, it can be clearly stated that while Cloud Computing is the future of technology, the fact remains that Cloud Computing brings with it various legal, regulatory and policy issues and challenges for its service providers in the context of law in India. It will be best advisable for all relevant stake-holders who are providing any service in respect of Cloud Computing in the context of use of iPads, Tablets, Smart Phones and Smart Devices that they comply with the law prevailing for the time being in force and have all the relevant documentation in place. This is likely to act as an umbrella of security for them and could potentially safeguard the legal interests of the service providers, in the event of any computer emergency or legal challenge as time passes by.

CHAPTER 5
LEGAL ISSUES PERTAINING TO SOCIAL MEDIA IN INDIA

Today, social networking is a popular activity on smart phone ipads, tablets and other smart devices. The users spend most of their time on smart phones/ smart devices for accessing the social networking sites in comparison to traditional web access.

The future of social networking is mobile. A report from comScore shows that both Facebook and Twitter users spend more time using those networks on mobile devices than they do on traditional computers or laptops. According to CNET, Facebook mobile users spent more than 7 hours engaging *via* browsers or apps in March, as compared to six hours *via* the computer. Twitter mobile users, meanwhile, spent more than 2 hours engaging on mobile devices, as compared to just 20.4 minutes on Twitter.com (with the caveat that doesn't track usage on third-party desktop clients like TweetDeck).[83]

With the usage of social networking sites on the smart phones, it has exposed millions to cybercrime. Around 5.4 million people were targeted by online criminals over the past 12 months, according to Norton's annual Cybercrime report. More than one in three Australians active on social media say they've been a victim of cybercrime on platforms like Facebook and Twitter. Cybersecurity expert Adam Palmer, who advises the FBI and Norton, said criminals were rapidly shifting away from traditional PC-based virus attacks and toward "easier targets" on mobile devices. The report estimates cybercrime costs Australians $1.65 billion a year and $110 billion worldwide, with the average victim being fleeced of $306 – almost double the global average.[84]

All social media websites are seeing a dramatic increase in their adoption across the world. Specifically in India, some have run down while others like Facebook have become predominant. Now seeing from a national perspective, there are couple of things that hits one's mind. *First*, social media as a phenomenon is not directly covered by the law, you don't find the usage of the words "social media" in the law. However, the Indian Cyberlaw being the Information Technology Act, 2000 has been amended by the Information Technology (Amendment) Act, 2008. The new amendments have come up with the concept of intermediary and the term intermediary is defined to mean any person

83. http://www.forbes.com/sites/jondube/2012/05/08/why-smartphones-are-the-future-of-social-networking/
84. http://www.theaustralian.com.au/media/social-media-and-smartphones-exposing-millions-to-cybercrime-says-study/story-e6frg996-1226466419501

with respect to any particular electronic record who on behalf of another person receives, stores or transmits that record or provides any service with respect to the said record and specifically includes telecom service providers, internet service providers, network service providers, web hosting service providers, online auction portals, online market places, online payment sites, search engines and cyber cafes.

Today, social networking sites allow everyone to become a creator, a publisher, a transmitter as also a repository for information including third party data or information as also sensitive personal data or information.

In India, the relevant legislation applicable to the electronic form is the Information Technology Act, 2000. The Information Technology Act, 2000 has been amended by the Information Technology (Amendment) Act, 2008 and the same has come into effect from October 27, 2009.

This legislation deals with all kinds of data and information in the electronic form as also the use of iPads, Tablets, Smart Phones and Smart Devices.

It is important to note that all social media service providers are intermediaries under section 2(1)(w) of the Information Technology Act, 2000. Section 79 of the Information Technology Act, 2000, mandates that these intermediaries have to exercise due diligence while discharging their obligations under the law. The Information Technology Rules, 2011 mandate parameters of due diligence which say that these service providers must have detailed terms and conditions informing their users not to publish or transmit information which is violative of the law. If they still publish the said information and either an affected party complains or the government notifies about such content, the intermediaries are duty bound to act within 36 hours and remove the offending content.

Legally, the social media service providers may be located in different jurisdictions. Most of these social media companies are considered as content providers or platform providers and most of them being located in the US are covered under the US laws. US does not make them liable for third party information but the position in India is substantially different. In India, all these social media service providers are intermediaries under section 2(1)(w) of the Information Technology Act, 2000. The moment they are an intermediary, under section 79 of the Information Technology Act, they are not made liable for any third party data, information or communication link made available by them provided they comply with the law, provided they exercise due diligence while discharging their obligations under the Act, provided they do not conspire or abet in the commission of any offence and provided once they are notified of any illegal content, they remove it within 36 hours.

It is pertinent to note that whatever one writes on social media websites is legal evidence and can be used against the concerned person in legal proceedings and for legal purposes.

Misuse of social media has two kinds of consequences – civil exposure to liability by paying damages way of compensation upto Rs. 5 crore (INR 50 million) under the amended Information Technology Act, 2000 and beyond five crores (INR 50 million) in a court of competent jurisdiction.

In addition, there is criminal exposure of criminal liability of punishment from three years to life imprisonment and fine from Rs. 1 lakh to Rs. 10 lakh (INR 1 million).

It is imperative for social media websites to ensure that while they deal with sensitive personal information in their capacity as an intermediary, they are duty bound to observe reasonable security practices and procedures in order to safeguard and protect the said information from unauthorized access or exposure.

The law has now specifically talked about content which is offensive or which has got menacing character. So under section 66A of the Information Technology Act, if you send any information from iPads, Tablets, Smart Phones and Smart Devices that is offensive or has menacing character, then that is an offence punishable with three years imprisonent and fine. Further, this section also covers information which is sent, which a person knows is false, but has been sent for the purpose of causing insult, injury, hatred or ill will, annoyance. Section 66A does not talk about what is offensive and does not give any illustrations in that regard. Similarly, section 67 of the Information Technology Act does not define what is obscenity or what is obscene, but uses lofty words like publishing or transmitting information electronically, which is lascivious or which appeals to the prurient interests or the effect of which is to tend to deprave and corrupt the minds of those who are likely to see, read or hear the same. Under the Information Technology Rules, 2011 that were notified in April 2011 the Government of India have come up with Information Technology (Intermediary Guidelines) Rules, 2011. Rule 3 of Information Technology (Intermediary Guidelines) Rules, 2011 categorically now provides that the service providers as intermediaries shall have detailed terms and conditions which specify that any user shall not host, display, upload, modify, publish, transmit, update or share any information that—

(a) belongs to another person and to which the user does not have any right to;

(b) is grossly harmful, harassing, blasphemous, defamatory, obscene, pornographic, paedophilic, libellous, invasive of another's privacy, hateful, or racially, ethnically objectionable, disparaging, relating or encouraging money laundering or gambling, or otherwise unlawful in any manner whatever;

(c) harm minors in any way;

(d) infringes any patent, trademark, copyright or other proprietary rights;

(e) violates any law for the time being in force;

(f) deceives or misleads the addressee about the origin of such messages or communicates any information which is grossly offensive or menacing in nature;

(g) impersonate another person;

(h) contains software viruses or any other computer code, files or programs designed to interrupt, destroy or limit the functionality of any computer resource;

(i) threatens the unity, integrity, defence, security or sovereignty of India, friendly relations with foreign States, or or public order or causes incitement to the commission of any cognisable offence or prevents investigation of any offence or is insulting any other nation.

After doing that, if still somebody believes that some information is offensive or defamatory or violative of the rules and the law, the affected person has a right to complain or the government has a right to notify about such content. Once either of these two situations happen, the service provider or intermediary is duty bound to mandatorily act within 36 hours and work with the user to disable access to that content. If the service provider or intermediary does not do so, it becomes a co-accused in the said crime.

Thus, a perusal of the aforesaid itself clearly shows that users of iPads, Tablets, Smart Phones and Smart Devices need to be extremely careful that they should not use iPads, Tablets, Smart Phones and Smart Devices for the purposes of uploading, posting or receiving content of the various kinds which are stipulated under rule 3 of the Information Technology (Intermediary Guidelines) Rules, 2011. If they do so, they could expose themselves to potential legal exposure. Further, such content could be removed or disabled by the service provider of the relevant social media website, once he receives the complaint from the affected person or a notification in that regard from the government.

As mobiles ipads, tablets, smart phones and smart devices are increasingly becoming *de facto* modes of accessing social media websites, users will have to be careful and duly diligent. Any carelessness or negligence on the part of the users of iPads, Tablets, Smart Phones and Smart Devices is likely to expose them and potentially social media service providers to legal liability. The Information Technology Act, 2000 as amended by the Information Technology (Amendment) Act, 2008 as also rules and regulations made thereunder including the Information Technology (Intermediary Guidelines) Rules, 2011 will continue to be applicable in respect of all acts done using mobiles for accessing social media and doing various activities thereon.

CHAPTER 6
LEGAL ISSUES PERTAINING TO MOBILE APPS

Today iPads, Tablets, Smart Phones and Smart Devices are increasingly being used by a large number of people. As the mobile revolution is continuing to grow, various new kinds of mobile handsets, new operating systems are hitting the market. Mobile today is a multi-dimensional computing device which has got various facilities.

Further, a large number of other utilitarian functions that computers provide on desktops are also sought to be provided on mobile phones through various applications known as Apps. Mobile Apps today are the rage of the times.

The word "Apps" is a short form of application. A Mobile Application or Mobile App is a software application designed to run on various communication devices, smart phones, tablets, iphones, ipads and other mobile devices. These mobile applications are available across the world through various application distribution platforms. Some of these platforms include Apple App Store, Google Play, Windows Phone Marketplace and BlackBerry App World.

A mobile application (or mobile app) is a software application designed to run on smart phones, tablets and other smart devices. They are available through application distribution platforms, which are typically operated by the owner of the mobile operating system, such as the Apple AppStore, Google Play, Windows Phone Marketplace and BlackBerry App World.

The term "app" has become popular, and in 2010 was listed as "Word of the Year" by the American Dialect Society. Technologist Michael Saylor has referred to the newer mobile app enabled smart phones as "app-phones" for their distinction from the earlier smart phone models.

The popularity of mobile applications has continued to rise, as their usage has become increasingly more prevalent across mobile phone users. A comScore study done in May, 2012 reported that mobile app usage was actually higher than web browsing; 51.1% vs. 49.8% respectively.

There are various definitions of mobile apps which are provided by different sources. Let us examine some of these definitions:

> "A mobile app is a software program you can download and access directly using your phone or another mobile device, like a tablet or music player.
>
> A mobile application, also known as mobile app, is a term used to describe software that runs on smartphones and mobile phones. Mobile

applications are designed to educate, entertain, or assist consumers in their daily lives"[85].

"Mobile application also called mobile apps, it is a term used to describe Internet applications that run on smart phones and other mobile devices. Mobile applications usually help users by connecting them to Internet services more commonly accessed on desktop or notebook computers, or help them by making it easier to use the Internet on their portable devices. A mobile app may be a mobile Web site bookmarking utility, a mobile-based instant messaging client, Gmail for mobile, and many other applications."[86]

"Mobile applications or mobile apps are applications developed for small handheld devices, such as mobile phones, smartphones, PDAs and so on. Mobile apps can come preloaded on the handheld device as well as can be downloaded by users from app stores or the Internet.

You can find mobile apps on both feature phones and smartphones. The most popular smartphone platforms that support mobile apps are Windows Mobile, Android, Symbian, Java ME and Palm[87]".

These mobile applications are currently being provided by various mobile application platforms. Some of the platforms which currently exist in the market for distribution of these mobile apps, as listed by Wikipedia, are as follows:

Amazon Appstore[88]: The Amazon Appstore is an American mobile application store for the Google Android operating system. It was opened in March, 2011, with 3800 applications.

Apple App Store[89]: The Apple App Store opened on July 10, 2008, and as of January, 2011, reported over 10 billion downloads. As of June 6, 2011, there are 425,000 third-party apps available, which are downloaded by 200 million iOS users.

BlackBerry App World[90]: Apps for the BlackBerry mobile devices are available through the BlackBerry App World application distribution service. It opened in April, 2009, and as of February, 2011, was claiming the largest revenue per app: $9,166.67 compared to $6,480.00 at the Apple App Store and $1,200 in the Android market. In July, 2011, it was reporting 3 million downloads per day and one billion total downloads.

Google Play[91]: Google Play is an international online software store developed by Google for Android devices. It was opened in October, 2008. In late April of 2012, AppBrain reported that there are over 430,000 available apps, with 10 billion apps downloaded and installed as of December, 2011.

---

85. http://www.hudsonhorizons.com/Our-Company/Internet-Glossary/Mobile-Applications.htm
86. http://www.webopedia.com/TERM/M/mobile_application.html
87. http://mobiledevices.about.com/od/glossary/g/What-Is-A-Mobile-Application.htm
88. http://en.wikipedia.org/wiki/Mobile_app
89. http://en.wikipedia.org/wiki/Mobile_app
90. http://en.wikipedia.org/wiki/Mobile_app
91. http://en.wikipedia.org/wiki/Mobile_app

Nokia Store:[92] An app store for the Nokia phone was launched internationally in May, 2009. As of April, 2011, there were 50,000 apps, and as of August, 2011, Nokia was reporting 9 million downloads per day. In February 2011, Nokia reported that it would start using Windows Phone 7 as its primary operating system. In May, 2011, Nokia announced plans to rebrand its Ovi product line under the Nokia brand and Ovi Store was renamed Nokia Store in October, 2011. Nokia Store remains as the distribution platform for its previous lines of mobile operating systems, while Nokia's Windows Phone 7 offering has been integrated into the Microsoft Marketplace.

Windows Phone Marketplace[93]**:** The Windows Phone Marketplace is a service by Microsoft for its Windows Phone 7 platform, which was launched in October, 2010. As of January, 2012, it has over 60,000 apps available.

Applications or Mobile Apps started really becoming popular with the advent of iPhones. The iPhone, being the proprietary technology of Apple, heralded the coming of the new era with new kinds of Mobile Apps. These Mobile Apps are being sold on Apple's iTunes.

At the time of writing, more than 4,00,000 Mobile Apps are available on the iTunes website. Some of the Mobile Apps belong to deliver functions while others provide interesting functionality of distinctive use to users.

While Mobile Apps have increased our convenience, productivity and adaptability of communication devices, yet at the same time, there are a large number of legal issues surrounding Mobile Apps. Some of these legal issues are just beginning to be highlighted at the time of writing.

A report from the research and consulting firm Strategy Analytics says global smart phone sales have gone past the 1 billion mark, 1.038 billion to be precise for the first time in the third quarter of 2012 and the numbers are set to double by 2015 end. The figures translate into the fact that one out of every seven people globally, carries a Smart phone.[94]

When one analyses the impact of Mobile Apps and their significance, various legal issues surrounding Mobile Apps come to one's mind.

The singular biggest important legal issue in today's context is that of privacy. People have inherent expectation of privacy whenever they talk on the phone. Generally, users are aware of the sovereign right of interception, monitoring and blocking that any sovereign government may exercise. Normally, a genuine *bona fide* lay user of a mobile communication device has invariably little expectation of his privacy being compromised.

Yet with the coming of Mobile Apps, there are very complex legal issues around privacy and Mobile Apps.

A recent study showed that most people are unaware of the fact that the photos and videos taken with their smart phones or cameras contain geolocation

92. http://en.wikipedia.org/wiki/Mobile_app

93. http://en.wikipedia.org/wiki/Mobile_app

94. http://www.thinkdigit.com/Mobiles-PDAs/Number-of-smartphones-in-use-worldwide-surpasses_11096.html

information. This information can be used to localise them while they are travelling, or even reveal their home address. This may be considered as a potential source of information leakage and may lead to a privacy breach. The service launched in the UK by World-Tracker, allows users to track any mobile phone around the globe and follow its movements from your computer. While the benefits provided by these systems are indisputable, they unfortunately pose a considerable threat to location privacy.[95]

There are no fixed standards that are applicable in the context of Mobile Apps and neither is there any burning desire or intention to comply with respecting and preserving the privacy of individual users of communication devices.

As such, one finds that there are virtually no audits available on Mobile Apps and hence these Mobile Apps, virtually out of their own sweet-will, have their own respective terms regarding requiring of service irrespective of privacy, personal and data of consumers and customers of the communication devices.

A July, 2012 study by the mobile security company Lookout found that, ads from advertising networks running on some apps may change smart phone settings and take contact information without your permission. The study tested 384,000 apps and found that 19,200 of those apps used malicious ad networks.[96]

In 2011, we saw malware families, such as Opfake; migrate from older platforms to Android. Android marketplace for apps has central control over what is published, it is easy for malware authors to create trojans that are very similar to popular apps, although Android users must explicitly approve the set of permissions that is outlined for each app. Currently more than half of all Android threats, collect device data or track users' activities. Almost a quarter of the mobile threats identified in 2011 were designed to send content and one of the most popular ways for phone malware authors to make money is by sending premium SMS messages from infected phones. This technique was used by 18% of mobile threats identified in 2011. Increasingly, phone malware does more than send SMSs. For example, we see attacks that track the user's position with GPS and steal information[97].

In case Mobile Apps are utilizing the platform provided by telecom service providers, in the event of violation of privacy or further rights of the users, the said platform of the telecom service providers could also be made liable for potential legal consequences, both civil and criminal.

There are further issues pertaining to violation of intellectual property rights by Mobile Apps. The Mobile App might use (*i.e.* display, reproduce, publish, modify, or make a derivative work of, etc.) copyrighted content such as images, videos, and sound recordings of others. Developers need to procure "rights clearance" from copyright owners in order to be protected against infringement claims. Clearance may exist for certain uses, such as in-store, but it is important to receive permission for use where such rights have not already been licensed.

---

95. Privacy, Accountability and Trust – Challenges and Opportunities by The European Network and Information Security Agency (ENISA).
96. https://www.privacyrights.org/fs/fs2b-cellprivacy.htm
97. INTERNET SECURITY THREAT REPORT, 2011 Trends Volume 17 Published April, 2012 by Symantec

Trademark issues might also arise if the App or its features are similar to a prior registered or otherwise recognized trademark. Trademark is a branding tool, and so the true test of infringement is whether the use of another's trademark confuses the end user regarding the origin of the App. Thus, an App could infringe another trademark in a number of ways, including (i) if the name of the App is similar to an existing trademark, (ii) if the look, feel, and layout of the App is similar to that of a recognized mark, or (iii) if an existing trademark is used in the marketing or description of the App such that the end user is likely to be confused about the source of the App. If the App allows for user contribution, then it is important to protect against vicarious liability from users who post infringing content.[98]

There are legal issues pertaining to the applicability of jurisdiction, in the event of dispute with the Mobile Apps service providers. Technically speaking, the jurisdiction would be determined by the terms and conditions entered between the customer and Mobile Apps service provider. Further, in case the said terms and conditions are silent, the dispute can be raised in any jurisdiction where the Mobile App is downloadable, used or is available on mobile platforms. Jurisprudence on this issue has yet to evolve at the time of writing.

In certain countries, in the context of the cyber legal legislation, Mobile Apps specifically come under some specific provisions. Mobile Apps service provider is an intermediary within the meaning of section 2(1)(w) of the amended Information Technology Act, 2000. The Indian Cyberlaw being the Information Technology Act, 2000 mandates a duty of exercise of due diligence upon intermediaries, while discharging their obligations under the law. Exercise of due diligence by Mobile Apps service provider would distinctly involve not to violate the privacy of its users. It will be interesting to see jurisprudence around Mobile Apps is developed in countries like India.

India's mobile phone industry is one of the fastest growing industries in the world.This is due to its high population and fast rate of growth. The Indian mobile phone industry has entered a phase of boom due to many proactive measures taken by various licensors and regulators.

Clearly as time passes by, in the countries where the mobile penetration is extremely high, Mobile Apps will continue to be used on a much more frequent, regular basis. The chances of arising of disputes are high. At the time of writing, we have not yet seen much evolution in jurisprudence on this new subject. It will be interesting to see how the jurisprudence on this subject evolves, as time passes by. Mobile Apps could open up a Pandora's Box of legal issues and legal exposure in the event of violations of rights of end users or customers and also violation of established law, prevailing over the national jurisdictions for the time being in force.

---

98. http://www.auxiliumlaw.com/content/legal-issues-mobile-applications-1

CONCLUSION

The various chapters of this book have tried to examine the different legal, policy and regulatory challenges that are likely to be faced by all relevant stakeholders and users of smart devices and connected services. The smart devices are the future of technology. Tomorrow belongs to smart devices as also mobile applications. In fact, this present decade is a decade belonging to the mobile bandwagon. Lot of new dramatic changes are continuing to happen with the advent of new kinds of technologies in these communication devices and iPads, Tablets, Smart Phones and Smart Devices. New kinds of models are emerging with each passing month, bringing far more computing capacities and capabilities in the hands of users. While the said smart devices are intending to make the users more smart, productive and efficient, the fact still remains that misuses of these devices are already beginning to happen. We are only scratching the tip of the iceberg but a lot of far more momentous legal, policy and regulatory challenges in this regard are likely to emerge, as time passes by.

The author is conscious of the fact that given the speed of technology, technology invariably leaves law ten steps behind itself. Law is always trying to catch up and is never being successful. However, in India, till such time that the law is changed, the law prevailing for the time being in force being the Information Technology Act, 2000 as amended by the Information Technology (Amendment) Act, 2008 and also various rules and regulations made thereunder, shall apply to all activities done using iPads, Tablets, Smart Phones and Smart Devices as also data and information in the electronic form resident therein. Given the intrinsic challenges that are likely to emerge in this regard, it is also possible that the Central Government could come up with more appropriate rules, regulations and notifications in this regard, which could help further, to prescribe the specific activities that should not be done using these iPads, Tablets, Smart Phones and Smart Devices. It is hard to predict how the jurisprudence around the use of iPads, Tablets, Smart Phones and Smart Devices is going to be evolved in India. However, the foundation for the said jurisprudence will have to be the Indian Cyberlaw.

A perusal of the Indian Cyberlaw clearly shows that it is not all comprehensive and it still has various loopholes. Given the fact that this law was enacted in the year 2000 and amended only after 9 years thereafter in the year 2009 when the Information Technology (Amendment) Act, 2008 came into force on 27th October, 2009, clearly this law has not even begun examining in a comprehensive manner, emerging legal issues pertaining to use, misuse and abuse of iPads, Tablets, Smart Phones and Smart Devices. The law has only managed to touch some of the aspects.

This becomes all the more relevant since communication devices have been brought within the ambit of the law with effect from 2008. But while the Information Technology (Amendment) Act, 2008 made only some changes in the said Information Technology law, the fact remains that these changes have been monumental in terms of expanding the scope of the legislaation to cover activities connected with use of iPads, Tablets, Smart Phones and Smart Devices. As time passes by, there will be need for far more amendments in the Information Technology Act, 2000 more so in the context of activities using iPads, Tablets, Smart Phones and Smart Devices. Clearly, the advent of iPads, Tablets, Smart Phones and Smart Devices are going to likely usher in the culture of smart computing. While it is expected that self-regulation is going to be a preferred mode as far as governments are concerned in the context of use of smart devices, self-regulation alone may not suffice. Governments of the world would increasingly be required to intervene and regulate the aspects pertaining to undesirable and criminal activities done using iPads, Tablets, Smart Phones and Smart Devices.

The advent of iPads, Tablets, Smart Phones and Smart Devices is further likely to enhance the scope of criminal activities specifically smart terrorism. The Indian Government has done a good job in bringing in place the Information Technology (Amendment) Act, 2008. However, a lot of amendments are now required as time passes by.

In conclusion, it can definitely be stated that India is beginning to see the emergence of jurisprudence of case-law around "smart devices". Given the peculiar customized requirements of the Indian ecosystem, more and more legal, policy and regulatory challenges are likely to emerge in the context of use of iPads, Tablets, Smart Phones and Smart Devices, which will further warrant coming up of appropriate, enabling, effective, deterrent provisions of law in this regard.

The future belongs to iPads, Tablets, Smart Phones and Smart Devices. The legislation needs to be up-to-date for dealing with all legal, policy and regulatory challenges posed by the use of iPads, Tablets, Smart Phones and Smart Devices. This is the very topical space of jurisprudence that needs to be watched. It will be interesting to see how the law is going to be evolved. Needless to say, it will suffice to conclude that the second decade of the 21st century will be the defining decade in terms of evolution and development of jurisprudence around use of iPads, Tablets, Smart Phones and Smart Devices in India. This decade is also likely to see tremendous advances in law and more significantly, is likely to see a complete change in the way, smart computing emerges as an integral part of human life and smart governance in India.

THE INFORMATION TECHNOLOGY ACT, 2000

(21 of 2000)

[*9th June, 2000*]

An Act to provide legal recognition for transactions carried out by means of electronic data interchange and other means of electronic communication, commonly referred to as "electronic commerce", which involve the use of alternatives to paper-based methods of communication and storage of information, to facilitate electronic filing of documents with the Government agencies and further to amend the Indian Penal Code, the Indian Evidence Act, 1872, the Banker's Books Evidence Act, 1891 and the Reserve Bank of India Act, 1934 and for matters connected therewith or incidental thereto;

WHEREAS the General Assembly of the United Nations by resolution A/RES/51/162, dated 30th January, 1997 has adopted the Model Law on Electronic Commerce adopted by the United Nations Commission on International Trade Law;

AND WHEREAS the said resolution recommends, *inter alia,* that all States give favourable consideration to the said Model Law when they enact or revise their laws, in view of the need for uniformity of the law applicable to alternatives to paper-based methods of communication and storage of information;

AND WHEREAS it is considered necessary to give effect to the said resolution and to promote efficient delivery of Government services by means of reliable electronic records;

BE it enacted by Parliament in the Fifty-first Year of the Republic of India as follows:—

CHAPTER I
PRELIMINARY

1. Short title, extent, commencement and application.—(1) This Act may be called the Information Technology Act, 2000.

(2) It shall extend to the whole of India and, save as otherwise provided in this Act, it applies also to any offence or contravention thereunder committed outside India by any person.

(3) It shall come into force on such date[1] as the Central Government may, by notification, appoint and different dates may be appointed for different provisions of this Act and any reference in any such provision to the commencement of this Act shall be construed as a reference to the commencement of that provision.

[2][(4) Nothing in this Act shall apply to documents or transactions specified in the First Schedule:

Provided that the Central Government may, by notification in the Official Gazette, amend the First Schedule by way of addition or deletion of entries thereto.

(5) Every notification issued under sub-section (4) shall be laid before each House of Parliament.]

---

1. Came into force on 17-10-2000 *vide* G.S.R. 788(E), dated 17th October, 2000.
2. Subs. by Act 10 of 2009, sec. 3, for sub-section (4) (w.e.f. 27-10-2009). Sub-section (4), before substitution, stood as under:

"(4) Nothing in this Act shall apply to—

(a) a negotiable instrument (other than a cheque) as defined in section 13 of the Negotiable Instruments Act, 1881 (26 of 1881);

(b) a power-of-attorney as defined in section 1A of the Powers-of-Attorney Act, 1882 (7 of 1882);

(c) a trust as defined in section 3 of the Indian Trusts Act, 1882 (2 of 1882);

(d) a Will as defined in clause (h) of section (2) of the Indian Succession Act, 1925 (39 of 1925), including any other testamentary disposition by whatever name called;

(e) any contract for the sale or conveyance of immovable property or any interest in such property;

(f) any such class of documents or transactions as may be notified by the Central Government in the Official Gazette."

2. Definitions.—(1) In this Act, unless the context otherwise requires,—

(a) "access", with its grammatical variations and cognate expressions, means gaining entry into, instructing or communicating with the logical, arithmetical or memory function resources of a computer, computer system or computer network;

(b) "addressee" means a person who is intended by the originator to receive the electronic record but does not include any intermediary;

(c) "adjudicating officer" means an adjudicating officer appointed under sub-section (1) of section 46;

(d) "affixing [1][electronic signature]", with its grammatical variations and cognate expressions means adoption of any methodology or procedure by a person for the purpose of authenticating an electronic record by means of [1][electronic signature];

(e) "appropriate Government" means as respects any matter,—

(i) enumerated in List II of the Seventh Schedule to the Constitution;

(ii) relating to any State law enacted under List III of the Seventh Schedule to the Constitution,

the State Government and in any other case, the Central Government;

(f) "asymmetric crypto system" means a system of a secure key pair consisting of a private key for creating a digital signature and a public key to verify the digital signature;

(g) "Certifying Authority" means a person who has been granted a licence to issue a [1][electronic signature] Certificate under section 24;

(h) "certification practice statement" means a statement issued by a Certifying Authority to specify the practices that the Certifying Authority employs in issuing [2][Electronic Signature] Certificates;

[3][(ha) "communication device" means cell phones, personal digital assistance or combination of both or any other device used to communicate, send or transmit any text, video, audio or image;]

(i) "computer" means any electronic, magnetic, optical or other high-speed data processing device or system which performs logical, arithmetic and memory functions by manipulations of electronic, magnetic or optical impulses, and includes all input, output, processing, storage, computer software or communication facilities which are connected or related to the computer in a computer system or computer network;

[4][(j) "computer network" means the inter-connection of one or more computers or computer systems or communication device through—

(i) the use of satellite, microwave, terrestrial line, wire, wireless or other communication media; and

(ii) terminals or a complex consisting of two or more inter-connected computers or communication device whether or not the inter-connection is continuously maintained;]

(k) "computer resource" means computer, computer system, computer network, data, computer data base or software;

---

1. Subs. by Act 10 of 2009, sec. 2, for "digital signature" (w.e.f. 27-10-2009).
2. Subs. by Act 10 of 2009, sec. 2, for "Digital Signature" (w.e.f. 27-10-2009).
3. Ins. by Act 10 of 2009, sec. 4(A) (w.e.f. 27-10-2009).
4. Subs. by Act 10 of 2009, sec. 4(B), for clause (j) (w.e.f. 27-10-2009). Clause (j), before substitution, stood as under:

'(j) "computer network" means the interconnection of one or more computers through—

(i) the use of satellite, microwave, terrestrial line or other communication media; and

(ii) terminals or a complex consisting of two or more interconnected computers whether or not the interconnection is continuously maintained;'

(l) "computer system" means a device or collection of devices, including input and output support devices and excluding calculators which are not programmable and capable of being used in conjunction with external files which contain computer programmes, electronic instructions, input data and output data that performs logic, arithmetic, data storage and retrieval, communication control and other functions;

(m) "Controller" means the Controller of Certifying Authorities appointed under sub-section (l) of section 17;

(n) "Cyber Appellate Tribunal" means the Cyber [1][***] Appellate Tribunal established under sub-section (1) of section 48;

[2][(na) "cyber cafe" means any facility from where access to the internet is offered by any person in the ordinary course of business to the members of the public;]

[2][(nb) "cyber security" means protecting information, equipment, devices computer, computer resource, communication device and information stored therein from unauthorised access, use, disclosure, disruption, modification or destruction;]

(o) "data" means a representation of information, knowledge, facts, concepts or instructions which are being prepared or have been prepared in a formalised manner, and is intended to be processed, is being processed or has been processed in a computer system or computer network, and may be in any form (including computer printouts magnetic or optical storage media, punched cards, punched tapes) or stored internally in the memory of the computer;

(p) "digital signature" means authentication of any electronic record by a subscriber by means of an electronic method or procedure in accordance with the provisions of section 3;

(q) "Digital Signature Certificate" means a Digital Signature Certificate issued under sub-section (4) of section 35;

(r) "electronic form", with reference to information, means any information generated, sent, received or stored in media, magnetic, optical, computer memory, micro film, computer generated micro fiche or similar device;

(s) "Electronic Gazette" means the Official Gazette published in the electronic form;

(t) "electronic record" means data, record or data generated, image or sound stored, received or sent in an electronic form or micro film or computer generated micro fiche;

[3][(ta) "electronic signature" means authentication of any electronic record by a subscriber by means of the electronic technique specified in the Second Schedule and includes digital signature;]

[3][(tb) "Electronic Signature Certificate" means an Electronic Signature Certificate issued under section 35 and includes Digital Signature Certificate;]

(u) "function", in relation to a computer, includes logic, control, arithmetical process, deletion, storage and retrieval and communication or telecommuni-cation from or within a computer;

[4][(ua) "Indian Computer Emergency Response Team" means an agency established under sub-section (1) of section 70B;]

(v) "information" includes [5][data, message, text], images, sound, voice, codes, computer programmes, software and data bases or micro film or computer generated micro fiche;

[6][(w) "intermediary", with respect to any particular electronic records, means any person who on behalf of another person receives, stores or transmits that record

1. The word "Regulations" omitted by Act 10 of 2009, sec. 4(C) (w.e.f. 27-10-2009).
2. Ins. by Act 10 of 2009, sec. 4(D) (w.e.f. 27-10-2009).
3. Ins. by Act 10 of 2009, sec. 4(E) (w.e.f. 27-10-2009).
4. Ins. by Act 10 of 2009, sec. 4(F) (w.e.f. 27-10-2009).
5. Subs. by Act 10 of 2009, sec. 4(G), for "data, text" (w.e.f. 27-10-2009).
6. Subs. by Act 10 of 2009, sec. 4(H), for clause (w) (w.e.f. 27-10-2009). Clause (w), before substitution, stood as under:

Contd. on next page

or provides any service with respect to that record and includes telecom service providers, network service providers, internet service providers, web-hosting service providers, search engines, online payment sites, online-auction sites, online-market places and cyber cafes;]

(x) "key pair", in an asymmetric crypto system, means a private key and its mathematically related public key, which are so related that the public key can verify a digital signature created by the private key;

(y) "law" includes any Act of Parliament or of a State Legislature, Ordinances promulgated by the President or a Governor, as the case may be, Regulations made by the President under article 240, Bills enacted as President's Act under sub-clause (a) of clause (1) of article 357 of the Constitution and includes rules, regulations, bye-laws and orders issued or made thereunder;

(z) "licence" means a licence granted to a Certifying Authority under section 24;

(za) "originator" means a person who sends, generates, stores or transmits any electronic message; or causes any electronic message to be sent, generated, stored or transmitted to any other person but does not include an intermediary;

(zb) "prescribed" means prescribed by rules made under this Act;

(zc) "private key" means the key of a key pair used to create a digital signature;

(zd) "public key" means the key of a key pair used to verify a digital signature and listed in the Digital Signature Certificate;

(ze) "secure system" means computer hardware, software, and procedure that—

(a) are reasonably secure from unauthorised access and misuse;

(b) provide a reasonable level of reliability and correct operation;

(c) are reasonably suited to performing the intended functions; and

(d) adhere to generally accepted security procedures;

(zf) "security procedure" means the security procedure prescribed under section 16 by the Central Government;

(zg) "subscriber" means a person in whose name the [1][Electronic Signature] Certificate is issued;

(zh) "verify", in relation to a digital signature, electronic record or public key, with its grammatical variations and cognate expressions, means to determine whether—

(a) the initial electronic record was affixed with the digital signature by the use of private key corresponding to the public key of the subscriber;

(b) the initial electronic record is retained intact or has been altered since such electronic record was so affixed with the digital signature.

(2) Any reference in this Act to any enactment or any provision thereof shall, in relation to an area in which such enactment or such provision is not in force, be construed as a reference to the corresponding law or the relevant provision of the corresponding law, if any, in force in that area.

CHAPTER II

[2][DIGITAL SIGNATURE AND ELECTRONIC SIGNATURE]

3. Authentication of electronic records.—(1) Subject to the provisions of this section, any subscriber may authenticate an electronic record by affixing his digital signature.

(2) The authentication of the electronic record shall be effected by the use of asymmetric crypto system and hash function which envelop and transform the initial electronic record into another electronic record.

Contd. from previous page

'(w) "intermediary", with respect to any particular electronic message, means any person who on behalf of another person receives, stores or transmits that message or provides any service with respect to that message;'

1. Subs. by Act 10 of 2009, sec. 2, for "Digital Signature" (w.e.f. 27-10-2009).
2. Subs. by Act 10 of 2009, sec. 5, for the heading "DIGITAL SIGNATURE" (w.e.f. 27-10-2009).

Explanation.—For the purposes of this sub-section, "hash function" means an algorithm mapping or translation of one sequence of bits into another, generally smaller, set known as "hash result" such that an electronic record yields the same hash result every time the algorithm is executed with the same electronic record as its input making it computationally infeasible—

(a) to derive or reconstruct the original electronic record from the hash result produced by the algorithm;

(b) that two electronic records can produce the same hash result using the algorithm.

(3) Any person by the use of a public key of the subscriber can verify the electronic record.

(4) The private key and the public key are unique to the subscriber and constitute a functioning key pair.

[1][**3A. Electronic signature.**—(1) Notwithstanding anything contained in section 3, but subject to the provisions of sub-section (2), a subscriber may authenticate any electronic record by such electronic signature or electronic authentication technique which—

(a) is considered reliable; and

(b) may be specified in the Second Schedule.

(2) For the purposes of this section any electronic signature or electronic authentication technique shall be considered reliable if—

(a) the signature creation data or the authentication data are, within the context in which they are used, linked to the signatory or, as the case may be, the authenticator and to no other person;

(b) the signature creation data or the authentication data were, at the time of signing, under the control of the signatory or, as the case may be, the authenticator and of no other person;

(c) any alteration to the electronic signature made after affixing such signature is detectable;

(d) any alteration to the information made after its authentication by electronic signature is detectable; and

(e) it fulfils such other conditions which may be prescribed.

(3) The Central Government may prescribe the procedure for the purpose of ascertaining whether electronic signature is that of the person by whom it is purported to have been affixed or authenticated.

(4) The Central Government may, by notification in the Official Gazette, add to or omit any electronic signature or electronic authentication technique and the procedure for affixing such signature from the Second Schedule:

Provided that no electronic signature or authentication technique shall be specified in the Second Schedule unless such signature or technique is reliable.

(5) Every notification issued under sub-section (4) shall be laid before each House of Parliament.]

CHAPTER III

ELECTRONIC GOVERNANCE

4. Legal recognition of electronic records.—Where any law provides that information or any other matter shall be in writing or in the typewritten or printed form, then, notwithstanding anything contained in such law, such requirement shall be deemed to have been satisfied if such information or matter is—

(a) rendered or made available in an electronic form; and

(b) accessible so as to be usable for a subsequent reference.

5. Legal recognition of [2][electronic signature].—Where any law provides that information or any other matter shall be authenticated by affixing the signature or any document shall be signed or bear the signature of any person, then, notwithstanding anything contained in such law, such requirement shall be deemed to have been satisfied, if such information or matter is

1. Ins. by Act 10 of 2009, sec. 6 (w.e.f. 27-10-2009).
2. Subs. by Act 10 of 2009, sec. 2, for "digital signatures" (w.e.f. 27-10-2009).

authenticated by means of [1][electronic signature] affixed in such manner as may be prescribed by the Central Government.

Explanation.—For the purposes of this section, "signed", with its grammatical variations and cognate expressions, shall, with reference to a person, mean affixing of his hand written signature or any mark on any document and the expression "signature" shall be construed accordingly.

6. Use of electronic records and [2][electronic signatures] in Government and its agencies.—(1) Where any law provides for—

(a) the filing of any form, application or any other document with any office, authority, body or agency owned or controlled by the appropriate Government in a particular manner;

(b) the issue or grant of any licence, permit, sanction or approval by whatever name called in a particular manner;

(c) the receipt or payment of money in a particular manner,

then, notwithstanding anything contained in any other law for the time being in force, such requirement shall be deemed to have been satisfied if such filing, issue, grant, receipt or payment, as the case may be, is effected by means of such electronic form as may be prescribed by the appropriate Government.

(2) The appropriate Government may, for the purposes of sub-section (1), by rules, prescribe—

(a) the manner and format in which such electronic records shall be filed, created or issued;

(b) the manner or method of payment of any fee or charges for filing, creation or issue any electronic record under clause (a).

[3]**[6A. Delivery of services by service provider.**—(1) The appropriate Government may, for the purposes of this Chapter and for efficient delivery of services to the public through electronic means authorise, by order, any service provider to set-up, maintain and upgrade the computerised facilities and perform such other services as it may specify by notification in the Official Gazette.

Explanation.—For the purposes of this section, service provider so authorised includes any individual, private agency, private company, partnership firm, sole proprietor firm or any such other body or agency which has been granted permission by the appropriate Government to offer services through electronic means in accordance with the policy governing such service sector.

(2) The appropriate Government may also authorise any service provider authorised under sub-section (1) to collect, retain and appropriate such service charges, as may be prescribed by the appropriate Government for the purpose of providing such services, from the person availing such service.

(3) Subject to the provisions of sub-section (2), the appropriate Government may authorise the service providers to collect, retain and appropriate service charges under this section notwithstanding the fact that there is no express provision under the Act, rule, regulation or notification under which the service is provided to collect, retain and appropriate e-service charges by the service providers.

(4) The appropriate Government shall, by notification in the Official Gazette, specify the scale of service charges which may be charged and collected by the service providers under this section:

Provided that the appropriate Government may specify different scale of service charges for different types of services.]

7. Retention of electronic records.—(1) Where any law provides that documents, records or information shall be retained for any specific period, then, that requirement shall be deemed to have been satisfied if such documents, records or information are retained in the electronic form, if—

---

1. Subs. by Act 10 of 2009, sec. 2, for "digital signature" (w.e.f. 27-10-2009).
2. Subs. by Act 10 of 2009, sec. 2, for "digital signatures" (w.e.f. 27-10-2009).
3. Ins. by Act 10 of 2009, sec. 7 (w.e.f. 27-10-2009).

(a) the information contained therein remains accessible so as to be usable for a subsequent reference;

(b) the electronic record is retained in the format in which it was originally generated, sent or received or in a format which can be demonstrated to represent accurately the information originally generated, sent or received;

(c) the details which will facilitate the identification of the origin, destination, date and time of despatch or receipt of such electronic record are available in the electronic record:

Provided that this clause does not apply to any information which is automatically generated solely for the purpose of enabling an electronic record to be despatched or received.

(2) Nothing in this section shall apply to any law that expressly provides for the retention of documents, records or information in the form of electronic records.

[1][**7A. Audit of documents, etc., maintained in electronic form.**—Where in any law for the time being in force, there is a provision for audit of documents, records or information, that provision shall also be applicable for audit of documents, records or information processed and maintained in the electronic form.]

8. Publication of rule, regulation, *etc.*, in Electronic Gazette.—Where any law provides that any rule, regulation, order, bye-law, notification or any other matter shall be published in the Official Gazette, then, such requirement shall be deemed to have been satisfied if such rule, regulation, order, bye-law, notification or any other matter is published in the Official Gazette or Electronic Gazette:

Provided that where any rule, regulation, order, by-law, notification or any other matter is published in the Official Gazette or Electronic Gazette, the date of publication shall be deemed to be the date of the Gazette which was first published in any form.

9. Sections 6, 7 and 8 not to confer right to insist document should be accepted in electronic form.—Nothing contained in sections 6, 7 and 8 shall confer a right upon any person to insist that any Ministry or Department of the Central Government or the State Government or any authority or body established by or under any law or controlled or funded by the Central or State Government should accept, issue, create, retain and preserve any document in the form of electronic records or effect any monetary transaction in the electronic form.

10. Power to make rules by Central Government in respect of [2][electronic signature].—The Central Government may, for the purposes of this Act, by rules, prescribe—

(a) the type of [2][electronic signature];

(b) the manner and format in which the [2][electronic signature] shall be affixed;

(c) the manner or procedure which facilitates identification of the person affixing the [1][electronic signature];

(d) control processes and procedures to ensure adequate integrity, security and confidentiality of electronic records or payments; and

(e) any other matter which is necessary to give legal effect to [3][electronic signatures].

[4][**10A. Validity of contracts formed through electronic means.**—Where in a contract formation, the communication of proposals, the acceptance of proposals, the revocation of proposals and acceptances, as the case may be, are expressed in electronic form or by means of an electronic record, such contract shall not be deemed to be unenforceable solely on the ground that such electronic form or means was used for that purpose.]

CHAPTER IV

ATTRIBUTION, ACKNOWLEDGEMENT AND DESPATCH OF ELECTRONIC RECORDS

11. Attribution of electronic records.—An electronic record shall be attributed to the originator,—

1. Ins. by Act 10 of 2009, sec. 8 (w.e.f. 27-10-2009).
2. Subs. by Act 10 of 2009, sec. 2, for "digital signature" (w.e.f. 27-10-2009).
3. Subs. by Act 10 of 2009, sec. 2, for "digital signatures" (w.e.f. 27-10-2009).
4. Ins. by Act 10 of 2009, sec. 9 (w.e.f. 27-10-2009).

(a) if it was sent by the originator himself;

(b) by a person who had the authority to act on behalf of the originator in respect of that electronic record; or

(c) by an information system programmed by or on behalf of the originator to operate automatically.

12. Acknowledgement of receipt.—(1) Where the originator has not [1][stipulated] that the acknowledgement of receipt of electronic record be given in a particular form or by a particular method, an acknowledgement may be given by—

(a) any communication by the addressee, automated or otherwise; or

(b) any conduct of the addressee, sufficient to indicate to the originator that the electronic record has been received.

(2) Where the originator has stipulated that the electronic record shall be binding only on receipt of an acknowledgement of such electronic record by him, then, unless acknowledgement has been so received, the electronic record shall be deemed to have been never sent by the originator.

(3) Where the originator has not stipulated that the electronic record shall be binding only on receipt of such acknowledgement, and the acknowledgement has not been received by the originator within the time specified or agreed or, if no time has been specified or agreed to within a reasonable time, then, the originator may give notice to the addressee stating that no acknowledgement has been received by him and specifying a reasonable time by which the acknowledgement must be received by him and if no acknowledgement is received within the aforesaid time limit he may after giving notice to the addressee, treat the electronic record as though it has never been sent.

13. Time and place of despatch and receipt of electronic record.—(1) Save as otherwise agreed to between the originator and the addressee, the despatch of an electronic record occurs when it enters a computer resource outside the control of the originator.

(2) Save as otherwise agreed between the originator and the addressee, the time of receipt of an electronic record shall be determined as follows, namely:—

(a) if the addressee has designated a computer resource for the purpose of receiving electronic records,—

(i) receipt occurs at the time when the electronic record enters the designated computer resource; or

(ii) if the electronic record is sent to a computer resource of the addressee that is not the designated computer resource, receipt occurs at the time when the electronic record is retrieved by the addressee;

(b) if the addressee has not designated a computer resource along with specified timings, if any, receipt occurs when the electronic record enters the computer resource of the addressee.

(3) Save as otherwise agreed to between the originator and the addressee, an electronic record is deemed to be despatched at the place where the originator has his place of business, and is deemed to be received at the place where the addressee has his place of business.

(4) The provisions of sub-section (2) shall apply notwithstanding that the place where the computer resource is located may be different from the place where the electronic record is deemed to have been received under sub-section (3).

(5) For the purposes of this section,—

(a) if the originator or the addressee has more than one place of business, the principal place of business, shall be the place of business;

(b) if the originator or the addressee does not have a place of business, his usual place of residence shall be deemed to be the place of business;

(c) "usual place of residence", in relation to a body corporate, means the place where it is registered.

---

1. Subs. by Act 10 of 2009, sec. 10, for "agreed with the addressee" (w.e.f. 27-10-2009).

CHAPTER V

SECURE ELECTRONIC RECORDS AND SECURE [1][ELECTRONIC SIGNATURES]

14. Secure electronic record.—Where any security procedure has been applied to an electronic record at a specific point of time, then such record shall be deemed to be a secure electronic record from such point of time to the time of verification.

[2][**15. Secure electronic signature.**—An electronic signature shall be deemed to be a secure electronic signature if—

(i) the signature creation data, at the time of affixing signature, was under the exclusive control of signatory and no other person; and

(ii) the signature creation data was stored and affixed in such exclusive manner as may be prescribed.

Explanation.—In case of digital signature, the "signature creation data" means the private key of the subscriber.]

[3][**16. Security procedures and practices.**—The Central Government may, for the purposes of sections 14 and 15, prescribe the security procedures and practices:

Provided that in prescribing such security procedures and practices, the Central Government shall have regard to the commercial circumstances, nature of transactions and such other related factors as it may consider appropriate.]

CHAPTER VI

REGULATION OF CERTIFYING AUTHORITIES

17. Appointment of Controller and other officers.—(1) The Central Government may, by notification in the Official Gazette, appoint a Controller of Certifying Authorities for the purposes of this Act and may also by the same or subsequent notification, appoint such number of Deputy Controllers [4][Assistant Controllers, other officers and employees] as it deems fit.

(2) The Controller shall discharge his functions under this Act subject to the general control and directions of the Central Government.

(3) The Deputy Controllers and Assistant Controllers shall perform the functions assigned to them by the Controller under the general superintendence and control of the Controller.

(4) The qualifications, experience and terms and conditions of service of Controller, Deputy Controllers [5][Assistant Controllers, other officers and employees] shall be such as may be prescribed by the Central Government.

---

1. Subs. by Act 10 of 2009, sec. 2, for "**DIGITAL SIGNATURES**" (w.e.f. 27-10-2009).
2. Subs. by Act 10 of 2009, sec. 11, for section 15 (w.e.f. 27-10-2009). Section 15, before substitution, stood as under:

   "**15. Secure digital signature.**—If, by application of a security procedure agreed to by the parties concerned, it can be verified that a digital signature, at the time it was affixed, was—
   (a) unique to the subscriber affixing it;
   (b) capable of identifying such subscriber;
   (c) created in a manner or using a means under the exclusive control of the subscriber and is linked to the electronic record to which it relates in such a manner that if the electronic record was altered the digital signature would be invalidated,

   then such digital signature shall be deemed to be a secure digital signature."
3. Subs. by Act 10 of 2009, sec. 11, for section 16 (w.e.f. 27-10-2009). Section 16, before substitution, stood as under:

   "**16. Security procedure.**—The Central Government shall, for the purposes of this Act, prescribe the security procedure having regard to commercial circumstances prevailing at the time when the procedure was used, including—
   (a) the nature of the transaction;
   (b) the level of sophistication of the parties with reference to their technological capacity;
   (c) the volume of similar transactions engaged in by other parties;
   (d) the availability of alternatives offered to but rejected by any party;
   (e) the cost of alternative procedures; and
   (f) the procedures in general use for similar types of transactions or communications."
4. Subs. by Act 10 of 2009, sec. 12(a), for "and Assistant Controllers" (w.e.f. 27-10-2009).
5. Subs. by Act 10 of 2009, sec. 12(b), for "and Assistant Controllers" (w.e.f. 27-10-2009).

(5) The Head Office and Branch Office of the office of the Controller shall be at such places as the Central Government may specify, and these may be established at such places as the Central Government may think fit.

(6) There shall be a seal of the Office of the Controller.

18. Functions of Controller.—The Controller may perform all or any of the following functions, namely:—

(a) exercising supervision over the activities of the Certifying Authorities;

(b) certifying public keys of the Certifying Authorities;

(c) laying down the standards to be maintained by the Certifying Authorities;

(d) specifying the qualifications and experience which employees of the Certifying Authority should possess;

(e) specifying the conditions subject to which the Certifying Authorities shall conduct their business;

(f) specifying the contents of written, printed or visual materials and advertisements that may be distributed or used in respect of a [1][Electronic Signature] Certificate and the public key;

(g) specifying the form and content of a [1][Electronic Signature] Certificate and the key;

(h) specifying the form and manner in which accounts shall be maintained by the Certifying Authorities;

(i) specifying the terms and conditions subject to which auditors may be appointed and the remuneration to be paid to them;

(j) facilitating the establishment of any electronic system by a Certifying Authority either solely or jointly with other Certifying Authorities and regulation of such systems;

(k) specifying the manner in which the Certifying Authorities shall conduct their dealings with the subscribers;

(l) resolving any conflict of interests between the Certifying Authorities and the subscribers;

(m) laying down the duties of the Certifying Authorities;

(n) maintaining a database containing the disclosure record of every Certifying Authority containing such particulars as may be specified by regulations, which shall be accessible to public.

19. Recognition of foreign Certifying Authorities.—(1) Subject to such conditions and restrictions as may be specified, by regulations, the Controller may, with the previous approval of the Central Government, and by notification in the Official Gazette, recognise any foreign Certifying Authority as a Certifying Authority for the purposes of this Act.

(2) Where any Certifying Authority is recognised under sub-section (1), the [1][Electronic Signature] Certificate issued by such Certifying Authority shall be valid for the purposes of this Act.

(3) The Controller may, if he is satisfied that any Certifying Authority has contravened any of the conditions and restrictions subject to which it was granted recognition under sub-section (1) he may, for reasons to be recorded in writing, by notification in the Official Gazette, revoke such recognition.

[2][**20. Controller to act as repository.**—[*Rep. by the Information and Technology (Amendment) Act, 2008, sec. 13 (w.e.f. 27-10-2009).*]

1. Subs. by Act 10 of 2009, sec. 2, for "Digital Signature" (w.e.f. 27-10-2009).
2. Section 20, before omission, stood as under:

"**20. Controller to act as repository.**—(1) The Controller shall be the repository of all Digital Signature Certificates issued under this Act.

(2) The Controller shall—

(a) make use of hardware, software and procedures that are secure from intrusion and misuse;

Contd. on next page

21. Licence to issue [1][Electronic Signature] Certificates.—(1) Subject to the provisions of sub-section (2), any person may make an application to the Controller for a licence to issue [1][Electronic Signature] Certificates.

(2) No licence shall be issued under sub-section (1), unless the applicant fulfills such requirements with respect to qualification, expertise, manpower, financial resources and other infrastructure facilities, which are necessary to issue [1][Electronic Signature] Certificates as may be prescribed by the Central Government.

(3) A licence granted under this section shall—

(a) be valid for such period as may be prescribed by the Central Government;

(b) not be transferable or heritable;

(c) be subject to such terms and conditions as may be specified by the regulations.

22. Application for licence.—(1) Every application for issue of a licence shall be in such form as may be prescribed by the Central Government.

(2) Every application for issue of a licence shall be accompanied by—

(a) a certification practice statement;

(b) a statement including the procedures with respect to identification of the applicant;

(c) payment of such fees, not exceeding twenty-five thousand rupees as may be prescribed by the Central Government;

(d) such other documents, as may be prescribed by the Central Government.

23. Renewal of licence.—An application for renewal of a licence shall be—

(a) in such form;

(b) accompanied by such fees, not exceeding five thousand rupees,

as may be prescribed by the Central Government and shall be made not less than forty-five days before the date of expiry of the period of validity of the licence.

24. Procedure for grant or rejection of licence.—The Controller may, on receipt of an application under sub-section (1) of section 21, after considering the documents accompanying the application and such other factors, as he deems fit, grant the licence or reject the application:

Provided that no application shall be rejected under this section unless the applicant has been given a reasonable opportunity of presenting his case.

25. Suspension of licence.—(1) The Controller may, if he is satisfied after making such inquiry, as he may think fit, that a Certifying Authority has—

(a) made a statement in, or in relation to, the application for the issue or renewal of the licence, which is incorrect or false in material particulars;

(b) failed to comply with the terms and conditions subject to which the licence was granted;

[2][(c) failed to maintain the procedures and standards specified in section 30;]

(d) contravened any provisions of this Act, rule, regulation or order made thereunder;

revoke the licence:

Provided that no licence shall be revoked unless the Certifying Authority has been given a reasonable opportunity of showing cause against the proposed revocation.

Contd. from previous page

(b) observe such other standards as may be prescribed by the Central Government,

to ensure that the secrecy and security of the digital signatures are assured.

(3) The Controller shall maintain a computerised data base of all public keys in such a manner that such data base and the public keys are available to any member of the public.

1. Subs. by Act 10 of 2009, sec. 2, for "Digital Signature" (w.e.f. 27-10-2009).
2. Subs. by S.O. 1015(E), dated 19th September, 2002, for clause (c) (w.e.f. 19-9-2002). Clause (c), before substitution, stood as under:

   "(c) failed to maintain the standards specified under clause (b) of sub-section (2) of section 20;" (w.e.f. 19-9-2002).".

(2) The Controller may, if he has reasonable cause to believe that there is any ground for revoking a licence under sub-section (1), by order, suspend such liecnce pending the completion of any enquiry ordered by him:

Provided that no licence shall be suspended for a period exceeding ten days unless the Certifying Authority has been given a reasonable opportunity of showing cause against the proposed suspension.

(3) No Certifying Authority whose licence has been suspended shall issue any [1][Electronic Signature] Certificate during such suspension.

26. Notice of suspension or revocation of licence.—(1) Where the licence of the Certifying Authority is suspended or revoked, the Controller shall publish notice of such suspension or revocation, as the case may be, in the data base maintained by him.

(2) Where one or more repositories are specified, the Controller shall publish notices of such suspension or revocation, as the case may be, in all such repositories:

Provided that the data base containing the notice of such suspension or revocation, as the case may be, shall be made available through a web site which shall be accessible round the clock:

Provided further that the Controller may, if he considers necessary, publicise the contents of data base in such electronic or other media, as he may consider appropriate.

27. Power to delegate.—The Controller may, in writing, authorise the Deputy Controller, Assistant Controller or any officer to exercise any of the powers of the Controller under this Chapter.

28. Power to investigate contraventions.—(1) The Controller or any officer authorised by him in this behalf shall take up for investigation any contravention of the provisions of this Act, rules or regulations made thereunder.

(2) The Controller or any officer authorised by him in this behalf shall exercise the like powers which are conferred on Income-tax authorities under Chapter XIII of the Income-tax Act, 1961 (43 of 1961), and shall exercise such powers, subject to such limitations laid down under that Act.

29. Access to computers and data.—(1) Without prejudice to the provisions of sub-section (1) of section 69, the Controller or any person authorised by him shall, if he has reasonable cause to suspect that [2][any contravention of the provisions of this Chapter] has been committed, have access to any computer system, any apparatus, data or any other material connected with such system, for the purpose of searching or causing a search to be made for obtaining any information or data contained in or available to such computer system.

(2) For the purposes of sub-section (1), the Controller or any person authorised by him may, by order, direct any person incharge of, or otherwise concerned with the operation of, the computer system, data apparatus or material, to provide him with such reasonable technical and other assistance as he may consider necessary.

30. Certifying Authority to follow certain procedures.—Every Certifying Authority shall,—

(a) make use of hardware, software, and procedures that are secure from intrusion and misuse;

(b) provide a reasonable level of reliability in its services which are reasonably suited to the performance of intended functions;

(c) adhere to security procedures to ensure that the secrecy and privacy of the [3][electronic signatures] are assured; [4][***]

[5][(ca) be the repository of all Electronic Signature Certificates issues under this Act;]

[5][(cb) publish information regarding its practices, Electronic Signature Certificates and current status of such certificate; and]

(d) observe such other standards as may be specified by regulations.

1. Subs. by Act 10 of 2009, sec. 2, for "Digital Signature" (w.e.f. 27-10-2009).
2. Subs. by Act 10 of 2009, sec. 14, for "any contravention of the provisions of this Act, rules or regulations made thereunder" (w.e.f. 27-10-2009).
3. Subs. by Act 10 of 2009, sec. 2, for "digital signatures" (w.e.f. 27-10-2009).
4. The word "and" omitted by Act 10 of 2009, sec. 15(i) (w.e.f. 27-10-2009).
5. Ins. by Act 10 of 2009, sec. 15(ii) (w.e.f. 27-10-2009).

31. Certifying Authority to ensure compliance of the Act, *etc.*—Every Certifying Authority shall ensure that every person employed or otherwise engaged by it complies, in the course of his employment or engagement, with the provisions of this Act, rules, regulations or orders made thereunder.

32. Display of licence.—Every Certifying Authority shall display its licence at a conspicuous place of the premises in which it carries on its business.

33. Surrender of licence.—(1) Every Certifying Authority whose licence is suspended or revoked shall immediately after such suspension or revocation, surrender the licence to the Controller.

(2) Where any Certifying Authority fails to surrender a licence under sub-section (1), the person in whose favour a licence is issued, shall be guilty of an offence and shall be punished with imprisonment which may extend up to six months or a fine which may extend up to ten thousand rupees or with both.

34. Disclosure.—(1) Every Certifying Authority shall disclose in the manner specified by regulations—

(a) its [1][Electronic Signature] Certificate [2][***]

(b) any certification practice statement relevant thereto;

(c) notice of the revocation or suspension of its Certifying Authority certificate, if any; and

(d) any other fact that materially and adversely affects either the reliability of a [1][Electronic Signature] Certificate, which that Authority has issued, or the Authority's ability to perform its services.

(2) Where in the opinion of the Certifying Authority any event has occurred or any situation has arisen which may materially and adversely affect the integrity of its computer system or the conditions subject to which an [1][Electronic Signature] Certificate was granted, then, the Certifying Authority shall—

(a) use reasonable efforts to notify any person who is likely to be affected by that occurrence; or

(b) act in accordance with the procedure specified in its certification practice statement to deal with such event or situation.

CHAPTER VII

[3][ELECTRONIC SIGNATURE] CERTIFICATES

35. Certifying authority to issue [1][Electronic Signature] Certificate.—(1) Any person may make an application to the Certifying Authority for the issue of an [1][Electronic Signature] Certificate in such form as may be prescribed by the Central Government.

(2) Every such application shall be accompanied by such fee not exceeding twenty-five thousand rupees as may be prescribed by the Central Government, to be paid to the Certifying Authority:

Provided that while prescribing fees under sub-section (2) different fees may be prescribed for different classes of applicants.

(3) Every such application shall be accompanied by a certification practice statement or where there is no such statement, a statement containing such particulars, as may be specified by regulations.

(4) On receipt of an application under sub-section (1), the Certifying Authority may, after consideration of the certification practice statement or the other statement under sub-section (3) and after making such enquiries as it may deem fit, grant the [4][Electronic Signature] Certificate or for reasons to be recorded in writing, reject the application:

---

1. Subs. by Act 10 of 2009, sec. 2, for "Digital Signature" (w.e.f. 27-10-2009).
2. The words "which contains the public key corresponding to the private key used by that Certifying Authority to digitally sign another Digital Signature Certificate;" omitted by Act 10 of 2009, sec. 16 (w.e.f. 27-10-2009).
3. Subs. by Act 10 of 2009, sec. 2, for "**DIGITAL SIGNATURE**" (w.e.f. 27-10-2009).
4. Subs. by Act 10 of 2009, sec. 2, for "Digital Signature" (w.e.f. 27-10-2009).

[1][***]

[2][Provided] that no application shall be rejected unless the applicant has been given a reasonable opportunity of showing cause against the proposed rejection.

36. Representations upon issuance of Digital Signature Certificate.—A Certifying Authority while issuing a Digital Signature Certificate shall certify that—

(a) it has complied with the provisions of this Act and the rules and regulations made thereunder;

(b) it has published the Digital Signature Certificate or otherwise made it available to such person relying on it and the subscriber has accepted it;

(c) the subscriber holds the private key corresponding to the public key, listed in the Digital Signature Certificate;

[3][(ca) the subscriber holds a private key which is capable of creating a digital signature;]

[3][(cb) the public key to be listed in the certificate can be used to verify a digital signature affixed by the private key held by the subscriber;]

(d) the subscriber's public key and private key constitute a functioning key pair;

(e) the information contained in the Digital Signature Certificate is accurate; and

(f) it has no knowledge of any material fact, which if it had been included in the Digital Signature Certificate would adversely affect the reliability of the representations in clauses (a) to (d).

37. Suspension of Digital Signature Certificate.—(1) Subject to the provisions of sub-section (2), the Certifying Authority which has issued a Digital Signature Certificate may suspend such Digital Signature Certificate,—

(a) on receipt of a request to that effect from—

(i) the subscriber listed in the Digital Signature Certificate; or

(ii) any person duly authorised to act on behalf of that subscriber;

(b) if it is of opinion that the Digital Signature Certificate should be suspended in public interest.

(2) A Digital Signature Certificate shall not be suspended for a period exceeding fifteen days unless the subscriber has been given an opportunity of being heard in the matter.

(3) On suspension of a Digital Signature Certificate under this section, the Certifying Authority shall communicate the same to the subscriber.

38. Revocation of Digital Signature Certificate.—(1) A Certifying Authority may revoke a Digital Signature Certificate issued by it—

(a) where the subscriber or any other person authorised by him makes a request to that effect; or

(b) upon the death of the subscriber; or

(c) upon the dissolution of the firm or winding up of the company where the subscriber is a firm or a company.

(2) Subject to the provisions of sub-section (3) and without prejudice to the provisions of sub-section (1), a Certifying Authority may revoke a Digital Signature Certificate which has been issued by it at any time, if it is of opinion that—

---

1. First Proviso omitted by Act 10 of 2009, sec. 17(a) (w.e.f. 27-10-2009). First Proviso, before omission, stood as under:

   "Provided that no Digital Signature Certificate shall be granted unless the Certifying Authority is satisfied that—

   (a) the applicant holds the private key corresponding to the public key to be listed in the Digital Signature Certificate;

   (b) the applicant holds a private key, which is capable of creating a digital signature;

   (c) the public key to be listed in the certificate can be used to verify a digital signature affixed by the private key held by the applicant:"

2. Subs. by Act 10 of 2009, sec. 17(b), for "Provided further" (w.e.f. 27-10-2009).
3. Ins. by Act 10 of 2009, sec. 18 (w.e.f. 27-10-2009).

(a) a material fact represented in the Digital Signature Certificate is false or has been concealed;

(b) a requirement for issuance of the Digital Signature Certificate was not satisfied;

(c) the Certifying Authority's private key or security system was compromised in a manner materially affecting the Digital Signature Certificate's reliability;

(d) the subscriber has been declared insolvent or dead or where a subscriber is a firm or a company, which has been dissolved, wound-up or otherwise ceased to exist.

(3) A Digital Signature Certificate shall not be revoked unless the subscriber has been given an opportunity of being heard in the matter.

(4) On revocation of a Digital Signature Certificate under this section, the Certifying Authority shall communicate the same to the subscriber.

39. Notice of suspension or revocation.—(1) Where a Digital Signature Certificate is suspended or revoked under section 37 or section 38, the Certifying Authority shall publish a notice of such suspension or revocation, as the case may be, in the repository specified in the Digital Signature Certificate for publication of such notice.

(2) Where one or more repositories are specified, the Certifying Authority shall publish notices of such suspension or revocation, as the case may be, in all such repositories.

CHAPTER VIII

DUTIES OF SUBSCRIBERS

40. Generating key pair.—Where any Digital Signature Certificate, the public key of which corresponds to the private key of that subscriber which is to be listed in the Digital Signature Certificate has been accepted by a subscriber, [1][***] the subscriber shall generate [2][that key] pair by applying the security procedure.

[3]**[40A. Duties of subscriber of Electronic Signature Certificate.**—In respect of Electronic Signature Certificate the subscriber shall perform such duties as may be prescribed.]

41. Acceptance of Digital Signature Certificate.—(1) A subscriber shall be deemed to have accepted a Digital Signature Certificate if he publishes or authorises the publication of a Digital Signature Certificate—

(a) to one or more persons;

(b) in a repository; or

otherwise demonstrates his approval of the Digital Signature Certificate in any manner.

(2) By accepting a Digital Signature Certificate the subscriber certifies to all who reasonably rely on the information contained in the Digital Signature Certificate that—

(a) the subscriber holds the private key corresponding to the public key listed in the Digital Signature Certificate and is entitled to hold the same;

(b) all representations made by the subscriber to the Certifying Authority and all material relevant to the information contained in the Digital Signature Certificate are true;

(c) all information in the Digital Signature Certificate that is within the knowledge of the subscriber is true.

42. Control of private key.—(1) Every subscriber shall exercise reasonable care to retain control of the private key corresponding to the public key listed in his Digital Signature Certificate and take all steps to prevent its disclosure [4][***].

(2) If the private key corresponding to the public key listed in the Digital Signature Certificate has been compromised, then, the subscriber shall communicate the same without any delay to the Certifying Authority in such manner as may be specified by the regulations.

---

1. The word "then" omitted by S.O. 1015(E), dated 19th September, 2002 (w.e.f. 19-9-2002).
2. Subs. by S.O. 1015(E), dated 19th September, 2002, for "the key" (w.e.f. 19-9-2002).
3. Ins. by Act 10 of 2009, sec. 19 (w.e.f. 27-10-2009).
4. The words "to a person not authorised to affix the digital signature of the subscriber" omitted by S.O. 1015(E), dated 19th September, 2002 (w.e.f. 19-9-2002).

Explanation.—For the removal of doubts, it is hereby declared that the subscriber shall be liable till he has informed the Certifying Authority that the private key has been compromised.

CHAPTER IX

[1][PENALTIES, COMPENSATION AND ADJUDICATION]

43. [2][Penalty and compensation] for damage to computer, computer system, etc.—If any person without permission of the owner or any other person who is incharge of a computer, computer system or computer network,—

(a) accesses or secures access to such computer, computer system or computer network [3][or computer resource];

(b) downloads, copies or extracts any data, computer data base or information from such computer, computer system or computer network including information or data held or stored in any removable storage medium;

(c) introduces or causes to be introduced any computer contaminant or computer virus into any computer, computer system or computer network;

(d) damages or causes to be damaged any computer, computer system or computer network, data, computer data base or any other programmes residing in such computer, computer system or computer network;

(e) disrupts or causes disruption of any computer, computer system or computer network;

(f) denies or causes the denial of access to any person authorised to access any computer, computer system or computer network by any means;

(g) provides any assistance to any person to facilitate access to a computer, computer system or computer network in contravention of the provisions of this Act, rules or regulations made thereunder;

(h) charges the services availed of by a person to the account of another person by tampering with or manipulating any computer, computer system, or computer network,

[4][(i) destroys, deletes or alters any information residing in a computer resource or diminishes its value or utility or affects it injuriously by any means;]

[4][(j) steal, conceals, destroys or alters or causes any person to steal, conceal, destroy or alter any computer source code used for a computer resource with an intention to cause damage;]

[5][he shall be liable to pay damages by way of compensation to the person so affected].

Explanation.—For the purposes of this section,—

(i) "computer contaminant" means any set of computer instructions that are designed—

(a) to modify, destroy, record, transmit data or programme residing within a computer, computer system or computer network; or

(b) by any means to usurp the normal operation of the computer, computer system, or computer network;

(ii) "computer database" means a representation of information, knowledge, facts, concepts or instructions in text, image, audio, video that are being prepared or have been prepared in a formalised manner or have been produced by a computer, computer system or computer network and are intended for use in a computer, computer system or computer network;

(iii) "computer virus" means any computer instruction, information, data or programme that destroys, damages, degrades or adversely affects the

1. Subs. by Act 10 of 2009, sec. 20, for "PENALTIES AND ADJUDICATION" (w.e.f. 27-10-2009).
2. Subs. by Act 10 of 2009, sec. 21(a), for "**Penalty**" (w.e.f. 27-10-2009).
3. Ins. by Act 10 of 2009, sec. 21(b) (w.e.f. 27-10-2009).
4. Ins. by Act 10 of 2009, sec. 21(c) (w.e.f. 27-10-2009).
5. Subs. by Act 10 of 2009, sec. 21(d), for "he shall be liable to pay damages by way of compensation not exceeding one crore rupees to the person so affected" (w.e.f. 27-10-2009).

performance of a computer resource or attaches itself to another computer resource and operates when a programme, data or instruction is executed or some other event takes place in that computer resource;

(iv) "damage" means to destroy, alter, delete, add, modify or rearrange any computer resource by any means;

[1][(v) "computer source code" means the listing of programmes, computer commands, design and layout and programme analysis of computer resource in any form.]

[2][**43A. Compensation for failure to protect data.**—Where a body corporate, possessing, dealing or handling any sensitive personal data or information in a computer resource which it owns, controls or operates, is negligent in implementing and maintaining reasonable security practices and procedures and thereby causes wrongful loss or wrongful gain to any person, such body corporate shall be liable to pay damages by way of compensation to the person so affected.

Explanation.—For the purposes of this section,—

(i) "body corporate" means any company and includes a firm, sole proprietorship or other association of individuals engaged in commercial or professional activities;

(ii) "reasonable security practices and procedures" means security practices and procedures designed to protect such information from unauthorised access, damage, use, modification, disclosure or impairment, as may be specified in an agreement between the parties or as may be specified in any law for the time being in force and in the absence of such agreement or any law, such reasonable security practices and procedures, as may be prescribed by the Central Government in consultation with such professional bodies or associations as it may deem fit;

(iii) "sensitive personal data or information" means such personal information as may be prescribed by the Central Government in consultation with such professional bodies or associations as it may deem fit.]

44. Penalty for failure to furnish information, return, etc.—If any person who is required under this Act or any rules or regulations made thereunder to—

(a) furnish any document, return or report to the Controller or the Certifying Authority fails to furnish the same, he shall be liable to a penalty not exceeding one lakh and fifty thousand rupees for each such failure;

(b) file any return or furnish any information, books or other documents within the time specified therefor in the regulations fails to file return or furnish the same within the time specified therefor in the regulations, he shall be liable to a penalty not exceeding five thousand rupees for every day during which such failure continues;

(c) maintain books of account or records, fails to maintain the same, he shall be liable to a penalty not exceeding ten thousand rupees for every day during which the failure continues.

45. Residuary penalty.—Whoever contravenes any rules or regulations made under this Act, for the contravention of which no penalty has been separately provided, shall be liable to pay a compensation not exceeding twenty-five thousand rupees to the person affected by such contravention or a penalty not exceeding twenty-five thousand rupees.

46. Power to adjudicate.—(1) For the purpose of adjudging under this Chapter whether any person has committed a contravention of any of the provisions of this Act or of any rule, regulation, [3][direction or order made thereunder which renders him liable to pay penalty or compensation] the Central Government shall, subject to the provisions of sub-section (3), appoint any officer not below the rank of a Director to the Government of India or an equivalent officer of a State Government to be an adjudicating officer for holding an inquiry in the manner prescribed by the Central Government.

1. Ins. by Act 10 of 2009, sec. 21(e) (w.e.f. 27-10-2009).
2. Ins. by Act 10 of 2009, sec. 22 (w.e.f. 27-10-2009).
3. Subs. by Act 10 of 2009, sec. 23(a), for "direction or order made thereunder" (w.e.f. 27-10-2009).

[1][(1A) The adjudicating officer appointed under sub-section (1) shall exercise jurisdiction to adjudicate matters in which the claim for injury or damage does not exceed rupees five crore:

Provided that the jurisdiction in respect of the claim for injury or damage exceeding rupees five crore shall vest with the competent court.]

(2) The adjudicating officer shall, after giving the person referred to in sub-section (1) a reasonable opportunity for making representation in the matter and if, on such inquiry, he is satisfied that the person has committed the contravention, he may impose such penalty or award such compensation as he thinks fit in accordance with the provisions of that section.

(3) No person shall be appointed as an adjudicating officer unless he possesses such experience in the field of Information Technology and legal or judicial experience as may be prescribed by the Central Government.

(4) Where more than one adjudicating officers are appointed, the Central Government shall specify by order the matters and places with respect to which such officers shall exercise their jurisdiction.

(5) Every adjudicating officer shall have the powers of a civil court which are conferred on the Cyber Appellate Tribunal under sub-section (2) of section 58, and—

(a) all proceedings before it shall be deemed to be judicial proceedings within the meaning of sections 193 and 228 of the Indian Penal Code (45 of 1860);

(b) shall be deemed to be a civil court for the purposes of sections 345 and 346 of the Code of Criminal Procedure, 1973 (2 of 1974);

[2][(c) shall be deemed to be a civil court for purposes of Order XXI of the Civil Procedure Code, 1908 (5 of 1908).]

47. Factors to be taken into account by the adjudicating officer.—While adjudging the quantum of compensation under this Chapter, the adjudicating officer shall have due regard to the following factors, namely:—

(a) the amount of gain of unfair advantage, wherever quantifiable, made as a result of the default;

(b) the amount of loss caused to any person as a result of the default;

(c) the repetitive nature of the default.

CHAPTER X

THE CYBER [3][***] APPELLATE TRIBUNAL

48. Establishment of Cyber Appellate Tribunal.—(1) The Central Government shall, by notification, establish one or more appellate tribunals to be known as the Cyber [4][***] Appellate Tribunal.

(2) The Central Government shall also specify, in the notification referred to in sub-section (1), the matters and places in relation to which the Cyber Appellate Tribunal may exercise jurisdiction.

[5]**[49. Composition of Cyber Appellate Tribunal.**—(1) The Cyber Appellate Tribunal shall consist of a Chairperson and such number of other Members, as the Central Government may, by notification in the Official Gazette, appoint:

1. Ins. by Act 10 of 2009, sec. 23(b) (w.e.f. 27-10-2009).
2. Ins. by Act 10 of 2009, sec. 23(c) (w.e.f. 27-10-2009).
3. The word "**REGULATIONS**" omitted by Act 10 of 2009, sec. 24 (w.e.f. 27-10-2009).
4. The word "Regulations" omitted by Act 10 of 2009, sec. 25 (w.e.f. 27-10-2009).
5. Subs. by Act 10 of 2009, sec. 26, for sections 49 to 52 (w.e.f. 27-10-2009). Sections 49 to 52, before substitution, stood as under:

"**49. Composition of Cyber Appellate Tribunal.**—A Cyber Appellate Tribunal shall consist of one person only (hereinafter referred to as the Presiding Officer of the Cyber Appellate Tribunal) to be appointed, by notification, by the Central Government.

"**50. Qualifications for appointment as Presiding Officer of the Cyber Appellate Tribunal.**—A person shall not be qualified for appointment as the Presiding Officer of a Cyber Appellate Tribunal unless he—

Contd. on next page

Provided that the person appointed as the Presiding Officer of the Cyber Appellate Tribunal under the provisions of this Act immediately before the commencement of the Information Technology (Amendment) Act, 2008 shall be deemed to have been appointed as the Chairperson of the said Cyber Appellate Tribunal under the provisions of this Act as amended by the Information Technology (Amendment) Act, 2008.

(2) The selection of Chairperson and Members of the Cyber Appellate Tribunal shall be made by the Central Government in consultation with the Chief Justice of India.

(3) Subject to the provisions of this Act—

(a) the jurisdiction, powers and authority of the Cyber Appellate Tribunal may be exercised by the Benches thereof;

(b) a Bench may be constituted by the Chairperson of the Cyber Appellate Tribunal with one or two Members of such Tribunal as the Chairperson may deem fit;

(c) the Benches of the Cyber Appellate Tribunal shall sit at New Delhi and at such other places as the Central Government may, in consultation with the Chairperson of the Cyber Appellate Tribunal, by notification in the Official Gazette, specify;

(d) the Central Government shall, by notification in the Official Gazette, specify the areas in relation to which each Bench of the Cyber Appellate Tribunal may exercise its jurisdiction.

(4) Notwithstanding anything contained in sub-section (3), the Chairperson of the Cyber Appellate Tribunal may transfer a Member of such Tribunal from one Bench to another Bench.

(5) If at any stage of the hearing of any case or matter it appears to the Chairperson or a Member of the Cyber Appellate Tribunal that the case or matter is of such a nature that it ought to be heard by a Bench consisting of more Members, the case or matter may be transferred by the Chairperson to such Bench as the Chairperson may deem fit.

50. Qualifications for appointment as Chairperson and Members of Cyber Appellate Tribunal.—(1) A person shall not be qualified for appointment as a Chairperson of the Cyber Appellate Tribunal unless he is, or has been, or is qualified to be, a Judge of a High Court.

(2) The Members of the Cyber Appellate Tribunal, except the Judicial Member to be appointed under sub-section (3), shall be appointed by the Central Government from amongst persons, having special knowledge of, and professional experience in, information technology, telecommunication, industry, management or consumer affairs:

Provided that a person shall not be appointed as a Member, unless he is, or has been, in the service of the Central Government or a State Government, and has held the post of Additional Secretary to the Government of India or any equivalent post in the Central Government or State Government for a period of not less than one year or Joint Secretary to the Government of India or any equivalent post in the Central Government or State Government for a period of not less than seven years.

(3) The Judicial Members of the Cyber Appellate Tribunal shall be appointed by the Central Government from amongst persons who is or has been a member of the Indian Legal Service and has held the post of Additional Secretary for a period of not less than one year or Grade I post of that Service for a period of not less than five years.

51. Term of office, conditions of service, etc., of Chairperson and Members.—(1) The Chairperson or Member of the Cyber Appellate Tribunal shall hold office for a term of five

---

Contd. from previous page

(a) is, or has been, or is qualified to be, a Judge of a High Court; or

(b) is, or has been, a member of the Indian Legal Service and is holding or has held a post in Grade I of that Service for at least three years.

"**51. Term of office.**—The Presiding Officer of a Cyber Appellate Tribunal shall hold office for a term of five years from the date on which he enters upon his office or until he attains the age of sixty-five years whichever is earlier.

"**52. Salary, allowances and other terms and conditions of service of Presiding Officer.**— The salary and allowances payable to, and the other terms and conditions of service including pension, gratuity and other retirement benefits of, the Presiding Officer of a Cyber Appellate Tribunal shall be such as may be prescribed:

Provided that neither the salary and allowances nor the other terms and conditions of service of the Presiding Officers shall be varied to his disadvantage after appointment."

years from the date on which he enters upon his office or until he attains the age of sixty-five years, whichever is earlier.

(2) Before appointing any person as the Chairperson or Member of the Cyber Appellate Tribunal, the Central Government shall satisfy itself that the person does not have any such financial or other interest as is likely to affect prejudicially his functions as such Chairperson or Member.

(3) An officer of the Central Government or State Government on his selection as the Chairperson or Member of the Cyber Appellate Tribunal, as the case may be, shall have to retire from service before joining as such Chairperson or Member.

52. Salary, allowances and other terms and conditions of service of Chairperson and Members.—The salary and allowances payable to, and the other terms and conditions of service including pension, gratuity and other retirement benefits of, the Chairperson or a Member of the Cyber Appellate Tribunal shall be such as may be prescribed.

52A. Powers of superintendence, direction, etc.—The Chairperson of the Cyber Appellate Tribunal shall have powers of general superintendence and directions in the conduct of the affairs of that Tribunal and he shall, in addition to presiding over the meetings of the Tribunal, exercise and discharge such powers and functions of the Tribunal as may be prescribed.

52B. Distribution of business among Benches.—Where Benches are constituted, the Chairperson of the Cyber Appellate Tribunal may, by order, distribute the business of that Tribunal amongst the Benches and also the matters to be dealt with by each Bench.

52C. Power of Chairperson to transfer cases.—On the application of any of the parties and after notice to the parties, and after hearing such of them as he may deem proper to be heard, or *suo motu* without such notice, the Chairperson of the Cyber Appellate Tribunal may transfer any case pending before one Bench, for disposal to any other Bench.

52D. Decision by majority.—If the Members of a Bench consisting of two Members differ in opinion on any point, they shall state the point or points on which they differ, and make a reference to the Chairperson of the Cyber Appellate Tribunal who shall hear the point or points himself and such point or points shall be decided according to the opinion of the majority of the Members who have heard the case, including those who first heard it.]

53. Filling up of vacancies.—If, for reason other than temporary absence, any vacancy occurs in the office of the [1][Chairperson or Member, as the case may be] of a Cyber Appellate Tribunal, then the Central Government shall appoint another person in accordance with the provisions of this Act to fill the vacancy and the proceedings may be continued before the Cyber Appellate Tribunal from the stage at which the vacancy is filled.

54. Resignation and removal.—(1) The [2][Chairperson or the Member] of a Cyber Appellate Tribunal may, by notice in writing under his hand addressed to the Central Government, resign his office:

Provided that the said Presiding Officer shall, unless he is permitted by the Central Government to relinquish his office sooner, continue to hold office until the expiry of three months from the date of receipt of such notice or until a person duly appointed as his successor enters upon his office or until the expiry of his term of office, whichever is the earliest.

(2) The Presiding Officer of a Cyber Appellate Tribunal shall not be removed from his office except by an order by the Central Government on the ground of proved misbehaviour or incapacity after an inquiry made by a Judge of the Supreme Court in which the Presiding Officer concerned has been informed of the charges against him and given a reasonable opportunity of being heard in respect of these charges.

(3) The Central Government may, by rules, regulate the procedure for the investigation of misbehaviour or incapacity of the aforesaid Presiding Officer.

55. Orders constituting Appellate Tribunal to be final and not to invalidate its proceedings.—No order of the Central Government appointing any person as the [3][Chairperson or Member] of a Cyber Appellate Tribunal shall be called in question in any manner and no act or proceeding before a Cyber Appellate Tribunal shall be called in question

1. Subs. by Act 10 of 2009, sec. 27, for "Presiding Officer" (w.e.f. 27-10-2009).
2. Subs. by Act 10 of 2009, sec. 28, for "Presiding Officer" (w.e.f. 27-10-2009).
3. Subs. by Act 10 of 2009, sec. 29, for "Presiding Officer" (w.e.f. 27-10-2009).

in any manner on the ground merely of any defect in the constitution of a Cyber Appellate Tribunal.

56. Staff of the Cyber Appellate Tribunal.—(1) The Central Government shall provide the Cyber Appellate Tribunal with such officers and employees as that Government may think fit.

(2) The officers and employees of the Cyber Appellate Tribunal shall discharge their functions under general superintendence of the [1][Chairperson].

(3) The salaries, allowances and other conditions of service of the officers and employees of the Cyber Appellate Tribunal shall be such as may be prescribed by the Central Government.

57. Appeal to Cyber Appellate Tribunal.—(1) Save as provided in sub-section (2), any person aggrieved by an order made by controller or an adjudicating officer under this Act may prefer an appeal to a Cyber Appellate Tribunal having jurisdiction in the matter.

(2) No appeal shall lie to the Cyber Appellate Tribunal from an order made by an adjudicating officer with the consent of the parties.

(3) Every appeal under sub-section (1) shall be filed within a period of forty-five days from the date on which a copy of the order made by the Controller or the adjudicating officer is received by the person aggrieved and it shall be in such form and be accompanied by such fee as may be prescribed:

Provided that the Cyber Appellate Tribunal may entertain an appeal after the expiry of the said period of forty-five days if it is satisfied that there was sufficient cause for not filing it within that period.

(4) On receipt of an appeal under sub-section (1), the Cyber Appellate Tribunal may, after giving the parties to the appeal, an opportunity of being heard, pass such orders thereon as it thinks fit, confirming, modifying or setting aside the order appealed against.

(5) The Cyber Appellate Tribunal shall send a copy of every order made by it to the parties to the appeal and to the concerned Controller or adjudicating officer.

(6) The appeal filed before the Cyber Appellate Tribunal under sub-section (1) shall be dealt with by it as expeditiously as possible and endeavour shall be made by it to dispose of the appeal finally within six months from the date of receipt of the appeal.

58. Procedure and powers of the Cyber Appellate Tribunal.—(1) The Cyber Appellate Tribunal shall not be bound by the procedure laid down by the Code of Civil Procedure, 1908 (5 of 1908), but shall be guided by the principles of natural justice and, subject to the other provisions of this Act and of any rules, the Cyber Appellate Tribunal shall have powers to regulate its own procedure including the place at which it shall have its sittings.

(2) The Cyber Appellate Tribunal shall have, for the purposes of discharging its functions under this Act, the same powers as are vested in a civil court under the Code of Civil Procedure, 1908 (5 of 1908), while trying a suit, in respect of the following matters, namely:—

(a) summoning and enforcing the attendance of any person and examining him on oath;

(b) requiring the discovery and production of documents or other electronic records;

(c) receiving evidence on affidavits;

(d) issuing commissions for the examination of witnesses or documents;

(e) reviewing its decisions;

(f) dismissing an application for default or deciding it *ex parte*;

(g) any other matter which may be prescribed.

(3) Every proceeding before the Cyber Appellate Tribunal shall be deemed to be a judicial proceeding within the meaning of sections 193 and 228, and for the purposes of section 196 of the Indian Penal Code (45 of 1860) and the Cyber Appellate Tribunal shall be deemed to be a civil court for the purposes of section 195 and Chapter XXVI of the Code of Criminal Procedure, 1973 (2 of 1974).

59. Right to legal representation.—The appellant may either appear in person or authorise one or more legal practitioners or any of its officers to present his or its case before the Cyber Appellate Tribunal.

1. Subs. by Act 10 of 2009, sec. 30, for "Presiding Officer" (w.e.f. 27-10-2009).

60. Limitation.—The provisions of the Limitation Act, 1963 (36 of 1963), shall, as far as may be, apply to an appeal made to the Cyber Appellate Tribunal.

61. Civil court not to have jurisdiction.—No court shall have jurisdiction to entertain any suit or proceeding in respect of any matter which an adjudicating officer appointed under this Act or the Cyber Appellate Tribunal constituted under this Act is empowered by or under this Act to determine and no injunction shall be granted by any court or other authority in respect of any action taken or to be taken in pursuance of any power conferred by or under this Act.

62. Appeal to High Court.—Any person aggrieved by any decision or order of the Cyber Appellate Tribunal may file an appeal to the High Court within sixty days from the date of communication of the decision or order of the Cyber Appellate Tribunal to him on any question of fact or law arising out of such order:

Provided that the High Court may, if it is satisfied that the appellant was prevented by sufficient cause from filing the appeal within the said period, allow it to be filed within a further period not exceeding sixty days.

63. Compounding of contraventions.—(1) Any contravention under this [1][Act] may, either before or after the institution of adjudication proceedings, be compounded by the Controller or such other officer as may be specially authorised by him in this behalf or by the adjudicating officer, as the case may be, subject to such conditions as the Controller or such other officer or the adjudicating officer may specify:

Provided that such sum shall not, in any case, exceed the maximum amount of the penalty which may be imposed under this Act for the contravention so compounded.

(2) Nothing in sub-section (1) shall apply to a person who commits the same or similar contravention within a period of three years from the date on which the first contravention, committed by him, was compounded.

Explanation.—For the purposes of this sub-section, any second or subsequent contravention committed after the expiry of a period of three years from the date on which the contravention was previously compounded shall be deemed to be a first contravention.

(3) Where any contravention has been compounded under sub-section (1), no proceeding or further proceeding, as the case may be, shall be taken against the person guilty of such contravention in respect of the contravention so compounded.

64. Recovery of [2][penalty and compensation].—A [3][penalty imposed or compensation awarded] under this Act, if it is not paid, shall be recovered as an arrear of land revenue and the licence or the [4][Electronic Signature] Certificate, as the case may be, shall be suspended till the penalty is paid.

CHAPTER XI

OFFENCES

65. Tampering with computer source documents.—Whoever knowingly or intentionally conceals, destroys or alters or intentionally or knowingly causes another to conceal, destroy, or alter any computer source code used for a computer, computer programme, computer system or computer network, when the computer source code is required to be kept or maintained by law for the time being in force, shall be punishable with imprisonment up to three years, or with fine which may extend up to two lakh rupees, or with both.

Explanation.—For the purposes of this section, "computer source code" means the listing of programmes, computer commands, design and layout and programme analysis of computer resource in any form.

[5][**66. Computer related offences.**—If any person, dishonestly or fraudulently, does any act referred to in section 43, he shall be punishable with imprisonment for a term which may extend to three years or with fine which may extend to five lakh rupees or with both.

1. Subs. by S.O. 1015(E), dated 19th September, 2002, for "Chapter" (w.e.f. 19-9-2002).
2. Subs. by Act 10 of 2009, sec. 31(ii), for "**penalty**" (w.e.f. 27-10-2009).
3. Subs. by Act 10 of 2009, sec. 31(i), for "penalty imposed" (w.e.f. 27-10-2009).
4. Subs. by Act 10 of 2009, sec. 2, for "digital Signature" (w.e.f. 27-10-2009).
5. Subs. by Act 10 of 2009, sec. 32, for sections 66 and 67 (w.e.f. 27-10-2009). Sections 66 and 67, before substitution, stood as under:

Contd. on next page

Explanation.—For the purposes of this section,—

(a) the word "dishonestly" shall have the meaning assigned to it in section 24 of the Indian Penal Code (45 of 1860);

(b) the word "fraudulently" shall have the meaning assigned to it in section 25 of the Indian Penal Code (45 of 1860).

66A. Punishment for sending offensive messages through communication service, etc.— Any person who sends, by means of a computer resource or a communication device,—

(a) any information that is grossly offensive or has menacing character; or

(b) any information which he knows to be false, but for the purpose of causing annoyance, inconvenience, danger, obstruction, insult, injury, criminal intimidation, enmity, hatred or ill will, persistently by making use of such computer resource or a communication device; or

(c) any electronic mail or electronic mail message for the purpose of causing annoyance or inconvenience or to deceive or to mislead the addressee or recipient about the origin of such messages,

shall be punishable with imprisonment for a term which may extend to three years and with fine.

Explanation.—For the purpose of this section, terms "electronic mail" and "electronic mail message" means a message or information created or transmitted or received on a computer, computer system, computer resource or communication device including attachments in text, image, audio, video and any other electronic record, which may be transmitted with the message.

66B. Punishment for dishonestly receiving stolen computer resource or communication device.—Whoever dishonestly received or retains any stolen computer resource or communication device knowing or having reason to believe the same to be stolen computer resource or communication device, shall be punished with imprisonment of either description for a term which may extend to three years or with fine which may extend to rupees one lakh or with both.

66C. Punishment for identity theft.—Whoever, fraudulently or dishonestly make use of the electronic signature, password or any other unique identification feature of any other person, shall be punished with imprisonment of either description for a term which may extend to three years and shall also be liable to fine which may extend to rupees one lakh.

66D. Punishment for cheating by personation by using computer resource.—Whoever, by means for any communication device or computer resource cheats by personating, shall be punished with imprisonment of either description for a term which may extend to three years and shall also be liable to fine which may extend to one lakh rupees.

66E. Punishment for violation of privacy.—Whoever, intentionally or knowingly captures, publishes or transmits the image of a private area of any person without his or her consent, under circumstances violating the privacy of that person, shall be punished with imprisonment which may extend to three years or with fine not exceeding two lakh rupees, or with both.

Contd. from previous page

"**66 Hacking with Computer System.**—(1) Whoever with the intent to cause or knowing that he is likely to cause wrongful loss or damage to the public or any person destroys or deletes or alters any information residing in a computer resource or diminishes its value or utility or affects it injuriously by any means, commits hacking.

(2) Whoever commits hacking shall be punished with imprisonment up to three years, or with fine which may extend upto two lakh rupees, or with both.

67. Publishing of information which is obscene in electronic form.—Whoever publishes or transmits or causes to be published in the electronic form, any material which is lascivious or appeals to the prurient interest or if its effect is such as to tend to deprave and corrupt persons who are likely, having regard to all relevant circumstances, to read, see or hear the matter contained or embodied in it, shall be punished on first conviction with imprisonment of either description for a term which may extend to five years and with fine which may extend to one lakh rupees and in the event of a second or subsequent conviction with imprisonment of either description for a term which may extend to ten years and also with fine which may extend to two lakh rupees."

Explanation.—For the purposes of this section—

(a) "transmit" means to electronically send a visual image with the intent that it be viewed by a person or persons;

(b) "capture", with respect to an image, means to videotape, photograph, film or record by any means;

(c) "private area" means the naked or undergarment clad genitals, pubic area, buttocks or female breast;

(d) "publishes" means reproduction in the printed or electronic form and making it available for public;

(e) "under circumstances violating privacy" means circumstances in which a person can have a reasonable expectation that;—

(i) he or she could disrobe in privacy, without being concerned that an image of his private area was being captured; or

(ii) any part of his or her private area would not be visible to the public, regardless of whether that person is in a public or private place.

66F. Punishment for cyber terrorism.—(1) Whoever,—

(A) with intent to threaten the unity, integrity, security or sovereignty of India or to strike terror in the people or any section of the people by—

(i) denying or cause the denial of access to any person authorized to access computer resource; or

(ii) attempting to penetrate or access a computer resource without authorisation or exceeding authorised access; or

(iii) introducing or causing to introduce any computer contaminant;

and by means of such conduct causes or is likely to cause death or injuries to persons or damage to or destruction of property or disrupts or knowing that it is likely to cause damage or disruption of supplies or services essential to the life of the community or adversely affect the critical information infrastructure specified under section 70 or

(B) knowingly or intentionally penetrates or accesses a computer resource without authorisation or exceeding authorised access, and by means of such conduct obtains access to information, data or computer database that is restricted for reasons of the security of the State or foreign relations; or any restricted information, data or computer database, with reasons to believe that such information, data or computer database so obtained may be used to cause or likely to cause injury to the interests of the sovereignty and integrity of India, the security of the State, friendly relations with foreign States, public order, decency or morality, or in relation to contempt of court, defamation or incitement to an offence, or to the advantage of any foreign nation, group of individuals or otherwise,

commits the offence of cyber terrorism.

(2) Whoever commits or conspires to commit cyber terrorism shall be punishable with imprisonment which may extend to imprisonment for life.'

67. Punishment for publishing or transmitting obscene material in electronic form.—Whoever publishes or transmits or causes to be published or transmitted in the electronic form, any material which is lascivious or appeals to the prurient interest or if its effect is such as to tend to deprave and corrupt persons who are likely, having regard to all relevant circumstances, to read, see or hear the matter contained or embodied in it, shall be punished on first conviction with imprisonment of either description for a term which may extend to three years and with fine which may extend to five lakh rupees and in the event of second or subsequent conviction with imprisonment of either description for a term which may extend to five years and also with fine which may extend to ten lakh rupees.

67A. Punishment for publishing or transmitting of material containing sexually explicit act, etc., in electronic form.—Whoever publishes or transmits or causes to be published or transmitted in the electronic form any material which contains sexually explicit act or conduct shall be punished on first conviction with imprisonment of either description for a term which may extend to five years and with fine which may extend to ten lakh rupees and in the event of second or subsequent conviction with imprisonment of either description for a term which may extend to seven years and also with fine which may extend to ten lakh rupees.

67B. Punishment for publishing or transmitting of material depicting children in sexually explicit act, etc., in electronic form.—Whoever—

(a) publishes or transmits or causes to be published or transmitted material in any electronic form which depicts children engaged in sexually explicit act or conduct; or

(b) creates text or digital images, collects, seeks, browses, downloads, advertises, promotes, exchanges or distributes material in any electronic form depicting children in obscene or indecent or sexually explicit manner; or

(c) cultivates, entices or induces children to online relationship with one or more children for and on sexually explicit act or in a manner that may offend a reasonable adult on the computer resource; or

(d) facilitates abusing children online, or

(e) records in any electronic form own abuse or that of others pertaining to sexually explicit act with children,

shall be punished on first conviction with imprisonment of either description for a term which may extend to five years and with fine which may extend to ten lakh rupees and in the event of second or subsequent conviction with imprisonment of either discription for a term which may extend to seven years and also with fine which may extend to ten lakh rupees:

Provided that provisions of section 67, section 67A and this section does not extend to any book, pamphlet, paper, writing, drawing, painting representation or figure in electronic form—

(i) the publication of which is proved to be justified as being for the public good on the ground that such book, pamphlet, paper, writing drawing, painting representation or figure is in the interest of science, literature, art or learning or other objects of general concern; or

(ii) which is kept or used for *bona fide* heritage or religious purposes.

Explanation.—For the purposes of this section "children" means a person who has not completed the age of 18 years.

67C. Preservation and retention of information by intermediaries.—(1) Intermediary shall preserve and retain such information as may be specified for such duration and in such manner and format as the Central Government may prescribe.

(2) Any intermediary who intentionally or knowingly contravenes the provisions of sub-section (1) shall be punished with an imprisonment for a term which may extend to three years and also be liable to fine.]

68. Power of Controller to give directions.—(1) The Controller may, by order, direct a Certifying Authority or any employee of such Authority to take such measures or cease carrying on such activities as specified in the order if those are necessary to ensure compliance with the provisions of this Act, rules or any regulations made thereunder.

[1][(2) Any person who intentionally or knowingly fails to comply with any order under sub-section (1) shall be guilty of an offence and shall be liable on conviction to imprisonment for a term not exceeding two years or a fine not exceeding one lakh rupees or both.]

[2][**69. Power to issue directions for interception or monitoring or decryption of any information through any computer resource.**—(1) Where the Central Government or a State

1. Subs. by Act 10 of 2009, sec. 33, for sub-section (2) (w.e.f. 27-10-2009). Sub-section (2), before substitution, stood as under:

"(2) Any person who fails to comply with any order under sub-section (1) shall be guilty of an offence and shall be liable on conviction to imprisonment for a term not exceeding three years or to a fine not exceeding two lakh rupees or to both."

2. Subs. by Act 10 of 2009, sec. 34, for section 69 (w.e.f. 27-10-2009). Section 69, before substitution, stood as under:

"**69. Directions of Controller to a subscriber to extend facilities to decrypt information.**—(1) If the Controller is satisfied that it is necessary or expedient so to do in the

Contd. on next page

Government or any of its officers specially authorised by the Central Government or the State Government, as the case may be, in this behalf may, if satisfied that it is necessary or expedient to do in the interest of the sovereignty or integrity of India, defence of India, security of the State, friendly relations with foreign States or public order or for preventing incitement to the commission of any cognizable offence relating to above or for investigation of any offence, it may, subject to the provisions of sub-section (2), for reasons to be recorded in writing, by order, direct any agency of the appropriate Government to intercept, monitor or decrypt or cause to be intercepted or monitored or decrypted any information generated, transmitted, received or stored in any computer resource.

(2) The procedure and safeguards subject to which such interception or monitoring or decryption may be carried out, shall be such as may be prescribed.

(3) The subscriber or intermediary or any person in-charge of the computer resource shall, when called upon by any agency referred to in sub-section (1), extend all facilities and technical assistance to—

(a) provide access to or secure access to the computer resource generating, transmitting, receiving or storing such information; or

(b) intercept, monitor, or decrypt the information, as the case may be; or

(c) provide information stored in computer resource.

(4) The subscriber or intermediary or any person who fails to assist the agency referred to in sub-section (3) shall be punished with imprisonment for a term which may extend to seven years and shall also be liable to fine.

69A. Power to issue directions for blocking for public access of any information through any computer resource.—(1) Where the Central Government or any of its officer specially authorised by it in this behalf is satisfied that it is necessary or expedient so to do, in the interest of sovereignty and integrity of India, defence of India, security of the State, friendly relations with foreign States or public order or for preventing incitement to the commission of any cognizable offence relating to above, it may subject to the provisions of sub-section (2) for reasons to be recorded in writing, by order, direct any agency of the Government or intermediary to block for access by the public or cause to be blocked for access by the public any information generated, transmitted, received, stored or hosted in any computer resource.

(2) The procedure and safeguards subject to which such blocking for access by the public may be carried out, shall be such as may be prescribed.

(3) The intermediary who fails to comply with the direction issued under sub-section (1) shall be punished with an imprisonment for a term which may extend to seven years and shall also be liable to fine.

69B. Power to authorise to monitor and collect traffic data or information through any computer resource for cyber security.—(1) The Central Government may, to enhance cyber security and for identification, analysis and prevention of intrusion or spread of computer contaminant in the country, by notification in the Official Gazette, authorise any agency of the Government to monitor and collect traffic data or information generated, transmitted, received or stored in any computer resource.

(2) The intermediary or any person in-charge of the computer resource shall, when called upon by the agency which has been authorised under sub-section (1), provide technical assistance and extend all facilities to such agency to enable online access or to secure and provide online access to the computer resource generating, transmitting, receiving or storing such traffic data or information.

Contd. from previous page

interest of the sovereignty or integrity of India, the security of the State, friendly relations with foreign States or public order or for preventing incitement to the commission of any cognizable offence, for reasons to be recorded in writing, by order, direct any agency of the Government to intercept any information transmitted through any computer resource.

(2) The subscriber or any person incharge of the computer resource shall, when called upon by any agency which has been directed under sub-section (1), extend all facilities and technical assistance to decrypt the information.

(3) The subscriber or any person who fails to assist the agency referred to in sub-section (2) shall be punished with an imprisonment for a term which may extend to seven years."

(3) The procedure and safeguards for monitoring and collecting traffic data or information, shall be such as may be prescribed.

(4) Any intermediary who intentionally or knowingly contravenes the provisions of sub-section (2) shall be punished with an imprisonment for a term which may extend to three years and shall also be liable to fine.

Explanation.—For the purposes of this section,—

(i) "computer contaminant" shall have the meaning assigned to it in section 43;

(ii) "traffic data" means any data identifying or purporting to identify any person, computer system or computer network or location to or from which the communication is or may be transmitted and includes communications origin, destination, route, time, data, size, duration or type of underlying service or any other information.]

70. Protected system.—[1][(1) The appropriate Government may, by notification in the Official Gazette, declare any computer resource which directly or indirectly affects the facility of Critical Information Infrastructure, to be a protected system.

Explanation.—For the purposes of this section, "Critical Information Infrastructure" means the computer resource, the incapacitation or destruction of which, shall have debilitating impact on national security, economy, public health or safety.]

(2) The appropriate Government may, by order in writing, authorise the persons who are authorised to access protected systems notified under sub-section (1).

(3) Any person who secures access or attempts to secure access to a protected system in contravention of the provisions of this section shall be punished with imprisonment of either description for a term which may extend to ten years and shall also be liable to fine.

[2][(4) The Central Government shall prescribe the information security practices and procedures for such protected system.]

[3]**[70A. National nodal agency.**—(1) The Central Government may, by notification published in the Official Gazette, designate any organisation of the Government as the national nodal agency in respect of Critical Information Infrastructure Protection.

(2) The national nodal agency designated under sub-section (1) shall be responsible for all measures including Research and Development relating to protection of Critical Information Infrastructure.

(3) The manner of performing functions and duties of the agency referred to in sub-section (1) shall be such as may be prescribed.]

[3]**[70B. Indian Computer Emergency Response Team to serve as national agency for incident response.**—(1) The Central Government shall, by notification in the Official Gazette, appoint an agency of the Government to be called the Indian Computer Emergency Response Team.

(2) The Central Government shall provide the agency referred to in sub-section (1) with a Director-General and such other officers and employees as may be prescribed.

(3) The salary and allowances and terms and conditions of the Director- General and other officers and employees shall be such as may be prescribed.

(4) The Indian Computer Emergency Response Team shall serve as the national agency for performing the following functions in the area of cyber security,—

(a) collection, analysis and dissemination of information on cyber incidents;

(b) forecast and alerts of cyber security incidents;

(c) emergency measures for handling cyber security incidents;

(d) coordination of cyber incidents response activities;

---

1. Subs. by Act 10 of 2009, sec. 35(a), for sub-section (1) (w.e.f. 27-10-2009). Sub-section (1), before substitution, stood as under:

   "(1) The appropriate Government may, by notification in the Official Gazette, declare that any computer, computer system or computer network to be a protected system."

2. Ins. by Act 10 of 2009, sec. 35(b) (w.e.f. 27-10-2009).
3. Ins. by Act 10 of 2009, sec. 36 (w.e.f. 27-10-2009).

(e) issue guidelines, advisories, vulnerability notes and whitepapers relating to information security practices, procedures, preventation, response and reporting of cyber incidents;

(f) such other functions relating to cyber security as may be prescribed.

(5) The manner of performing functions and duties of the agency referred to in sub-section (1) shall be such as may be prescribed.

(6) For carrying out the provisions of sub-section (4), the agency referred to in sub-section (1) may call for information and give direction to the service providers, intermediaries, data centres, body corporate and any other person.

(7) Any service provider, intermediaries, data centres, body corporate or person who fails to provide the information called for or comply with the direction under sub-section (6), shall be punishable with imprisonment for a term which may extend to one year or with fine which may extend to one lakh rupees or with both.

(8) No court shall take cognizance of any offence under this section, except on a complaint made by an officer authorised in this behalf by the agency referred to in sub-section (1).]

71. Penalty for misrepresentation.—Whoever makes any misrepresentation to, or suppresses any material fact from the Controller or the Certifying Authority for obtaining any licence or [1][Electronic Signature] Certificate, as the case may be, shall be punished with imprisonment for a term which may extend to two years, or with fine which may extend to one lakh rupees, or with both.

72. Penalty for breach of confidentiality and privacy.—Save as otherwise provided in this Act or any other law for the time being in force, if any person who, in pursuance of any of the powers conferred under this Act, rules or regulations made thereunder, has secured access to any electronic record, book, register, correspondence, information, document or other material without the consent of the person concerned discloses such electronic record, book, register, correspondence, information, document or other material to any other person shall be punished with imprisonment for a term which may extend to two years, or with fine which may extend to one lakh rupees, or with both.

[2][**72A. Punishment for disclosure of information in breach of lawful contract.**—Save as otherwise provided in this Act or any other law for the time being in force, any person including an intermediary who, while providing services under the terms of lawful contract, has secured access to any material containing personal information about another person, with the intent to cause or knowing that he is likely to cause wrongful loss or wrongful gain discloses, without the consent of the person concerned, or in breach of a lawful contract, such material to any other person, shall be punished with imprisonment for a term which may extend to three years, or with fine which may extend to five lakh rupees, or with both.]

73. Penalty for publishing [1][Electronic Signature] Certificate false in certain particulars.—(1) No person shall publish a [1][Electronic Signature] Certificate or otherwise make it available to any other person with the knowledge that—

(a) the Certifying Authority listed in the certificate has not issued it; or

(b) the subscriber listed in the certificate has not accepted it; or

(c) the certificate has been revoked or suspended,

unless such publication is for the purpose of verifying a [1][electronic signature] created prior to such suspension or revocation.

(2) Any person who contravenes the provisions of sub-section (1) shall be punished with imprisonment for a term which may extend to two years, or with fine which may extend to one lakh rupees, or with both.

74. Publication for fraudulent purpose.—Whoever knowingly creates, publishes or otherwise makes available a [1][Electronic Signature] Certificate for any fraudulent or unlawful purpose shall be punished with imprisonment for a term which may extend to two years, or with fine which may extend to one lakh rupees, or with both.

---

1. Subs. by Act 10 of 2009, sec. 2, for "Digital Signature" (w.e.f. 27-10-2009).
2. Ins. by Act 10 of 2009, sec. 37 (w.e.f. 27-10-2009).

75. Act to apply for offence or contravention committed outside India.—(1) Subject to the provisions of sub-section (2), the provisions of this Act shall apply also to any offence or contravention committed outside India by any person irrespective of his nationality.

(2) For the purposes of sub-section (1), this Act shall apply to an offence or contravention committed outside India by any person if the act or conduct constituting the offence or contravention involves a computer, computer system or computer network located in India.

76. Confiscation.—Any computer, computer system, floppies, compact disks, tape drives or any other accessories related thereto, in respect of which any provision of this Act, rules, orders or regulations made thereunder has been or is being contravened, shall be liable to confiscation:

Provided that where it is established to the satisfaction of the court adjudicating the confiscation that the person in whose possession, power or control of any such computer, computer system, floppies, compact disks, tape drives or any other accessories relating thereto is found is not responsible for the contravention of the provisions of this Act, rules, orders or regulations made thereunder, the court may, instead of making an order for confiscation of such computer, computer system, floppies, compact disks, tape drives or any other accessories related thereto, make such other order authorised by this Act against the person contravening of the provisions of this Act, rules, orders or regulations made thereunder as it may think fit.

[1][**77. Compensation, penalties or confiscation not to interfere with other punishment.**—No compensation awarded, penalty imposed or confiscation made under this Act shall prevent the award of compensation or imposition of any other penalty or punishment under any other law for the time being in force.

77A. Compounding of offences.—A court of competent jurisdiction may compound offences, other than offences for which the punishment for life or imprisonment for a term exceeding three years has been provided, under this Act:

Provided that the court shall not compound such offence where the accused is, by reason of his previous conviction, liable to either enhanced punishment or to a punishment of a different kind:

Provided further that the court shall not compound any offence where such offence affects the socio economic conditions of the country or has been committed against a child below the age of 18 years or a woman.

(2) The person accused of an offence under this Act may file an application for compounding in the court in which offence is pending for trial and the provisions of sections 265B and 265C of the Code of Criminal Procedure, 1973 shall apply.

77B. Offences with three years imprisonment to be bailable.—Notwithstanding anything contained in the Code of Criminal Procedure, 1973 (2 of 1974), the offence punishable with imprisonment of three years and above shall be cognizable and the offence punishable with imprisonment of three years shall be bailable.]

78. Power to investigate offences.—Notwithstanding anything contained in the Code of Criminal Procedure, 1973 (2 of 1974), a police officer not below the rank of [2][Inspector] shall investigate any offence under this Act.

[3][*CHAPTER XII*

INTERMEDIARIES NOT TO BE LIABLE IN CERTAIN CASES

79. Exemption from liability of intermediary in certain cases.—(1) Notwithstanding anything contained in any law for the time being in force but subject to the provisions of sub-

1. Subs. by Act 10 of 2009, sec. 38, for section 77 (w.e.f. 27-10-2009). Section 77, before substitution, stood as under:

   "**77. Penalties or confiscation not to interfere with other punishments.**—No penalty imposed or confiscation made under this Act shall prevent the imposition of any other punishment to which the person affected thereby is liable under any other law for the time being in force."

2. Subs. by Act 10 of 2009, sec. 39, for "Deputy Superintendent of Police" (w.e.f. 27-10-2009).
3. Subs. by Act 10 of 2009, sec. 40, for Chapter XII (w.e.f. 27-10-2009). Chapter XII, before substitution stood, as under:

Contd. on next page

sections (2) and (3), an intermediary shall not be liable for any third party information, data, or communication link made available or hosted by him.

(2) The provisions of sub-section (1) shall apply if—

(a) the function of the intermediary is limited to providing access to a communication system over which information made available by third parties is transmitted or temporarily stored or hosted; or

(b) the intermediary does not—

(i) initiate the transmission,

(ii) select the receiver of the transmission, and

(iii) select or modify the information contained in the transmission;

(c) the intermediary observes due diligence while discharging his duties under this Act and also observes such other guidelines as the Central Government may prescribe in this behalf.

(3) The provisions of sub-section (1) shall not apply if—

(a) the intermediary has conspired or abetted or aided or induced, whether by threats or promise or otherwise in the commission of the unlawful act;

(b) upon receiving actual knowledge, or on being notified by the appropriate Government or its agency that any information, data or communication link residing in or connected to a computer resource, controlled by the intermediary is being used to commit the unlawful act, the intermediary fails to expeditiously remove or disable access to that material on that resource without vitiating the evidence in any manner.

Explanation.—For the purpose of this section, the expression "third party information" means any information dealt with by an intermediary in his capacity as an intermediary.

CHAPTER XIIA

EXAMINER OF ELECTRONIC EVIDENCE

79A. Central Government to notify Examiner of Electronic Evidence.—The Central Government may, for the purposes of providing expert opinion on electronic form evidence before any court or other authority specify, by notification in the Official Gazette, any Department, body or agency of the Central Government or a State Government as an Examiner of Electronic Evidence.

Explanation.—For the purposes of this section, "electronic form evidence" means any information of probative value that is either stored or transmitted in electronic form and includes computer evidence, digital audio, digital video, cell phones, digital fax machines.]

CHAPTER XIII

MISCELLANEOUS

80. Power of police officer and other officers to enter, search, etc.—(1) Notwithstanding anything contained in the Code of Criminal Procedure, 1973 (2 of 1974), any police officer, not

---

Contd. from previous page

'*CHAPTER XII*

NETWORK SERVICE PROVIDERS NOT TO BE LIABLE IN CERTAIN CASES

79. Network service providers not to be liable in certain cases.—For the removal of doubts, it is hereby declared that no person providing any service as a network service provider shall be liable under this Act, rules or regulations made thereunder for any third party information or data made available by him if he proves that the offence or contravention was committed without his knowledge or that he had exercised all due diligence to prevent the commission of such offence or contravention.

Explanation.—For the purposes of this section,—

(a) "network service provider" means an intermediary;

(b) "third party information" means any information dealt with by a network service provider in his capacity as an intermediary.'

below the rank of a [1][Inspector], or any other officer of the Central Government or a State Government authorised by the Central Government in this behalf may enter any public place and search and arrest without warrant any person found therein who is reasonably suspected of having committed or of committing or of being about to commit any offence under this Act.

Explanation.—For the purposes of this sub-section, the expression "public place" includes any public conveyance, any hotel, any shop or any other place intended for use by, or accessible to the public.

(2) Where any person is arrested under sub-section (1) by an officer other than a police officer, such officer shall, without unnecessary delay, take or send the person arrested before a magistrate having jurisdiction in the case or before the officer-in-charge of a police station.

(3) The provisions of the Code of Criminal Procedure, 1973 (2 of 1974), shall, subject to the provisions of this section, apply, so far as may be, in relation to any entry, search or arrest, made under this section:

81. Act to have overriding effect.—The provisions of this Act shall have effect notwithstanding anything inconsistent therewith contained in any other law for the time being in force.

[2][Provided that nothing contained in this Act shall restrict any person from exercising any right conferred under the Copyright Act, 1957 (14 of 1957) or the Patents Act, 1970 (39 of 1970).]

[3]**[81A. Application of the Act to electronic cheque and truncated cheque.**—(1) The provisions of this Act, for the time being in force, shall apply to, or in relation to, electronic cheques and the truncated cheques subject to such modifications and amendments as may be necessary for carrying out the purposes of the Negotiable Instruments Act, 1881 (26 of 1881), by the Central Government, in consultation with the Reserve Bank of India, by notification in the Official Gazette.

(2) Every notification made by the Central Government under sub-section (1) shall be laid, as soon as may be after it is made, before each House of Parliament, while it is in session, for a total period of thirty days which may be comprised in one session or in two or more successive sessions, and if, before the expiry of the session immediately following the session or the successive sessions aforesaid, both Houses agree in making any modification in the notification or both Houses agree that the notification should not be made, the notification shall thereafter have effect only in such modified form or be of no effect, as the case may be; so, however, that any such modification or annulment shall be without prejudice to the validity of anything previously done under that notification.

Explanation.—For the purposes of this Act, the expressions "electronic cheque" and "truncated cheque" shall have the same meaning as assigned to them in section 6 of the Negotiable Instruments Act, 1881 (26 of 1881).]

82. [4][Chairperson, Members, Officers and employees to be public servants].—The [5][Chairperson, Members] and other officers and employees of a Cyber Appellate Tribunal, the Controller, the Deputy Controller and the Assistant Controllers shall be deemed to be public servants within the meaning of section 21 of the Indian Penal Code (45 of 1860).

83. Power to give directions.—The Central Government may give directions to any State Government as to the carrying into execution in the State of any of the provisions of this Act or of any rule, regulation or order made thereunder.

84. Protection of action taken in good faith.—No suit, prosecution or other legal proceeding shall lie against the Central Government, the State Government, the Controller or any person acting on behalf of him, the [6][Chairperson, Members], adjudicating officers and the staff of the Cyber Appellate Tribunal for anything which is in good faith done or intended to be done in pursuance of this Act or any rule, regulation or order made thereunder.

---

1. Subs. by Act 10 of 2009, sec. 41, for "Deputy Superintendent of Police" (w.e.f. 27-10-2009).
2. Ins. by Act 10 of 2009, sec. 42 (w.e.f. 27-10-2009).
3. Ins. by Act 55 of 2002, sec. 13 (w.e.f. 6-2-2003).
4. Subs. by Act 10 of 2009, sec. 43(a), for the heading "**Controller, Deputy Controller and Assistant Controllers to be public servants**" (w.e.f. 27-10-2009).
5. Subs. by Act 10 of 2009, sec. 43(b), for "Presiding Officer" (w.e.f. 27-10-2009).
6. Subs. by Act 10 of 2009, sec. 44, for "Presiding Officer" (w.e.f. 27-10-2009).

[1][**84A. Modes or methods for encryption.**—The Central Government may, for secure use of the electronic medium and for promotion of e-governance and e-commerce, prescribe the modes or methods for encryption.]

[1][**84B. Punishment for abetment of offences.**—Whoever abets any offence shall, if the act abetted is committed in consequence of the abetment, and no express provision is made by this Act for the punishment of such abetment, be punished with the punishment provided for the offence under this Act.

Explanation.—An act or offence is said to be committed in consequence of abetment, when it is committed in consequence of the instigation, or in pursuance of the conspiracy, or with the aid which constitutes the abetment.]

[1][**84C. Punishment for attempt to commit offences.**—Whoever attempts to commit an offence punishable by this Act or causes such an offence to be committed, and in such an attempt does any act towards the commission of the offence, shall, where no express provision is made for the punishment of such attempt, be punished with imprisonment of any description provided for the offence, for a term which may extend to one-half of the longest term of imprisonment provided for that offence, or with such fine as is provided for the offence, or with both.]

85. Offences by companies.—(1) Where a person committing a contravention of any of the provisions of this Act or of any rule, direction or order made thereunder is a company, every person who, at the time the contravention was committed, was in charge of, and was responsible to, the company for the conduct of business of the company as well as the company, shall be guilty of the contravention and shall be liable to be proceeded against and punished accordingly:

Provided that nothing contained in this sub-section shall render any such person liable to punishment if he proves that the contravention took place without his knowledge or that he exercised all due diligence to prevent such contravention.

(2) Notwithstanding anything contained in sub-section (1), where a contravention of any of the provisions of this Act or of any rule, direction or order made thereunder has been committed by a company and it is proved that the contravention has taken place with the consent or connivance of, or is attributable to any neglect on the part of, any director, manager, secretary or other officer of the company, such director, manager, secretary or other officer shall also be deemed to be guilty of the contravention and shall be liable to be proceeded against and punished accordingly.

Explanation.—For the purposes of this section,—

(i) "company" means any body corporate and includes a firm or other association of individuals; and

(ii) "director", in relation to a firm, means a partner in the firm.

86. Removal of difficulties.—(1) If any difficulty arises in giving effect to the provisions of this Act, the Central Government may, by order published in the Official Gazette, make such provisions not inconsistent with the provisions of this Act as appear to it to be necessary or expedient for removing the difficulty:

Provided that no order shall be made under this section after the expiry of a period of two years from the commencement of this Act.

(2) Every order made under this section shall be laid, as soon as may be after it is made, before each House of Parliament.

87. Power of Central Government to make rules.—(1) The Central Government may, by notification in the Official Gazette and in the Electronic Gazette, make rules to carry out the provisions of this Act.

(2) In particular, and without prejudice to the generality of the foregoing power, such rules may provide for all or any of the following matters, namely:—

1. Ins. by Act 10 of 2009, sec. 45 (w.e.f. 27-10-2009).

[1][(a) the conditions for considering reliability of electronic signature or electronic authentication technique under sub-section (2) of section 3A;]

[1][(aa) the procedure for ascertaining electronic signature or authentication under sub-section (3) of section 3A;]

[1][(ab) the manner in which any information or matter may be authenticated by means of electronic signature under section 5;]

(b) the electronic form in which filing, issue, grant or payment shall be effected under sub-section (1) of section 6;

(c) the manner and format in which electronic records shall be filed, or issued and the method of payment under sub-section (2) of section 6;

[2][(ca) the manner in which the authorised service provider may collect, retain and appropriate service charges under sub-section (2) of section 6A;]

(d) the matters relating to the type of [3][electronic signature], manner and format in which it may be affixed under section 10;

[4][(e) the manner of storing and affixing electronic signature creation data under section 15;]

[4][(ea) the security procedures and practices under section 16;]

(f) the qualifications, experience and terms and conditions of service of Controller, Deputy Controllers [5][, Assistant Controllers, other officers and employees] under section 17;

[6][***]

(h) the requirements which an applicant must fulfil under sub-section (2) of section 21;

(i) the period of validity of licence granted under clause (a) of sub-section (3) of section 21;

(j) the form in which an application for licence may be made under sub-section (1) of section 22;

(k) the amount of fees payable under clause (c) of sub-section (2) of section 22;

(l) such other documents which shall accompany an application for licence under clause (d) of sub-section (2) of section 22;

(m) the form and the fee for renewal of a licence and the fee payable thereof under section 23;

[7][(ma) the form of application and fee for issue of Electronic Signature Certificate under section 35;]

(n) the form in which application for issue of a [8][Electronic Signature] Certificate may be made under sub-section (1) of section 35;

(o) the fee to be paid to the Certifying Authority for issue of a [7][Electronic Signature] Certificate under sub-section (2) of section 35;

---

1. Subs. by Act 10 of 2009, sec. 46(A)(i), for clause (a) (w.e.f. 27-10-2009). Clause (a), before substitution, stood as under:
   "(a) the manner in which any information or matter may be authenticated by means of digital signature under section 5;"
2. Ins. by Act 10 of 2009, sec. 46(A)(ii) (w.e.f. 27-10-2009).
3. Subs. by Act 10 of 2009, sec. 2, for "digital signature" (w.e.f. 27-10-2009).
4. Subs. by Act 10 of 2009, sec. 46(A)(iii), for clause (e) (w.e.f. 27-10-2009). Clause (e), before substitution, stood as under:
   "(e) the security procedure for the purpose of creating secure electronic record and secure digital signature under section 16;"
5. Subs. by Act 10 of 2009, sec. 46(A)(iv), for "and Assistant Controller" (w.e.f. 27-10-2009).
6. Clause (g) omitted by Act 10 of 2009, sec. 46(A)(v) (w.e.f. 27-10-2009). Clause (g), before omission, stood as under:
   "(g) other standards to be observed by the Controller under clause (b) of sub-section (2) of section 20;"
7. Ins. by Act 10 of 2009, sec. 46(A)(vi) (w.e.f. 27-10-2009).
8. Subs. by Act 10 of 2009, sec. 2, for "Digital Signature" (w.e.f. 27-10-2009).

[1][(oa) the duties of subscribers under section 40A;]

[1][(ob) the reasonable security practices and procedures and sensitive personal data or information under section 43A;]

(p) the manner in which the adjudicating officer shall hold inquiry under sub-section (1) of section 46;

(q) the qualification and experience which the adjudicating officer shall possess under sub-section (3) of section 46;

(r) the salary, allowances and the other terms and conditions of service of the [2][Chairperson and Members] under section 52;

(s) the procedure for investigation of misbehaviour or incapacity of the [3][Chairperson and Members] under sub-section (3) of section 54;

(t) the salary and allowances and other conditions of service of other officers and employees under sub-section (3) of section 56;

(u) the form in which appeal may be filed and the fee thereof under sub-section (3) of section 57;

(v) any other power of a civil court required to be prescribed under clause (g) of sub-section (2) of section 58; and

[4][(w) the powers and functions of the Chairperson of the Cyber Appellate Tribunal under section 52A;]

[4][(x) the information, duration, manner and form of such information to be retained and preserved under section 67C;]

[4][(y) the procedures and safeguards and interception, monitoring, or decryption under sub-section (2) of section 69;]

[4][(z) the procedure and safeguards for blocking for access by the public under sub-section (2) of section 69A;]

[4][(za) the procedure and safeguards for monitoring and collecting traffic data or information under sub-section (3) of section 69B;]

[4][(zb) the information security practices and procedures for protected system under section 70;]

[4][(zc) manner of performing functions and duties of the agency under sub-section (3) of section 70A;]

[4][(zd) the officers and employees under sub-section (2) of section 70B;]

[4][(ze) salaries and allowances and terms and conditions of service of the Director-General and other officers and employees under sub-section (3) of section 70B;]

[5][(zf) the manner in which the functions and duties of agency shall be performed under sub-section (5) of section 70B;]

[5][(zg) the guidelines to be observed by the intermediaries under sub-section (2) of section 79;]

[5][(zh) the modes or methods for encryption under section 84A.]

(3) [6][Every notification made by the Central Government under sub-section (1) of section 70A and every rule made by] shall be laid, as soon as may be after it is made, before each House of Parliament, while it is in session, for a total period of thirty days which may be comprised in one session or in two or more successive sessions, and if, before the expiry of the session immediately following the session or the successive sessions aforesaid, both Houses

1. Ins. by Act 10 of 2009, sec. 46(A)(vii) (w.e.f. 27-10-2009).
2. Subs. by Act 10 of 2009, sec. 46(A)(viii), for "Presiding Officer" (w.e.f. 27-10-2009).
3. Subs. by Act 10 of 2009, sec. 46(A)(viii), for "Presiding Officer" (w.e.f. 27-10-2009).
4. Subs. by Act 10 of 2009, sec. 46(A)(ix), for clause (w) (w.e.f. 27-10-2009). Clause (w), before substitution, stood as under:

   "(w) any other matter which is required to be, or may be, prescribed."
5. Subs. by Act 10 of 2009, sec. 46(A)(ix), for clause (w) (w.e.f. 27-10-2009). Clause (w), before substitution, stood as under:

   "(w) any other matter which is required to be, or may be, prescribed."
6. Subs. by Act 10 of 2009, sec. 46(B)(i), for "Every notification made by the Central Government under clause (f) of sub-section (4) of section 1 and every rule made by it" (w.e.f. 27-10-2009).

agree in making any modification in [1][***] the rule or both Houses agree that [1][***] the rule should not be made, [1][***] the rule shall thereafter have effect only in such modified form or be of no effect, as the case may be; so, however, that any such modification or annulment shall be without prejudice to the validity of anything previously done under that notification or rule.

88. Constitution of Advisory Committee.—(1) The Central Government shall, as soon as may be after the commencement of this Act, constitute a Committee called the Cyber Regulations Advisory Committee.

(2) The Cyber Regulations Advisory Committee shall consist of a Chairperson and such number of other official and non-official members representing the interests principally affected or having special knowledge of the subject-matter as the Central Government may deem fit.

(3) The Cyber Regulations Advisory Committee shall advise—

(a) the Central Government either generally as regards any rules or for any other purpose connected with this Act;

(b) the Controller in framing the regulations under this Act.

(4) There shall be paid to the non-official members of such Committee such travelling and other allowances as the Central Government may fix.

89. Power of Controller to make regulations.—(1) The Controller may, after consultation with the Cyber Regulations Advisory Committee and with the previous approval of the Central Government, by notification in the Official Gazette, make regulations consistent with this Act and the rules made thereunder to carry out the purposes of this Act.

(2) In particular, and without prejudice to the generality of the foregoing power, such regulations may provide for all or any of the following matters, namely:—

(a) the particulars relating to maintenance of data-base containing the disclosure record of every Certifying Authority under clause [2][(n)] of section 18;

(b) the conditions and restrictions subject to which the Controller may recognise any foreign Certifying Authority under sub-section (1) of section 19;

(c) the terms and conditions subject to which a licence may be granted under clause (c) of sub-section (3) of section 21;

(d) other standards to be observed by a Certifying Authority under clause (d) of section 30;

(e) the manner in which the Certifying Authority shall disclose the matters specified in sub-section (1) of section 34;

(f) the particulars of statement which shall accompany an application under sub-section (3) of section 35.

(g) the manner by which the subscriber shall communicate the compromise of private key to the Certifying Authority under sub-section (2) of section 42.

(3) Every regulation made under this Act shall be laid, as soon as may be after it is made, before each House of Parliament, while it is in session, for a total period of thirty days which may be comprised in one session or in two or more successive sessions, and if, before the expiry of the session immediately following the session or the successive sessions aforesaid, both Houses agree in making any modification in the regulation or both Houses agree that the regulation should not be made, the regulation shall thereafter have effect only in such modified form or be of no effect, as the case may be; so, however, that any such modification or annulment shall be without prejudice to the validity of anything previously done under that regulation.

90. Power of State Government to make rules.—(1) The State Government may, by notification in the Official Gazette, make rules to carry out the provisions of this Act.

(2) In particular, and without prejudice to the generality of the foregoing power, such rules may provide for all or any of the following matters, namely:—

(a) the electronic form in which filing, issue, grant, receipt or payment shall be effected under sub-section (1) of section 6;

(b) for matters specified in sub-section (2) of section 6;

---

1. The words "the notification or" omitted by Act 10 of 2009, sec. 46(B)(ii) (w.e.f. 27-10-2009).
2. Subs. by S.O. 1015(E), dated 19th September, 2002, for "(m)" (w.e.f. 19-9-2002).

[1][***]

(3) Every rule made by the State Government under this section shall be laid, as soon as may be after it is made, before each House of the State Legislature where it consists of two Houses, or where such Legislature consists of one House, before that House.

[2][**91. Amendment of Act 45 of 1860.**—[*Rep. by the Information Technology (Amendment) Act, 2008 (10 of 2009), sec. 48.*]]

[2][**92. Amendment of Act 1 of 1872.**—[*Rep. by the Information Technology (Amendment) Act, 2008 (10 of 2009), sec. 48.*]]

[2][**93. Amendment of Act 18 of 1891.**—[*Rep. by the Information Technology (Amendment) Act, 2008 (10 of 2009), sec. 48.*]]

[2][**94. Amendment of Act 2 of 1934.**—[*Rep. by the Information Technology (Amendment) Act, 2008 (10 of 2009), sec. 48.*]]

[3][*THE FIRST SCHEDULE*

[*See* sub-section (4) of section 1]

DOCUMENTS OR TRANSACTIONS TO WHICH THE ACT SHALL NOT APPLY

Sl. No.	Description of documents or transactions
1.	A negotiable instrument (other than a cheque) as defined in section 13 of the Negotiable Instruments Act, 1881 (26 of 1881).
2.	A power-of-attorney as defined in section 1A of the Powers-of-Attorney Act, 1882 (7 of 1882).
3.	A trust as defined in section 3 of the Indian Trusts Act, 1882 (2 of 1882).
4.	A Will as defined in clause (h) of section 2 of the Indian Succession Act, 1925 (39 of 1925) including any other testamentary disposition by whatever name called.
5.	Any contract of the sale of conveyance of immovable property or any interest in such property.]

[4][*THE SECOND SCHEDULE*

[*See* sub-section (1) of section 3A]

ELECTRONIC SIGNATURE OR ELECTRONIC AUTHENTICATION TECHNIQUE AND PROCEDURE

Sl. No.	Description	Procedure
(1)	(2)	(3)

[5][***]

1. Clause (c) omitted by Act 10 of 2009, sec. 47 (w.e.f. 27-10-2009). Clause (c), before omission, stood as under:

   (c) any other matter which is required to be provided by rules by the State Government.

2. Sections 91 to 94, before omission, stood as under:

   "**91. Amendment of Act 45 of 1860.**—The Indian Penal Code shall be amended in the manner specified in the First Schedule to this Act.

   92. Amendment of Act 1 of 1872.—The Indian Evidence Act, 1872 shall be amended in the manner specified in the Second Schedule to this Act.

   93. Amendment of Act 18 of 1891.—The Bankers' Books Evidence Act, 1891 shall be amended in the manner specified in the Third Schedule to this Act.

   94. Amendment of Act 2 of 1934.—The Reserve Bank of India Act, 1934 shall be amended in the manner specified in the Fourth Schedule to this Act."

3. Subs. by Act 10 of 2009, sec. 49, for the First Schedule (w.e.f. 27-10-2009).
4. Subs. by Act 10 of 2009, sec. 49, for the Second Schedule (w.e.f. 27-10-2009).
5. The Third Schedule and the Fourth Schedule omitted by Act 10 of 2009, sec. 50 (w.e.f. 27-10-2009).

THE INFORMATION TECHNOLOGY (ELECTRONIC SERVICE DELIVERY) RULES, 2011[1]

In exercise of the powers conferred by clause (ca) of sub-section (2) of section 87, read with sub-section (2) of section 6A of the Information Technology Act, 2000 (21 of 2000), the Central Government hereby makes the following rules, namely:—

1. Short title and commencement.—(1) These rules may be called the Information Technology (Electronic Service Delivery) Rules, 2011.

(2) They shall come into force on the date[2] of their publication in the Official Gazette.

2. Definitions.—In these rules, unless the context otherwise requires,—

(a) "Act" means the Information Technology Act, 2000 (21 of 2000);

(b) "appropriate Government" means the Central Government or the State Government or an Union Territory Administration;

(c) "authorised agent" means an agent of the appropriate Government or service provider and includes an operator of an electronically enabled kiosk who is permitted under these rules to deliver public services to the users with the help of a computer resource or any communication device, by following the procedure specified in the rules;

(d) "certificate" means a certificate required to be issued by a statutory authority empowered under any Act, rule, regulation or Order of the appropriate Government to issue a certificate to confirm the status, right or responsibility of a person, either natural or artificial, and includes a certificate in electronic form printed and delivered in such form as may be specified by the appropriate authority;

(e) "Certifying Authority" means certifying authority as defined in clause (g) of sub-section (1) of section 2 of the Act;

(f) "communication device" means the communication device as defined in clause (ha) of sub-section (1) of section 2 of the Act;

(g) "computer resource" means the computer resource as defined in clause (k) of sub-section (1) of section 2 of the Act;

(h) "Electronically enabled kiosk" means the cyber cafe as defined in clause (na) of sub-section (1) of section 2 of the Act;

(i) "Electronic Service Delivery" means the delivery of public services in the form of filing receipt of forms and applications, issue or grant of any license, permit, certificate, sanction or approval and the receipt or payment of money by electronic means by following the procedure specified under rule 3;

(j) "electronic signature" means the electronic signature as defined in clause (ta) of sub-section (1) of section 2 of the Act;

(k) "Electronic Signature Certificate" means the electronic signature certificate as defined in clause (tb) of sub-section (1) of section 2 of the Act;

(l) "Repository of Electronically Signed Electronic Records" means a collection of all electronically signed electronic records, stored and managed in accordance with these rules;

(m) "service provider" means a service provider as referred to in *Explanation* to sub-section (1) of section 6A of the Act;

(n) "signing authority" means an authority empowered under any Act, rules, regulations or Order of the appropriate Government to issue a certificate.

---

1. *Vide* G.S.R. 316(E), dated 11th April, 2011, published in the Gazette of India, Extra., Pt. II, Sec. 3(i), dated 13th April, 2011.
2. Came into force on 13-4-2011.

3. System of electronic service delivery.—(1) The appropriate Government may on its own or through an agency authorised by it, deliver public services through electronically enabled kiosks or any other electronic service delivery mechanism.

(2) The appropriate Government or its agencies may specify the form and the manner of electronic service delivery.

(3) The appropriate Government may determine the manner of encrypting sensitive electronic records requiring confidentiality, while they are electronically signed.

(4) The appropriate Government shall notify the service providers and their agents authorised for electronic service delivery.

(5) The appropriate Government may allow receipt of payments made by adopting the Electronic Service Delivery System to be a deemed receipt of payment effected in compliance with the financial code and treasury code of such Government.

(6) The appropriate Government may authorise service providers or their authorised agents to collect, retain and appropriate such service charges as may be specified by the appropriate Government for the purpose of providing such services from the person availing such services:

Provided that the apportioned service charges shall be clearly indicated on the receipt to be given to the person availing the services.

(7) The appropriate Government shall by notification specify the scale of service charges which may be charged and collected by the service providers and their authorised agents for various kinds of services.

(8) The appropriate Government may also determine the norms on service levels to be complied with by the service provider and the authorised agents.

4. Notification of electronic service delivery.—(1) The appropriate Government may notify the services that shall be delivered electronically from time-to-time.

(2) The appropriate Government may identify and notify, from time-to-time, the list or signing authorities in respect of different classes of licenses, permits, certificates, sanctions, payment receipt approvals and local limits of their respective jurisdictions.

(3) The notification shall specify the nature of certificate, the names of the signing authorities, as approved by the appropriate Government, the period of effectiveness of the authority and the extent of their jurisdiction.

(4) The appropriate Government may notify changes to the list of signing authorities from time-to-time, taking into consideration the terms and conditions of the services of employees holding positions of signing authorities.

5. Creation of repository of electronically signed electronic records by Government Authorities.—(1) All authorities that issue any license, permit, certificate, sanction or approval electronically, shall create, archive and maintain a repository of electronically signed electronic records of such licenses, permits, certificates, sanctions or approvals, as the case may be, online with due time- stamps of creation of these individual electronic records.

(2) The appropriate Government may specify the manner of creating, establishing, archiving and maintaining the repository of electronically signed electronic records referred to in sub-rule (1).

(3) The authorities may electronically sign the electronic records of such licenses, permits, certificates, sanctions or approvals for each record or as a whole for a specific duration and shall be responsible in administering them online.

(4) The appropriate Government may specify the security procedures in respect of the electronic data, information, applications, repository of digitally signed electronic records and information technology assets under their respective control and that security procedures shall be followed by the Head of the Department and the signing authorities.

Explanation.—The expression "security procedures" referred to in sub-rule (4) shall include requirements for the storage and management of cryptographic keys, restrictions for downloading the certificates on to browsers, and of complying with the requirements of certifying authorities.

6. Procedure for making changes in a repository of electronically signed electronic records.—(1) The appropriate Government may either *suo moto* or after receiving an application from an interested party, make or order to make an appropriate change in a repository of electronically signed electronic records along with recording the reasons for making such a change.

(2) Any change effected to any record in a repository of electronically signed electronic records and any addition or deletion of a record from such repository shall be electronically signed by the person who is authorised to make such changes along with the time stamps of original creation and modification times.

(3) The appropriate Government may determine the manner of electronically signing the event of deletion of a record from the repository of electronically signed electronic records.

(4) The appropriate Government may also determine the manner of provisioning secure access to the repository of digitally signed electronic records.

(5) The appropriate Government may also determine the requirements for maintaining audit trails of all changes made to repository of digitally signed electronic records.

7. Responsibility of service provider and authorised agents for financial management and accounting.—The appropriate Government may direct every service provider and authorised agent to keep an updated and accurate account of the transactions, receipts, vouchers and specify the formats for maintaining accounts of transactions and receipt of payment in respect of the electronic services delivered and the said records shall be produced for inspection and audit before an agency or person nominated by the appropriate Government.

8. Audit of the Information System and Accounts of service provider and authorised agents.—(1) The appropriate Government may cause an audit to be conducted of the affairs of the service providers and authorised agents in the State at such intervals as deemed necessary by nominating such audit agencies.

(2) The audit may cover aspects such as the security, confidentiality and the privacy of information, the functionality and performance of any software application used in the electronic service delivery and the accuracy of accounts kept by the service providers and authorised agents.

(3) The service providers and the authorised agents shall provide such information and assistance to the audit agencies nominated by the appropriate authority, to comply with the directions given by the audit agencies and to rectify the defects and deficiencies pointed out by the audit agencies within the time-limit specified by the audit agency.

(4) All service providers and the authorised agents shall submit a due declaration for protecting the data of every individual transaction and citizen and any unauthorised disclosure to anyone without the written consent of either the individual or the appropriate Government shall be debarred from providing such a service any further and the provisions of section 45 of the Act shall be applicable in such cases.

9. Use of special stationery in electronic service delivery.—The appropriate Government may specify different types of special stationery, with accompanying security features for forms, applications, licenses, permits, certificates, receipts of payment and such other documents as part of electronic service delivery.

THE INFORMATION TECHNOLOGY (REASONABLE SECURITY PRACTICES AND PROCEDURES AND SENSITIVE PERSONAL DATA OR INFORMATION) RULES, 2011[1]

In exercise of the powers conferred by clause (ob) of sub-section (2) of section 87 read with section 43A of the Information Technology Act, 2000 (21 of 2000), the Central Government hereby makes the following rules, namely:—

1. Short title and commencement.—(1) These rules may be called the Information Technology (Reasonable Security Practices and Procedures and Sensitive Personal Data or Information) Rules, 2011.

(2) They shall come into force on the date[2] of their publication in the Official Gazette.

2. Definitions.—(1) In these rules, unless the context otherwise requires,—

(a) "Act" means the Information Technology Act, 2000 (21 of 2000);

(b) "Biometrics" means the technologies that measure and analyse human body characteristics, such as 'fingerprints', 'eye retinas and irises', voice patterns', facial patterns', 'hand measurements' and 'DNA' for authentication purposes;

(c) "Body corporate" means the body corporate as defined in clause (i) of *explanation* to section 43A of the Act;

(d) "Cyber incidents" means any real or suspected adverse event in relation to cyber security that violates an explicitly or implicitly applicable security policy resulting in unauthorised access, denial of service or disruption, unauthorised use of a computer resource for processing or storage of information or changes to data, information without authorisation;

(e) "Data" means data as defined in clause (o) of sub-section (1) of section 2 of the Act;

(f) "Information" means information as defined in clause (v) of sub-section (1) of section 2 of the Act;

(g) "Intermediary" means an intermediary as defined in clause (w) of sub-section (1) of section 2 of the Act;

(h) "Password" means a secret word or phrase or code or passphrase or secret key, or encryption or decryption keys that one uses to gain admittance or access to information;

(i) "Personal information" means any information that relates to a natural person, which, either directly or indirectly, in combination with other information available or likely to be available with a body corporate, is capable of identifying such person.

(2) All other words and expressions used and not defined in these rules but defined in the Act shall have the meanings respectively assigned to them in the Act.

3. Sensitive personal data or information.—Sensitive personal data or information of a person means such personal information which consists of information relating to:—

(i) password;

(ii) financial information such as Bank account or credit card or debit card or other payment instrument details;

(iii) physical, physiological and mental health condition;

(iv) sexual orientation;

(v) medical records and history;

1. *Vide* G.S.R. 313(E), dated 11th April, 2011 published in the Gazette of India, Extra., Pt. II, Sec. 3(i), dated 13th April, 2011.
2. Came into force on 13-4-2011.

(vi) Biometric information;

(vii) any detail relating to the above clauses as provided to body corporate for providing service; and

(viii) any of the information received under above clauses by body corporate for processing, stored or processed under lawful contract or otherwise:

Provided that, any information that is freely available or accessible in public domain or furnished under the Right to Information Act, 2005 or any other law for the time being in force shall not be regarded as sensitive personal data or information for the purposes of these rules.

4. Body corporate to provide policy for privacy and disclosure of information.—(1) The body corporate or any person who on behalf of body corporate collects, receives, possess, stores, deals or handle information of provider of information, shall provide a privacy policy for handling of or dealing in personal information including sensitive personal data or information and ensure that the same are available for view by such providers of information who has provided such information under lawful contract. Such policy shall be published on website of body corporate or any person on its behalf and shall provide for—

(i) clear and easily accessible statements of its practices and policies;

(ii) type of personal or sensitive personal data or information collected under rule 3;

(iii) purpose of collection and usage of such information;

(iv) disclosure of information including sensitive personal data or information as provided in rule 6;

(v) reasonable security practices and procedures as provided under rule 8.

5. Collection of information.—(1) Body corporate or any person on its behalf shall obtain consent in writing through letter or fax or email from the provider of the sensitive personal data or information regarding purpose of usage before collection of such information.

(2) Body corporate or any person on its behalf shall not collect sensitive personal data or information unless—

(a) the information is collected for a lawful purpose connected with a function or activity of the body corporate or any person on its behalf; and

(b) the collection of the sensitive personal data or information is considered necessary for that purpose.

(3) While collecting information directly from the person concerned, the body corporate or any person on its behalf shall take such steps as are, in the circumstances, reasonable to ensure that the person concerned is having the knowledge of —

(a) the fact that the information is being collected;

(b) the purpose for which the information is being collected;

(c) the intended recipients of the information; and

(d) the name and address of —

(i) the agency that is collecting the information; and

(ii) the agency that will retain the information.

(4) Body corporate or any person on its behalf holding sensitive personal data or information shall not retain that information for longer than is required for the purposes for which the information may lawfully be used or is otherwise required under any other law for the time being in force.

(5) The information collected shall be used for the purpose for which it has been collected.

(6) Body corporate or any person on its behalf shall permit the providers of information, as and when requested by them, to review the information they had provided and ensure that any personal information or sensitive personal data or information found to be inaccurate or deficient shall be corrected or amended as feasible:

Provided that a body corporate shall not be responsible for the authenticity of the personal information or sensitive personal data or information supplied by the provider of information to such body corporate or any other person acting on behalf of such body corporate.

(7) Body corporate or any person on its behalf shall, prior to the collection of information including sensitive personal data or information, provide an option to the provider of the

information to not to provide the data or information sought to be collected. The provider of information shall, at any time while availing the services or otherwise; also have an option to withdraw its consent given earlier to the body corporate. Such withdrawal of the consent shall be sent in writing to the body corporate. In the case of provider of information not providing or later on withdrawing his consent, the body corporate shall have the option not to provide goods or services for which the said information was sought.

(8) Body corporate or any person on its behalf shall keep the information secure as provided in rule 8.

(9) Body corporate shall address any discrepancies and grievances of their provider of the information with respect to processing of information in a time bound manner. For this purpose, the body corporate shall designate a Grievance Officer and publish his name and contact details on its website. The Grievance Officer shall redress the grievances of provider of information expeditiously but within one month from the date of receipt of grievance.

6. Disclosure of information.—(1) Disclosure of sensitive personal data or information by body corporate to any third party shall require prior permission from the provider of such information, who has provided such information under lawful contract or otherwise, unless such disclosure has been agreed to in the contract between the body corporate and provider of Information, or where the disclosure is necessary for compliance of a legal obligation:

Provided that the information shall be shared, without obtaining prior consent from provider of information, with Government agencies mandated under the law to obtain information including sensitive personal data or information for the purpose of verification of identity, or for prevention, detection, investigation including cyber incidents, prosecution, and punishment of offences. The Government agency shall send a request in writing to the body corporate possessing the sensitive personal data or information stating clearly the purpose of seeking such information. The Government agency shall also state that the information so obtained shall not be published or shared with any other person.

(2) Notwithstanding anything contained in sub-rule (1), any sensitive personal data or information shall be disclosed to any third party by an order under the law for the time being in force.

(3) The body corporate or any person on its behalf shall not publish the sensitive personal data or information.

(4) The third party receiving the sensitive personal data or information from body corporate or any person on its behalf under sub-rule (1) shall not disclose it further.

7. Transfer of information.—A body corporate or any person on its behalf may transfer sensitive personal data or information including any information, to any other body corporate or a person in India, or located in any other country, that ensures the same level of data protection that is adhered to by the body corporate as provided for under these rules. The transfer may be allowed only if it is necessary for the performance of the lawful contract between the body corporate or any person on its behalf and provider of information or where such person has consented to data transfer.

8. Reasonable Security Practices and Procedures.—(1) A body corporate or a person on its behalf shall be considered to have complied with reasonable security practices and procedures, if they have implemented such security practices and standards and have a comprehensive documented information security programme and information security policies that contain managerial, technical, operational and physical security control measures that are commensurate with the information assets being protected with the nature of business. In the event of an information security breach, the body corporate or a person on its behalf shall be required to demonstrate, as and when called upon to do so by the agency mandated under the law, that they have implemented security control measures as per their documented information security programme and information security policies.

(2) The international Standard IS/ISO/IEC 27001 on "Information Technology – Security Techniques - Information Security Management System - Requirements" is one such standard referred to in sub-rule (1).

(3) Any industry association or an entity formed by such an association, whose members are self-regulating by following other than IS/ISO/IEC codes of best practices for data

protection as per sub-rule (1), shall get its codes of best practices duly approved and notified by the Central Government for effective implementation.

(4) The body corporate or a person on its behalf who have implemented either IS/ISO/IEC 27001 standard or the codes of best practices for data protection as approved and notified under sub-rule (3) shall be deemed to have complied with reasonable security practices and procedures provided that such standard or the codes of best practices have been certified or audited on a regular basis by entities through independent auditor, duly approved by the Central Government. The audit of reasonable security practices and procedures shall be carried out by an auditor at least once a year or as and when the body corporate or a person on its behalf undertake significant upgradation of its process and computer resource.

THE INFORMATION TECHNOLOGY (INTERMEDIARIES GUIDELINES) RULES, 2011[1]

In exercise of the powers conferred by clause (zg) of sub-section (2) of section 87 read with sub-section (2) of section 79 of the Information Technology Act, 2000 (21 of 2000), the Central Government hereby makes the following rules, namely:—

1. Short title and commencement.—(1) These rules may be called the Information Technology (Intermediaries Guidelines) Rules, 2011.

(2) They shall come into force on the date[2] of their publication in the Official Gazette.

2. Definitions.—(1) In these rules, unless the context otherwise requires,—

(a) "Act" means the Information Technology Act, 2000 (21 of 2000);

(b) "Communication link" means a connection between a hypertext or graphical element (button, drawing, image) and one or more such items in the same or different electronic document wherein upon clicking on a hyperlinked item, the user is automatically transferred to the other end of the hyperlink which could be another document or another website or graphical element.

(c) "Computer resource" means computer resource as defined in clause (k) of sub-section (1) of section 2 of the Act;

(d) "Cyber security incident" means any real or suspected adverse event in relation to cyber security that violates an explicitly or implicitly applicable security policy resulting in unauthorised access, denial of service or disruption, unauthorised use of a computer resource for processing or storage of information or changes to data, information without authorisation;

(e) "Data" means data as defined in clause (o) of sub-section (1) of section 2 of the Act;

(f) "Electronic Signature" means electronic signature as defined in clause (ta) of sub-section (1) of section 2 of the Act;

(g) "Indian Computer Emergency Response Team" means the Indian Computer Emergency Response Team appointed under sub-section (1) of section 70(B) of the Act;

(h) "Information" means information as defined in clause (v) of sub-section (1) of section 2 of the Act;

(i) "Intermediary" means an intermediary as defined in clause (w) of sub-section (1) of section 2 of the Act;

(j) "User" means any person who access or avail any computer resource of intermediary for the purpose of hosting, publishing, sharing, transacting, displaying or uploading information or views and includes other persons jointly participating in using the computer resource of an intermediary.

(2) All other words and expressions used and not defined in these rules but defined in the Act shall have the meanings respectively assigned to them in the Act.

3. Due diligence to be observed by intermediary.—The intermediary shall observe following due diligence while discharging his duties, namely:—

(1) The intermediary shall publish the rules and regulations, privacy policy and user agreement for access or usage of the intermediary's computer resource by any person.

(2) Such rules and regulations, terms and conditions or user agreement shall inform the users of computer resource not to host, display, upload, modify, publish, transmit, update or share any information that—

(a) belongs to another person and to which the user does not have any right to;

(b) is grossly harmful, harassing, blasphemous, defamatory, obscene, pornographic, paedophilic, libellous, invasive of another's privacy, hateful, or racially, ethnically objectionable, disparaging, relating or encouraging money laundering or gambling, or otherwise unlawful in any manner whatever;

---

1. *Vide* G.S.R. 314(E), dated 11th April, 2011 published in the Gazette of India, Extra., Pt. II, Sec. 3(i), dated 13th April, 2011.
2. Came into force on 13-4-2011.

(c) harm minors in any way;

(d) infringes any patent, trademark, copyright or other proprietary rights;

(e) violates any law for the time being in force;

(f) deceives or misleads the addressee about the origin of such messages or communicates any information which is grossly offensive or menacing in nature;

(g) impersonate another person;

(h) contains software viruses or any other computer code, files or programs designed to interrupt, destroy or limit the functionality of any computer resource;

(i) threatens the unity, integrity, defence, security or sovereignty of India, friendly relations with foreign states, or public order or causes incitement to the commission of any cognisable offence or prevents investigation of any offence or is insulting any other nation.

(3) The intermediary shall not knowingly host or publish any information or shall not initiate the transmission, select the receiver of transmission, and select or modify the information contained in the transmission as specified in sub-rule (2):

Provided that the following actions by an intermediary shall not amount to hosting, publishing, editing or storing of any such information as specified in sub-rule (2)—

(a) temporary or transient or intermediate storage of information automatically within the computer resource as an intrinsic feature of such computer resource, involving no exercise of any human editorial control, for onward transmission or communication to another computer resource;

(b) removal of access to any information, data or communication link by an intermediary after such information, data or communication link comes to the actual knowledge of a person authorised by the intermediary pursuant to any order or direction as per the provisions of the Act;

(4) The intermediary, on whose computer system the information is stored or hosted or published, upon obtaining knowledge by itself or been brought to actual knowledge by an affected person in writing or through email signed with electronic signature about any such information as mentioned in sub-rule (2) above, shall act within thirty-six hours and where applicable, work with user or owner of such information to disable such information that is in contravention of sub-rule (2). Further the intermediary shall preserve such information and associated records for at least ninety days for investigation purposes.

(5) The Intermediary shall inform its users that in case of non-compliance with rules and regulations, user agreement and privacy policy for access or usage of intermediary computer resource, the Intermediary has the right to immediately terminate the access or usage rights of the users to the computer resource of Intermediary and remove non-compliant information.

(6) The intermediary shall strictly follow the provisions of the Act or any other laws for the time being in force.

(7) When required by lawful order, the intermediary shall provide information or any such assistance to Government Agencies who are lawfully authorised for investigative, protective, cyber security activity. The information or any such assistance shall be provided for the purpose of verification of identity, or for prevention, detection, investigation, prosecution, cyber security incidents and punishment of offences under any law for the time being in force, on a request in writing stating clearly the purpose of seeking such information or any such assistance.

(8) The intermediary shall take all reasonable measures to secure its computer resource and information contained therein following the reasonable security practices and procedures as prescribed in the Information Technology (Reasonable Security Practices and Procedures and Sensitive Personal Information) Rules, 2011.

(9) The intermediary shall report cyber security incidents and also share cyber security incidents related information with the Indian Computer Emergency Response Team.

(10) The intermediary shall not knowingly deploy or install or modify the technical configuration of computer resource or become party to any such act which may change or has the potential to change the normal course of operation of the computer resource than what it is supposed to perform thereby circumventing any law for the time being in force:

Provided that the intermediary may develop, produce, distribute or employ technological means for the sole purpose of performing the acts of securing the computer resource and information contained therein.

(11) The intermediary shall publish on its website the name of the Grievance Officer and his contact details as well as mechanism by which users or any victim who suffers as a result of access or usage of computer resource by any person in violation of rule 3 can notify their complaints against such access or usage of computer resource of the intermediary or other matters pertaining to the computer resources made available by it. The Grievance Officer shall redress the complaints within one month from the date of receipt of complaint.

THE INFORMATION TECHNOLOGY (GUIDELINES FOR CYBER CAFE) RULES, 2011[1]

In exercise of the powers conferred by clause (zg) of sub-section (2) of section 87 read with sub-section (2) of section 79 of the Information Technology Act, 2000 (21 of 2000), the Central Government hereby makes the following rules, namely:—

1. Short title and commencement.—(1) These rules may be called the Information Technology (Guidelines for Cyber Cafe) Rules, 2011.

(2) They shall come into force on the date[2] of their publication in the Official Gazette.

2. Definitions.—(1) In these rules, unless the context otherwise requires,—

(a) "Act" means the Information Technology Act, 2000 (21 of 2000);

(b) "Appropriate Government" means the Central Government or the State Government or an Union Territory Administration;

(c) "Cyber Cafe" means cyber café as defined in clause (na) of sub-section (1) of section 2 of the Act;

(d) "computer resource" means a computer resource as defined in clause (k) of sub-section (1) of section 2 of the Act;

(e) "Data" means data as defined in clause (o) of sub-section (1) of section 2 of the Act;

(f) "Information" means information as defined in clause (v) of sub-section (1) of section 2 of the Act;

(g) "Intermediary" means an intermediary as defined in clause (w) of sub-section (1) of section 2 of the Act;

(h) "Registration Agency" means an agency designated by the Appropriate Government to register cyber café for their operation;

(i) "Log Register" means a register maintained by the Cyber Café for access and use of computer resource;

(j) "User" means a person who avails or access the computer resource and includes other persons jointly participating in availing or accessing the computer resource in a cyber café.

(2) All other words and expressions used and not defined in these rules but defined in the Act shall have the meanings respectively assigned to them in the Act.

3. Agency for registration of cyber café.—(1) All cyber cafes shall be registered with a unique registration number with an agency called as registration agency as notified by the Appropriate Government in this regard. The broad terms of registration shall include:

(i) name of establishment;

(ii) address with contact details including email address;

(iii) whether individual or partnership or sole proprietorship or society or company;

(iv) date of incorporation;

(v) name of owner/partner/proprietor/director;

(vi) whether registered or not (if yes, copy of registration with Registrar of Firms or Registrar of Companies or Societies); and

(vii) type of service to be provided from cyber café.

Registration of cyber café may be followed up with a physical visit by an officer from the registration agency.

(2) The details of registration of cyber café shall be published on the website of the registration agency.

---

1. *Vide* G.S.R. 315(E), dated 11th April, 2011 published in the Gazatte of India, Extra., Pt. II, Sec. 3(i), date 13th April, 2011.
2. Came into force on 13-4-2011.

(3) The Appropriate Government shall make an endeavour to set up on-line registration facility to enable cyber café to register on-line.

(4) The detailed process of registration to be mandatorily followed by each Registration Agency notified by the Appropriate Government shall be separately notified under these rules by the Central Government.

4. Identification of user.—(1) The cyber café shall not allow any user to use its computer resource without the identity of the user being established. The intending user may establish his identify by producing a document which shall identify the users to the satisfaction of the cyber café. Such document may include any of the following:—

(i) Identity card issued by any School or College; or

(ii) Photo Credit Card or debit card issued by a Bank or Post Office; or

(iii) Passport; or

(iv) Voter Identity Card; or

(v) Permanent Account Number (PAN) card issued by Income-Tax Authority; or

(vi) Photo Identity Card issued by the employer or any Government Agency; or

(vii) Driving License issued by the Appropriate Government; or

(viii) Unique Identification (UID) Number issued by the Unique Identification Authority of India (UIDAI).

(2) The cyber café shall keep a record of the user identification document by either storing a photocopy or a scanned copy of the document duly authenticated by the user and authorised representative of cyber cafe. Such record shall be securely maintained for a period of at least one year.

(3) In addition to the identity established by an user under sub-rule (1), he may be photographed by the cyber cafe using a web-camera installed on one of the computers in the cyber café for establishing the identity of the user. Such web-camera photographs, duly authenticated by the user and authorised representative of cyber café, shall be part of the log register which may be maintained in physical or electronic form.

(4) A minor without photo Identity card shall be accompanied by an adult with any of the documents as required under sub-rule (1).

(5) A person accompanying a user shall be allowed to enter cyber café after he has established his identity by producing a document listed in sub-rule (1) and record of same shall be kept in accordance with sub-rule (2).

(6) The cyber café shall immediately report to the concerned police, if they have reasonable doubt or suspicion regarding any user.

5. Log Register.—(1) After the identity of the user and any person accompanied with him has been established as per sub-rule (1) of rule 4, the cyber Café shall record and maintain the required information of each user as well as accompanying person, if any, in the log register for a minimum period of one year.

(2) The cyber café may maintain an online version of the log register. Such online version of log register shall be authenticated by using digital or electronic signature. The log register shall contain at least the following details of the user, namely:—

(i) Name

(ii) Address

(iii) Gender

(iv) Contact Number

(v) Type and detail of identification document

(vii) Date

(vii) Computer terminal identification

(viii) Log in Time

(ix) Log out Time.

(3) Cyber café shall prepare a monthly report of the log register showing date-wise details on the usage of the computer resource and submit a hard and soft copy of the same to the person or agency as directed by the registration agency by the 5th day of next month.

(4) The cyber café owner shall be responsible for storing and maintaining backups of following log records for each access or login by any user of its computer resource for at least one year:—

(i) History of websites accessed using computer resource at cyber café;

(ii) Logs of proxy server installed at cyber café.

Cyber café may refer to "Guidelines for auditing and logging – CISG-2008-01" prepared and updated from time-to-time by Indian Computer Emergency Response Team (CERT-In) for any assistance related to logs. This document is available at www.cert-in.org.in

(5) Cyber café shall ensure that log register is not altered and maintained in a secure manner for a period of at least one year.

6. Management of Physical Layout and computer resource.—(1) Partitions of Cubicles built or installed if any, inside the cyber café, shall not exceed four and half feet in height from the floor level.

(2) The screen of all computers installed other than in Partitions or Cubicles, shall face 'outward', *i.e.*, they shall face the common open space of the cyber café.

(3) Any cyber café having cubicles or partitions shall not allow minors to use any computer resource in cubicles or partitions except when they are accompanied by their guardians or parents.

(4) All time clocks of the computer systems and servers installed in the cyber café shall be synchronised with the Indian Standard Time.

(5) All the computers in the cyber cafe may be equipped with the commercially available safety or filtering software so as to the avoid, as far as possible, access to the websites relating to pornography including child pornography or obscene information.

(6) Cyber café shall take sufficient precautions to ensure that their computer resource are not utilised for any illegal activity.

(7) Cyber café shall display a board, clearly visible to the users, prohibiting them from viewing pornographic sites as well as copying or downloading information which is prohibited under the law.

(8) Cyber café shall incorporate reasonable preventive measures to disallow the user from tampering with the computer system settings.

(9) Cyber café shall maintain the user identity information and the log register in a secure manner.

(10) Cyber café shall also maintain a record of its staff for a period of one year.

(11) Cyber cafe shall not misuse or alter the information in the log register.

7. Inspection of cyber café.—(1) An officer authorised by the registration agency, is authorised to check or inspect cyber cafe and the computer resource or network established therein at any time for the compliance of these rules. The cyber café owner shall provide every related document, registers and any necessary information to the inspecting officer on demand.

SUBJECT INDEX

•••